Rituals, Runaways, and the Haitian Revolution

The Haitian Revolution was perhaps the most successful slave rebellion in modern history; it created the first and only free and independent Black nation in the Americas. This book tells the story of how enslaved Africans forcibly brought to colonial Haiti through the trans-Atlantic slave trade used their cultural and religious heritages, social networks, and labor and militaristic skills to survive horrific conditions. They built webs of networks between African and 'creole' runaways, slaves, and a small number of free people of color through rituals and marronnage — key aspects to building the racial solidarity that helped make the revolution successful. Analyzing underexplored archival sources and advertisements for fugitives from slavery, Crystal Eddins finds indications of collective consciousness and solidarity, unearthing patterns of resistance. Considering the importance of the Haitian Revolution and the growing scholarly interest in exploring it, Eddins fills an important gap in the existing literature. This title is also available as Open Access on Cambridge Core.

CRYSTAL NICOLE EDDINS is Assistant Professor in the Department of Africana Studies at the University of North Carolina at Charlotte. Her research has been supported by the Ruth J. Simmons Postdoctoral Fellowship, the John Carter Brown Library, and the National Science Foundation.

Cambridge Studies on the African Diaspora

General Editor: Michael A. Gomez, New York University

Using the African Diaspora as its core defining and launching point for examining the historians and experiences of African-descended communities around the globe, this series unites books around the concept of migration of peoples and their cultures, politics, ideas, and other systems from or within Africa to other nations or regions, focusing particularly on transnational, transregional, and transcultural exchanges.

Titles in the series

Crystal Nicole Eddins, *Rituals, Runaways, and the Haitian Revolution: Collective Action in the African Diaspora*

Merle L. Bowen, *For Land and Liberty: Black Struggles in Rural Brazil*

Michael A. Gomez, *Reversing Sail: A History of the African Diaspora, Second Edition*

Jorge L. Giovannetti-Torres, *Black British Migrants in Cuba: Race, Labor, and Empire in the Twentieth-Century Caribbean, 1898–1948*

Daniel B. Domingues da Silva, *The Atlantic Slave Trade from West Central Africa, 1780–1867*

Rashauna Johnson, *Slavery's Metropolis: Unfree Labor in New Orleans during the Age of Revolutions*

Rituals, Runaways, and the Haitian Revolution

Collective Action in the African Diaspora

CRYSTAL NICOLE EDDINS

CAMBRIDGE
UNIVERSITY PRESS

CAMBRIDGE
UNIVERSITY PRESS

University Printing House, Cambridge CB2 8BS, United Kingdom

One Liberty Plaza, 20th Floor, New York, NY 10006, USA

477 Williamstown Road, Port Melbourne, VIC 3207, Australia

314–321, 3rd Floor, Plot 3, Splendor Forum, Jasola District Centre, New Delhi – 110025, India

103 Penang Road, #05–06/07, Visioncrest Commercial, Singapore 238467

Cambridge University Press is part of the University of Cambridge.

It furthers the University's mission by disseminating knowledge in the pursuit of education, learning, and research at the highest international levels of excellence.

www.cambridge.org
Information on this title: www.cambridge.org/9781009256155
DOI: 10.1017/9781009256148

© Crystal Nicole Eddins 2022
Reissued as Open Access, 2022

First published 2022

A catalogue record for this publication is available from the British Library.

Library of Congress Cataloging-in-Publication Data
NAMES: Eddins, Crystal Nicole, 1984- author.
TITLE: Rituals, runaways, and the Haitian Revolution : collective action in the African diaspora / Crystal Nicole Eddins.
DESCRIPTION: Cambridge, United Kingdom ; New York, NY : Cambridge University Press, 2022. | Series: Cambridge studies on the African diaspora | Includes bibliographical references and index.
IDENTIFIERS: LCCN 2021027125 (print) | LCCN 2021027126 (ebook) | ISBN 9781108843720 (hardback) | ISBN 9781009256155 (paperback) | ISBN 9781009256148 (epub)
SUBJECTS: LCSH: Slave insurrections–Haiti–History. | Blacks–Race identity–Haiti. | Maroons–Haiti–Ethnic identity. | Rites and ceremonies–Haiti. | Blacks–Haiti–Social life and customs. | Group identity–Haiti. | Social movements–Haiti–History. | Haiti–History–Revolution, 1791-1804–Causes. | BISAC: HISTORY / Latin America / General
CLASSIFICATION: LCC F1923 .E23 2022 (print) | LCC F1923 (ebook) | DDC 305.896/07294–dc23
LC record available at https://lccn.loc.gov/2021027125
LC ebook record available at https://lccn.loc.gov/2021027126

ISBN 978-1-009-25615-5 Paperback

I give thanks and praise to God
Love and appreciation to my family and ancestors
Onè and respè *to the people of Haiti*

Contents

Figures

IMAGES

MAPS

GRAPHS AND CHARTS

Tables

Acknowledgements

My sincere appreciation goes to Studies on the African Diaspora series editor Michael A. Gomez, Cecelia Cancellaro, Cambridge University Press staff, James Warren, Denise Bannerman, Frantz Zéphirin, and the anonymous reviewers for their support, assistance, guidance, and labor in bringing this book to fruition.

Thank you to my University of North Carolina at Charlotte colleagues for their support: Julia Jordan-Zachery, Akin Ogundiran, Dorothy Smith-Ruiz, Oscar de la Torre, Debra Smith, Veronica Robinson, Oweeta Shands, Rosie Wickham, Danielle Boaz, Tanure Ojaide, Honoré Missihoun, Erika Edwards, Gregory Mixon, Sonya Ramsey, Jürgen Buchenau, Christopher Cameron, Christine Haynes, Kendra Jason, Janaka Bowman-Lewis, Elisabeth Paquette, Andrea Pitts, Eddy Souffrant, Felix Jean-Louis, Huma Ibrahim, and Reese Manceaux.

My year at the Center for the Study of Slavery and Justice as the Ruth J. Simmons Postdoctoral Fellow provided a great community to think through and discuss the ideas for the book, revisit materials at the John Carter Brown Library, and host a manuscript workshop where Michael Gomez, Rory McVeigh, and Center Director Anthony Bogues provided critical feedback. I am happy to also have had the support of Professor Bogues, Shana Weinberg, Maiyah Gamble-Rivers, Catherine Van Amburgh, Nic John Ramos, Zach Sell, Felicia Bevel, Felicia Denaud, and Ricarda Hammer.

Many faculty, staff, and colleagues were an important part of my undergraduate and graduate journey at Michigan State University: Aaron McCright, Glenn Chambers, Steve Gold, Brendan Mullan, Carl Taylor, Yomaira Figueroa, David Wheat, Rita Edozie, Soma Chaudhuri,

Safoi Babana-Hampton, Clifford Broman, Stephanie Nawyn, Ray Jussaume, John McClendon, Roseanne Bills, Tammy Spangler, Patience Adibe, Marilyn Duke, John Duda, Nwando Achebe, Michael Largey, Sohba Ramanand, Debbie Jesswein, David Wiley, Logan Williams, Roger Bresnahan, Tony Nunez, Julius Jackson, Beronda Montgomery, Steven Thomas, Pero Dagbovie, Kyana Young, Gwendolyn Midlo Hall, John Lee, Thomas Padilla, Devin Higgins, Alissa Lyon, Agnes Widder, Nicole Jess, Dean Rehberger, Jualynne Dodson, Sonya Johnson, Samina Hamidi, Will Escalante, Christian Ramirez, Blair Zaid, Shanti Zaid, Alexandra Gelbard, Matthew Pettway, Harry Odamtten, Julene Wilson, Renee Canady, Ola Nwabara, Jasmine Cooper, Janelle Edwards, Kelly Birch, Jamil Scott, Jeff Oliver, John Girdwood, Maria Martin, Fayana Richards, Ashley Sanderlin, Khalfani Herman, Paula Miller, and Summer Allen.

Over the years, a number of scholars and colleagues, archive buddies, and travel friends and hosts offered their support, advice, and nuggets of insights and wisdom that encouraged me, stimulated or challenged my thinking, and helped push my work forward: John K. Thornton, Carolyn Fick, Alex Dupuy, Mimi Sheller, Jane Landers, J. Cameron Monroe, Keisha Blain, Ashley Currier, Vanessa Holden, Jessica M. Johnson, Julia Gaffield, Chelsea Steiber, Rob Taber, Zophia Edwards, Matthew J. Smith, Cheryl Hicks, David Geggus, Patrick Bellegarde-Smith, Rudolph Ware, Jason Daniels, Rachel Yales, Ademide Adeluyi, Amy M. Johnson, Nicole Truesdell, Mamyrah Dougé-Prosper, Kishauna Soljour, Daniel Auguste, Patrick Sylvain, Joel Theodot, Jean Lesly Rene, Marc Prou, Mari Evans, Dave Glovsky, Jesus Ruiz, Jonathan Krause, Wendy Guillaume, Marc Joseph, Kyrah Daniels, Marvin Chocotte, Amber Gray, Joanna de Hora, Rodrigo Bulamah, Constance, Wamabale, Paulette and Cleophat at the Jeff Cherubin Domond Foundation Home in Port-au-Prince, Habitation Lauriers in Cap Haïtien, Michael D. Rogers, Reggie Turner, the Avril family, David Ingleman, Ebby Louis, Tahina Vatel, David Rocourt, Rebecca Olivier, Eziaku Nwokocha, Ernesto Mercado, Leo Carrio Cataldi, Linda Rupert, Alex Borucki, Jesse Dorst, Mary Draper, Aysha Pollnitz, Larry Tise, Josh Fitzgerald, Timo McGregor, Andrew Dial, Miguel Cruz, Mark Kelley, Marcy Norton, Diogo Ramada Curto and Renzo Baldasso, Daniel Ruppel, and Bruno Feitler.

Many thanks go to archivists and staff members at the French Archives Nationale and Archives Nationale d'Outre-Mer, the John Carter Brown Library, the Schomburg Center for Research in Black Culture, the Library

Company of Philadelphia, University of Florida George A. Smathers Libraries, University of Michigan William L. Clements Library, the UK College of Arms, the British National Archives, and the British Library. Several Haitian scholars and librarians patiently answered my questions and were critically helpful in identifying local sources of knowledge about my work: Patrick Tardieu, head archivist of the Bibliothèque des Pères du Saint-Esprit; Erol Josué, Director of the Bureau Nationale d'Ethnologie; Mr. Cezar and staff at the Archives Nationale d'Haïti (Poste Marchand); Laënnec Hurbon; Maurice Etienne at Lakou Lakay in Milot; and Evains Wêche at the library of Jérémie.

Various entities have supported this project at each stage of inception: the Center for the Study of Slavery and Justice and John Carter Brown Library at Brown University, the University of North Carolina-Duke Consortium in Latin American and Caribbean Studies, the University of Florida Center for Latin American Studies, the African American Intellectual History Society, the National Science Foundation Sociology Program, the University of North Carolina at Charlotte Faculty Research Grant and the Department of Africana Studies, and Michigan State University's Graduate School, Departments of Sociology and African American & African Studies, and Center for Latin American and Caribbean Studies.

This book has benefitted greatly from the support of, and inspiration from, several organizations, conferences, and workshops: the Association for the Study of the Worldwide African Diaspora, the African American Intellectual History Society, the Social Science History Association, the Du Bois Scholars Network, the Slavery's Hinterlands Symposium, the Revolutionary Era Consortium, the Association for the Study of African American Life and History, the North Carolina Conference on Latin American Studies, the (En)gendering the Atlantic World Workshop, the International Sociological Association, and the University of Notre Dame Center for the Study of Social Movements Young Scholars Conference.

Finally, my sincerest thanks, love, and appreciation go to my parents Eddie and Edith Eddins, brothers Eddie and Greg, sister-in-law Adina, nieces, nephews, cousins, aunts, uncles, my godmother Cheryl Garnett, Carolyn Arnold, friends Jasmine Gary Oke, Tiffany Samuel, Kevin Post, and other friends and family for their encouragement, patience, love, and support.

This title is part of the Cambridge University Press *Flip it Open* Open Access Books program and has been "flipped" from a traditional book to an Open Access book through the program.

Flip it Open sells books through regular channels, treating them at the outset in the same way as any other book; they are part of our library collections for Cambridge Core, and sell as hardbacks and ebooks. The one crucial difference is that we make an upfront commitment that when each of these books meets a set revenue threshold we make them available to everyone Open Access via Cambridge Core.

This paperback edition has been released as part of our Open Access commitment and we would like to use this as an opportunity to thank the libraries and other buyers who have helped us flip this and the other titles in the program to Open Access.

To see the full list of libraries that we know have contributed to *Flip it Open*, as well as the other titles in the program please visit https://www.cambridge.org/core/services/open-research/open-access/oa-book-pilot-flip-it-open/flip-it-open-acknowledgements

Introduction

...Come eat this food
Rada, Mondongue, Don Petro, Mussondi, Ammine
Come, come and eat this food,
Motokolo, the earth is shaking, where are you?

This song excerpt from the Haitian Vodou religious tradition recites a roll call for the *lwa* (spirits) from various African ethnic groups to gather, partake in offerings, and be recognized during a ceremony.[1] In Vodou, the *lwa* are divided into *nanchons* representing the African "nations"; however, in the song above, we see a coming together of culturally and regionally disparate spirits – the Rada (Arada) from the Bight of Benin, Mondongues and Moussondis of West Central Africa, and the Ammine (Mina), who originated from areas between the Bight of Benin and the Gold Coast. This assembly of distinct African *lwa* is an instructive lens through which we can interrogate the historical nature of interactions and relationships between diverse enslaved Africans of colonial Haiti, then called Saint-Domingue. Though divided by their geographic, religious, cultural, and linguistic origins, enslaved Africans in Saint-Domingue shared in the experience of forced migration and subjugation under a violent, repressive colonial regime. African captives were the majority of Saint-Domingue's enslaved population; they retained consciousness about and historical memory of polities, economies, and social structures that existed on the African continent since many were victims or veterans of political and religious coups, civil wars, and inter-state military conflicts that were directly and indirectly connected to the trans-Atlantic slave

I

trade (Thornton 1991). Africans struggled to re-create themselves and re-create home in the Americas by relying on their knowledge bases to make sense of their circumstances and build solidarity with each other to ensure survival.

Solidarity initially formed among the enslaved population during the Middle Passage, then during "seasoning" process of introducing new African captives to the plantation system. The collective need for enslaved people to survive the material conditions of plantation society required enculturation into the structure of expected norms and behaviors, while at the same time offering one another protection from retribution for small transgressions against the labor system (Casimir 2001, 2015). Their micro-level interactions with each other in the colony helped to cultivate, over time, an accumulated sense of collective consciousness, solidarity and relationship networks, and power to organize resistance against subjugation (Lovejoy 1997). Aradas, Mondongues, Minas, and the multitude of other African captives who survived the Middle Passage indelibly shaped the colony's landscape economically through their involuntary labor value; socially with their network relationships, cultural productions, and sacred practices; and politically through the articulation of political expressions from the African continent that re-emerged as resistance, revolts, marronnage and fugitive slave communities, and the Haitian Revolution.

The central argument of *Rituals, Runaways, and the Haitian Revolution: Collective Action in the African Diaspora* is that the web of networks between African and creole runaways, those who were enslaved, and a small number of free people of color built through rituals and marronnage was a key aspect to building an emerging sense of racial solidarity that helped make the Haitian Revolution successful. Shared African ethnic identity among the "Kongo," "Rada," and "Nagô" insurgent bands was important for facilitating trust through common language, political ideologies, or religious orientation. However, this book also brings attention to racial solidarity – cooperation among individuals beyond their cultural, linguistic, or political boundaries – as a strategically important aspect of collective consciousness. I explicate collective consciousness, and racial solidarity, by exploring the complicated relationships between groups previously believed to be politically and socially opposed or uncooperative. False dichotomies between slaves and runaway maroons; Africans and creoles; and short-term *petit* and permanent *grand* maroons are linked to the earliest enslaved blacks present on the island. When Hispanicized black *ladinos* escaped slavery soon after their early sixteenth-century arrival, Spanish colonists cast them as wild beasts or *cimarróns*. Colonists preferred continent-born Africans, who they called *bozales*, and perceived them as more docile than *ladinos* due to the lack of exposure to European lifeways – only for African Wolofs to stage the island's first black-led revolt in 1521. Recent scholarship suggests the Spanish colonial definition of *cimarrón* conceals the Taíno origins of the term *simaran*, which signifies the ongoing action of an arrow in flight and perhaps symbolizes "the intentionality of . . . enslaved or colonized people extricating themselves from conditions of oppression."[2] The black *ladinos* and African *bozales* who labored alongside the Taíno in Spanish mines and on sugar plantations, and collaborated with them in marronnage and rebellions, likely would have adopted the Taíno understanding of the term *cimarrón*, engendering a solidarity-based tradition of resistance. Yet, colonial histories and memory of resistance in colonial Haiti continue to inform conceptions of an inherent binary between the *ladino* or creole versus the African *bozale*, the runaway maroon versus the slave, and free and unfree. These erroneous presumptions about the nature of black people's claim-staking to freedom and the relationships between these categories deserve correction. By problematizing these dichotomized categories of human actors, this book presents a broader conceptualization of participation in resistance activity that pushes us beyond silences around and disavowals of enslaved people's social and political agency (Trouillot 1995), and centers collective actions as the source of structural transformations.

It is important to provide nuance to the process by which racial solidarity developed, especially in such a highly stratified colonial society as Saint-Domingue. Racial solidarity between enslaved creoles and Africans was largely situational, but as the 1791 uprising and war for independence unfolded, it was the liberation impulses generated from maroons and African rebels that pushed creole leadership to take a collective stance against white control of the nation. Solidarity was also constructed through the interactive processes involved in marronnage, which was considered an egregious offense because runaways' self-defined freedom entailed a counteraction to the logic of racial slavery and disrupted plantation work gangs' labor output. After a person or a group of people set off as fugitives, those who remained on plantations safeguarded the missing runaway by concealing their absence; conversely, runaways at times hid on plantations and took shelter in bondspeople's housing quarters. Most maroons were continent-born Africans who often escaped with members of their ethnic group, but there were situations in which it was more beneficial to flee with others. People from various backgrounds and experiences within the plantation system could bring together a wider range of knowledge, resources, and skills that could aid in escape and rebellion. For example, there was significant ethnic diversity on southwestern Saint-Domingue plantations, including enslaved people trafficked from Jamaica, meaning there was likely a heterogeneous resistance mounted by the Platons maroon kingdom against French incursions in 1792.[3] When Toussaint Louverture enacted strict labor codes that resembled slavery during his tenure as colonial leader and governor, many of the newly emancipated cultivators constantly rebelled and escaped plantations as maroons to send the message that forced labor would not be tolerated under any circumstances. Finally, it was largely continent-born Africans and maroons who led the resistance against Napoleon Bonaparte's army in 1802, forcing mobilization toward independence.

The rebels' resistance was not limited to military fighting, but they also resisted the prevailing Atlantic world economic order by creating what Haitian sociologist Jean Casimir (2001, 2015, 2020) calls the "counter-plantation" system of family landownership networks, subsistence farming, and the proliferation of Vodou – all of which were the foundation of the country's sense of popular sovereignty in the independence era. These ontological shifts and collective efforts "from below" negated white-dominated capitalist structures and demanded the reconceptualization of freedom, citizenship, property, and identity on a wider scale. Aspects of the counter-plantation logic have antecedents in the colonial era: participation in the sacred rituals that eventually coalesced into Vodou and micro-level "sociogenic" marronnage were "shaped by cognition, metaphysics, egalitarianism, hope for refuge, and the experiences of the masses" and were grounded in various African ethnic sensibilities. These practices made possible "sovereign" marronnage, the macro-level project of emancipation and nation-building during the Haitian Revolution, which was in part shaped by an emerging racial identity that was a necessary component to contesting the inherent contradictions of white supremacy and Enlightenment ideals (Roberts 2015: 117, chapter 3). Once the 1805 Haitian Constitution was ratified, it explicitly stated that all of the nation's citizens would be generally regarded as black people.[4] The Haitian revolutionaries had subverted colonial era norms and policies that enslaved and oppressed individuals according to race, birth origin, skin color, or status, and affirmed blackness as their singular national and racial identity.

Slavery in Saint-Domingue was codified into law by the *Code Noir*, which attempted to constrain the lives of bondspeople in nearly every imaginable way. Though planters and enslaved people alike oftentimes ignored the *Code Noir*, it dictated that Africans and their descendants would be baptized as Christians, it prohibited the enslaved from bearing arms or buying and selling items at market, and it forbade them from participating in any civil or criminal matters. The *Code Noir* did not officially recognize marriages between enslaved people and determined children's slave status according to that of the mother, meaning parents had no reproductive rights over their children or immediate familial networks. One way to mediate these social controls, or to disavow them altogether, was through marronnage. Whether they were seeking to permanently escape – *grand* marronnage – or needed a brief respite from the brutal plantation regime – *petit* marronnage – runaways relied on knowledge, tools, resources, and relationships within their immediate grasp to facilitate their escape. Marronnage afforded a flexibility of movement, familiarity with landscape, and the maintenance or construction of social ties between maroons, slaves, and free people that in some ways diminished the differences between these categories of social actors – especially in the face of increasing racial discrimination and repression. These groups were often in contact, and individuals could move between the states of being in marronnage, slavery, and freedom at different points of their lives; it was not impossible for an enslaved person to become a maroon, return to slavery, then become legally free. For example, recent research suggests Toussaint Louverture did just that, escaping temporarily on more than one occasion during his youth then eventually earning his freedom decades before the Haitian Revolution. Jean-François Papillon, and his romantic partner Charlotte, had been a fugitive at the time of the northern plain uprising for three years.[5] We may never know whom they encountered, what they discussed, or if they were aware of events occurring in France and the implications for Saint-Domingue. But we can speculate, as this book will in later chapters, that Jean-François, Charlotte, and many others used marronnage to cultivate relationships that would help them to organize the revolt. To be clear, this book is not attempting to assert that the masses of insurrectionists were maroons, a claim that has been debated enough. However, many maroons hid in plain sight and were often indistinguishable from those who were enslaved; therefore, maroons conceivably were present and participatory in the revolution. The influence of marronnage on the Haitian revolutionaries was also exemplified when the "indigenous" army under Jean-Jacques Dessalines named the newly independent country "Haiti," reclaiming the island's original name *Ayiti* from the Taínos, who, along with enslaved Africans, were arguably the first maroons of the Atlantic world.

Marronnage itself can be considered, in general terms, as an act and process of reclamation and redirection. When enslaved people moved about, voluntarily walking or running away from plantations, they not only made internal decisions regarding their reasons for leaving, or to where and with whom they would escape; runaways were reclaiming parts of their lives that enslavers intended to wholly control and own. Enslavers extracted labor value and wealth from enslaved people, but they also looked to extract intangible aspects of enslaved people's consciousness and identity, including their cultural connections to a homeland; time and energy; sense of self and dignity; power and self-control; social relationships; and usage of land and resources. Uncovering the ways maroons exhibited collective consciousness through acts of reclamation and redirection, especially considering they did not leave behind writings of their own, requires an inter- or multi-disciplinary approach that can help interpret archival data sources in unconventional ways. Jean Fouchard's (1972) *The Haitian Maroons*, Carolyn Fick's (1990) *The Making of Haiti*, and Michael Gomez's (1995) *Exchanging Our Country Marks* provide methodological insights and models for subversively reading marronnage and runaway slave advertisements as a lens through which to understand identity and cultural dynamics, as well as collective action, among enslaved populations. The present study employs protest event content analysis (Koopmans and Rucht 2002; Hutter 2014) of the thousands of fugitive advertisements originally published in Saint-Domingue's newspapers, primarily *Les Affiches américaines*, and draws on insights from Black/African Diaspora Studies[6] and the sociology of social movements to unveil hints and clues about escapees' innermost worlds. Rather than accept the conditions of enslavement that prescribed social death and alienation for racialized chattel laborers, maroons and their actions during flight initiated significant changes in their daily lived experiences.

This book offers a look at how, where, when, and with whom African women, men, and children collectively resisted enslavement before the Haitian Revolution, giving us a deeper knowledge of the patterns of resistance that contributed to the Revolution. Additionally, our understanding of marronnage as an anti-colonial, anti-slavery political project elevates when we study Haiti from a *longue-durée* perspective, since the island already had a significant population of self-liberated black people by the early seventeenth century. The onset of French colonization required the suppression and incorporation of maroons and enslaved captives alike into the sugar plantation economy; but just as the Spanish conquest of the island's black population through sugar slavery failed, so would the French – the Haitian Revolution of 1791 being an astounding success of black resistance against empire. A significant aim of this work is to go beyond quantifying marronnage toward comprehending the relationships that it created, and the potentiality of the tangible and intangible resources shared through those connections. I analyze variables induced from *Les Affiches* advertisements in a temporal fashion to illuminate how structural factors shaped, or were shaped by, maroons' and rebel slaves' micro-level actions. Maroons' actions reclaimed their identities, energy, and effort from behaviors that benefitted the plantocracy and redirected them toward their individual, familial, or collective interests and needs. They sought to maintain and create family ties by escaping with their children, with their countrywomen and men, or with people of other ethnic groups; and they visited or hid with free or enslaved family members and loved ones. They assumed African surnames or nicknames, or used their artisanal and language skills to forge documents and present themselves as free persons. Runaways armed themselves with guns, machetes, and other weapons to protect themselves from the *maréchaussée* (fugitive slave police) and to sack planters' properties in search of needed resources like food and clothing. They carved out geographic spaces for maroon settlements within the colony, and at times fled Saint-Domingue altogether to find refuge in the neighboring Spanish colony of Santo Domingo. These indications of behavior, reclamation of social and human capital, and knowledge of the colonial landspace are embedded in the advertisements and, when aggregated over time, they can exhibit evidence of collective consciousness, patterns of collective responses to social conditions, and the seeds of what would become the Black Radical Tradition.

CONSCIOUSNESS AND COLLECTIVE ACTION, REVOLUTIONS, AND THE BLACK RADICAL TRADITION

Collective action is any activity that brings people together for a common purpose, usually to solve a social problem (Oliver 2013). Collective consciousness is a foundational aspect of collective action because it heightens understanding of the reasons for taking part in protest activities. Shared consciousness requires both comprehension of injustices and inequalities within a material context, and having common interests with others who share positionality. Through interactive processes, social movement actors raise consciousness and construct forms of resistance befitting their context or situation (Snow and Lessor 2013). Consciousness has been the subject of sociological study since early theorists examined the impact of industrialism and modernity on patterns of relations in human communities. Marx and Engels' *German Ideology* ([1846] 2001) defined shared consciousness as a world of ideas and conceptions that emerged from, and was conditioned by, proletarian workers' common relation to capitalist modes of production. With greater inequality, class consciousness would heighten and eventually lead the working class to overthrow the bourgeoisie in a social revolution. Émile Durkheim's *Elementary Forms of Religious Life* (1912) argued that shared ritual behavior enhanced a shared sense of effervescent emotions among participants. Decades later, in *The Making of the English Working Class*, E. P. Thompson ([1963] 1980) extended Marx's definition to show how class consciousness not only arises from tense interactive processes between groups of opposed interests, but is also embedded in workers' traditions, values, and institutions. Subsequent cultural studies (Swidler 1986; Hall 1990; Kane 2000) and social movement studies (Fantasia 1988; Steinberg 1999) relied on these 'traditional' conceptions of consciousness; but sociology largely ignored the work of W. E. B. Du Bois and his consideration of other variables, primarily race, as the basis for Black[7] people's consciousness, agency, and strivings for freedom (Du Bois [1903] 1994; Morris 2007).

Sociological omission of theorizing about racial inequality, slavery, and legacies of colonialism date to the earliest work on consciousness and revolution. Cedric J. Robinson's (1983) *Black Marxism: The Making of the Black Radical Tradition* turned Marxist analysis of social movements on its head by re-assessing the development of industrial capitalism and working-class consciousness in Europe. Robinson asserts that Marx and Engels, and later E. P. Thompson, did not fully recognize ethnic, cultural, and political heterogeneity in early modern Europe, specifically overlooking the contributions of Irish migrant workers in English labor organizing efforts. This unification between the English and Irish did not last, however, resulting in the separation of "the races" and the rise of English nationalism. England's colonial dominance over Ireland engendered long-standing racial chauvinism toward the Irish from English elites, which was further inflamed among the working classes by the presence of low-wage Irish workers in England. Marx's and Thompson's incorrect assumption that the English proletariat was a cohesive group based on class entailed a failure to acknowledge the interconnectedness of racial (or proto-racial) identity, legacies of colonization, and class-based identity within contestations to capitalist formations, laying the foundation for later theorizing about collective consciousness and social movements being ill-equipped to comprehend the complexity of black mobilizations.

The origins of the Black Radical Tradition call for bringing more attention to the fundamental significance of enslaved African labor in the development of industrial capitalism, and an understanding of the deeply transformational nature of Black mobilizations in contrast to industrial wage earners or agrarian peasants that are typically considered the vanguard in revolutionary successes against dominant-class landlords. Theda Skocpol's 1979 *States & Social Revolutions* focused on peasantries in France, Russia, and China, and defined peasants as agricultural culti-vators alienated from claims to their production – but not necessarily alienated from claims to wages or land. Peasants paid taxes and rents, and according to Skocpol, peasant families in rentier agrarian systems who possessed and worked their own land were particularly inclined to rebel (1979: 116). On the other hand, enslaved people were alienated from their labor value and products, as well as any claim to wages, land, citizenship, and at the most basic level, ownership of themselves. In addition to the surplus labor value that enslaved African workers gener-ated, having been bought and sold as commodities they themselves were the foremost form of capital in the Atlantic world. When enslaved people committed marronnage, they were in effect "stealing back" themselves and their labor value, rejecting the commodification and enslavement they faced and re-humanizing themselves through various forms of expression (Wynter n.d.: 72–74). Marronnage and overt rebellions recovered enslaved people from a life of social death: complete isolation from one's own social, cultural, religious, economic, and political networks (Patterson 1982). Maroons fled in groups, sought out family members who were free – attempting to restore linkages broken by domestic slave trades – and attempted to live life, precarious as it may have been, on their own terms.

Robinson (1983: chapter 7) points out that the nature of the Black Radical Tradition, particularly African-led slave rebellions, was grounded in the worldviews that bondspeople carried with them from the continent. Enslaved people's expression of the tradition was often articulated through spiritual, cultural, and metaphysical idioms and stood in complete opposition to their position as chattel slaves and the epistemological underpinnings of racial capitalism itself. Indeed, Africans held ideologies and conceptions about the nature and purpose of political structures, monarchal rule, and slavery and freedom before their forcible transport to the Americas. John K. Thornton's (1993b) work shows that loyalty to the King of Kongo was present among West Central Africans during the Haitian Revolution.[8] While some black leaders of the early and post-Haitian Revolution era embraced both republican and monarchal forms of government, the notion that either political ideology "trickled down" from the French Revolution cannot fully account for the masses of African and African descendants and their political worldviews. It therefore cannot be taken for granted that Saint-Domingue's half million African Diasporans immediately attached themselves to European political philosophies because they had none of their own. The present study argues, in part inspired by the work of Carolyn Fick, that the women and men who were forced to labor on sugar, coffee, indigo, and cotton plantations had a collective consciousness opposed to slavery and racial capitalism that shaped their forms of resistance, and urged Haitian Revolution leaders Georges Biassou, Jean-François Papillon, Toussaint Louverture, and Jean-Jacques Dessalines to continually push the envelope for general emancipation and Haitian independence. This book therefore grapples with common perceptions that the driving ideologies of the Haitian Revolution were indigenized versions of French republicanism or royalism.

The anti-monarchal revolutions in France and in North America drastically changed the social and political landscape of the Atlantic world, infusing in it ideas of liberty and independence. Yet neither country seriously engaged the question of how to extend freedom and rights to the enslaved Africans who propelled both nations' economic prosperity and ability to leverage power against their respective monarchal rulers. As early as 1896 in his doctoral dissertation *The Suppression of the African Slave Trade*, W. E. B. Du Bois claimed it was the Haitian Revolution that "intensified and defined the anti-slavery movement" and was one of several major factors that led to the eventual abolition of the transAtlantic slave trade in 1807.[9] The prohibition of the trade, and the abolition of slavery in Saint-Domingue, did not directly result from either the American or French Revolutions, both of which were hindered from fully actualizing and universalizing republican political ideals by their unwavering commitment to slavery as the primary mode of economic enterprise. This is the argument that Anna Julia Cooper and C. L. R. James put forth, placing directly on the shoulders of enslaved Africans the impetus for radical social, economic, and political changes not only in the Caribbean but in France as well. Some 13 years before James' ([1938] 1989) foundational text *The Black Jacobins*, Anna Julia Cooper ([1925] 1988) defended her doctoral dissertation *L'attitude de la France à l'égard l'esclavage pendant la révolution [Slavery and the French Revolutionists, 1788–1805]*, arguing that France's persistence in ignoring questions about race and enslavement in Saint-Domingue forced the black revolutionaries to pursue their own liberties and shift conceptualizations of rights and freedom in France. The analyses from Cooper and James – and later from scholars like Du Bois ([1935] 1992), Herbert Aptheker ([1943] 1969), and Eric Williams (1944) – held powerful implications for what was widely accepted about the Age of Revolutions and the modern era: that it was people of African descent, their labor value, and struggles for freedom and racial equality that were the true source of the most transformative social, economic, and political changes seen to date. Despite it being the most radical political event of the Age of Revolutions (Knight 2000), few sociologists have studied the Haitian Revolution or the African Diaspora writ large, missing their wider implications and contributions to the development of, and disruptions to, European capital accumulation in the early modern era (Magubane 2005; Martin 2005).

To address the theoretical and methodological silences resulting from Eurocentric, nationally-bound, and presentist sociological scholarship, there has been a growing contingency of "third wave" historical sociologists whose work takes seriously the contributions of Cooper, James, Du Bois, Williams, and Robinson by bringing issues of racial capitalism and colonialism to the forefront of the sociology discipline (Adams, Clemens and Orloff 2005; Magubane 2005; Bhambra 2011, 2014; Morris 2015; Go 2016; Go and Lawson 2017; Itzigsohn and Brown 2020). Recent considerations in sociology and political science now accept the centrality of the Haitian Revolution in engendering alternate streams of ideals and values that would come to define the modern era for enslaved and colonized peoples. Without analysis of the Haitian Revolution, narratives about the global structuring of nation-state development – "First" and "Third Worlds," cores and peripheries, and the "Global North" and "South" – can tend to overlook and inadvertently reify the histories of European colonialism, racialized hierarchies, and slavery that engendered economic and political inequalities between states (Shilliam 2008, 2017).

The Haitian Revolution not only raises questions about what scholars mean by "development," it also urges the redefinition of concepts of freedom, equality, and independence that are not grounded in the colonial, slave-holding histories of the American and French Revolutions (Bhambra 2015, 2016). Indeed, rather than having realized already existing revolutionary ideals from Europe, the Haitian Revolution propagated its own revolutionary ideals of individual and collective autonomy through subsistence farming and establishing a free and independent nation (Getachew 2016).

Theorization about the politics of colonialism, slavery, and race within dominant paradigmatic perspectives in the social sciences is needed in the sociology of revolutions and social movements field, therefore the current study contributes to the postcolonial "turn" in sociology by bringing it into already existing conversation within Black/African Diaspora Studies about the origins and nature of racial capitalism and the Black Radical Tradition. The global protest cycle of the late 1960s invigorated intellectual interests in and Marxist analyses of conflicts, collective action, social movements, and revolutions, with theorists arguing any understanding of revolutionary circumstances must engage structural realities, including the connections between international and world-historical contexts (Tilly 1978; Skopcol 1979; Goldstone 1991; Skopcol 1994; Sewell 1996b; Beck 2017; Lawson 2017). Such a macro-level approach is indeed highly appropriate for understanding events in Saint-Domingue given the rapidly changing social, economic, and political dynamics of the Atlantic world. Change and transformation were commonplace due to both European and African states' consolidation of resources and power, and because of the increasingly tenuous economic and political relationship between the Caribbean colonies and the French metropole. Yet, preeminent studies of revolutions overlooked the Haitian Revolution – an event widely silenced throughout historical and philosophical considerations of the Age of Revolutions. For example, few if any sociological studies of the French Revolution acknowledge that the capital generated from slave labor and the slave trade contributed a substantial portion of the French bourgeoisie's wealth and therefore "were the economic basis of the French Revolution," as C. L. R. James observed.[10] Without theoretical consideration of the Haitian Revolution, the sociology of revolutions misses the integrated nature of slavery, racial capitalism, and colonialism in producing structures against which Black people and others of the formerly colonized world have fought. Comparative analysis of twentieth-century Latin American revolutions combines analyses of race, class, and gender, but the framework does not fully account for the long-term legacies of Spanish colonialism in producing inequalities in places like Mexico, Cuba, and Nicaragua (Foran 2001). Later studies (Foran 2009) broadened the number of cases beyond France, Russia, and China to include revolutions of the "Third World," but little attention is paid to racialized power dynamics that shape domestic and international relations.

Structural approaches to revolutions also tend to marginalize analysis of mobilizers' motivations or actions "from below," to which a fourth wave of revolution studies have responded by highlighting culture, agency, and identity in ways that are similar to approaches social movement scholars use (Foran 1993; Selbin 1997; Foran 2001; Sohrabi 2005; Selbin 2010; Beck 2017). Lines between revolutions and social movements have increasingly blurred theoretically, and in cases where insurgents respond to similarly weakened economic and political conditions with similar forms of protest and resistance. Yet, the study of collective actions of the past that cannot be neatly defined as classical "social movements," such as enslaved people's rebellions, tends not to be as popular (McAdam, Tarrow, and Tilly 1996; Gould 2005; Peterson 2013; Goldstone and Ritter 2019). Marronnage was not a social movement in the most classically defined sense, but an aggregate look at micro-level patterns of resistance actions against enslavement, particularly in the years leading to a revolutionary upheaval, could be considered tantamount to protracted struggle that ideas from the social movements field can help explain. Though specific concepts from the field related to collective consciousness and the temporality of tactics are helpful and are utilized in this study, there are certain limitations to relying on social movement theories in their entirety.

Prevailing social movement frameworks deal with questions surrounding the timing and emergence of collective action, but have not fully incorporated analyses that account for racist principles that structure society and intentionally exclude Black people from having access to power and resources. Doug McAdam's ([1982] 1999) analysis of the US Civil Rights Movement developed the political process model, but it has been critiqued for lack of engagement with issues of race and racial oppression, and Black mobilizers' comprehension of their racialized social conditions (Bracey 2016). The model is based on a conception of power and wealth that is concentrated in the hands of a few (McAdam [1982] 1999: 36), but it does not acknowledge that those minority stakeholders are, and historically have been, white people. Like the structuralist models used in studies of revolutions, the political process model focuses on movements' long-term development until they can exploit social, economic, and political cleavages at the macro-level. McAdam argues that political opportunities and social movement organizations help facilitate the development of "cognitive liberation," or collective consciousness; however, this book reverses this assertion and assumes collective consciousness grew primarily due to the shared social conditions under slavery and guided group interactions and insurgent activity.

The resource mobilization model foregrounds organizations, networks, institutions, and resources that social movement actors galvanize to organize a movement. Part of the difficulty with this framework, in the case of colonial Haiti and many, though not all, early modern slave societies, is that those held in bondage did not have access to, nor were they allowed to create, formal organizations or institutions that could provide the fundamental basis for mobilizing and generating resources to support a movement. This does not preclude, however, the relevance of non-tangible, social psychological resources such as collective consciousness and identity, solidarity, or cultural tools that mobilizers can employ in rallying participants toward an action or series of actions. The present study is equally as concerned with aspects of the social psychological realm as with its outward manifestations in the form of marronnage. Micromobilization theories focus on the socially constructed process of collective action by locating actors, and those whom they influence and recruit, within their structural realities (Morris 1992; Morris and Mueller 1992; Ward 2015, 2016). To understand mobilization from this perspective, I draw on the work of Aldon Morris, which advances theorizing about indigenous resources among dominated groups – Black communities in particular – their oppositional consciousness, and social spaces that situate mobilizers' efforts within their localized identities and struggles against interlocking systems of racial, economic, and gendered oppression (Morris 1984, 1992; Morris and Braine 2001).

THEORETICAL FRAMEWORK

As Gurminder Bhambra and Adom Getachew have suggested, new meanings of revolution are needed to suit the Haitian Revolution's distinctiveness, and the breadth of its post-1804 reverberations in slave rebellions, abolition movements, anti-colonial struggles, and revolutionary ideals. The Haitian Revolution and its wider implications in the Atlantic world were products of and challenges to the context in "which modernity has been constituted and developed" (Bhambra 2016: 3); that is, anti-Black racism, colonial expansion, and capitalist extraction. "Three sites of domination – the plantation, race, and imperialism – constituted the political grounds from which the [Haitian] revolution emerged … and they were also the terrain on which alternative visions of the universal were formulated" (Getachew 2016: 10), thus, in its success, the Haitian Revolution de-commodified humans and their labor, abolished racial barriers to political participation, retreated from the global capitalist order, and symbolically restored land to original inhabitants (Bhambra 2015, 2016). In that case, I propose that an alternative definition of modern revolution could be: mass collective actions that undermine, transform, and reverse conditions of concentrated power and widespread powerlessness; capitalist-driven commodification of humans, labor, land and natural resources; and racial dispossession and hierarchy upheld by white supremacist ideology and violence. Enslaved people experimented with these revolutionary ideals of freedom during the colonial era by "rejecting a plantation economy in which their labor was directed toward the production of cash crops (Bhambra 2016: 12)." This book offers marronnage as the most fundamental and historically grounded individual and collective action that advanced this rejection, aligned with Jean Fouchard's assertion that "marooning is the dominant feature of all Haitian history."[11] Not only does this book attempt to account for the relationship between marronnage and the Haitian Revolution, I also build on the work of John Gaventa (1980) to propose a causal model for collective action among people who live under severe repression. To keep people enslaved and to maintain the appearance of quiescence to bondage, enslavers of Saint-Domingue employed multiple dimensions of power that included violence and force, economic and political apparatuses that actively served the powerful, as well as cultural and ideological structures of power. To transcend and dismantle these layers of extreme economic and power inequities, it is important for potential mobilizers to first develop counterhegemonic collective consciousness.

This book pairs insights from Black/African Diaspora Studies with scholarship in the sociology of social movements and revolutions, but departs from previous sociological studies in several ways. First, it draws on constructionist/interactionist approaches to understand how people who share structural positionality and patterns of interaction develop a collective consciousness. Politicized consciousness can also be expressed through dynamics of collective action, solidarity work, organization, institutional arrangements, and the values and attitudes that emerge from within those formations (Fantasia 1988). While any group that shares material conditions can develop a political consciousness that advances their interests, systemic oppression produces consciousness that specifically addresses the unequal nature of their social conditions. Individuals' and groups' identities are lodged within the racial, gendered, and economic structures of their historical moment – interrelated domains rooted in the colonial matrix of power (Mignolo 2011). These systems of domination, the "constellation of institutions, ideas, and practices that successfully enables a group to achieve and maintain power and privilege through the control and exploitation of another group" (Morris 1992: 362–363) shape the social, economic, and political realities that marginalize certain groups rather than others. Awareness of this marginalization creates a counterhegemonic consciousness that transforms *political* consciousness to one that is *oppositional* to oppressive social forces. As such, oppositional consciousness constitutes the foundation from which oppressed groups attempt to resist and dismantle systems of domination. Within the context of European conquest, oppositional consciousness might also seek to replace dominating structures with macro-level polities that address the needs of masses and are based on their historical memory of, and historical experiences with, states and political forces (Stern 1987). As members of an involuntary diaspora, it becomes important to engage the worldviews, cultural and religious practices, and modes of thought about social, economic, and political relations that enslaved Africans carried with them from the continent and re-assembled in Saint-Domingue (Cohen 1992; Vertovec 1997; Shuval 2000; Brubaker 2005; Cohen 2008; Dufoix 2008; Sheffer 2012). Sociologist Ruth Simms Hamilton (1988: 18; 2007: 29–31) argues that oppositional consciousness and the cultural and ideological tools to organize liberation struggles are cultivated within networks of African Diaspora communities. This provides an inroad to deeper engagement with forced migrant diasporans' mobilization potential – particularly African Diasporans in the Americas – using a paradigm that can account for race, stratification, and oppression (Bracey 2016) in the early modern period.

    Second, this text posits that interaction processes not only indicated and helped form a collective oppositional consciousness, but contributed to an emerging sense of racial solidarity among enslaved African and African descended people of various ethnic and geographic backgrounds. Solidarity is an important aspect of how groups from disparate political, economic, cultural, or religious identities come together for a shared purpose. European colonial societies in the Americas relied on a "many-headed hydra" of widely diverse pools of laborers (Linebaugh and Rediker 2000), including Africans from vast regions spanning western lands referred to as Senegambia, down to Angola, then around the southern tip and up to the eastern shores of Mozambique. These groups were largely foreign to one another until they collided in the colonial context, where in work gangs, housing quarters, sacred ritual gatherings, and in maroon bands they interacted, grappled with each other, and came to common understandings of their common situation. While respecting linguistic, cultural, and religious differences, enslaved people forged political and cultural solidarities that became useful for perceiving exploitative social conditions and interpreting the salience of race and racial inequality in Saint Domingue as the basis for leveraging power during their collective actions (Skocpol 1979: 115; Melucci 1989; Taylor and Whittier 1992; Gomez 1998; Kane 2011). The book's assertion that racial solidarity was forming as people took part in sacred rituals and marronnage has an important implication for understanding post-independence Haitian national identity, which by 1805 was equated with blackness. Racial identity in the early modern era cannot be taken for granted as a social category; policies like the *Code Noir* and the 1805 Haitian Constitution concretized race, but it also developed through social norms and interactional processes.

Any study of oppositional consciousness leading to the Haitian Revolution must also begin with theorizing the ways in which racial and economically exploitative social structures shaped the conditions for Africans and African descendants' collective action. Race was a social construct to delineate the boundaries of who would be considered human (Wynter 2003), and it "has been a constitutive element, an organizational principle ... that has constructed and reconstructed world society since the emergence of modernity," signaled by the rise of European imperial expansion and enslavement of Africans (Winant 2001: 19). Saint-Domingue represented the height of racial oppression and exploitation as what can be described as a slave society: one in which many if not all social institutions are shaped by the deliberate denial of enslaved people to be self-determining (Stinchcombe 1995). Political, economic, and social relations in Saint-Domingue established and maintained powerlessness among enslaved Africans and African descendants as the status quo. The enslaved were regarded as non-human chattel and were forced to work for little to no compensation. Social structures of the wider Atlantic world organized skin color, phenotypes, and national birth origin into near impenetrable racial hierarchies with white Europeans representing the pinnacle of humanity and ownership, and black Africans associated with slave status. The *Code Noir* of 1685 outlined racial boundaries for French colonies, including Saint-Domingue, and in effect produced a stratified society where color, race, and ethnicity were inextricably linked to social class, status, citizenship, freedom, and power (Trouillot 1982; Garrigus 1993; King 2001; Garrigus 2006; Midy 2006). The masses of the enslaved population were black people born on the African continent and their progeny; while many – though not all – members of the small mixed-race population were free, amassed wealth, and attained social prominence. This work locates the impetus for the Haitian revolutionary insurgency with enslaved Africans and African descendants, in contrast to others that give primary importance to the attempts of mixed-race individuals to achieve French citizenship.

The fourth major intervention this book makes in the body of work about revolutions is a long-term approach to resistance and action before the actual event itself. A selection of long-term time frames is important to fully understand changes in resistance patterns as an explanatory tool. Social actors, during both peaceful and eventful times, ongoingly engage in politicized behaviors whether they are initiating new actions or adapting to new social forces (Stern 1987). Oppressive conditions notwithstanding, Africans in bondage found ways to be continuous initiators of politicized actions, or "weapons of the weak" (Scott 1985), through everyday challenges to the enslavement system, such as work tool sabotage, feigning illness, suicide, poison, or temporary escapes. These individualized tactics, along with collective, group-based behaviors, made up a repertoire of contention – a collection of distinctive resistance tactics that become culturally grounded; routine actions that are born from previous struggle and are temporally convenient – learned, adapted, and performed at participants' choosing (Traugott 1995; Taylor and Van Dyke 2004; Tilly 2006; della Porta 2013). According to Carolyn Fick, "of the many and diverse forms of resistance, marronnage proved in the end to be the most viable and certainly the most consistent" (1990: 49), and it represented a rupture in a social system predicated on black subservience. "Ruptures" are surprising breaks from routine practices that are typically neutralized or absorbed into the structure, disavowed or denied. But when accumulated, collective ruptures can lead to transformational historical events (Sewell 1996b) such as the Haitian Revolution. Therefore, revolutions can emerge through consciousness, solidarity, and long-term struggle.

HISTORIOGRAPHY

Part of the difficulty of writing about Haiti, the Haitian Revolution, and the country's colonial history involves the politicized nature of writing history itself. Even as the Revolution was unfolding, white Saint-Dominguans seemed to disregard its occurrence, evidenced by the fact that the August 21–22, 1791 revolt in the north was not mentioned in the *Gazette de Saint Domingue* newspaper until almost two weeks later.[12] Since that time, the Haitian Revolution has haunted social and political thought (Buck-Morss 2009) but was not given full treatment in several areas of scholarship until fairly recently. For example, historical literature on the Age of Revolutions has increasingly accepted that the Haitian Revolution holds a central place and influence in an era of monumental societal changes (Scott [1986] 2018; Klooster [2009] 2018; West, Martin, and Wilkins 2009; Landers 2010; Scott and Hebrard 2012). But, since Carolyn Fick's *The Making of Haiti* (1990), few historians have attempted to re-construct a narrative about the masses of enslaved people who participated in the Haitian Revolution. Part of this difficulty is due to a lack of primary source data left behind by the insurgents themselves.[13] This dearth of information has motivated others to attempt to identify forms of pre-revolutionary resistance (Girard 2013). Yet, the effort to uncover a tradition of rebellion in Saint-Domingue proves difficult for two reasons. First, ongoing slave revolts or maroon wars seem to not have been as common in Saint-Domingue as they were in other Caribbean locations (Turner 2011). Second, historical archives offer little evidence of formal organizations such as *confrères* – Catholic brotherhoods and sisterhoods that were often the centers of diasporic Africans' collective actions and identity formation in Spanish and Portuguese colonies of the Americas (Berlin 1996; Peabody 2002; Dewulf 2015). Therefore, several historians have probed the significance of marronnage as a contributing factor to the emergence of the Haitian Revolution.

The debate surrounding the role, or lack thereof, of runaway bands in the Haitian Revolution seems to have reached a stalemate. As some (Manigat 1977, 2007; Daniels 2012; Joseph 2012; Girard 2013) observe, the intellectual conflict has tended to fall along national lines. Members of the "Haitian school" view marronnage as an ongoing socio-political movement linked to the revolution (Fouchard 1972; Laguerre 1989). In the "French school," others (Debach [1973] 1996; Debien [1973] 1996; Geggus 1986) argue that marronnage was a passive form of resistance devoid of any collective consciousness toward freedom. Jacques Cauna (1996) also argues that marronnage and Africa-inspired rituals provided the organizational tools to develop a growing consciousness of resistance that preceded the Haitian Revolution, yet he denies that the enslaved population held any ideas of liberty or revolution. Rather than revive these intellectual contentions, the present book attempts to understand the dynamics of marronnage not yet fully explored by previous scholarship. Haitian scholar and politician Leslie Manigat (1977, 2007) affirms marronnage embodied an independence-oriented, "ethno-nationalist" conscious-ness, and suggests an integrated micro- and macro-level approach is necessary to studying marronnage over time to discern this conscious-ness. Manigat, and later Fick (1990), theorized that the propensity of some runaways, particularly women, to temporarily leave and return to the plantation repeatedly (*petit* marronnage) may have been a tactic to develop relationships and create an informal, loosely organized mobil-ization structure of enslaved individuals and self-liberated communities (*grand* marronnage) who shared and circulated ideas, resources, and strategies for escape and overthrowing enslavement. These insights by Manigat and Fick, as well as other works on marronnage that give new advances in the comprehension of maroon consciousness, help guide the methodology of this book.

Neil Roberts' (2015) *Freedom as Marronage* theoretically frames mar-ronnage as a liminal space between slavery and freedom where there is mobility, further deconstructing the boundaries between maroon and slave, and potentiality for agency. Roberts offers four pillars of marron-nage that help inform dynamic conceptions of marronnage and its utility as an organizing tool: (1) it involves distance, the separation of individ-uals between a physical place or a condition of being; (2) there is a movement that gives people the ability to be agents over their most immediate actions and the direction of their motions – this flight is not only physical but can be cognitive or metaphysical; (3) it is dependent on property; and (4) it has a purpose or a goal of an act as determined by an individual or collective. Moreover, Roberts gives new conceptual categor-ies of marronnage – sovereign and sociogenic – to give primacy to the overarching socio-political aims of maroon communities and the emerging Haitian nation-state itself. One of the most important sovereign maroon communities was *Le Maniel* of the Baoruco mountains, most recently studied by Charlton Yingling (2015). *Le Maniel* maintained an independent community throughout the eighteenth century, bringing needed attention to their socio-political consciousness to leverage inter-imperial fights over the French Saint-Domingue–Spanish Santo Domingo border for their formal recognition as a free community.

METHODOLOGY AND OUTLINE OF STUDY

The issues of lacking primary sources, a contentious historiography, and the role of Haitian cultural imagination – historical memory embedded in oral history, religious, cultural, and literary traditions – have signaled the challenges to historical paradigms and methodology that face scholars of Saint-Domingue-Haiti (Dayan 1995; Daut 2015). However, questions about the politics of writing history are not isolated to colonial Saint-Domingue, especially when attempting to understand the perspective of people who were deliberately written out of history, such as captured Africans dispersed across the Atlantic Ocean. Reconstructing narratives of their lives is an arduous task that requires knowledge of the African continent itself, the transAtlantic slave trade, and the colonial contexts of the Americas into which European traders transported captives (Lovejoy 1997; Palmer 2000; Mann 2001). Scholars have rightly pointed out that in doing such research, it is important not to treat the African continent as a monolithic place frozen in its pre-colonial time (Palmer 2000). Transformations in African histories, polities, economies, and cultures shaped social structures locally and globally, and influenced the progress and outcomes of the European slave trade (Thornton 1992). Therefore, framing the African continent as not just a historically stagnant source of captives *to* the Americas, but as a stream of ongoing history happening *in* the Americas is a critical challenge of this work and any other study focused on African descendant peoples during enslavement. A critical issue in linking Africa to its diaspora is attempting to identify captives from a multitude of ethnic, religious, political, or geographic groups whose true self-designations were either unknown or misrepresented in European slave trading and plantation records (Morgan 1997; Hall 2005). To add to this existing data on slavery, I use content analysis of over 10,000 runaway advertisements from colonial newspapers that often describe African ethnonyms to examine micromobilization patterns through shared liberation consciousness, identity work, and solidarity building. I interpret each reported incident of marronnage as a form of protest that can be analyzed across time and space (Koopmans and Rucht 2002; Hutter 2014).

The advertisements contain qualitative information that lend to wider understandings of how enslaved runaways exhibited oppositional consciousness, and conceptualized and enacted freedom on their terms. I identified several behaviors described in the advertisements that help give insight to the runaway's mindset – of course bearing in mind that plantation owners or managers wrote these advertisements, which therefore reflect their point of view. However, because enslaved people themselves were the singularly important form of capital in Saint-Domingue, enslavers had a financial incentive to provide as much accurate detail as possible to aid in identifying, locating, and recovering absconders whom enslavers considered valuable "lost property." Thus, the speculative information provided in the advertisements about the runaways and their actions can carry some legitimacy despite enslavers' implicit and explicit biases. Though the original intent of these advertisements was to surveil, track, and re-enslave black people, I aim to subvert the texts by discerning the ways in which runaways created or used previously existing social ties, and forms of their African-Atlantic human capital, to facilitate their escape and respond to structural conditions. Examination of how those patterns changed over time gives a sense of African Diasporic oppositional consciousness.

This book is an interdisciplinary case study that draws on theoretical concepts and perspectives from historical sociology and social movements scholarship and uses comparative and quantitative methods of analysis to identify collective consciousness in ways that highlight agency and self-determination. Though the voices of the masses of enslaved have yet to be unearthed, an aggregate quantitative study of their micro-level social marronnage actions might reveal temporal and geographic patterns that indicate a liberation orientation before the Haitian Revolution began. This goal aligns with historian Vincent Brown's (2016) idea of "going against the grain" of using quantitative work in slavery studies during the age of databases. Rather than reduce human processes to a "numbers game," Brown points out that quantitative analysis can support the socio-cultural interpretive tradition of Black/African Diaspora Studies and explain intentionality in ways the sources were never meant to convey. The present "database age" in which we live has provided me a unique advantage to employ tools created by digital humanists to aggregate pieces of archival data that likely would have taken previous generations of scholars a considerably longer period of time to access, collect, and analyze. The *Marronnage dans le Monde Atlantique* (Marronnage in the Atlantic World) database not only allows me to look at fugitive advertisements from eighteenth-century Saint Domingue individually, but I cross-referenced findings from those advertisements with other sources to hopefully create a fuller picture of marronnage. Similarly, the W. E. B. Du Bois Institute's *Trans-Atlantic Slave Trade Database* contains what historians consider to be a strong representation of nearly all known French slave trade voyages. These two searchable, open-source tools provide users with access to materials that have taken decades for researchers, archivists, and coders to congregate; and they are critical to understanding enslavement and resistance in the Americas from both micro- and macro-levels.

This book is organizationally and theoretically arranged to connect the interplay between structures, social action, and historical change – particularly concerning how collective consciousness (1) is shaped by history, culture, and other social forces; (2) is reinforced by shared social conditions, common experiences, and processes of interaction; and (3) informs and guides collective action. The first of these three parts explores the social forces that prompted forced diaspora migrations to Saint-Domingue and the social, political, and religious institutions with which enslaved Africans were familiar prior to their dispersals. Chapter 1 begins with African histories as the headspring of cultural and political expressions in Saint-Domingue, with the hopes of uncovering Africans and African descendants' epistemological and ontological core. There were local conceptions of slavery and the slave trade and a legacy of resistance to it. From the Upper Guinea region to Angola, captive Africans being funneled from the hinterland to the coasts – as well as those who were bonded by domestic forms of enslavement – escaped their owners, staged revolts and raids, and formed self-protective communities in geographically isolated zones. Slave ship revolts also occurred regularly and with greater intensity after 1750 when the French trade escalated. The survivors of African revolts, civil wars, and inter-state conflicts were sold into slavery in the Americas, where maroon community formations and open rebellion may have been an extension of the defensive and offensive strategies that were employed on the African continent to resist the slave trade. Chapter 2 establishes the nature of the "host society" that enslaved Africans encountered when they arrived at Saint-Domingue and provides a historical background of the French colony within the wider context of European colonization of the Caribbean. This chapter frames the island originally known to the Taíno as *Ayiti* as a space of human commodification, death, and slave resistance since the first Africans arrived in 1503. In less than 20 years, enslaved Africans were consistently escaping, taking up residence with remaining Taínos in the mountains, and participating in organized revolts. These rebellions occurred within the context of the divisions of labor during slavery, the development of the sugar and coffee economies, and the exorbitant death rates of enslaved people. In examining enslaved people's immediate social world, I look at their social lives and recreation, particularly cultural and spiritual creations, considering them as processes of enculturation that introduced new Africans to local idioms and modes of survival.

The second part of the book, Chapters 3–6, is interested in enslaved Africans' patterns of interaction with each other and their immediate environment and how these interactions gave rise to or indicated collective consciousness. To detect evidence of "movement-like" activities, these chapters focus on networks, significant protest events, key individuals, and cultural artifacts (Clemens and Hughes 2002). Chapter 3 looks at the relationship between ritual free spaces and resistance, and argues that enslaved people infused the spiritual world and ritual practices with politicized consciousness and resistance. Key primary sources by late eighteenth-century writers such as Moreau de Saint-Méry and Michel Descourtilz portrayed Africa-inspired rituals as dangerous because of the perceived association with rebelliousness. Writers and enslavers alike perceived ritualists as haughty, unruly, and having undue influence over other enslaved people who adhered to African belief systems, took part in ritual gatherings, and used or carried sacred objects to demonstrate allegiance with leadership and non-human sources of power. One of the most well-known cases of a ritualist operating as a campaigner for rebellion is Mackandal, who, in 1758, stood accused of organizing a plot to poison the whites in northern Saint-Domingue. The central argument is that by participating in ritual actions, Africans and African descendants summoned the cultural heritage(s) that they brought to Saint-Domingue with them as captives in the transAtlantic slave trade. Though the enslaved population was culturally and geographically diverse, they interacted with each other and exchanged sacred forms of power, developing social relationships in ritual gatherings that enhanced and politicized their collective consciousness. The gatherings and related activities were tools to affirm humanity and re-connect with spirit beings that could influence everyday life situations. Moreover, maroons used these opportunities to recruit potential insurgents and to preach for liberation. As such, ritual spaces functioned as zones that fostered opposition to the enslavement that was foundational to the social order.

Chapter 4 uses content analysis of over 10,000 runaway slave advertisements in an in-depth look at marronnage through the lens of network building, identity formation, and race and solidarity work. Since diaspora communities tend to create networks based on some shared identity from their host societies, I draw on diaspora studies and social movements studies by quantitatively analyzing runaway slave advertisement data from *Les Affiches américaines* colonial newspaper. Nearly half of the thousands of runaways described in the *Les Affiches* advertisements fled within a small group of two or more people. Many were racially or ethnically homogeneous maroon groups that rallied around their collective identity, while groups composed of diverse ethnic backgrounds bridged their differences to forge pan-African identity at a minimum, or at most an emerging racial solidarity that lingered and later solidified during particular moments of the Haitian Revolution. The chapter also explores the complex relationships between enslaved people, maroons and free people of color, since absconders often had previous relationships with and sought refuge with people beyond their immediate plantation, highlighting the importance of social capital in finding success at marronnage. Chapter 5 similarly relies on the *Les Affiches* advertisements to examine the ways maroons reclaimed themselves, their identities, their time, and other tangible and intangible resources. Runaways exhibited more oppositional behaviors such as passing for free, appropriating material goods, bearing arms, and escaping for longer durations of time – leading to escalating *grand* marronnage before the Haitian Revolution. Chapter 6 explores the geographic and spatial dimensions of marronnage. Enslaved people and maroons had intimate knowledge of their immediate locales and geopolitical borders that they sought as places of refuge. Planters constantly worried about the presence of runaways in the mountains as well as those who crossed the border into Spanish territory, and the colony's local topography contained several cave systems that provided spaces for runaways and enslaved people to establish linkages and plan rebellion. Not only were maroons spatially pervasive throughout Saint-Domingue, their presence had a significant impact on the landscape and on the Santo Domingo border itself.

Part III of the book then turns to the ways collective consciousness influenced social actions and impacted social structures. Chapter 7 contextualizes the rates and nature of marronnage within changing social, economic, political, and environmental factors. I frame marronnage as a part of enslaved people's repertoire of contention, a collection of organic forms of resistance tactics that are sustained over time, yet adapted for new contextual circumstances (Traugott 1995; Taylor and Van Dyke 2004; Tilly 2006; della Porta 2013). Here it is important to identify the structural contexts, especially the political developments, plantation production, policing and repression, and natural environment that shaped marronnage. Chapter 8 traces the continuation of oppositional consciousness into the revolutionary period. Over time, more connections developed between runaways and plantation slaves, and small-scale uprisings occurred increasingly before the Haitian Revolution began, feeding into the solidarity that eventually formed around a shared racial identity.

I

HOMELANDS, DIASPORA, AND SLAVE SOCIETY

"We Have a False Idea of the Negro": Legacies of Resistance and the African Past

Weary from war with the formerly enslaved rebel army and having lost thousands of French troops to fighting and yellow fever, by the end of 1802, the infamous expedition of General Victoire Leclerc to reimpose slavery in Saint-Domingue was failing. Approaching death himself, that fall Leclerc sent several desperate letters to the mainland requesting additional resources and reconsideration of the mission, including one in which he pleaded:

We have ... a false idea of the Negro ... We have in Europe a false idea of the country in which we fight and the men whom we fight against.[1]

The statement reads as a deathbed confession of a military incursion gone embarrassingly awry in part from having underestimated enemy forces. But a deeper excavation of Leclerc's sentiment reveals a potential moment of awakening from Europe's three-centuries-old ontological belief in the supposedly inferior nature, identity, and intellectual capacity of the "negro." As Michel-Rolph Trouillot (1995) has argued, until – and indeed, even after the Haitian Revolution, Europeans failed to conceive of Africans as humans, as thinkers, as planners, or as revolutionaries. Early nationalistic chauvinism embedded in both early Christianity and capitalism fueled the reimagination of African polities, cultures, and individuals into a flattened, singular "negro," or black identity void of any distinctions (Robinson 1983: 99–100; Wynter 2003; Bennett 2018). Cedric J. Robinson's (1983) now foundational *Black Marxism: The Making of the Black Radical Tradition* has offered that the "negro" was an invention of racial capitalism, manufactured through

Christianity, commodification and the transatlantic slave trade, and enslavement in the Americas.

Enslavers' imposition of an inferior racial identity did little to alter the self-defined identities of diasporic Africans who, in many ways, retained knowledge of and appreciation for who they were and the ways they understood the world – despite the traumatic experience of the Middle Passage and enslavement. Africans embodied their own biographies, histories, and worldviews that shaped their human activities – especially within political, economic, and military realms – and this ontological and epistemological core with which Africans operated represented the source of their opposition to racial capitalism (Robinson 1983). Scholars have increasingly given attention to the dimensions of West African and West Central African cultural, religious, militaristic, and political influences on the Haitian Revolution (Thornton 1991, 1993b; Gomez 1998; Diouf 2003; Mobley 2015). This turn provides a growing baseline of historical data that problematizes previous beliefs that France alone bestowed Enlightenment ideals upon enslaved African people. Reading the archives of enslavers' records that labeled captives according to their geographic locations – though oftentimes incorrectly – reveals that African ethnicities and cultural identities were not only linked to specific locations of origin, but to political projects.

Africans were not able to fully retain entirely cohesive social, political, or religious structures due to the trauma of separation from their homes and the Middle Passage; but they re-created elements of their institutions and transmitted them through interactions on plantations, in ritual spaces, in self-liberated maroon communities, and in the bellies of slave ships. Prior to the colonial situation, African captives began bonding around coping with the horrifying conditions of the Middle Passage. The long voyages on foot or in small river boats from hinterlands to coastal port cities, and the waiting period in slave castles at the ports, could take several months to a year. In addition, slave ship voyages across the Atlantic Ocean also took up to three to four months. Ship captains, traders, and sailors tightly packed captives into ships, usually head-to-foot to fit as many people as possible into the ship's belly. Food was meager and the sanitary conditions were loathsome. The Middle Passage was a harrowing experience where physical abuse, disease, and death; psychological disorientation; and sexual exploitation were ubiquitous. Captives commonly attempted suicide and at times collectively revolted on the ships (Richardson 2003; Smallwood 2008; Mustakeem 2016). Interactions between "shipmates" on the way to the ports and on slave ships were the only sources of human affirmation, and the beginnings of the social ties that would spawn collective identity formation and cultural production after disembarkation (Mintz and Price 1976; Borucki 2015).

This type of violent extraction from families, communities, and societal structures would have stimulated in slave trade victims an affinity for their real (rather than mythical) homelands that was the basis of their attempts to actively preserve, re-formulate, or construct oppositional conscious-ness, identities, network relationships, and cultural and religious practices to maintain self-understanding and integrity in host societies that were hostile to their presence (Vertovec 1997; Shuval 2000; Butler 2001; Brubaker 2005; Hamilton 2007; Dufoix 2008). As such, maintaining a sense of self and creating community relationships, behaviors, norms, and ideologies to affirm the collective was essential to African Diasporans' survival and acts of resistance against enslavement (Hamilton 2007: 29–31). African ethnic or "New World" identities that were linked to specific cultural, religious, and racial formations influenced several col-lective action rebellions throughout the Americas. Rather than assume these formations were "backward-looking" or somehow lacking progres-sive ideals as Eugene Genovese (1979) suggested, I argue that rebellions among the enslaved and maroons were based on the political, economic, and cultural practices of those who themselves were avoiding capture or otherwise resisting the violence of the transAtlantic slave trade. Rebellions and revolts like Tacky's Revolt in Jamaica and the Haitian Revolution were indeed progressive, transformative factors that altered the course of European struggles for hegemonic power (Santiago-Valles 2005) and broadened discourses around freedom, equality, and citizenship.

Who were the "negroes," "rebels," "brigands," "insurgents," and "masses," as C. L. R. James ([1938] 1989) referred to them, of the Haitian Revolution? From where did they originate, what was the shape and character of the social forces into which they were socialized, and how did elements of their African origins inform collective action? This chapter attempts to contextualize forms of resistance tactics that appeared in Saint-Domingue from the perspective of Africans who "lived in their ethnicity as much as anyone else" (Winant 2001: 55), and therefore were influenced by their respective socio-political and cultural worldviews. Though it was a French and white creole colony in name and political economy, the social world of Saint-Domingue was essentially African. Approximately 90 percent of the colony's population was black, and over two-thirds of those black people were of immediate African extraction. Enslavers purchased or kidnapped captives from several African societies that practiced indigenous forms of enslavement, although these systems were qualitatively different from the racialized slavery Europeans implemented in the Americas. African forms of slavery add another dimension to the socio-economic and political realities that captives lived with on the continent, and it constituted part of their collective consciousness. Yet the incongruence between African and European slaveries, the commodification that rendered human life expendable, and processes of racialization were radicalizing forces that further heightened and politicized collective consciousness. The persistent influence of African social, political, and religious formations – especially the Bight of Benin and West Central Africa – helped inform the ways enslaved people in Saint-Domingue coped with their situation and attempted to reconstruct their lives in ways that were alternative to the dictates of Western modernity.

The transAtlantic slave trade and African rulers' responses to it were leading causes of societal transformations that affected the everyday lived experiences of women, men, and children who were either victimized by the trade in some capacity or were aware of the potential to be victimized. African state leaders increasingly consolidated power and wealth, which they gained from trading captives with Europeans. The growing chasm between the elite classes and those who were most vulnerable to capture led to conflict and revolt over the trade, making eighteenth-century African wars and uprisings an important scene of the Age of Revolutions (Ware 2014; Green 2019; Brown 2020). Discontent over the trade, warfare and upheaval, and shifting paradigms over the nature and scope of African rulers' absolute power created space for more egalitarian political philosophies to emerge "from below" and challenge existing regimes. Politically progressive ideals sought to place limits on monarchal authority through decentralized governance, and placed higher expectations on kings to act with fairness, unselfishness, and restraint. These changing beliefs were often understood and articulated through socio-religious idioms as people attempted to rectify societal imbalances through ritual, resistance, and the development of egalitarian social forms on both sides of the Atlantic (Thornton 1993b). Individuals responded to the increasing encroachment of the trade by attempting to defend or fortify themselves or their communities. Africans' discontent over violent capture and strategies for attempting to resist the trafficking process were also expressed through coastal marronnage and slave ship insurrections. Those who were unsuccessful at self-protection and funneled into the trade carried with them not only the trauma of their personal experiences, but undoubtedly held anecdotes about neighbors, kith, and kin affected by the trade and attitudes about whether they were justifiably or unjustifiably being held captive according to local custom, and for what reasons. Many of the rituals and spiritual beliefs, political ideas, and acts of rebellion that would later become prominent during the Haitian Revolution predated the Middle Passage and therefore serve as important antecedents that deserve exploration. What follows is an attempt to explicate and trace the Black Radical Tradition to Saint-Domingue, from its inception in African political formations and socio-religious worldviews, its containment and transformations due to commodification and contact with the French Atlantic slave trade, and expressions during coastal and slave ship rebellions.

DOMESTIC AFRICAN SLAVERY AND THE FRENCH TRADE

Slavery was part of many African societies and was based on inequality, but it operated differently than the racialized slavery Europeans initiated in the Americas. Domestically enslaved Africans – and their labor – were a concrete form of privately-owned property and were considered subordinate family members. Despite not owning themselves or their labor value and performing labor that would be considered degrading, enslaved people typically were not denied their humanity and at times were allowed relative freedoms, social mobility, and property ownership. Various societies had their own socially constructed norms surrounding eligibility for enslavement. Captives included prisoners of war, the financially indebted, and cultural or religious outsiders. For example, those who had knowledge of the Qu'ran at areas of Senegambia could be protected from the slave trade; native-born Dahomeans were not supposed to be enslaved; and Kongolese bondspeople were typically from outside the kingdom and could be physically punished for disobedience or for being absent without prior permission.[2] Buying people was a way of accumulating wealth and state officials used many of the enslaved for government or military services to increase their political power. It was relatively easy for enslavers to trade with Europeans, since they were likely to be wealthy merchants, rulers, or state officials. In exchange for European manufactured guns, alcohol, salt, clothing and jewelry, African kings and merchants sold war captives from neighboring polities, criminals, and other individuals who were most peripheral to centers of power.[3] As the demands for enslaved labor on Caribbean and Brazilian sugar plantations increased and trade with Europeans became costlier, African kings resorted to waging wars to meet the demands for more captives.

The Portuguese were the first Europeans to sustain contact with parts of Africa through trade and conquest in the mid-fifteenth century; they first explored the Bight of Benin in 1472 and were shortly followed by Spaniards who procured slaves from Portuguese and Dutch traders. With the founding of the Dutch West India Company in 1625, the French West India Company in 1664, and English Royal African Company in 1672, captive Africans quickly became the foremost form of capital – even more valuable than land or gold by the eighteenth century, according to Walter Rodney – and the international slave trade accelerated.[4] The French slave trade was relatively obscure and illegal during this period. Early in the eighteenth century, French ships supplied Spanish colonies with African captives, but few of these voyages resulted in trafficking bondspeople to French territories in the Americas, leaving a dearth of French slave trading records. Before the Treaty of Utrecht officially sanctioned the French slave trade in 1713, the Dutch and English sold many Africans to French Caribbean islands, and the French took other captives during raids on English ships and territories. The number of slave ship voyages and disembarked Africans gradually increased in the early part of the century, then exploded in the 1770s and 1780s.

European slave traders relied on established commercial networks and a range of actors who facilitated negotiations, financial exchanges, and the procurement of human bodies, typically through brutal means. The levels of violence used to extract and traffic Africans to the coasts and onto slave ships cannot be understated. Sowande Mustakeem's (2016) *Slavery at Sea* has illuminated the micro-level processes of the Middle Passage, beginning with the moment of capture and ending at the point of sale at ports of the Americas, emphasizing the effects of violence, illness, and psychological despair on individual captives as well as the larger collective of captives as they witnessed traumas inflicted on others. In addition to engaging in warfare, captors leveled raids on families, communities, and villages unexpectedly, and by the eighteenth century nearly 70 percent of captive Africans had been victims of kidnapping. Though by some local conventions slavery was associated with criminality or being born within a low status group, increasing demand from plantations in the Americas during the eighteenth century meant that on the African continent, "escalating value placed upon black bodies created a threatening environment in which every person in African society, regardless of status, became a potential target."[5] It is estimated that during the eighteenth century, the French transported between 1.1 and 1.25 million captive Africans, bound for port cities of the Americas. Of those captured, nearly 800,000 embarked on ships headed to Saint-Domingue but only 691,116 survived the Middle Passage and were counted among those who disembarked.[6] The loss of life during the voyages is only part of the total experience of African deaths, which also included fatalities "between the time of capture and time of embarkation, especially in cases where captives had to travel hundreds of miles to the coast ... [and] the number of people killed and injured so as to extract the millions who were taken alive and sound."[7]

As the trade ratcheted up around mid-century, a seemingly unending stream of Africans were brought to the colony, resulting in the enslaved population approaching 500,000 just before the Haitian Revolution, two-thirds of whom were continent-born.[8] In the first half of the eighteenth century, the majority of captives were taken from the Bight of Benin with West Central Africans and Senegambians, respectively, representing the second and third most common groups. After 1750, however, French slave trading moved southward along the West Central African coast. These inhabitants became the largest proportion of captives to Saint-Domingue and were increasingly desired to labor in the colony's quickly growing coffee industry. For example, one family in Port-au-Prince stated in 1787 that their affairs were so prosperous that the estate went from owning 5 to 36 slaves in a matter of only 18 months.[9] Once a ship was financed to take sail from one of the French ports, most likely Nantes since it was the busiest slaving port, the captain took wares to be sold for African captives at the coast. Guns were one of the most highly valued trade items, as they gave the perception of technological advancement and amplified strength and power in warfare to capture more slaves; for example, a petition from a "citoyen," Sudreau, appears to request permission to exchange African captives for 700 guns.[10] The growing abundance of captives at the coast meant that prices for slaves were cheaper than in the Caribbean colonies. Eighty Africans from the Guinea coast destined for Les Cayes were bought for 800 *livres*, approximately half the value that planters placed on healthy enslaved adults.[11] Other highly valued captives were black sailors and other ship hands, whose nautical skills and familiarity with coastal cultures could aid slave ship captains in completing transactions. One sailor, described as a "Frenchified" black, was valued at 2,400 *livres*, significantly higher than the average price of a Saint Dominguan enslaved person.[12] In order to ensure the voyages' profitability, ship captains procured as many slaves as possible, sometimes tarrying along the African coast and visiting multiple ports to find available human cargo, but typically slavers secured captives from one

African port to reduce the length of the voyage and the probability of illness and insurrection.

Archival data show a clear dominance of African men over women during the height of the French trade to Saint-Domingue, consistent with findings from other European nations' trading activity more generally. Between 1750 and 1791, the highest level of gender parity existed among captives from the Bight of Biafra, where 53.9 percent were male and the remaining 46.1 percent women and children. Children represented a sizable proportion in French slaving records, accounting for nearly 27 percent of captives. Lower sex ratios were often due to raiding and kidnapping, and women and children were often the victims of these activities, as seen in the Bights of Biafra and Benin areas. Higher levels of gender imbalance occurred between captives from the West Central and Southeastern African regions. This disparity, especially among West Central Africans, can be attributed to women's value as local agricultural laborers, which kept them from being vulnerable to the trade in higher numbers. Other reasons for the low presence of women in the French trade relate to local needs for women in matrilineal societies; additionally, the hardships of the journey from the interior to the coasts made women and children less desirable to slavers.[13] Such gender dynamics – as well as responses to the slave trade – varied by culture, political structure, and region. What follows is an exploration of those variations, and considerations of religion, economy and political systems in areas that were most impacted by the French slave trade to Saint-Domingue.

POLITICAL SYSTEMS, THE SLAVE TRADE, AND RELIGION

During the height of the slave trade, several African polities were consolidating power and wealth at the highest levels, leaving communities, clans, and towns vulnerable to warfare and raids. Popular contestations to abuses of power not only influenced revolts and resistance to the slave trade, they informed political consciousness about the nature of rule, inequality, and unjust forms of slavery. As Africans from various regions encountered each other in Saint-Domingue, they found compatibility and solidarity in their experiences and perspectives on the imbalances of power and resources that resulted in enslavement. In the Dahomey Kingdom, ancestral and nature-related deities indicated the religious reach of monarchal rulers into the everyday lives of their subjects, including the enslaved. These imperial deities, as well as local spirits, migrated with people through the Middle Passage to the Americas. Other coastal African religious systems were less tolerant of the realities of slavery and informed ethical dimensions against the slave trade. Muslims at Senegambia, as well as Vili traders based at the Loango Coast, exemplify a major thrust of this chapter: that African peoples had local conceptions of slavery and the damage caused by the European slave trade, and that spiritual sensibilities informed those ideas. Yet, despite these systems of thought that opposed the fundamentally exploitative and dehumanizing nature of the slave trade, African participation in the vast commercial network allowed the European slave trade to function by relying on local knowledge and trade relationships. These and a multitude of other African-born people represent the complexity of local complicity with the trade, the power imbalances between Europeans and Africans, and opposition to the slave trade.

The Bight of Benin

According to the *Trans-Atlantic Slave Trade Database*, deportees from the Bight of Benin comprised over 35 percent of those taken to Saint-Domingue in the early part of the eighteenth century. The French settled a trading base at Ouidah, one of the most utilized slaving ports at the Bight of Benin, a region that eventually came to be known as the "Slave Coast" due to its convenient geography and low purchase prices for captives. One of the most prolific slave trading polities at the Bight of Benin was the Dahomey Kingdom, which originated in the sixteenth century in a small, geographically dismal area 60 miles from the coast. Its capital was Abomey, but the land had little to no natural resources and the climate of the area was not conducive to habitation. The nation's dependence on the slave trade to obtain guns pushed them towards the coast, dominating other cultural groups, such as the Yoruba-speaking Nagôs and Fon/Gbe-speaking Aradas, along the way.[14] By the 1730s, Dahomey had emerged on the Guinea Coast, after having conquered Allada in 1724, Ouidah in 1727, and Jankin in 1732.[15] With direct Dahomean presence on the coast, there was a steady supply of captives for the trade. The yearly number of captives from the Bight of Benin to Saint-Domingue increased from 8,577 to 10,970 between 1721 and 1730, corresponding to Dahomey's conquest of Ouidah in 1727 (Table 1.1). Similar to West Central African conceptions that equated the slave trade to witchcraft or cannibalism, which will be discussed below, seventeenth-century recordings in Dahomey suggest some captives believed that traders would

TABLE 1.1. *Embarked captives to Saint-Domingue by African region, 1700–1750*

	1701–1705	1706–1710	1711–1715	1716–1720	1721–1725	1726–1730	1731–1735	1736–1740	1741–1745	1746–1750	Total
Senegambia	0	160	2,096	2,431	2,063	1,221	3,805	5,168	4,835	768	22,547
Sierra Leone	0	0	0	0	0	0	0	177	220	0	397
Windward Coast	0	0	80	0	0	0	0	922	2,164	395	3,561
Gold Coast	0	0	0	149	273	0	1,102	5,354	8,699	1,116	16,693
Bight of Benin	0	1,408	4,899	8,059	8,577	10,970	6,152	15,453	9,371	3,665	68,554
Bight of Biafra	0	0	370	1,027	0	0	0	320	484	0	2,201
WC Africa & St. Helena	0	0	840	2,875	2,993	593	3,172	10,809	13,696	8,956	43,931
SE Africa & Indian Ocean	0	0	0	0	386	0	386	0	0	0	772
Other	607	0	1,718	4,412	1,222	2,238	2,380	7,157	6,018	3,240	28,992
Total	607	1,568	10,003	18,593	15,514	15,022	16,997	45,360	45,484	18,140	187,648

eat them. Other beliefs included the idea that "the cowry shells which were used locally as money were obtained by fishing with the corpses of slaves, who were killed and thrown into the sea, to be fed upon by sea snails, and then hauled back out to retrieve the shells."[16] The metaphors of people being eaten by sea animals or other people, or being transformed into material objects, reflected the harsh reality of the exchange between humans and commodities, and expressed widespread fear and indignation about the slave trade.

Fon/Gbe-speaking peoples turned to their local spirit forces, the *vodun*, to intervene on their behalf. The thousands of *vodun* at the Bight of Benin can be generally categorized into two groups: those derived from family networks, including ancestors, and founders of clans and towns; and those associated with the forces of nature such as fire, the sea, and thunder. While most *vodun* were based in local communities, powerful *vodun* attracted followers from other locales. The oldest *vodun* that had long-standing roots in one community received the most reverence. The snake spirit, Dangbe, was considered part of Ouidah's royal pantheon prior to Dahomey's emergence. People presented Dangbe with gifts such as silk, food and drink, and foreign commodities, with hopes that he would provide protection to society from outside forces. The spiritual power of the local *vodun* translated into social capital and political strength that could undermine imperial Dahomey's ideological and cultural dominance, and the priests of Dangbe were nearly equivalent in power and status to the king of Ouidah. Dahomeans destroyed and ate the sacred snakes of Ouidah during their 1727 campaign to publicly demonstrate their hostility and military dominance over the people and their gods.[17] Although Ouidah had suffered defeat, signaling to some the spiritual inferiority of Ouidah's *vodun*, members of the conquered Fon/Gbe-speaking peoples who were exiled to Saint-Domingue maintained a close relationship with the snake spirit and became the progenitors of what would become Haitian Vodou. Oral histories reveal there was continued unrest in the 1730s and 1740s, as followers of Sakpata, a group of *vodun* associated with the land, were rumored to use spiritual means to plot against King Agaja in retaliation for his sale of so many of Sakpata's adherents into slavery.[18]

The Dahomean monarchy responded with active measures to re-shape religious life by appropriating local *vodun*, while introducing new *vodun* from the royal lineage for public reverence to "more effectively control the followers of popular gods."[19] Members of the royal family were strictly prohibited from participating in worship of *vodun* outside of the king's ancestral lineage. However, "commoner" clans – groups of royal subjects – could associate with and worship the monarch's ancestral *vodun*. Dahomey's religious consolidation helped facilitate its growing domination, and the kings' ability to centralize and wield political, economic, and military power deeply relied on the manipulation of existing religious beliefs and practices. The *kpojito* queen mother, a political and symbolic position held by a woman related to the Dahomean king by birth or marriage, influenced religious relations. One of the longest serving kings of Dahomey, Tegbesu, reigned from 1740 to 1774 and was accompanied by his *kpojito*, Hwanjile, who is credited with re-organizing religious hierarchy in Dahomey. Hwanjile introduced several *vodun* to the kingdom, most notably the creator couple Mawu and Lisa, in 1740, which were ranked above all other local *vodun*. Mawu and Lisa represented an ideological message that power and authority came from both male and female figures, which may have helped satisfy remaining followers of Dangbe – many of whom were women who could attain priesthood and other statuses of rank, even if they were of the commoner or slave class.[20] This move was instrumental in aiding King Tegbesu gain power and control over Dahomean religious life, thereby undermining the mechanisms by which protest could emerge.[21]

In addition to religious legitimation, the power of the slave trade bolstered Dahomey's state-building capacity and wealth, particularly during Tegbesu's tenure. Tegbesu personally supervised trade relations at European forts and with the Oyo Empire. But, up to and after his death, the fundamental Dahomean law that banned the sale of anyone born within the kingdom was no longer upheld, as slaves became the primary overseas export good.[22] Dahomean kings lived lavishly as a result of slave trading profits, which they displayed at "customs" ceremonies where festivities included distributing food, drink, trade goods, and well as military performances.[23] Figures from the *Trans-Atlantic Slave Trade Database* (Tables 1.1 and 1.2) help create a more complex picture of the volume of the slave trade from the Bight of Benin. There seems to have been a drop in the slave trade from the Bight of Benin between 1741 and 1750, the first years of Tegbesu's power, then an even more drastic drop between 1755 and 1760. Though Ouidah continued to be a forerunning port for the French well into the latter half of the eighteenth century, ongoing warfare between Dahomey and the neighboring Oyo Empire between the 1760s and 1780s was a dominant factor in generating large numbers of captives from the Bight of Benin to Saint-Domingue.

The Oyo Empire and its Yoruba-speaking inhabitants trace their origin to the city Ile Ife, which was first ruled by the common ancestor and king

TABLE 1.2. *Embarked captives to Saint-Domingue by African regions, 1751–1800*

	1751–1755	1756–1760	1761–1765	1766–1770	1771–1775	1776–1780	1781–1785	1786–1790	1791–1795	1796–1800	Total
Senegambia	3,964	0	1415	2,222	2,306	1,961	2,248	7,459	837	0	22,412
Sierra Leone	1,301	263	1,991	4,487	255	1,698	4,083	6,676	1,644	0	22,418
Windward Coast	772	0	344	456	241	196	573	2,010	206	0	4,798
Gold Coast	1,006	230	109	1,377	1,111	630	2,145	8,029	431	0	15,068
Bight of Benin	21443	577	5757	12,785	18,423	18,224	7,926	30,809	3,366	0	119,310
Bight of Biafra	1,676	626	1,502	4,097	1,686	5,179	2,891	13,263	4,535	0	35,455
WC Africa & St. Helena	20,881	2,673	14,292	48,003	44,086	27,887	37,318	76,235	15,120	540	287,035
SE Africa & Indian Ocean	0	0	0	0	333	2,189	2,513	19,473	4,901	0	29,409
Other	7,216	250	4,060	9,093	7,842	7,038	9,598	19,325	6,148	0	70,570
Total	58,259	4,619	29,470	82,520	76,283	65,002	69,295	183,279	37,208	540	606,475

Oduduwa prior to the sixteenth century. After being sacked by the Nupes in the sixteenth century, and later by the Bariba, the Oyo Empire reorganized itself, laying the foundation for expansion in the seventeenth and eighteenth centuries.[24] In contrast to the centrality of monarchical power in kingdoms like Dahomey, Loango, or Kongo, the Oyo Empire was composed of smaller units of political power based in Yoruba towns that operated autonomously but were subordinate to the Oyo king. Town "chiefs" gained power through the accumulation of wealth and followers, and this power was passed down through lineage. Chiefs represented the interests of their families and followers within their wards to the king; however, members of the wards could shift allegiances from one chief to another depending on the efficacy and generosity of the latter. Many chiefs commanded the military, while a group of seven elite chiefs composed a religious council to control the spiritual sects. There was also a Muslim ward of the city of Oyo, established between the sixteenth and seventeenth centuries, which was under the control of one of the non-royal chiefs.[25] The Oyo Yoruba and Aradas had similar cosmologies, and in fact several Yoruba nature spirits, the *orisha*, such as Ogou, Eshu-Elegba, Olorun, Oshun, and Oshumare, were incorporated into *vodun* due to expansion, trade, demographic shifts, and conflict between Dahomey and the Yoruba peoples.[26]

The Oyo Empire went to war with Allada in 1698 and fought Dahomey in 1726–1730 in response to Dahomey's aggressive attempts to control the slave trade at the coasts, which stood in opposition to Oyo's commercial interests. Oyo's campaign to provide aid to smaller nations resisting Dahomey successfully resulted in Dahomey becoming a tributary to Oyo, and Oyo supplied slaves to Ouidah through Dahomey.[27] From 1739 to 1748, Dahomey again revolted against Oyo, which was not a long-term success since by the 1770s Dahomey was paying tribute to Oyo and the two empires fought alongside each other to invade smaller polities like Mahi and Badagri.[28] The height of Oyo's power was between 1754 and 1774, when the empire expanded to the north, then from 1774 to 1789, when it conquered Egbado, Mahi, and Porto Novo. Major interrelated factors that led to the rise of the empire included its military might and the use of highly trained cavalry and archers; economically it grew due to participation in the expansion of long-distance trade and commerce, most notably the Atlantic slave trade, which then financed military resources. Other captives that the Oyo empire enslaved or traded were the Oyo Yoruba, non-Oyo Yoruba, and neighbors of the Yoruba such as the Hausas, Nupe, Borgu, Mahi, and the Bariba.[29]

The Yoruba-speaking Nagôs were a key group from the Bight of Benin taken to Saint-Domingue. While Yoruba captives taken to Cuba were referred to as the Lucumí, in Portuguese Brazil and French Saint-Domingue, the Yoruba collectively were called Nagô.[30] Archival data from Saint-Domingue's plantation records and runaway slave advertisements indicate that the Nagôs actually outnumbered the Aradas by the end of the eighteenth century.[31] There is some confusion about the origins of the term "Nagô"; historians have suggested that Fon-speakers applied the term to all Yoruba slaves and any captives handled by Oyo. Other evidence points to the Anagô as a smaller society of merchants that occupied southwestern Yorubaland, which was subject of the Oyo Empire from as early as the late seventeenth century. In the early eighteenth century, the Nagô traded slaves for firearms at Porto Novo and its towns paid tribute to Oyo in tobacco, gunpowder, European cloth, and flints.[32] As a subsidiary nation of Oyo, the Nagô were dispatched to send provisions and armies led by "Kossu, a Nago chief, belonging to Eyeo [Oyo]" to assist Dahomey in raids against Bagadri in 1784. The Nagô themselves were also targets for the trade during periods of heightened warfare between Dahomey and Oyo. Nagôs were sold from Ouidah as early as 1725 and again in 1750; from Porto Novo in 1780 and 1789; and during three campaigns waged by Dahomey against the Nagôs in 1788 and 1789.[33] As the Oyo Empire weakened and Dahomey ascended, between one-fourth and one-third of captives from the Bight of Benin were Nagôs/Yorubas, making them one of Saint-Domingue's ethnic majorities whose numbers increased during the time period leading to the Haitian Revolution.[34]

The Nagôs' militaristic experience, as both participants in and victims of the slave trade, seems to be reflected in contemporary Haitian Vodou, as Nagô is a significant "nation" or ethnically organized pantheon of spirits that includes important warrior-oriented deities like Ogou and Agwé.[35] Combat skills acquired through the Anagô military background were essentially transferred to Saint-Domingue through war captives, traded as slaves, who later put their knowledge to use during the Haitian Revolution – for example, the rebel leader Alaou. Accounts from Cap Français in 1793 described Nagô rebels as a "valiant nation" of fierce fighters who skillfully prevented an incursion of armed free people of color and put down attempts to recruit local plantation slaves into the ranks of the free troops. Jean-Jacques Dessalines was said to have been a devoted follower of Ogou, the god of warfare and iron. After his assassination in 1806, he was deified in Vodou as Ogou Dessalines within the

Nagô tradition.[36] Nagô influence in the Haitian Revolution predates the "Nagoization" of nineteenth-century Brazil and Cuba in the wake of the Oyo Empire's collapse, which brought a flood of enslaved Yoruba-speakers into the sugar-producing nations through illegal trafficking and triggered several Nagô-led slave rebellions (Barcia 2014). As I discuss in Chapters 3 and 8, Nagô/Yoruba conceptions of weaponry, war, and religion became a key component of enslaved people's collective consciousness during Saint-Domingue's pre-revolutionary era and the 1791 uprising. Their experiences with the transAtlantic slave trade as victims and traffickers would have been thrown into sharp relief in a foreign colony where slave status was synonymous with race and African origin, rather than with relationship to powerful states.

Senegambia and Other Areas

Intra-European, intra-African, and European-African conflict over control of the slave trade destabilized many coastal and interior societies and affected the regional outflows of African ethnic groups over time. In addition to the Bight of Benin Coast, the French held Senegambian slave posts at Gorée Island, near Dakar, and Saint Louis, between the Senegal and Gambian rivers. Given its geographic proximity to Europe, Senegambia was the first sub-Saharan region to establish direct commercial contact with Portugal in the fifteenth century and was one of the first leading sources of captives to Iberia and the Americas.[37] At that time, the Jolof Empire controlled much of the region from the Senegal River to Sierra Leone and was composed of several ethnic and linguistic groupings including the Wolofs, "Mandingues," and "Bambara" Mande-speakers, and "Poulards" or Fulbe-speakers. When the empire disintegrated in the middle of the fifteenth century, several of its vassal states broke for independence, in part to determine the terms of their relationship with the slave trade and to protect their constituents from capture. Aggressive slave trading led to economic, social, and political crises such as increasing militarization and inter-state violence.[38] Armed military forces known as the *ceddo* operated alongside oppressive regimes and unleashed violence throughout Senegambia during their raids for slaves. The kings protected the *ceddo* regimes as they captured their own subjects in exchange for guns and liquor, and to satisfy indebtedness to European traders.[39] As a result of the rife violence associated with the trans-Atlantic slave trade, Senegambian captives were the third largest regional group brought to Saint-Domingue by the early eighteenth century (Table 1.1).

Soon, Muslim clerics would lead anti-slavery religious movements at Futa Jallon and Futa Tooro that would disrupt the slave trade and influence rebellions in the Americas. By the second half of the eighteenth century, the Bight of Biafra exceeded Senegambia as the third source of African captives to Saint-Domingue. Generally lacking a centralized political structure to regulate the trade, the swampy coastal regions surrounding the Niger and Cross Rivers were particularly vulnerable to small-scale raids, kidnapping, and legal and religious justification for enslaving the Igbo and Ibibio populations.[40]

Gold Coast captives were not very common in the colony, and their number in the trade seems to have remained under 30,000 throughout the eighteenth century. But, as planters in Saint-Domingue's southern peninsula struggled to keep productivity in pace with the prosperous northern and central plains, they turned to brokers who procured slaves from diverse regions. A 1790 accounting statement from the captain of the ship *L'Agréable* shows that several planters from Port-au-Prince, Croix-des-Bouquets, Mirebalais, Léogâne, and as far as Nippes and Jérémie purchased 26 of the ship's 187 souls originating from Little Popo.[41] These captives from Little Popo may have been counted as members of the Mina nation, who are often confused by scholars as originating from the El Mina fort in present-day Accra, Ghana, since the port town borders the Bight of Benin and the Gold Coast. Eighteenth-century people known as the Mina were often polyglots who spoke both the Fon/Gbe language of the Bight of Benin and the Gold Coast Akan language. The Mina were reputed to be excellent fishermen, gold and saltminers, and mercenaries proficient in using firearms. Mina armies were in high demand, migrating to places that called for their services including the Bight of Benin/Slave Coast, where many were captured and sold to the Americas.[42]

As the slave trade progressed and the French lost their West African colonies Senegal and Gorée to the British during the Seven Years War, French traders moved their bases beyond West Central Africa toward Southeastern African shores. Sofala, a province of Mozambique, was a major East African trading entrepôt, where captives were funneled into the Atlantic and Indian Ocean slave trades.[43] To supply their Caribbean sugar and coffee plantations with enslaved laborers, the French exchanged firearms and coinage, and their eighteenth-century economic activities in East Africa rivaled those of the Portuguese.[44] Though the number of enslaved Mozambicans and others from Southeastern African/ Indian Ocean regions in Saint-Domingue was not nearly as large as those from the Bight of Benin or West Central Africa, after 1750 their numbers actually exceeded Senegambians, Biafrans and others from less exploited regions (Table 1.2). Familiarity with the Arabic language and Islamic beliefs and practices was a commonality that connected significant portions of Senegambia and Sierra Leone as well as Mozambique, since the religion had been a mainstay in Mozambique from as early as the ninth century. It is highly likely that enslaved Mozambicans who also were of the Islamic faith were sold to Saint-Domingue.[45] Islam influenced anti-slavery mobilization both in Senegambia and in Saint-Domingue, as discussed below and in Chapters 2 and 3. Therefore, when considering an emergent racial solidarity, as this book attempts to do, it is interesting and necessary to note the Mozambican presence as part of Saint-Domingue's wider enslaved population (study of which is oftentimes reduced to its numerical majorities), and to be attentive to possible cultural and religious connections between enslaved Africans prior to their disembarkation in the Americas. According to the *Trans-Atlantic Slave Trade Database*, the average Middle Passage journey for ships voyaging between France, the Southeast African–Indian Ocean littoral, and on to Saint-Domingue was over 20 days longer than trips from other African regions. These longer voyages were riskier due to the increasing likelihood of illness or insurrection, but traders nonetheless viewed trips to the Southeast African–Indian Ocean littoral to purchase captives as a profitable endeavor. Enslaver Louis Monneron agreed to sell between 150 and 300 Mozambicans in February 1781 with the exception of the sick captives who presented a financial risk to the expedition.[46] Another trader contacted Monneron in 1782, seeking to order 1,000 Mozambicans in order to sell them at a later date and ameliorate his "disastrous" financial situation.[47] In 1787, an inquiry was made to buy a Saint-Domingue coffee plantation in exchange for blacks from Mozambique, likely implying that the captives were of significant value since the plantation in Moka, presumably in Mauritius, was described as "a superbe operation."[48]

West Central Africa

At the beginning of the eighteenth century, the West Central African zone already constituted a main trading destination, secondary to the Bight of Benin, for French ships headed to Saint-Domingue (Table 1.1). Aggression from other European traders in the Western coastal regions had pushed French activity south from the Bight of Benin to West Central Africa and, in turn, the French attempted to encroach on ports controlled by other European nations. In 1705, the French were accompanied by rulers from the Dombe in an attack on neighboring Benguela, a Portuguese-controlled port near Angola, likely because they were attracted to the region for its widely purported wealth in captives and gold. Though the Portuguese maintained control over the southern Angolan ports Benguela and Luanda, the French also continued an illegal trade from southern coasts without paying Portuguese duties.[49] As Saint-Domingue surpassed Cuba and Brazil as the world's leading sugar producer, and became a prominent coffee producer around mid-century, the demand for enslaved Africans increased and the Loango Coast became the French traders' primary source of captives.[50] Ports north of the Congo River – Malemba, Loango, and Cabinda – had become primary French slave trading posts, far exceeding those of other regions. Numbers of trafficked West Central Africans doubled those from the Bight of Benin and made up well over one-third of Saint-Domingue's Africa-born population (Table 1.2).[51] These included groups from the Loango Bay and deep into the interior, such as the Mondongues, Montequets or "Tekes," Mayombés and Mousombes.

The Loango Coast basin was an ecologically diverse region containing rivers, swamps, forests, and savannahs, and it was home to several cultural groups and languages that shared a relationship with an abundance of water and the Bantu language system, especially the KiKongo language. The various groups using this language system are collectively known as the BaKongo peoples, although their political and religious systems differed. The Loango Kingdom emerged to prominence in the sixteenth century, originally as subsidiary of the Kongo Kingdom. After establishing trading in ivory, copper, rubber, and wood with the Portuguese, the Loango Kingdom broke away and became an independent state that held power over the smaller state of Ngoyo, Cabinda, and the Kakongo Kingdom, which controlled the port of Malemba.[52] In the earliest periods of contact with Europeans, trading from the Loango Bay was essentially controlled by the king, who lived directly near the coast in order to assert dominance without interference from middlemen. As trading systems developed, the Vili rose in prominence as partners to European traders who exchanged cloth, guns, and alcohol for human captives. Though the Portuguese were dominant in regions south of the river, the Vili preferred to operate with French, Dutch, and English traders who brought a wider variety of goods for lower prices.[53]

Vili traders captured slaves from the southern Kongo Kingdom, who were referred to as "Franc-Congos" in shipping data, and took them northward to the Loango Coast outposts.[54] Political instability within the Kongo Kingdom increasingly led to Kongolese citizens being subject to enslavement, which was previously reserved for foreigners in the kingdom.[55] The Kongo civil wars had their roots in the mid-seventeenth century, but peace was brought to the kingdom for several decades after two warring factions agreed to share and alternate leadership. The Kingdom of Kongo had developed contact and trade relations with Portugal in 1483, and King Afonso V was the first ruler to fully implement a European-style royal court with Christianity as its official religion. Members of the Kongolese elite were educated in Europe and built local schools where wealthy children learned Latin and Portuguese. To finance this cultural and religious revolution, Afonso and subsequent kings traded slaves and eventually resorted to waging war with neighboring states to capture slaves. Over the course of the sixteenth and seventeenth centuries, warfare dramatically increased the number of slaves brought to the Kongo Kingdom from foreign markets. But as the eighteenth century approached, financial demands following civil wars over succession claims to the throne and other conflicts led to expanding justifications to enslave freeborn Kongolese. Spikes in the numbers of Kongolese captives taken to Saint-Domingue overlap with royal coups of the 1760s and 1780s that overthrew Dom Pedro V and, later, his remaining allies (Table 1.2).[56]

Members of Pedro V's failed succession may have been captured and sold to Saint-Domingue. Pierre "Dom Pedro" was a Kongolese runaway from Petit Goâve who declared himself free – perhaps meaning he had been freeborn – and became the originator of Haitian Vodou's *petwo* dance, which was enlivened by rum, gunpowder, and a pantheon of "hot" spirits.[57] Understanding West Central African perspectives on the slave trade helps explain the sacred usage of rum and gunpowder in West Central African rituals in Saint-Domingue, which I further discuss in Chapter 3. The ongoing connections and transfers of goods, knowledge, and people between Africa and the Caribbean meant that there was an historical accumulation of meaning, sacrality and power, and connection to human lives lost to the slave trade. The slave trade consumed human life, and West Central Africans who were most vulnerable to capture and sale understood the trade in terms of cannibalization and witchcraft. This spiritual and metaphorical formulation made sense given the dynamics of the trade: traders took people, and in their stead appeared material objects like cowrie shells, alcohol, and gunpowder, which were assumed to hold the essence of the disappeared person and therefore took on additional sacred meaning. Commodities like cloths and metals already had social and spiritual significance, but took on new sacred meanings in the Americas as the slave trade increased and meanings of those items – and enslaved captives – were viewed, in European worldviews, solely for their economic value (Domingues 2017; Green 2019: 236–238).

West Central African societies defined "witchcraft" broadly, to include actions that indicated selfishness and the abuse of power – even by royal political authorities. The greed and abuses of power associated with the slave trade, especially the increasing capture and sale of freeborn people in addition to enslaved foreigners, stimulated political and religious institutions to check the authority of the kings who ruled over the trade. Though they shared the KiKongo language, in the sixteenth century Loango was culturally and religiously distinct from Kongo. North of the Congo River, there was minimal settlement of the European colonists, who exerted less cultural, religious, and political influence than was common at the Angolan Portuguese colony. Seventeenth-century Jesuit missions resulted in several conversions, but these had negligible effect on the overall religious life at Loango, in part allowing the kingdom to maintain religious, cultural, economic, and political autonomy. The city of Mbanza Loango served as the religious and political center of the Loango Kingdom, staffed by administrative nobles with relatives of the king ruling rural provinces.[58] Loango kings were held to a high moral standard of ruling with fairness and were typically seen as spiritual leaders bestowed with supernatural abilities by the *bunzi* priests who ruled earth and nature spirits. The kings' sacred power needed to be protected from the outside world through public isolation and a system of operating primarily at night.[59] Religious shrines doubled as judicial centers where judgement and law were determined; a series of spiritual authorities presided over these shrines and advised the king on important matters. *Ngangas* were priests of resurrected spirits whose broad range of responsibilities included leading ceremonies, practicing healing, and performing rituals to communicate with spiritual powers and eliminate the influence of the dead on the living. *Ngangas* were vital to the political realm, as their ritual power was deemed important during warfare and their sacred knowledge qualified them to be advisors to the king. Therefore, they were a constant presence in local rulers' entourages and at public events.[60]

Outside of the king's sphere of influence, a popular movement that emphasized healing and fairness grew among the Lemba society, which began in Loango and eventually reached regions southwest of the Malebo

Pool.[61] The Lemba believed that the slave trade was destroying society; they differed from surrounding states because of their approach to justice, the use of force, and the structure of economic resources. The Lemba specialized in trade on a decentralized, "horizontal" basis and encouraged locally-produced and traded goods. They maintained peace in the market-place via the use of priests and conflict resolution. Any conflict or mater-ial, social, economic, and political ills were attributed to spiritual imbalances that required a spiritual response using *nkisi* medicinal bundles.[62] Not all members of Lemba society where inherently opposed to the slave trade, however. Among Lemba adherents were Vili merchants from Loango who transported captives from the southern Kongo Kingdom to ports north of the Congo River – an exploitative economic practice that metaphorically cannibalized people and was associated with *kindoki* or spiritual witchcraft. The Vili's allegiance to Lemba served to counter the negative sacred implications of their slave trading enterprise as a "spiritual means to heal the evil released by their activities."[63]

THE MIDDLE PASSAGE AND RESISTANCE
TO THE SLAVE TRADE

Slave Ships: Sites of Illness, Death, and Intimacy

The Middle Passage was the initial process that conflated African lives with exchangeable commodities; it might also be considered the experi-ence that produced what would become a collective consciousness and feeling of solidarity among its survivors. The shared experience of violent extraction from one's homeland; being branded and chained to a person who may or may not share one's linguistic or cultural identity; the waiting period at the fortification castles; the long voyage in the belly of the slave ship; and hunger, disorientation, and death were all part of the material conditions of transport that left a lasting impression on Middle Passage survivors. Strangers bound together came to know each other in unspeak-able ways, creating bonds that lasted when they disembarked at ports on the other side of the Atlantic. These relationships with "shipmates" and other cultural or linguistic familiars would form the basis of kinship networks and collective identity in the Americas through the transmission of stories, memories, or songs about the homeland experience and the Middle Passage itself. Words from a song from the Haitian Vodou tradition, "Sou Lan Me," speak to the collective memory of the Middle Passage and the longing for liberation from the slave ship:

On the ocean we are sailing
Agwé in Oyo
There will come a time when they'll see us
On the ocean we are sailing/
They took our feet
They chained our two wrists
They dropped us in the bottom/
Slave ship under the water
The ocean is bad
The ship is broken
It's ready to sink/
Slave ship under the water
At the bottom of the ocean
It's covered in water
It's ready to sink/
In the bottom of the ship
We are all one/
In the bottom of the ship
If it sinks/
No one will be saved
Agwé in Oyo
We're all on board
Don't you see we're trapped/
We're trapped, papa, trapped
We're trapped Lasirèn, trapped.[64]

The traumatic experience of being trapped in the bottom of a slave ship left little help on which to depend, prompting a spiritual appeal to the spirits Agwé and Lasirèn that control the high seas and transoceanic travel, and a lament for the lives lost during the voyage.

Though scholars agree that approximately 12 million living Africans arrived in the Americas over the course of the slave trade, the mortality rates associated with each phase of the trade were undoubtedly much higher. Africans perished from warfare and raids at the moment of capture, during treks to the coast, and while bound in the fortification castles awaiting embarkation on the ships. Furthermore, the Middle Passage voyage itself incurred approximately 15–20 percent losses in human life aboard the slave ships.[65] During the voyages between the African continent and Saint-Domingue in the years 1751–1800, 66,273 individuals – or approximately 11 percent of those who were forcibly embarked on slave ships – died or were killed during the course of the Middle Passage. The total loss of life associated with the transAtlantic slave trade has yet to be determined, but a growing body of information provides insight into the hellish conditions of the slave ship. Individual voyages from the African continent to American ports could be as short as two to three months; however, some lasted for up to a year (or more) when ship captains waited to fill their boats with as many enslaved people as possible from various ports of the continent while the captives themselves languished in the ship's lower decks.

The captives were bound together by chains; they were naked and packed into the ship tightly to fit as many human bodies as possible in the bottom floor of the deck, which was dark, hot, and short of oxygen. Food consisted of a mixture of beans, millet, peas, and flour that ship hands distributed three times a day, along with a small drink of water. Exhaustion, diarrhea, vomiting, dysentery, contagions like smallpox and tuberculosis, and a wide array of other illnesses were ubiquitous among the captives, as was the overwhelming sense of despair that led many to cast themselves overboard. The population density at trading centers like Ouidah facilitated the spread of diseases such as smallpox and by the 1770s, European slavers were inoculating captives before they embarked on the ships.[66] Medical practitioners who treated the enslaved were often either underqualified or lacking in resources, and they treated the captives in exploitative ways to advance their medical knowledge as well as the commercial enterprise of slaving (Mustakeem 2016: 150–155). Similar to resistance tactics used in American colonies, individual efforts to avoid slavery also included feigning illness. In 1776, a young West Central African girl seems to have effectively avoided sale to Port-au-Prince on the *L'Utile* slave ship by pretending to be sick.[67] Women and girls were particularly vulnerable to rape by captains, sailors, and other ship hands. Ship hands held women separately from male captives and enslavers viewed them through stereotypical notions of black sexuality (ibid: 83). Though rape was common throughout the Middle Passage experience, it was rarely acknowledged in French records or reported to authorities. One case emerges from the historical record involving Second Captain Philippe Liot, who brutally "mistreated" a young woman, breaking two of her teeth and leaving her in such a state of decline that she perished shortly arriving at Saint-Domingue. Liot later inflicted his abuses on another girl, between ages 8 and 10, forcibly clasping her mouth for three days so she could not scream while he violated her. The child was sold in Saint-Domingue, but the violence she endured left her in a near "deathly state."[68]

Separated from their traditional modes of survival, homelands, communities, cultures, and ancestral spirits and living kinship ties, a pressing existential question was "how captives would sustain their humanity in the uniquely inhumane spatial and temporal setting of the slave ship at sea (Smallwood 2008: 125)." Africans kept track of time according to the moon cycles and formed intimate relationships with others who survived the ship voyages. They affirmed one another's humanity on ships through small acts that went undetected by slavers, like touching, decorating hair, or expressing desire. Women captives who were pregnant when they embarked, or became pregnant through rape, delivered babies on ships with the help of midwives or anyone in proximity who could aid the process. These relationships – some sexual, some not – seem to have survived the Middle Passage and were the basis of powerful "shipmate" social ties throughout the Americas that operated as family-like or otherwise intimate networks (Mintz and Price 1976, chapter 4; Tinsley 2008; Borucki 2015). The ports at Cap Français and Port-au-Prince by far received more slave ships than other ports. When captive Africans who survived the journey across the Atlantic Ocean landed in the urban centers of Saint-Domingue, they confronted a new reality: foreign geographic landscapes, social arrangements, and power dynamics. They disembarked the vessels while still chained to their "shipmates" – individuals whom they may or may not have known prior to capture but who most certainly shared the bonds of surviving the Middle Passage, regional origin, cultural identity, and political affiliation, and/or religion. The "clusters" (Hall 2005) of the newly arrived generally valued the literal and social psychological ties that bound them to their shipmates. After plantation owners purchased them at the ports, Africans gravitated to each other on respective plantations. Bight of Benin and West Central Africans could easily locate members of their ethnic, religious, or linguistic communities as they were the largest ethnic groups in the main ports in the major cities, as well as in less- utilized ports. Outside of Cap Français and Port-au-Prince, the densest proportion of Sierra Leoneans, Windward Coast Africans, and Bight of Biafrans were found at Les Cayes; Africans from the Gold Coast and Senegambians had significant numbers in Léogâne; and Saint Marc was a hub for Bight of Benin Africans, West Central Africans, and Southeast/Indian Ocean Africans (Table 1.3). Chapter 2 will further discuss the distribution of ethnic groups on Saint-Domingue's plantations and how their spatiality may have influenced patterns of resistance. Enslaved people and maroons' geographic location in the colony, together with their knowledge of the landscape, was an important part of their collective consciousness and this is explored in Chapter 6.

TABLE 1.3. *Disembarkations of African regional ethnicities across Saint-Domingue ports, 1750–1800*

	Arcahaye	Le Cap	Les Cayes	Fort Dauphin	Jacmel	Jérémie	Léogâne	Mole St. Nicolas	Petit Goâve	Port-au-Prince	Port-de-Paix	Saint-Marc	Port Unspecified	Total
Senegambia	0	8,425	730	416	131	0	2,597	0	0	5,608	0	1,352	1,009	20,268
Sierra Leone	204	7,861	4,053	0	143	0	244	0	0	5,700	204	972	985	20,366
Windward Coast	0	1,144	1,430	0	0	0	0	0	0	853	0	624	150	4,201
Gold Coast	0	7,356	1,182	0	0	107	2,274	0	0	763	0	1,062	1,725	14,469
Bight of Benin	0	36,810	4,248	0	0	0	13,518	0	313	31,507	626	17,228	2,029	105,919
Bight of Biafra	0	7,134	7,756	0	132	557	1,024	0	168	7,538	0	3,024	562	27,895
WC Africa	0	157,084	19,518	432	1,616	382	28,254	344	201	40,065	1930	10,196	5,074	265,096
SE Africa	0	13,340	1,7000	0	0	0	894	0	0	2,213	0	2,166	843	21,156
Other	0	25,496	3,893	0	506	270	3,295	0	0	15,400	382	5,964	5,626	60,832
Total	204	264,650	44,510	848	2,528	1,316	51,740	344	682	109,647	3,142	42,588	18,003	540,202

African Marronnage, Rebellion, and Revolution

The stark economic inequality between African aristocracies, merchant classes, and the masses contributed to a growing African oppositional consciousness and widespread revolt against the slave trade. Resistance to enslavement in the Americas did not spontaneously appear once captives disembarked from slave ships and reached plantations – it was predated by, and in some cases may be considered as an extension of, African wars and resistance to local forms of slavery and the onslaught of European trading. When centering Africa and Africans, marronnage, revolts, revolutions, and indeed the progressive human ideals that defined the Enlightenment era and the Age of Revolutions might be equally informed by African political sensibilities. Sylviane Diouf's *Fighting the Slave Trade: West African Warfare Strategies* (2003) offers insights into the little-known aspects of the defensive and offensive strategies Africans took to contest the slave trade, and African conceptions and practices of warfare. This chapter has highlighted the origins of what would become a politicized, oppositional consciousness in Saint-Domingue through a brief excavation of the African background and its role in shaping enslaved people's approaches to resistance. The shifting landscape of political ideology tilted African masses against forms of rule associated with the greed and violence of the slave trade, and the pervasiveness of war meant that some were armed with militaristic tools that, though unsuccessful on the continent, would prove useful in the Americas (Thornton 1991, 1993b; Barcia 2014).

Given the sheer volume of the slave trade and its duration, one wonders how social structures and institutions responded to its imbalanced nature and its destructive effects on local communities. Scholars agree that the collapse of several major states and empires prior to the eighteenth and nineteenth centuries meant that the vast majority of Atlantic Africa was composed of a multitude of fragmented states that could not mount a real defense against foreign powers. Europe's demand for gold, kola nuts, and other African products was not detrimental to the decentralized states, but as market demands called for human beings, violence escalated to levels that these smaller states were not fully equipped to handle. This is not to mention the commercial and politico-military advantage that European nations had over Africans, given a longer period of consolidation and world trade, which put African leaders in a reactionary position in relation to the changing needs of Western European economies. Class divisions also contributed to social cleavages, which Europeans were able to take advantage of when imposing the slave trade. Resistance to the trade from local African rulers was uncommon, since they and others of the merchant elite classes benefited financially and would not have been affected by the trade in any tangible way.[69]

Two women, Queen Njinga of Ndongo (Luanda) and Dona Beatriz of Kongo, led mid-seventeenth- and early eighteenth-century West Central African resistance movements that were notable exceptions to the notion that African rulers were complicit or failed to utilize their economic or military resources to resist the transAtlantic slave trade. After decades of peaceful trade relations between the Portuguese and the Kongo Kingdom, the Portuguese set out to conquer the kingdom of Angola, or Ndongo, in 1575. This campaign leveled a heavy blow to the kingdom's power in the region, which was based on a tributary system of surrounding polities paying dues. Though Ndongo withstood Portugal's incursions for a short while, the successive deaths of Njinga's father and brother led to a deepening of the slave trade and created a vacuum of power that she was fully prepared to fill in 1624. Njinga used a wide-ranging political repertoire, including diplomatic ploys, guerrilla warfare, and ritual symbolism, to position herself as a formidable military leader, pause the slave trade, and establish peace with the Portuguese in the mid-seventeenth century.[70]

Under the influence of Saint Anthony, Dona Beatriz led an early eighteenth-century spiritual and political movement to unify the Kongo Kingdom. To introduce broad reformations, she advocated for the exaltation of Saint Anthony and opposed local priests by asserting that Jesus and Mary were Kongolese people born in São Salvador. Dona Beatriz's movement was heavily supported by women, as she fashioned herself as a healer of fertility issues and attempted to create an order of nuns. Her message propagated widespread prosperity and the coming of an age of miracles. This was popular among the peasantry, who were eager for an end to the constant warfare that was feeding the slave trade. The Antonian movement's increasing relevance and political allegiances with opponents of King Pedro, and its calls for peace and an end to greed and abuses of power – which were considered to be manifestations of *kindoki* spiritual witchcraft – presented it as a target to the prevailing monarchy, which resulted in Dona Beatriz's execution.[71] Yet the movement did seem to have a measurable, though temporary, impact on the slave trade. The years of the Antonian movement correspond with the lowest levels of slave trading West Central Africa had seen since the 1650s and 1660s – a period that overlaps with peace treaties between Queen Njinga and the

Portuguese. The years after Dona Beatriz's death saw a gradual increase in the slave trade from West Central Africa. By the late eighteenth century this would become the most frequently exploited region, exceeding the Bight of Benin.[72]

Religious consolidation in West Central Africa, as well as Senegambia, helped to mount the solidarity needed to mobilize diverse groups into a united front that could oppose European armies who represented merchants involved in the slave trade. There was a long tradition of Senegambian resistance to the slave trade in the form of religious discontent among Muslims, who held Qu'ranic beliefs that they could not be enslaved. Islam had been present in West Africa from as early as the ninth century but was largely associated with long-standing merchant networks that bought and sold human captives, kola nuts, European imports, commercial activity, and political allegiances. Though not every Senegambian was Muslim, most were in some way familiar with or proximate to Islam, and as the religion spread so did upheavals on the African continent that had direct a influence on the slave trade. In the early seventeenth century, a more militant form of Islam emerged to counter the Atlantic slave trade and the growing instability that it engendered. Nasir Al Din led a religious movement to control local trade markets and to introduce a more righteous Islamic practice. With the aid of local factions and members of the *marabout* class of Islamic clerics, Al Din's short-lived movement deposed several kingdoms and replaced them with theocracies. Though Al Din's movement failed when Saint-Louis chose to continue the Atlantic trade and to support autocratic regimes, many *marabouts* migrated south to Futa Jallon, where they would continue to seek autonomy for Muslims in the early eighteenth century.[73]

The shared heritage of Islam, and the intensification of the trade at Senegambia, Sierra Leone, and the Windward Coast, may have contributed to the rise of revolts from those areas. Rising prices for captives led to a breakdown of local Senegambian conventions that were intended to protect free people, domestic slaves, and Muslims from the slave trade (Richardson 2003). Fighting between the Muslim Fulbe and the Mande-speaking Jallonke resulted in jihad that as early as the 1720s, and reaching its height in the 1760s–1780s, violently pushed Sierra Leoneans into the slave trade in increasing numbers.[74] By 1776, growing intolerance of the enslavement of Muslims resulted in a revolution against the slave trading nobility at Futa Tooro. A popular uprising against the trade developed, with Muslim clerics like Abdul-Qadir Kan at the helm, as the slave trade increased in volume at the end of the eighteenth century. The revolution nearly ended slavery and the slave trade from Futa Tooro by prohibiting French traders from traveling up the Senegal River to procure Arabic gum and captives. The abolition of the slave trade at Senegambia was widely known and even represented a model for white abolitionist Thomas Clarkson, who lauded Kan's actions. Despite the ban of slave trading activity at Futa Tooro, the French continued to work with the rebels' enemies to procure slaves and other resources from Gorée and Saint Louis, thus undermining the revolution.[75]

Resistance among potential captives was a regular occurrence, since – besides those who were already enslaved according to local custom for being a criminal or in debt – most individuals taken to the Americas were victims of some other financial crisis, or were either kidnapped or prisoners of war. These were free people who were losing their original liberty, personal dignity, familial and community networks, and connections to their homeland and ancestral deities due to the trade. Africans, especially those who lived in the interior lands, did not always have a clear idea of Europeans' intentions or the location of those who had disappeared. Despite the opaqueness of the nature of the slave trade, there was a general sense that malevolent forces were at work and a knowledge that lives were in imminent danger. Individuals, families, and entire communities took precautions to protect themselves.

Flight from communities that were vulnerable to raiding seems to have been a common form of resistance for those affected by French slaving. What is today the Ganvié lacustrine village in the Republic of Benin is an historical example of a community's flight to the waters to avoid the violent encroaching power of the Dahomey Kingdom's slaving of smaller polities and decentralized peoples. The Tofinu is a homogeneous ethnic group closely related to the Aja groups that developed from generations of migrants who, beginning in the late seventeenth century, settled along Lake Nokoué and surrounding swamplands within the coastal lagoon system. According to oral tradition, Ganvié means "safe at last," which references the earliest settlers' sense of refuge from the onslaught of slave trading that increased when Dahomey conquered Allada in 1724, Ouidah in 1727, and Jankin in 1732. Ganvié was a maroon community that fashioned its survival in ways that emerged alongside similar communities in the Americas. Upon arrival to Ganvié, newcomers who may have been local slaves were freed and protected from the pervasiveness of slaving. To protect the community, members utilized canoeing skills that were lacking among Dahomean armies, mounted expeditions to find wives, and used a wide array of weaponry, including javelins, sledgehammers, swords, and locally made and imported guns.[76]

West Central Africans also fortified themselves; as early as the sixteenth century, enslaved people at the plantation-based island São Tomé escaped into the mountains and revolted in 1595, convincing the Portuguese to move their sugar production operations to Brazil.[77] In the seventeenth and eighteenth centuries, there were known *quilombo* maroon communities such as Ndembo, just south of Loango near Luanda, who fled Portuguese slave trading at Benguela. *Quilombos* originally emerged in the seventeenth century as military structures associated with Imbangala (also referred to as the "Jaga") traveling warrior forces, some of whom sold captives to the Portuguese while others waged war against Ndongo and Matamba in revolt against the political and economic pressures that arose alongside the slave trade. The *quilombo* collectives allowed the Imbangala to "unite people from different lineages speaking different languages," a characteristic that would figure prominently in the Americas when *quilombos* were essentially exported to Brazil, most notably at Palmares, due to the growing slave trade.[78] By the early eighteenth century, *quilombos* on the West Central African coasts, especially at Luanda just south of the Loango Bay, were largely associated with communities of runaways who had evaded capture by slave traders. Several *quilombos* grew in part due to support from local African leaders and free individuals who were complicit in protecting the runaways, as well as from *quilombo* raids on Luanda residents who owned enslaved people. Accounts from the early eighteenth century record a series of attacks by *quilombo* members – who originated from Benguela – assaulting and robbing Luanda residents, taking goods, supplies, and enslaved captives. At Luanda, would-be slaves and enslaved domestic workers feared the slave trade; they used their kin networks to escape, taking windows of opportunity when their owners were out of sight. A group of 130 slaves escaped in 1782 when their owner made a trip in search of gold mines.[79] Despite regular attacks on maroons by Luanda officials, and attempts to offer amnesty to those who returned, these communities increased in number into the late eighteenth century. Luanda's maroons were incorporated into local rulers' armies and were used to attack members of the merchant class, as occurred in 1784 when traders reported "significant financial damage due to the large number of escaping Africans making their way to Ndembo."[80] These patterns of flight, armed resistance, and re-appropriation of forms of capital might be considered the antecedents to marronnage in the Americas.

Efforts to free themselves did not cease even after marronnage to prevent capture was ineffective. On the treks from the hinterlands to the coasts, captives tried to flee or threw themselves overboard from canoes and ships. The process of boarding the ships was especially frantic, as many were encountering the Atlantic Ocean for the first time and realized it may be their last chance to free themselves and see their families again. West Central Africans saw the ocean as the *kalunga*, the great body of water that separated the world of the living from the world that dead spirits occupied.[81] The walk from the ports to the ships not only represented a social death from being torn away from kith, kin, and ancestral lands, it also was a spiritual death in which captives would have believed they were crossing into the land of the dead, heightening an already existing sense of anxiety and fear. An example of a successful attempt to prevent a slave ship taking off from the African coast occurred on December 26, 1788, when 40 captives from Mayombé of West Central Africa overtook the slave ship *l'Augustine* that held 386 would-be slaves. The captives

took possession of a chest of arms and attacked seven men of the crew who were then on board, two were killed, the five others were injured and thrown into the sea; but they had the fortune to save themselves in the boat and took refuge at Mayombé ... Blacks once masters of the boat have raised the anchor and sailed."[82]

Slave trade resistance occurred on a wide scale, with African leaders mobilizing militaries, and at the micro-level, small groups and individuals attempting to avoid or disrupt the trade's centripetal force. Once ships set out to sea, African rulers were powerless to reverse the captives' destinies – but the captives themselves continued to struggle individually and collectively against capitalist-driven slaving practices.

Slave Ship Insurrections

Information from the *Trans-Atlantic Slave Trade Database* indicates that 79 slave ships intended to reach Saint-Domingue experienced some form of collective resistance by Africans. Data are only available beginning in the year 1710 but they confirm that the cases of revolt varied temporally, with the majority of insurrections occurring after 1750 in keeping with the growth of the slave trade and regionally distinguished by local political economies (Richardson 2003). Twenty-four of the 79 ships originated from the Bight of Benin, but given the volume of voyages between there and

Saint-Domingue, Bight of Benin ship revolts were in fact underrepresented. Similarly, even as West Central Africa was the leading source of enslaved people – especially after the mid-eighteenth century – only 12 ship revolts from that region occurred, making those revolts also underrepresented. Rather, ships with African insurrections from Senegambia to Saint-Domingue were overrepresented, with 21 ship revolts between the years 1711 and 1800. For the entirety of ships bound for the Americas, those that left Senegambia were eight times more likely to experience a slave ship revolt than those that departed from the Bight of Benin.[83]

The gradual increase of all slave ship insurrections is aligned with the increasing volume of seaborne ships as the slave trade grew over time and is linked to events on the African coast. For example, the number of eighteenth-century Senegambian slave ship revolts appears to have been connected to the Futa Jallon and Futa Tooro jihads of the 1720s–1730s and 1780s, respectively. Captives held in Gorée and Saint Louis' slaving prisons revolted, as well as a group of women who were sold to Saint-Domingue in 1729 for attacking the sous-lieutenant of *L'Annibal* (Johnson 2020: 39, 93–94). By the turn of the nineteenth century, Abdul-Qadir Kan's Islamic revolution had ended, and slaving from the region resumed. It appears that illegally purchased Muslims, or those who otherwise held anti-slavery sentiments, traveled from Gorée and Saint-Louis to Saint-Domingue and staged several slave ship insurrections between 1786 and 1788. The *Reverseau* left Saint-Louis in May 1786 and arrived at Port-au-Prince only a month later after 57 Senegambians and nine crew members died at sea. Africans bought at Saint-Louis and Gorée revolted on the *Fleury*, which also departed in May 1786 and similarly landed at Port-au-Prince in June, leaving 48 captives and five crew members dead. That these two ships departed from the same ports within days of each other and that captives on both ships attempted to stage uprisings is an unlikely coincidence and should not be overlooked. In November of 1786, the *Alexandre* vessel embarked on what would become a notably long and deadly journey from Gorée to Saint-Domingue. Initially, 229 Africans filled the ship's belly, while 29 men were part of the crew. Though details are unclear, during the nearly year-long voyage, the Africans revolted. By the time the ship arrived at Le Cap in October of 1787, 135 Africans and eight crew members were dead. In early 1787, the *Amitié* carried 227 captives from Saint-Louis and Gorée to Port-au-Prince, but not before 21 people were killed in their attempt to stage a revolt. The *Aimable Louise* had made previous trips to Saint-Domingue and Guadeloupe, but Senegambian resistance thwarted an early 1788 voyage and the ship never reached the Americas.

TABLE 1.4. *Slave ship voyages to Saint-Domingue with noted African resistance, 1711–1800*

	1711–1720	1721–1730	1731–1740	1741–1750	1751–1760	1761–1770	1771–1780	1781–1790	1791–1800	Totals
Senegambia	1	1	1	3	2	6	1	6	0	21
Sierra Leone	0	0	0	0	0	1	1	1	1	4
Windward Coast	0	0	0	0	0	0	0	0	0	0
Gold Coast	0	0	1	1	0	0	1	0	0	3
Bight of Benin	4	5	3	5	3	1	2	1	0	24
Bight of Biafra	0	0	0	0	0	1	1	5	0	7
WC Africa	0	0	1	2	0	3	0	5	1	12
SE Africa/Indian Ocean	0	0	0	0	0	0	0	2	0	2
Other	1	1	2	0	0	1	1	0	0	6
Totals	6	7	8	11	5	13	7	20	2	79

Whether or not we can effectively trace African resistance on the coasts to slave ship insurrections and to New World rebellion, resistance happened at every stage of the trade, including colonial ports in the Americas. Newly arrived African captives committed marronnage as soon as their feet touched land, oftentimes while still shackled, and were described in runaway advertisements as *nouveau* (new). In many cases, the *nouveau* label was used when the person's slave name, approximate age, or ethnic origin was not known because they may not have been fully integrated into the plantation system. According to the *Marronnage dans le Monde Atlantique* database, as many as 269 advertisements for runaway maroons mention the *navire* or slave ship from which *nouveau* Africans had disembarked. On March 10, 1773, two runaways were listed in *Les Affiches américaines* as cargo on the *Marie-Séraphique* ship that made several voyages between Nantes, the Loango Coast, and Cap Français between 1770 and 1774. The two men, along with 331 other captives, had survived a 51-day Middle Passage, were disembarked at Le Cap on January 6, 1773, and escaped after having been sold from Le Cap to a store in Saint Marc. Three other "nouveaux Congo" captives escaped directly after disembarking from the *Marie-Séraphique* in 1775.[84]

Several voyages of the *Saint Hilaire* were particularly hellish due to high mortality rates, which may have prompted survivors to escape once they disembarked in Saint-Domingue. During a four-month voyage from Ouidah, the *Saint Hilaire* landed at Port-au-Prince in April 1770 with only 323 of the 528 captives still alive. The January 1774 voyage of the *Saint Hilaire* started at Ouidah with 482 captives and, after 82 days, landed at Port-au-Prince on June 17 with only 411 souls, meaning 71 people perished during the voyage.[85] In the aftermath of the 1774 trip, several runaway advertisements were posted for individuals who were linked to the *Saint Hilaire*. Shortly after being introduced to Saint-Domingue, a "negre nouveau," having an "H" branded into his thigh, escaped on July 7, according to the advertisement posted on July 20. The following August, two "nouveaux" Aradas, who had been sold by the ship's captain La Causse, also escaped Port-au-Prince. Finally, in January 1775, a man named François, who was also described as "having the mark of the slave ship Saint Hilaire 'LH' intertwined," fled his owner in Port-au-Prince.[86]

CONCLUSION

The "false idea of the negro" against which General Leclerc cautioned belied the rich histories and traditions of African political ideas, spiritual inclinations, and collective resistance actions to enslaving. Due to the rise of the transAtlantic slave trade, expanding inequality in various African societies caused economic, political, social, and religious chasms that engendered new forms of political thought on the continent. For African captives who were the victims of raids, warfare, and greed, the Middle Passage compounded these experiences. Slaving practices on the African continent varied depending on geographic region and socio-political formations, however the Middle Passage process was the first step in homogenizing the experiences of "the negro." Middle Passage survivors, no matter their place of origin, endured incredible trauma but also carried their worldviews with them on the voyages across the Atlantic. Moreover, while the stark realities of violence and greed that undergirded enslavement in Saint-Domingue may have harkened to the African past, the added components of racialization likely further enflamed the collective consciousness of Middle Passage survivors. As Africans interacted with each other and formed respective ethnic clusters, collective oppositional consciousness and solidarity began to take shape.

This chapter has highlighted the ways in which coastal Africans responded to the rapidly changing conditions around them that shaped their lives in irreversible ways. To understand racial capitalism as a social process and a mode of economic production, the commodification of Africans from humans to cargo must first be considered (Robinson 1893, chapters 4–5). Conversely, as Robinson argues, the origins of the Black Radical Tradition lie in Africans' worldviews and their epistemological opposition to racial capitalism. Slavery existed in Africa, as in many human societies, but it was not premised on racialization and did not operate with the intense brutality involved in the trans-Atlantic slave trade. Those who were unfortunate enough to already have been familiar with domestic slavery would have faced an entirely new set of circumstances as a captive on a slave ship destined for the Americas. As the slave trade intensified throughout the eighteenth century, its victims were increasingly people who were free and, according to local customs, should have been invulnerable to capture. Africans' understandings about the ethics and limits of slaving would have informed a sense of indignation at the experience of displacement and bondage. Many interpreted their circumstances through supernatural terms, since oftentimes African leaders were also spiritual leaders, and social, economic, and political forces were believed to be either the consequences of happenings in the non-physical realm or violations of sacred rules of order. Accordingly, later in Saint-Domingue, resistance was articulated through idioms and rituals of the sacred, as will be explored in Chapter 3. Sacred rituals, and other forms of resistance, were often collective efforts between maroons and plantation slaves.

Though it is not yet possible to directly link African slave trade resistance to events in the Caribbean, it is important to recognize that the realities of the slave trade, and resistance to it, was part of the socio-economic and political context from which captives emerged and should be understood as part of their world. Moreover, this helps us revise our ideas about the making of revolution and modernity, when and where it occurred, and to decentralize Europe as its singular birthplace. Recent historical sociologists (Magubane 2005; Go and Lawson 2017) have argued for transnational analyses of modernity, abandoning previous generations of scholarship that tended to overlook colonial relationships in favor of methodological nationalism. As works by Anna Julia Cooper and C. L. R James have shown, the French Revolution perhaps would not have happened without the wealth from the Caribbean colonies, namely Saint-Domingue, and the ideological push of the Haitian Revolution. It then follows that due to the triangularity of the European slave trade, the Haitian Revolution most certainly would not have happened without Africa and Africans.

Africa, as a site of unfreedoms and freedoms and the foremost source of natural resources, lifeblood, and human labor in the Atlantic world, was a critical contributor to modern capitalism and must therefore be brought from the margins closer to the center when we consider the making of modernity. This is not even to speak of the Africans who were trafficked through the Arab slave trade across the Indian Ocean, but who yet labored on European plantations that contributed to capitalist development (Rodney 1982: 97). Further, European colonial domination of Africa lasted well into the twentieth century, after the 1885 Berlin Conference divided the continent and access to its resources, ensuring that "African economies are integrated into the very structure of the developed capitalist economies" (ibid.: 25). It is more historically accurate to place Africa and other parts of the formerly colonized world at the center of how we conceptualize the capitalist world economy rather than at the periphery. A recapitulation of the ways European capitalism developed through the exploitation of Africa and Africans is beyond the scope of the current work, but this understanding – as well as the ways that Africans re-defined freedom and emancipation through their self-initiated actions – means we can think of the existence of multiple modernities that developed in various times and places (Bhambra 2011).

2

In the Shadow of Death

"The stranger in San Domingo was awakened by the cracks of the whip, the stifled cries, and the heavy groans of the Negroes who saw the sun rise only to curse it for its renewal of their labours and their pains", this quote from C. L. R. James' foundational text *The Black Jacobins* ([1938] 1989: 9–10) serves as a helpful entry way point through which to understand colonial Haiti, known in the eighteenth century as French Saint-Domingue. As African captives disembarked at Saint-Domingue's ports – after surviving social, economic, and political upheaval in their homelands and months of trauma in the form of dislocation, violence, death, and illness – traffickers branded them and sold them off to plantations across the colony. From that moment forward, forced labor, daily acts of brutality and other indignities, and death characterized everyday life for the enslaved. The horrors of Saint-Domingue are infamous to readers who are already familiar with "New World" plantation societies, but sociologists who specialize in the study of race might be less familiar with Haiti's centrality in the making of racial capitalism. To fully understand the significance of a major rebellion like the Haitian Revolution in the context of what was once the most profitable and deadly slave colony in the Americas, it is important to understand the complex set of social relations that eventually led to the astounding collapse of racial slavery in Haiti. This chapter does not merely attempt to recount what is now a fairly well-known historical narrative about the colony's economic prosperity from sugar and coffee production, but to locate the experiences of enslaved Africans and African descendants within the island space on which Haiti sits (Ayiti/Española/Saint-Domingue/Haiti) – the nucleus of several "firsts" in early the modern history of the Americas:

- the first site of European "discovery," colonization, and indigenous genocide
- the first site of black enslavement
- the first site of indigenous and African collective resistance to European dominance
- the first site of a successful black revolt against slavery, and
- the first free and independent black nation.

Four tenets – human commodification, labor exploitation, death, and resistance – of Haiti's structural reality have persisted beyond Spanish and French colonial systems to the period of the United States' imperial influence. It might be argued that understanding Haiti from this perspective illuminates the ways in which black life throughout the Americas was and continues to be circumscribed by structural forces rooted in colonial encounters, slavery, and anti-blackness. After surviving the Middle Passage, enslaved Africans and their descendants experienced similar material conditions in Saint-Domingue. Africans also encountered each other and their respective cultural, social, and political heritages, and a landscape that was imbued with the Taíno presence and legacy, resulting in a deeper cultivation of collective consciousness and solidarity. To further comprehend how enslaved Africans responded to their newfound conditions in the Caribbean, I examine the immediate social world of enslaved people by looking at their social lives and recreation – particularly cultural and spiritual creations surrounding death – considering them as processes of enculturation that introduced new Africans to local idioms and modes of survival. These sacred ritual practices and symbolic remembrances of the dead eventually formed the "medium of the conspiracy" among enslaved Africans and African descendants to free themselves from slavery.[1]

AYITI

Prior to Spanish arrival to the Caribbean, autochthonous Taíno AmerIndians of the Arawak family inhabited several islands, including *Quisqueya* – meaning "vast country," or *Ayiti*, "land of the mountains" – the second largest island of the Greater Antilles. Moreau de Saint-Méry estimated that there were between 1 and 3 million inhabitants on the island, and during his travels noted the presence of indigenous ritual artifacts in the north.[2] The *Ayitian* indigenous population was divided into five kingdoms, each headed by *cacique* chiefs who were often connected to one another, and Taíno *caciques* from other parts of the Caribbean, through kinship networks.[3] *Cacique* Guarionex led the Kingdom of Magua, which began at the north-central shore and extended east. The Marien Kingdom, governed by Guacanario, occupied what later became the northern department of Saint-Domingue. A third kingdom, Higuey, was in the south-east portion of what later became the Spanish colony of Santo Domingo. The island's south-central zone was held by the Kingdom of Maguana, whose *cacique* was an indigenous Caraïbe of the Lesser Antilles named Caonabo, husband of Anacaona. Anacaona was the great-aunt of the famed rebel leader Enriquillo, and sister of one of the island's most powerful *caciques*, Behechio, who ruled the Xaragua Kingdom based on the island's southwestern peninsula, extending east toward what the French later dubbed the Cul-de-Sac plain.[4]

When Christopher Columbus and the European *conquistadors* arrived in 1492, they claimed ownership of the island from the indigenous people and renamed it Española. After his initial arrival, Columbus returned to the Americas on three occasions and visited Española, Cuba, the Bahamas, and the South and Central American coasts in search of gold before his death in 1506.[5] These first moments of contact between the Taíno and Europeans set in motion patterns of interaction and structures of dominance that shaped societal relations in the Americas for centuries to come. Religious sanctioning from the Catholic Church and European racialization of "others" informed the white supremacist logic of colonial conquest, which anchored the genocide of indigenous peoples of Española (Smith 2012: 69). By the first years of the sixteenth century, other Spanish *conquistadors* had invaded Española and bound the Taínos, and other indigenous captives from neighboring Caribbean islands, within a labor system to work in gold mining, agriculture and, later, sugarcane cultivation. However, slaughter in combat, starvation, and infectious disease stemming from contact with Europeans swiftly devastated the Taíno population.[6] To replenish their supply of an uncompensated labor force, the Catholic priest Bartholemé de las Casas suggested to the Spanish crown that the indigenous were "noble savages" that should not be enslaved. Instead, Africans who were not protected by negotiated agreements between the Spanish and Taíno *caciques* would be imported.[7] This second logic of white supremacy, slaveability, or anti-black racism, anchored capitalist development within one population pool – black people – who were seen as particularly vulnerable and suited to commodified labor (ibid.: 68–69).

The earliest of these Africans were free *ladinos* who were assimilated Catholics from the Iberian Coast of Spain; and later legal and illegal

channels of the slave trade carried African continent-born *bozales*.[8]
Records of the sixteenth- and seventeenth-century transAtlantic slave
trade to Española are minimal, but the earliest Africans that Spaniards
brought to the island worked in gold mines. As the mines became unpro-
ductive, sugar production signaled the rise of "New World" slave economies using involuntary African labor. Enslavers did not officially target
African women as potential laborers until 1504. But in June 1527, the
king of Spain permitted traders to bring in African women captives to
close the population gap between black men and women and to encourage marriage and families, which the king hoped would increase an
overall sense of contentment and dissuade men from escaping to the
mountains or staging uprisings.[9] The African population had overtaken
the Spanish and Taíno population as early as 1509, and by the 1540s,
Española held between 20,000 and 30,000 enslaved Africans and African
descendants, with Senegambians, West Central Africans, and Biafrans
making up the largest portions of captives during the sixteenth century
(Table 2.1).[10]

The rise of exploitative and oppressive social structures in Española
engendered the social conditions that the small population of Taíno and
growing number of Africans faced: forced removal from their homelands,
the experience of being used as exploited labor for European resource
extraction and protoindustrial production, commodification as a human
being, and exorbitant death rates. The deeply penetrating reach of these
structural realities shaped the terms of everyday life and everyday death,
yet despite foreboding structural determinism, human beings can and do
exhibit agency, as did the Taínos and Africans. Structures and agency are
co-constituted and only exist in relationship to each other. Structures
shape the lives of social actors, who in turn rely on elements from their
symbolic world and social interactions to generate collective actions that
minimally agitate or, at maximum, transform those structures (Hall 1990;
Sewell 1992; Kane 2000; Diehl and McFarland 2010). Even with the
institutionalization of social death at Española and alienation from
human connections, identity, and labor value (Patterson 1982) in gold
mines and on sugar plantations, some Taíno and enslaved Africans
exerted collective agency by consistently escaping, fleeing to the densely
forested mountains, and participating in organized attacks against the
Spanish *encomienda* labor system.

The island of *Ayiti* – and its subsequent geopolitical designation,
Española – can be thought of as a contact zone, a "space of colonial
encounters, the space in which peoples geographically and historically

TABLE 2.1. *Disembarkations to Española and Saint-Domingue by African regions, 1500–1700*

Year	Senegambia	Sierra Leone	Bight of Benin	Bight of Biafra	WC Africa & St. Helena	Other Africa	Total
1501–1525	0	0	0	287	0	0	287
1526–1550	1,547	0	0	861	0	0	2,408
1551–1575	3,816	279	0	1,377	0	561	6,033
1576–1600	3,352	0	0	1,133	643	3,278	8,406
1601–1625	0	0	0	0	4,530	1,883	6,413
1626–1650	0	0	319	380	1,060	287	2,046
1651–1675	0	0	882	0	225	0	1,107
1676–1700	1,861	0	0	0	272	821	2,954
Total	10,576	279	1,201	4,038	6,730	6,830	29,654

separated come into contact with each other and establish ongoing relations, usually involving conditions of coercion, radical inequality, and intractable conflict."[11] Taínos and other indigenous AmerIndians from the circum-Caribbean, Iberian black *ladinos* and African-born *bozales*, and Spanish and French colonists converged on the island and contributed – voluntarily and involuntarily, and to varying degrees – to *Ayiti's* culture, language, and legacy of resistance that eventually culminated in the 1791–1804 Haitian Revolution. As the island's original inhabitants, the Taíno influenced the enslaved African and African descendant population's collective consciousness, which was transmitted intergenerationally through sacred ritual practice and the memory of sixteenth century revolts against Spanish colonization (Beauvoir-Dominique 2009, 2010).

Less than 20 years after the arrival of enslaved laborers, slave resistance became a mainstay of *Ayiti* that coincided with the emergence of the Spanish sugar economy racialization processes, and the exorbitant death rates of enslaved people. By the early seventeenth century, however, Africans' persistent struggle against slavery in the form of maroon raids on plantations, combined with the Spanish policy of depopulating much of the island, directly contributed to the essential collapse of the growing sugar industry.[12] The first plantation society in the Americas was undermined by black insurgency, representing what we might thus think of as the first of several "*Ayitian* Revolutions" and new sites and temporalities of modernity. By the late seventeenth century, the Spanish Empire incorporated new laws into the *Siete Partidas* code regulating enslaved and free people of color, legalizing the racialized slavery and oppression that had already been in existence.[13] These policies not only concretized the racial order, they were mechanisms of social control to prevent the kind of resistance from maroons and the enslaved that had undermined the Spanish sugar enterprise. The French soon resumed and expanded sugar production – as well as their own version of laws and mores that codified racial hierarchy in the *Code Noir* – overwhelming its own plantation economy a century later with excesses that undergirded economic, social, and political crises that helped to spark the 1791–1804 Haitian Revolution.

THE FIRST *AYITIAN* REVOLUTION: AFRICAN RESISTANCE AND MARRONNAGE IN THE SIXTEENTH TO SEVENTEENTH CENTURIES

Enslaved Africans rebelled against their new circumstances from the moment of their arrival on what was then called Española. As early as

1503, the governor of Española, Nicolás de Ovando, lamented to the Spanish crown that the *ladinos* were consistently escaping after having learned "bad customs" from the Taíno.[14] Some of these self-liberated *ladinos* took up residence with members of the remaining Taíno population and participated in the *cacique* Enriquillo's war against the Spanish that lasted from 1519 to 1534. Proximity to the Taíno while working in the gold mines was assumed to have instilled in the *ladino* bondspeople a growing sense of discontent with enslavement; Ovando suggested that they be replaced with *bozales* – captive Africans born and socialized on the continent – assuming they would be easier to control because of their lack of exposure to the Spanish culture and language, and the Christian religion.[15] Ovando's presumption was also based on a growing belief that "Europeanness" was the pinnacle of human superiority, while its opposite – non-Christian Africanness – was solely eligible for the opposite of freedom – slavery. Spanish colonists racialized enslaved *ladinos* and *bozales* in contrasting ways that nonetheless denied their intelligence and the essence of their humanity. Colonists described runaways as *cimarrons*, meaning wild or untamed in Spanish. The denial of runaways' inherent impulses to be free by relegating their actions to those of unruly animals established a false dichotomy in slaveowners' thinking about enslaved people that would last for centuries to come: the notion that freedom was a foreign concept to African people and therefore any of their attempts to self-liberate were dismissed as impossible (Trouillot 1995).

This sentiment was proven incorrect when, on Christmas Day of 1521, African *bozales* staged the first black-led uprising against enslavement in the Americas. A group of twenty Wolofs from Diego Columbus' sugar mill recruited several other enslaved Africans and autochthonous individuals from a nearby plantation in an attempt to seize the town of Azua and then join Enriquillo in the Baoruco mountains.[16] By the second day of their escape, the rebels had secured weapons, killed several Spaniards, and mobilized a force of at least 400 black and indigenous people. The insurgents intended to kill all the "Christians" at the sugar mills, farms, and towns, including those at Enriquillo's former home at San Juan de la Maguana.[17] The early presence of Wolofs in the Americas was a result of Spanish-controlled commercial trading through the Damel of Kajoor in the Senegambia region during the early sixteenth century.[18] These Wolofs were part of region-wide warrior traditions, and possibly were Muslims who may have been carrying out a continuation of jihad against the Spanish Christians as vengeance for their bondage.[19]

Archival records indicate that even after the 1521 revolt, colonial officials downplayed repeated uprisings and Africans' active participation in them to conceal a gradual loss of control over the enslaved population and the countryside outside the capital city of Santo Domingo, where maroons increasingly reigned. For example, a group of Wolof runaways attacked various plantations on horseback; their riding skills impressed, or embarrassed, Spanish representatives in Española.[20] King Charles V of Spain wrote a letter in December 1523, suggesting colonists in Española arm themselves given the growing African population.[21] In April 1528, the Crown received notice that there were

blacks that are run-aways and of wicked life and wiles that are not domestic, nor do they work as they are obliged, and [they] induce and call the other blacks that are peaceful and working to leave and rebel and do other crimes and ills, from which it results that the said blacks that are in the mines and other farms and businesses rebel and commit other crimes.

The king issued an order to the governor of Española to investigate the number of escaped Africans in the colony so that they could be returned and placed under surveillance.[22] Some runaways were captured, jailed, and sentenced to execution, which the Spanish crown attempted to expedite as they awaited their punishment.[23] The Spanish implemented waves of ordinances aimed at controlling the enslaved and implemented new taxes to finance military expeditions, but these were largely unsuccessful. Well-known leaders Diego Guzman, Diego Ocampo – who negotiated his freedom along with some 30 others – Miguel Biafara, Juan Criollo, and Juan Canario descended from the Baoruco mountains and constantly harassed the Spanish. These incursions prevented Spanish expansion into the countryside and kept settlements contained to Santo Domingo.[24] Accounts from 1532 describe a privileged enslaved man who killed his owner, then prompted others to begin a "killing spree" – but the perpetrators went unpunished because no one wanted to admit the uprising had occurred.[25]

By the 1540s, there were as many as seven thousand maroons living, mining, and trading independently in the eastern country and mountains, and population imbalances between the increasing number of enslaved Kongolese and plantation personnel left sugar plantations vulnerable to raids.[26] Maroon presence had spread beyond the city of Santo Domingo and the Baoruco mountains, reaching as far northwest as what later became Môle Saint Nicolas.[27] Maroons developed subsistence spaces – called *montes* by Spanish colonists – for raising livestock, agriculture, and collecting drinking water. These spaces were attractive to enslaved people, runaways, and indigenous people who were seeking not only freedom but additional food to subsidize the inadequate provisions they received on plantations. Maroons shaped the island's ecological landscape by subverting Spanish authority, waging war, and financially benefitting from their production through trade.[28] In 1544, military squads were sent to fight two maroon groups roaming the island; one group was composed of 15 rebels and the other group had 37 members, but most were killed or captured then returned to their owners. These maroons seem to have had nearly complete control over the countryside and, in April 1545, Prince Philip of Spain expressed concern that there were so many rebellious blacks occupying the island's central zone that local Spaniards feared leaving their farms unless they were in groups, and that they had to sleep in shifts with weapons in their hands. Yet, despite the overwhelming presence of rebellious Wolofs in the 1521 uprising, Prince Philip continued to insist that the menace was due to *ladino* activity rather than that of the *bozales,* whom he believed did not have the ability to organize a revolt.[29]

Throughout the 1540s, black rebellion was so widespread that by 1548 maroons had destroyed two-thirds of the island's sugar plantations.[30] One such African rebel was Sebastian Lemba, a feared Kongolese maroon who led Baoruco encampments for 15 years. Spanish sources described him as a highly skilled blacksmith with extensive military knowledge, which he used to organize West Central African-style raids on nearby plantations, dispersing his forces of 140 small groups to attack from varying directions.[31] During one such incursion for food, clothing, salt, and women, he kidnapped another KiKongo-speaking blacksmith to aid with the production of weapons.[32] The Spanish initiated convoys into the mountains, where they found many Taínos and Africans; Lemba was caught and executed in 1547. Colonists propped his head on a city wall in Santo Domingo – Porta de Lemba – as a warning to repress other potential rebellions. Years after the execution, residents of Santo Domingo remembered Lemba as a military leader, regarding him as "Captain Lemba" whose confrontations with colonial forces were a "war."[33] Other rebels who rose up met a similar fate. Fernando Monteros and, later in Spring 1554, Juan Vaquero "the cowboy" were hung and quartered, and Monteros' body parts were displayed along the roads leading to Santo Domingo and in the city plaza.[34]

By the late sixteenth to mid-seventeenth century, the Spanish presence in western Española was declining, in part due to the constant threat of African rebellion. Maroons continued to establish strongholds throughout the island, especially in the regions that would become part of French Saint-Domingue. Not only were maroons a mainstay in the Baoruco mountains and Môle Saint Nicolas, they also settled in areas including Fort Dauphin, the Artibonite Valley, and the Grand Anse southern peninsula.[35] The Spanish could no longer sufficiently defend themselves against the encroachment of the English and the Dutch, but more particularly the French. A greater number of French travelers and *boucaneer* sea raiders descended on Tortuga, a small island off the northwestern coast. There the French *boucaneers* met and began trading with Senegambian and West Central African runaways who had made their way from the island's Spanish side. Two African maroons, presumably Senegambians based on their ethnonym-based surnames – Cristobal Fula and Antonio Mandinga – spoke in court testimonies that they hunted and skinned cattle and brought the skins to the island's northern coasts, where they traded textiles with the Portuguese and the French.[36] Kongo-Angolans were brought to the island in part because of the 1580 union between the Spanish and the Portuguese, who for over a century already had trade relations and presence in the Kongolands, resulting in West Central African captives becoming the dominant group transported to the island in the seventeenth century. In the 1590s, the Spanish sent cavalry troops against the absconders in the north, where they captured several of the most "dangerous" Angolans: Louis Angola, who ran away with his pregnant Biafran wife, Antonin Angola, and Sebastian Angola. Subsequent expeditions to capture maroons in the north were unsuccessful, and in the face of defeat the Spanish organized a program to depopulate the north and to relocate to the south in 1605, essentially ceding the west to the French – and to the maroons.[37]

The Española census indicated that black and white populations steeply decreased after the forced relocation policy and also after the decline in new African arrivals: in 1606 there were almost 10,000 free and enslaved people, then only 4,500 in 1681.[38] As early as the mid-seventeenth century, the French informally settled on the island's western region in larger numbers and illegally trafficked Africans to develop sugar enterprises in what was soon to become Saint-Domingue. This included raids on Spanish towns; for example, a *ladino* maroon was said to have participated in a 1644 French incursion on Azua where several enslaved people were taken.[39] African and African descended captives posed as much of a threat to the French as they had been to the Spanish, and as Chapter 6 will discuss further, they quickly took note of the contestation over the west–east border and exploited it and French–Spanish tensions to their benefit. A "gang of warriors," comprised of over 30 Africans, was captured in the Baoruco mountains; many of these were Senegambians, as signified by their names: Juan Faula, Juan Mandigo, Beatriz Mandinga, Maria Mandinga, Francisco Mandinga, Anton Xolofo, and Ana Mandinga.[40] In 1662, a Spanish archbishop was sent to peacefully reduce the number of runaways in the Baoruco mountains. There he found 600 self-liberated families encamped in four *palenques*, another Spanish term for runaway communities, along the southern coast. The archbishop attempted to compromise with them; however, these maroons were self-sufficient and did not feel the need to negotiate surrender. They had corn and other crops, livestock, and the women searched for gold in the rivers. The men traded these goods in Santo Domingo – possibly with various African ethnic Catholic brotherhoods – and made weapons from iron and steel they acquired.[41]

There is no official count of maroons on the island in the seventeenth century, but it is likely that the settlements in Môle Saint Nicolas, Fort Dauphin, Artibonite, and Grand Anse expanded like the Baoruco mountain communities. Once the French officially claimed lands in a largely deserted western Española, the island's population majority were politically and economically autonomous black people who had already waged a century-long struggle against enslavement on sugar plantations in the form of marronnage. Geographic spaces like Tête des Nègres at Môle Saint Nicolas and Fonds des Nègres in Grand Anse reflect the historical presence of maroons who probably remained in their settlements and reproduced families. The sixteenth- and seventeenth-century struggle against slavery had quickened the disruption of the Spanish colonial sugar industry, leading to broader legal and repressive measures in the 1680 *Siete Partidas* to constrain all black people including free blacks, *ladinos*, and *bozales*. Repression of free, enslaved, and maroon black people continued in the early eighteenth century as the French colonial state created its *maréchaussée* fugitive slave police force to support plantation economy development (also see Chapters 6 and 7). The historical memory of the maroon struggle, early collaboration with indigenous Taínos, and the significance of the Baoruco mountains and the countryside surrounding Santo Domingo as geographic scenes of action continued to be part of the cultural landscape that welcomed newly arrived Africans under French rule at the turn of the eighteenth century.

FRENCH SLAVERY AND RACE IN SAINT-DOMINGUE

Structures and processes of human commodification, labor exploitation, death, and resistance were present in the Spanish colonial period and escalated under the French. While African resistance contributed to dismantling the Spanish sugar industry at Española, French forces took advantage of the vacuum of imperial power and ushered in an intensified, crop-diverse plantation system that relied on human commodification, labor exploitation, and racial hierarchy, and engendered an invigorated wave of death and resistance among the enslaved. French imperial expansion began in the seventeenth century and spread to several colonies in North America and the Caribbean. Plantation owners and colonists included few settlers compared to the growing number of enslaved African laborers, furthering the economic productivity of slave-holding Caribbean colonies. Early seventeenth-century French slave trading activity was largely clandestine and/or illegal, thus much evidence for this period is lacking. Still, the French established several trading companies and claimed various locations within the Caribbean, including Guadeloupe, Martinique, St. Christopher and western Española, or Saint-Domingue. The development of the *Compagnie des Indes Occidentales* (West Indies Company) in 1664 expanded and elevated slave trading and commercialism for the French crown.[42] The king of France deemed enslaved labor in the Caribbean islands as an "absolute necessity" to increase cultivation of cocoa, indigo, coffee, tobacco, and especially sugar, so he issued "a government bounty . . . on every African slave exported to the Americas."[43] As profits from the Caribbean colonies, especially Martinique, grew, the French Crown's 1685 *Code Noir* implemented mandates to dictate the slave trade and the people who were trafficked as enslaved labor.

After decades of raids from French, British, and Dutch pirates on western Española, and conflict between the French and Spanish, the Spanish officially ceded the contested territory to the French with the signing of the 1697 Treaty of Ryswick (Figure 2.1).[44] Chapter 6 will explore in more depth the position of enslaved Africans during ongoing contestations over the borderlands between the Spanish and the French – struggles that continued even after the treaty's ratification. The treaty formally recognized French presence in the island's western area, which they named Saint-Domingue – while the eastern territory still under Spanish rule was generally referred to as Santo Domingo. As Julius Scott has argued, during the seventeenth century several Caribbean islands, including Española, were essentially frontier zones populated by members of the "masterless class" – maroons, pirates, and European immigrant laborers. The turn of the eighteenth century, however, marked the rise of sugar production in the Caribbean and the unprecedented surge of the transAtlantic slave trade.[45] Though more research on early

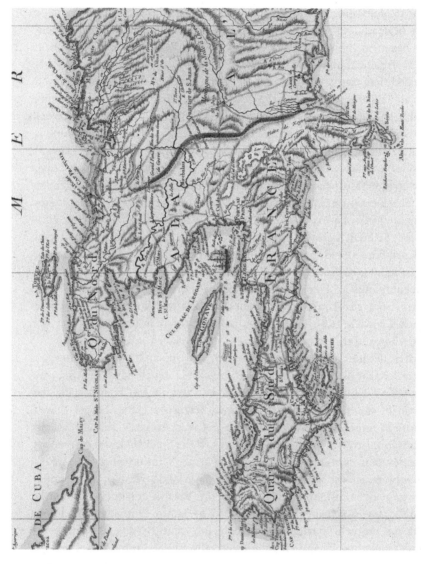

FIGURE 2.1. "Carte de l'Isle de St. Domingue", Courtesy of the John Carter Brown Library

eighteenth-century Saint-Domingue is needed, the French presence in western Española was solidified by the turn of the eighteenth century, and sugar and indigo production expanded. The steady output stimulated a growth in the enslaved population. In the century's first decade and a half, just over 10,000 African captives disembarked at Saint-Domingue. By 1716, the yearly number of Africans arriving was over 14,000, which more than doubled between 1736 and 1745. Cap Français was a main port site for the French trade, receiving over 9,000 ships in 1790 alone. In 1728 there were 50,000 enslaved Africans in Saint-Domingue; in 1754 that figure increased to 172,000, then reached 500,000 by the end of the century.[46] Approximately one-third of these newly arrived Africans arrived in the northern port city Cap Français, and other ports such as Port-au-Prince and Jérémie were used to a lesser extent. There remained a gender imbalance between enslaved men and women and the colonial living conditions for the enslaved were so deadly that the Africans did not sustain and reproduce themselves, which led plantation owners to continually replace that pool of laborers with new, Africa-born captives.[47] The unnaturally enormous and rapid growth of sugar production and of the enslaved African population transformed Saint-Domingue into a full-scale plantation-based slave society – completing the sugar revolution first initiated by the Spanish in the sixteenth century.

In contrast to slavery in Africa, or any other known slave society where social or economic status was usually the primary factor in being enslaved, the European slave trade introduced racial dynamics that drastically altered the nature of bondage in the "New World," simultaneously ushering in unequal power relations that permeated the fabric of the modern era (Winant 2001). Supported by evolving ideological and religious beliefs that Africans, especially those who were not baptized as Christians, were uncivilized, barbaric, and backwards, chattel slavery in the Americas generally operated on a polarity of opposing racial identities where blackness was equated with slave status, whiteness with liberty and freedom, and indigenous, Asian, and multi-racial individuals occupied intermediate spaces. The global political and economic forces of enslaving and capitalist development that deliberately precluded black people from power and other institutional resources to create change in their respective locations shaped the collective experiences of Africans in the early modern diaspora (Hamilton 1988, 2007). European colonies in the Americas, particularly sugar producing islands that were wholly dependent on slave labor, actively prevented African descendants from having full participation in or access to decision-making liberties within spheres of political representation, education, and social or economic development (Stinchcombe 1995).

As competition between the Portuguese, Spanish, Dutch, English, and French for control of the slave trade and demands for sugar intensified, so did the exploitation of unfree labor and the hardening of racial lines using legal and coercive means. Violence was the primary idiom that upheld economic, social, and political powerlessness among enslaved people and repressed acts of rebellion. The *Code Noir*, the French statute on slavery, legally codified the brute force of slavery as well as the racialization of freedom and slavery. The *Code Noir* allowed European men to marry enslaved and free African and African-descended women, creating a paternalistic racial structure that distributed power and resources according to racial identity and biological connectedness to whiteness. Coerced interracial relationships produced a small mixed-race population, the *gens du couleur libre* – or free people of color – who inherited wealth, land, and social mobility from their fathers. Though some mixed-race African descendants remained enslaved, many obtained manumission, educational opportunities in France, financial capital, and prosperous plantation estates and numbers of slaves that at times rivaled that of rich, white Saint-Dominguans.[48] Racial categorization of those who were not "purely" white was an obsession of sorts in Saint-Domingue – so much so that writer Moreau de Saint-Méry developed an elaborate schema describing 128 combinations of black, white, and AmerIndian mixtures, based on "classes" of skin tones, facial features, and hair types. Even the small number of free and enslaved sub-continental Indians were included in Moreau de Saint-Méry's model; though he compared them to whites in character, he also implied their susceptibility to downward mobility due to their darker skin or any intermingling with Africans.[49] The resulting overarching categories included the *mulâtre*, who was half-white, half-black; the *quarteron*, one-quarter black; and the *griffe*, three-quarters black.[50] Among the population of those who descended from Africans, there was considerable stratification according to skin color, ethnicity or lineage, slave status, and social class, which would later inform political struggles in the colony during the late 1780s and early 1790s.

The free people of color numbered over 27,000 and comprised 47 percent of the entire free population, accounting for a little over 5 percent of the colony. They found success in the coffee and, increasingly, the indigo niche markets, which required less start-up funds and smaller workforces, making them safer investments than sugar plantations.[51] Free women of color were especially entrepreneurial in Saint-Domingue's urban centers. Their economic activities in domestic work allowed them to accumulate capital and shift toward the buying and selling of slaves, real estate, and luxury goods distribution.[52] During the late eighteenth century, French laws increasingly excluded free people of color from various occupations and prevented them from accessing full political representation in France. Despite their small numbers, the frustrations of this wealthy and powerful group triggered their campaign for citizenship led by *quarterons* Vincent Ogé and Julian Raimond, who challenged the French national assembly in 1790.[53] In addition to the *gens du couleur*, some enslaved Africans and creoles in urban areas with artisanal trades could purchase their freedom or receive manumission from a family member. These former slaves – *affranchis* – were a modestly wealthy group who often maintained connections to the enslaved population through family, ethnic identity bonds, and work relations. For example, Toussaint Louverture was an *affranchi* before the Haitian Revolution, and his innermost circle was mostly comprised of free and enslaved Fon-speakers of the Arada nation.[54] In 1789, there were over one thousand free women and men of color living in Cap Français, many of whom owned homes, businesses, and enslaved Africans.[55] Cooks, carpenters, hairdressers, tailors, and other such workers from the Kongo and the Bight of Benin bought their liberty. Enslaved seamstresses also occupied the higher echelons of the bonded labor force. They trained in France to learn about the latest fashion trends and their owners leased them to other enslavers, allowing them to freely travel to markets or to see their clients. These women then used their geographic mobility and earned income to manumit themselves.[56]

No singular racial identity existed among the African-descended population in Saint-Domingue due to the colonial hierarchy and stratification. Though free people of color faced racial discrimination and oppression, only the lives and labor of enslaved Africans and African descendants were commodified and exploited for the profit of others. Enslaved people, formerly enslaved *affranchis* and privileged *gens du couleur*, and self-emancipated maroons were mostly disconnected, though there were moments and situations where cooperation and solidarity, however fraught, among these groups was forged. Except for a few, most *gens du couleur* separated themselves socially, economically, and politically from Africanness and blackness. Free people of color held economic interests grounded in plantation slavery and virulently fought against abolition until it became painfully clear that civil rights for free people of color were only viable with the contributions of an army of emancipated slaves. Before, during, and after the revolutionary era, racial solidarity between enslaved people, maroons, and free people of color was highly situational and vulnerable to cleavages along economic or political lines. Chapter 4 will explore aspects of solidarity building among maroons, and Chapter 7 will examine the temporal nature of marronnage and the interactive patterns forged through collective escape and rebellion. As this book argues, these were key processes that enhanced racial consciousness and solidarity, and informed both the struggle for independence in 1802 and post-revolutionary conceptions of race and citizenship. By declaring blackness as the undergirding qualifier for freedom and citizenship in the constitution, the Haitian revolutionary state became a "maroon nation" that had broken away from and subverted the racial capitalist order of the early modern Atlantic world (Roberts 2015; Gonzalez 2019).

THE SOCIAL CONDITIONS OF LABOR EXPLOITATION

The major city of Saint-Domingue, and the wealthiest of all the French colonies, was Cap Français, usually referred to as Le Cap, a port along the northern coast. Known as the Northern plain, an area that spanned 75 kilometers from east to west and 25 kilometers from north to south of Le Cap, the districts surrounding and including the bustling port were the most affluent and opulent in the colony.[57] The city was home to a mixture of people – poor and wealthy whites, enslaved people who leased themselves out for contracted work, the *gens du couleur*, and *affranchi* artisans. Its social life was vibrant and included masonic lodges, philosophical and scientific societies, cafés, dance halls and theaters, rum shops, and churches. The city was also an attraction for visitors and runaway slaves who sought refuge there by passing as free. In the years of the North American War for Independence, some 200 runaways were found renting rooms in houses owned by free people of color during a police sweep of the Petite Guinée (Little Guinea) neighborhood on the west side of Le Cap.[58] The city was home to the *marché des négres*, or the negro market, where, especially on Sundays, enslaved people from rural districts brought foodstuffs to buy and sell. The enslaved population for this region was about 170,000. Table 2.2[59] shows the population distribution of Le Cap's surrounding parishes as well as those outside Port-au-Prince, the colonial capital and next most populated city.[60]

By 1789, the nearly 500,000 enslaved African and African descendants in Saint-Domingue were held on over 7,800 plantations: over 3,000 that grew indigo; 3,000 coffee producers; nearly 800 that cultivated cotton;

TABLE 2.2. *Population distribution of enslaved African diasporans, 1789*

Province	Region	Parishes	Number of African Diasporans
North	Le Cap	Le Cap and its dependences	21,613
		Petite Anse and Plain of Le Cap	11,122
		L'Acul, Limonade and St. Susan	19,876
		Quartier Morin and Grand Rivière	18,554
		Dondon and Marmelade	17,376
		Limbé and Port Margot	15,978
		Plaisance and Le Borgne	15,018
	Fort Dauphin	Fort Dauphin	10,004
		Ouanaminthe and Vallière	9,987
		Terrier Rouge and Le Trou	15,476
	Port de Paix	Port de Paix, St. Louis, Jean Rabel, etc.	29,540
	Mole St. Nicholas	Mole and Bombarde	3,183
West	Port-au-Prince	Port au Prince	42,848
		Arcahaye	18,553
		Mirebalais	10,902
	Léogâne	Léogâne	14,896
	St. Marc	St. Marc, Petite Rivière, Verettes, and Gonaïves	57,216
	Petit Goâve	Petit Goâve, Grand Goâve, Le Fond des Nègres	18,829
		L'Anse a Vaux, le Petit Trou	13,229
	Jérémie	Jérémie and Cape Dame Marie	20,774
South	The Cayes	The Cayes and Torbuk/Torbeck	30,937
	Tiburon	Cape Tiburon and Les Côteaux	8,153
	St. Louis	St. Louis, Cavaillon, and Aquin	18,785
	Jacmel	Jacmel, Les Cayes, and Baynet	21,151
Total			464,000

and nearly 800 plantations that were producing sugar, which was the key to the colonial economy. Enslaved women, men, and children in this plantation economy lived within distinctly oppressive conditions. They were considered chattel that were commodities and forms of capital, typically counted alongside furniture and animals; they received no wages, nor did they have any political or legal rights or representation.[61] Depending on crop growth and geographic location, plantations had as many as 250 enslaved African and African-descended women and men who performed a range of tasks that were hierarchically ranked according to the level of arduousness associated with the work. "Field hands" were those who spent the most time performing physical tasks: cultivating the ground, cutting and harvesting crops, then processing crops in preparation for sale and transport. *Commandeurs*, or slave drivers, were typically enslaved men who sometimes carried a whip to monitor and discipline the work gangs in the stead of the plantation's owner. The *commandeur* was one of the most important positions on most plantations, since owners relied on them to guide the everyday labor practices and prevent any problems with enslaved workers. Though there were examples to the contrary, enslaved creole men typically occupied higher-ranked positions, including those that required artisanal apprenticeship, while women and Africans made up most of the field hands.

Men typically outnumbered women on plantations due to preferences for men during the early phases of the Atlantic trade, though the sex ratio came into balance in the years approaching the Haitian Revolution.[62] Despite, or perhaps due to, the apparent dominance of a male presence, the division of labor between enslaved men and women had little variance. Few women occupied the domestic arena labor force that had responsibilities for cooking, cleaning, laundry, and healthcare; generally, women rarely occupied specialized positions compared to those who performed strenuous field hand labor. Conversely, there were an array of specialized areas that enslaved men occupied, such as drivers, sugar boilers, watchmen or valets. On sugar plantations, it was regular for women and men to cut cane side-by-side as well as perform other tasks in the distilling and refining processes.[63] Gender compositions and divisions of labor were largely dependent on crop growth, as were ethnic divisions of labor. What follows is a description of plantation life, focusing on Saint-Domingue's major commodities: sugar, coffee, and indigo.

Indigo

Saint-Domingue began cultivating indigo in the early 1700s, though it was not wildly profitable, as potential planters initially considered the indigo trade to be an entryway to begin sugar and coffee production. However, since the start-up costs for indigo production were lower, Saint-Domingue's free people of color gained wealth in indigo development in the latter three decades of the eighteenth century. In the south, illegal trading between free planters and merchants from Curaçao and Jamaica bolstered indigo sales.[64] While most sugar plantations had as many as 250 enslaved workers, indigo plantations were smaller with between 30 and 80 workers in the 1780s. The 1784 sale of an indigo plantation in southern Torbeck included 72 enslaved people, indicating indigo estates were growing after the Seven Years War.[65] The workload was less arduous relative to sugar plantations. There was constant planting and weeding of the indigo shrubs, which laborers uprooted and re-planted several times beginning at the start of the annual rainy season. Men used hoes to dig the holes while women followed, placing the seeds and covering them. As laborers collected bundles of the plant, they were placed into a basin of water and allowed to ferment until the liquid dye emerged and the men drained the basin.

As Chapter 1 explained, geographic location seems to have influenced the ethnic composition of enslaved Africans on plantations, with more homogeneity in the north, an even mixture in the west, and more diversity in the south. The degree of ethnic diversity or cohesion among the enslaved work force depended on planters' proximity to major port cities, their financial ability to pay higher prices for "in-demand" ethnic groups, as well as their perceptions of each African ethnic group's health and diet, physical strength, agricultural experience, and overall disposition. Just as Moreau de Saint-Méry documented the perceived attitudes of multi-racial individuals, slave traders, plantation owners, and horticulturalists relied on stereotypes to populate their plantations. Planters surrounding Le Cap had their choice of bondspeople, since most African captives disembarked there, while toward the west and especially the south planters purchased captives from less commonly exploited regions. In the north, indigo plantations had over 60 percent of Central Africans, but only 16 percent from the Bight of Benin, and even less, 1 percent, from the Bight of Biafra. In the west, there was near parity between Central Africans and those from Benin; while in the south there was no clear majority: 33 percent Central Africans, 19 percent Biafrans, 18 percent from Benin.[66] The Torbeck plantation, owned by Lemoine-Drouet, included 33 men, 22 women, 12 boys and 5 girls. Twenty-one of the adults were colony-born creoles, but the others were African-born: 21 Kongos, 4 Cangas, 4 Mandigues, 2 Minas, 2 Thiambas/Quiambas, and 1 Senegalaise (Senegambian).[67] Among them were one creole *commandeur* Gerome, aged 28; an 18-year-old wig-maker named Philippe; 2 creole servants named Jeannette, aged 45, and Sanitte; and Marie Jeanne, a creole *hospitalière*, or healthcare provider to the enslaved, aged 45. On planta-tions like at Torbeck, various African ethnic groups interacted with each other and forged solidarity through labor and proximity. However, ethnic cohesion, rather than diversity, of especially sugar and coffee plantations in the north likely contributed to a sense of solidarity that facilitated the 1791 uprising (Geggus 1999).

Coffee

Coffee plantations tended to have fewer creoles and more enslaved Africans, specifically larger numbers of the African ethnic groups sugar producers deemed undesirable, such as the Kongo, Bibi, Mondongue, or the Igbo. P. J. Laborie's *The Coffee Planter of Saint Domingo* (1798) served as an instruction manual for British planters planning coffee cultivation in Jamaica and provided insights into common practices on Saint Dominguan *caféteries*. According to Laborie, Kongos, Aradas, and Thiambas were the most desirable groups; Kongos were considered especially docile. However, as Chapter 3 will explain, several rebellious ritualists were West Central Africans based in northern coffee plantations. Laborie made other suggestions, such as organizing work gangs by ethnicity, ensuring that they received warm baths to help them adjust to the climate, and having the enslaver, rather than other Africans, baptize the newly-arrived, serving as godparent in order to dissuade non-Christian "superstitious" rituals. Interestingly, he noted that women were not cooperative because they were accustomed to working for men in Africa, perhaps referring to the fact that women performed agricultural labor, especially in West Central Africa.[68]

Coffee rapidly became a leading crop in Saint-Domingue after the Seven Years War and prior to the Haitian Revolution. It grew to rival sugar production between 1767 and 1789, during which time coffee export profits boomed sixfold and served to loosen France's grip on the colony. As I discuss further below, the increase in imported Africans corresponded to the growth of coffee sales between the years 1783 and 1788 (Table 2.3). Whereas sugar required large, flat plots of land, Saint-Domingue's heavy rainfall and cool temperatures in the mountainous highlands supported coffee cultivation on smaller plots. Planter Elias Monnereau noted: "At present there are scarce any plantations upon the mountains without being planted with coffee."[69] For example, Port Margot had 24 coffee plantations or *caféteries*, at the top of the mountain, 15 on the slope, and none at the base.[70] The favorable climate and topography made it considerably easier to start a *caféterie* with less initial capital than one would need for a sugar plantation. Smaller labor forces allowed coffee production to be a low-cost investment. The numbers of

enslaved workers were much lower than the labor force on sugar plantations, which typically were over 200. Coffee plantations tended to be
larger in the west, averaging 76 people, than the north or south, averaging
43 and 38, respectively. In the west, coffee originated from Léogâne and
spread to Grand-Goâve and sections of Port-au-Prince. Northern parishes
that surrounded the Le Cap plains were coffee dominant; for example,
Marmelade had 7,000 enslaved on 160 *caféteries* and several provision
grounds, while Dondon had 9,000 on 219 *caféteries*. This coffee frontier
originated in Terrier-Rouge and eventually spread southwestward toward
l'Acul and Plaisance. In the southern peninsula region of Grand Anse, the
Jérémie parish contributed a substantial amount of coffee in the 1770s
and 1780s.[71]

Sugar

If coffee and indigo growth stimulated the raw wealth for capital accumulation throughout the early French Empire, sugar was its cash cow.
Sugar slowly gained popularity among Europeans, beginning as a delicacy
for the upper classes and becoming a dietary staple for members of
European societies. French traders and merchants established plantations
in the lesser Antilles islands, beginning in the late seventeenth century,
outfitted primarily for sugar cane cultivation. Sugar production was an
intensive, multi-step process, and necessary technology had not developed
sufficiently to make the sugar trade significant on a worldwide scale.
However, over the course of the seventeenth and eighteenth centuries,
cultivation processes became more refined and sugar exports from the
Americas to Europe multiplied exponentially.[72] Though other French and
English colonies were also substantial contributors to the sugar trade,
Saint-Domingue ascended to the top of the export chain by out-producing
all of them combined at the end of the eighteenth century. Saint-
Domingue became known as the "Pearl of the Antilles" by exporting
100 million pounds of sugar in 1765, and by 1788 sugar exports reached
200 million pounds.[73]

There were nearly 800 sugar plantations in Saint-Domingue by 1789.
While this may not seem like a substantial number compared to coffee,
sugar plantations were larger, more intensive operations that included a
diversified labor force. Sugar plantations dominated the north; they aver-
aged between 150 and 200 enslaved people, and were the largest in the
north but slightly smaller in the west.[74] For example, the five Galliffet
plantations, some of the most industrious in the colony, held a combined
total of over 1,000 enslaved people.[75] A wealthy class of planters known

as *grand blancs*, or the "big" whites, heavily invested in the industrialization of sugar. French merchants funded many of these *grand blancs*, who used their capital to develop and run large sugar plantations. These merchants also controlled international trade by dictating prices for products such as food and commodities, as well as the prices for enslaved Africans.[76] *Petit blancs*, or "small" whites were overseers, artisans, shopkeepers, managers, or small-scale plantation owners.

Sugar estates were akin to compounds, with several buildings including the main house for the plantation owner, several housing units – more like shacks – for the bondspeople, animal quarters, an infirmary, and sugar-processing buildings – all covering up to 750 acres. At the height of cultivation season, work days lasted for 24 hours as enslaved people worked in shifts, receiving as little as four hours of sleep per night and a small window for lunch that allowed them time to cultivate their own gardens. During work hours, sugar cultivation required all field hands to plant, fertilize, weed, and cut sugar cane stalks. Under the supervision of a *maître sucrier* – sugar boiler monitor, women fed sugar cane stalks into the mill where the juice was extracted that was then boiled several times until it hardened and was prepared for shipping.[77] This was a dangerous process, and it was not uncommon for enslaved laborers to endure accidents such as having limbs cut by machetes or a body part trapped in the sugar grinder. In addition to sugar cane cutting and boiling, estates included farming and ranching, hospital working, midwifery, clothes washing, and other artisanal tasks. The occupational diversity of sugar estates allowed for more social mobility than on coffee plantations, although creole men were preferred for most specialized work.[78] While coffee planters tended to favor captives from the Kongolands, Bight of Benin Africans were more prevalent on sugar plantations, especially in Saint-Domingue's western and southern regions. Planters regarded them as physically stronger and more capable of agricultural work than other ethnic groups. African ethnic cohesion and the proto-industrial nature of sugar production "proletarianized" the enslaved, contributing to the collective consciousness of the northern bondspeople who organized the August 1791 insurrection (James [1938] 1989, p. 86).

HUMAN COMMODIFICATION AND DEATH

Enslavement in the Americas forced people to work for no compensation, thus they were alienated from the value of the agricultural items they produced. Based on the work of scholars like C. L. R. James and Eric

Williams, it is generally accepted that the wealth generated from the trade of products extracted using slave labor is a clear connection between slavery and capitalist development in Europe. Recent scholarship also has given attention to the processes of trafficking and converting human beings into commodities to be bought, sold, traded, leased and disposed at the whims of the plantocracy. As the previous chapter discussed, the French procured African captives at coastal ports in exchange for rum, guns, and various other wares. Warfare and violent raids produced an abundance of captives available at African enslaving ports, which entailed a lower price point for human life on the continent than in the colony. Purchasing captive Africans was relatively cheap – according to records from the slave ship *Marie-Séraphique*, between the years 1770 and 1780 the average purchase price of a captive at the Loango Coast was 348 *livres*.[79] Survivors of the Middle Passage were purchased based on their potential productivity as laborers; during the time of the *Marie-Séraphique* voyages, the average price for enslaved people in Saint-Domingue was over four times the selling price in Africa (Table 2.4). The inflation of slave prices between the point of the slave ship's departure and disembarkation further shows that enslavers were interested in maximizing profits at each stage of captivity between the Middle Passage to the Americas (Smallwood 2008; Berry 2017). Not only were African lives perceived as inferior to European lives, they were considered to be *worth less* in economic value until enslavers stripped them of every aspect of their African-ness and converted them into racialized chattel. Planters protected their financial investments in enslaved people by branding their initials to indicate ownership of an enslaved person. To obfuscate their ownership, or the shame of having been commodified and branded like cattle, bondspeople in Saint-Domingue used herbs to heal their scabs and make the brands illegible.[80]

The newly emerging world capitalist system was in part dependent on the expendability of human life (Mignolo 2011), and nowhere was this truer than Saint-Domingue where the deaths of enslaved people was inescapable. Early sources claimed that between one-third and one half of Africans brought to the colony perished in a short time frame, making it one of the deadliest colonies in the Americas.[81] Mass fatalities were not uncommon. For example, an account about an aspiring coffee planter in Dondon claimed that he "set out with a coffee plantation and sixteen negroes; at the end of eighteen months ... he found himself reduced to a single negro, the fifteen being dead in so short a space of time."[82] Rather than examine plantation records to calculate death rates as a lens through

TABLE 2.3. *Captive African imports and coffee sales*

Year	Africans imported & sold	[Slave] sales revenue	Cafes sold	Sale prices in the colony
1783	9,370	15,650,000	44,573,000	33,429,750
1784	25,025	43,602,000	57,885, 000	44,951,250
1785	21,762	43,634,000	52,885,000	57,368,000
1786	27,648	54,420,000	52, 180,000	57,398,000
1787	30,839	60,563,000	70,003,000	91,003,900
1788	29,506	61,936,000	68,151,000	92,003,850

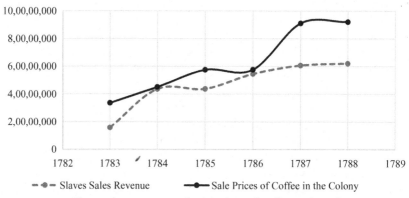

FIGURE 2.2. Slave sales revenue and sale prices of coffee in the colony

which to understand the lack of value of black life, I compare commodity prices to the monetary values associated with enslaved people to gain a glimpse into the ways economic trends reflected the lived reality of bondspeople who were similarly regarded as a commodity. Table 2.3, originally published in *Nouvelles de Saint Domingue*, compares the revenues from the sales of enslaved people ("Slave sales revenue") and the "sale prices of coffee in the colony."[83] The visualization of the relationship between "slave sales revenue" and "sale prices of coffee in the colony" represented in Figure 2.2 shows a slow growth of slave revenues while coffee sales quickly climbed toward the late 1780s. From these data points, we can speculate that the higher commodity prices rose, the relative value of black life declined. The growing demand for coffee and sugar in a global market stimulated the slave trade and likely was the cause for worsening conditions on plantations.

Table 2.4, originally published in *Les Affiches américaines*, similarly allows us to see the relationship between slave and sugar prices by

TABLE 2.4. *"Tableau de comparaison des* Négres, *depuis 1730, jusqu'à 1786, dans la Colonie de Saint-Domingue"*

Year	Average price of *négres*	Average price of raw sugar	Representative of the value of *négres* in quintals of sugar	Fractions of quintal
1730	1,000 *livres*	8 *livres*	125	
1740	1,200 *livres*	18	66	deux tiers
1750	1,300 *livres*	24	54	un seizième
1765	1,450 *livres*	35	41	trois septièmes
1770	1,600 *livres*	33	48	seize 33ème
1775	1,650 *livres*	35	47	un septième
1778	1,600 *livres*	36	44	quatre neuvièmes
1786	1,968 *livres*	31	63	quinze 31ème

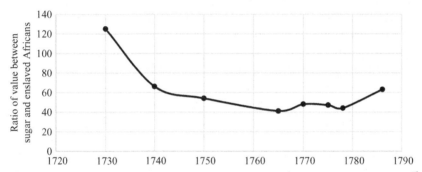

FIGURE 2.3. Representative of the value of enslaved africans in "quintals" of sugar

showing the trajectory of average slave prices over time, beginning with 1,000 *livres* in 1730 and ending with 1,968 *livres* in 1786.[84] While the price of slaves almost doubled over the 50-year period, the average price of raw sugar nearly quadrupled. The table column labelled "Representative of the value of *négres* in quintals of sugar" displays the ratio between the average prices of enslaved people and average prices of raw sugar, and indicates a steady decline of the slave value–sugar price ratio. Therefore, when the value of sugar increased, the value of enslaved people decreased in relation to that of sugar. This ratio was not merely an economic statistic; it had real-life implications, especially given the well-known rigor and dangerous life on plantations. The increased sugar and coffee prices created incentives to increase production, which meant more forced labor, longer workdays, and more brutal practices to squeeze every ounce of energy from the enslaved workers. Figure 2.3 displays the ratio between slave and sugar prices, "representative of the value of *négres* in quintals of sugar"; the ratio's decrease reflects the reality that the abundance of low-priced African captives combined with rapidly increasing demands for sugar essentially cheapened the value of black lives in Saint-Domingue, especially in the years leading to the Haitian Revolution.

The 1685 *Code Noir* was the official royal policy that claimed to provide protected treatment of slaves in the French colonies, and it included a minimum ration of food, clothing, and medical care for the disabled. Yet planters disregarded the *Code*, and plantations provided insufficient clothing, food, shelter, and little to no medical assistance. Only after the king of France reinforced *Code Noir* in 1784 were plantation owners required to provide the enslaved with land plots for cultivation. Newly arrived Africans were given a transition period of six to twelve months of "seasoning," which was a process of structured care to acclimate the captives to the unfamiliar environment. Despite these efforts, newly arrived Africans died at rapid rates – to the extent that death rates exceeded birth rates throughout the eighteenth century.[85] African women's fertility and overall health were particularly vulnerable to deterioration due to the trauma and violence of capture, the Middle Passage, and the relentless labor regimes on plantations.[86]

Death was ubiquitous in Saint-Domingue and was particularly unkind to the enslaved population. Diseases such as smallpox, typhoid and yellow fever, dysentery, syphilis, scurvy, and scabies were widespread in the Atlantic zone and prevalent on slave ships due to lack of nourishment, supplies, and sanitation. Sick captives from ships sometimes brought these illnesses to the colony; for example, a slave ship that arrived at Le Cap in 1772 held several smallpox-infected captives who spread the disease, which eventually killed nearly 1,200 people.[87] In addition near unending work schedules, and illness and hunger, brutality toward slaves was commonplace. Enslavers sexually exploited women and girls with regularity and they even sexually violated men. In Trou, group of enslaved domestic laborers killed a planter named Poncet – he was their biological father, who had castrated his sons and committed incest with and impregnated his daughter. Sannite, Poncet's pregnant daughter, was sentenced to a public hanging after the delivery of what was presumed to be his child.

Indiscretions of any kind were met with violence and torturous acts, some of which was documented by Baron de Vastey. Writing in 1814, de Vastey relayed horrific stories of planters' treatment of enslaved people, which occurred frequently and often with impunity. Bordering on sadism, planters buried slaves alive, used their blood to clarify sugar, mutilated their genitals and cut off their limbs, while bloodhounds were commonly trained to hunt and capture enslaved runaways.[88] Enslaved people escaped for a myriad of reasons, one of which was torturous and even murderous plantation owners. In 1741 a wealthy colonist was charged with murdering over 200 of his own slaves, five of whom had been mutilated. His restitution was a 150,000-pound donation to the public works fund.[89] At the Dame de l'Isle Adam property in Plaine du Nord, a former runaway named Thomas was interviewed about his experiences and the reasons he escaped. Thomas was a creole *commandeur* who fled before All Saint's Day in early November 1774, then returned in early January 1775. He fled because he feared retribution from the plantation agent M. Chapuzet for killing a mule, and the agent had a penchant for murdering enslaved people suspected of harming animals. Thomas testified that part of the reason he left was because he was trying to avoid the same fate as his own father, whom Chapuzet murdered for allegedly killing an enslaved woman.[90]

Conceptions of death in popular Kreyol sayings like "moun fêt pou mouri" (people are born to die) point to the overwhelming volume and nature of death that began with the mass casualties of the Taíno and extended into the French colonial period.[91] Death during the Middle Passage, from being overworked, illness, suicide or murder was a commonplace, and they were given the spiritual significance of death in West African and West Central African cosmologies, as were commemorations of the dead. Reverence of deceased familial ancestors and African royalty were and continue to be central to Haitian religious belief and practice. The Guedevi were the indigenous inhabitants of what later became the Dahomey Kingdom and may have been among Dahomey's first victims to slave trading upon losing power to the kingdom's growing imperial dominance. Known as the "children of Guede," individuals and spirits from the Guedevi formed the Guede rite of *lwa*, or Haitian deities, which today rules over and protects matters concerning the life cycle to ensure collective survival: life, death, health, children, and fertility.[92] Not only can the dead communicate important messages to the living about the mysteries of the material and non-material worlds, but death also represents freedom in the form of repatriation to Africa. The idea that one's soul would return to Africa upon death was a commonly held belief among enslaved people, and in Haiti this notion is made most explicit in that the sacred, "other-world" of spirits and the dead is referred to as Guinea – the West African coastal region from which most captives from the Bight of Benin were taken.[93] Rituals related to death or the dead figured prominently in the sacred practices of the enslaved, and the next chapter will further explore how death intersected with an ethos of liberation. Though we do not have many records of African Saint Dominguans' funerary practices, the few extant accounts give insights into the re-creation of ritual life in the colony.

AFRICAN-INSPIRED CULTURAL CREATIONS IN SAINT-DOMINGUE

Members of the African Diaspora did not lose their inherent understandings of themselves or the social and symbolic world(s) as they grappled with forceful separation from their African homelands and their respective social, economic, political, and religious institutions; new geographic locations; new societal structures; and unfamiliar human groups such as Europeans, AmerIndians, and other African ethnic groups. African Diaspora members constructed new and distinct identities and cultural formations that were largely rooted in their homeland worldviews and reformulated and re-articulated in the host society. Their collective ritual life connected them to Africa and to each other, and death rites and other practices helped integrate newly arrived enslaved people into the existing social fabric of the population, enculturating new arrivals and establishing the basis for collective consciousness, solidarity, and means of survival in the colony. Enslaved people in Saint-Domingue, when out of sight from plantation personnel, displayed unseen facets of their personalities through laughter and joking, satirical song, gossip, and storytelling.[94] Some plantation workers employed a communal style of hoeing, timing their strokes to African rhythms. Pierre de Vaissière noted food preparation and eating styles, reverence for the elderly, and cultural expressions through song, dance, and death rites as distinctly African and connected to non-Christian beliefs.[95] Enslaved women practiced extended breastfeeding, a common method of birth control in West and West Central African societies, and even referred to themselves as the mother of their oldest child, suggesting motherhood bestowed a sense of honor. There were strong emotional bonds and affectionate relationships between mothers and their children; enslaved mothers were meticulous in caring for children and took considerable pride in children's hygiene, appearance, and health.[96]

Saint-Domingue had no formal educational opportunities for the enslaved population, and enslavers and some commentators assumed Africans were intellectually inferior. Yet, the enslaved indeed exemplified intelligence and many were literate in their native languages, including Arabic.[97] African descendants brought to Saint-Domingue from other colonies were familiar with European languages spoken within the Atlantic world. Many advertisements placed in *Les Affiches américaines* made note of runaways' French, Spanish, English, Portuguese, or Dutch reading and writing skills as a form of human capital that could help the person pass for free. Enslaved Africans and African descendants had a "public face" in their contact with whites, but also shared an inner symbolic universe to which whites were not privy (Berger and Luckmann 1966; Gomez 1998).

Death Rites

One significant way that enslaved people humanized themselves and expressed their African-inspired practices was through funeral rites (Wynter n.d. :77–83). Enslaved people died rapidly and there were several burial sites for unbaptized blacks in Saint-Domingue, although they were not well tended. The law required the enslaved to be buried in alignment with the Catholic faith, but blacks often appropriated these rituals in their own styling and held funerals at night. Whites eventually abandoned the cemeteries, leaving Africans and African descendants to freely practice their sacred traditions for the dead. In a funeral procession in the southern Aquin, people carried with them *garde-corps*, or small figurine "body-guards." Women followed the body, singing and clapping their hands, while men came behind, playing slow drums. Afterward, family, friends, and members of the same ethnic group gathered for a repast. For several days after the funeral, mourners wore all-white clothing with kerchiefs on their heads.[98]

As a public practice, enslaved peoples' death rites were perhaps more visible to European eyes than other African-inspired cultural practices. As practices unfamiliar to European observers, they were still notable and thus survive in written records. In the 1760s, indigo planter Elias Monnereau documented a funeral ritual that culminated with a unique practice. Family and friends of the deceased invited associates to a Sunday ceremony to which everyone brought something to share, either food, rum, or another alcoholic beverage. As each person arrived, they paid respects and compliments to the dead, then formed a circle at the door opposite to where the corpse lay to collectively celebrate the person's life with drink. Participants then knelt and recited prayers one after the other, then laid down to kiss the ground. After another drink, they danced in pairs until dinner, at which time they consumed a sacrificed pig.[99]

Michel Descourtilz also observed a funeral that involved the *calenda* dance. A creole woman named Ursule had lost her friend François, and approached Descourtilz begging for a sheep, saying they already had the *banza* guitar and *bamboula* drums prepared for the dancing portion of François' burial ceremony. Ursule sang and wept for her friend: "François, he has gone! Poor François! Poor man who has died!" She suddenly began to dance the *chica*, which Moreau de Saint-Méry identified as having Kongolese origins, saying "let me dance for him, let me dance for him."[100] After the funeral proceedings, loved ones carefully cleaned and tended to corpses in preparation for sending them to burial sites. At times children led the procession in front of the coffin, carrying a large wooden cross to the feast and *calenda* dance.

Peyrac family plantation papers from Croix-de-Bouquet describe an interesting burial ritual wherein observers thought the ceremony was a spectacle or a game rather than a final farewell. Four men carried the deceased in her or his coffin on their shoulders and walked around

with a frightful spell, all at once running in zigzags, sometimes right, sometimes left, pretending that the spirit of the dead did not want to go through this or that road. The women uttered frightful cries, they wept, and conjured the evil spirit not to torment the soul of the deceased. Sometimes the carriers stopped, saying that the dead man did not want to go any further. Soon they resumed their contortions and pretended to let the coffin fall on the ground, but after a thousand exercises of address[ing the community], the body was restored to equilibrium and...deposit [ed] in its last abode. In reality, this strange race, corpse on the shoulder, [is to] "disorient the dead one to prevent him [from] find[ing] the way of his house."[101]

This funerary practice of allowing the dead person's spirit to visit members of the community before their final departure remarkably mirrors burial rites recorded in nineteenth-century Jamaica (Figure 2.4), where Bight of Biafran Igbos and Gold Coast Coromantees were most culturally influential. Processions for the dead on the Anglophone island had a social function of shaping values in the slave community by affirming the social status of the deceased, or by admonishing evil spirits and wrongdoers who were still alive. Some Africans in Jamaica believed that evil spirits could lure the newly dead into haunting the living, and that it was the responsibility of loved ones to ensure a proper burial so the

FIGURE 2.4. "Heathen practices at funerals, Schomburg Center for Research in Black Culture"

spirit could peacefully transition to the other world.[102] Bight of Benin/ Gold Coast Minas in Saint Croix reported to a missionary named Christian Oldendorp that only those who "belonged to God" could receive a proper burial and that opposing forces would prevent the bearers from carrying the corpse forward.[103] These beliefs would help explain why the women and pallbearers in the ceremony at the Peyrac plantation in Croix-de-Bouquet allowed the spirit of the deceased to maneuver its way around evil spirits toward its final resting place.

In northern Saint-Domingue, funerals were held at a burial mound called *Croix bossale* at Fossette in the south end of Le Cap. Fossette was a heavily used cemetery, averaging almost two burials per day and completely turning over the cemetery grounds every three years.[104] Fossette, along with the public square in Le Cap, was a gathering space for African-Saint Dominguans to hold services that were infused with Africa-inspired and Catholic practices. In accounts from 1777, Fossette was a center of dance and musical activity on Sunday nights and holidays.[105] The burial processions were organized affairs, and leaders were ranked as kings and queens with

sashes of different colors with different types of gold and silver braid that they wear on their jackets, and the women wear around their waist. They pay a subscription of several *portugaises* and burial fees which the others inflate as they feel like it. These funerals give rise to big processions, at which the sashes are worn.[106]

There was an informal system of inheritance, where a person's belongings were distributed in a hierarchical fashion to her or his children first, other family members second, then to other blacks who also had children.[107] The large parade, mutual aid effort, and uniform costumes are indicators of a lay brotherhood/sisterhood organization for and by black Catholics, as was the case in Afro-Iberian-influenced places like Brazil, Cuba, Rio de la Plata, and even New York and New England. These confraternities held ritual celebrations on Sundays and major holidays, ensured a proper burial for the dead, served as informal banks for enslaved blacks to purchase their freedom, and often were the nexus of identity formation and rebellion organization.[108]

Death was an inescapable reality in Saint-Domingue; therefore, commemorating it, preventing it, and at times inflicting death were core components of African-Saint Dominguans' ritual life. Naturally, the preoccupation with death was accompanied by supernatural powers that enslaved people drew upon to not only address personal concerns, but to critique and rectify the societal imbalances created by racialized enslavement. Thus, death rites, as a mode of enculturation, functioned as platform for resistance to the very racialized enslavement that commodified, exploited, and killed enslaved people. The François Mackandal affair (discussed below and in Chapter 3) and subsequent ritual events stand as examples of spiritual activities intersecting with seditious notions of freedom and liberation. However, participants of these rituals, as well as those rituals described below, came from various African ethnic backgrounds and statuses in the slave community, suggesting solidarity was beginning to form a collective identity around blackness and anti-slavery sentiments.

WORLDVIEWS AND RITUAL LIFE

Analysis of enslaved populations' lifeways, particularly religious practices, in the Americas must begin with an historical study of Africa – a difficult and complex task due to African geo-political processes and gaps in slave trade data (Lovejoy 1997; Morgan 1997). Africa was and continues to be extremely diverse, with thousands of languages and cultural groups. However, many of these distinct cultural expressions and identities were mutually intelligible through geographic proximity, political allegiance, and trade relations. As Chapter 1 demonstrated, the slave trade did not randomly distribute captive Africans, it trafficked them in homogeneous clusters alongside peoples from neighboring regions (Hall 2005). Further, several African groups shared undergirding worldview principles that informed their behaviors and practices (Herskovits 1958; Mbiti 1990). Christian Oldendorp, a Moravian missionary in eighteenth-century Danish St. Croix, documented findings from his observations, interactions, and conversations with enslaved Africans about their identities, homelands, cultures, and religious beliefs. While he acknowledged variance in Africans' beliefs and practices, there were several areas of overlapping spiritual tenets, including: (1) one supreme, benevolent deity; (2) lesser gods associated with forces of nature, territories, and family that mediate between humans and the supreme god; (3) the use of material objects imbued with sacrality; (4) the performance of prayers and sacrificial offerings to the supreme and lesser gods; (5) ritual leaders, male or female, who also operated as community healers and diviners; and (6) the transmigration of spirits post-mortem.[109]

This historical overview of African worldviews and emergent cultural connections focuses primarily, though not exclusively, on the Bight of Benin and West Central Africa. At the beginning of the eighteenth century, the Ouidah port on the Bight of Benin Coast provided the largest number of slaves to Saint-Domingue. The *vaudoux* – derived from the Fon term *vodun* – was the most well-known ritual in the colony, and the term was probably liberally applied to rituals and practitioners that may have been performing rites from another region. Due to the dominance of West African cultural and religious continuations in historical and contemporary accounts of Haitian Vodou, scholars argue that Bight of Benin groups (Arada/Fon, Nagô/Yoruba) established the mold for religiosity among the enslaved in Saint-Domingue into which later-arriving groups would be incorporated (Hebblethwaite 2014). After the 1750s, ports along the West Central African Loango Coast were most used in the French slave trade, and the broadly defined "Kongolese" became the majority ethnic group in the prosperous colony. Recent research has focused on the cultural influence of the Kongolese (Thornton 1993b, 1991; Vanhee 2002; Mobley 2015) and sheds new light on how their activities may have reflected a sense of militancy, particularly given the contentious history of the Kongo and its surrounding kingdoms in the late eighteenth century.

Members of the various African ethnic groups, along with creole African descendants born in the colony, formed ritual sects that were distinct from each other yet shared common worldviews. These groups were described as "nations," and were distinguished by dances, songs, association with spirit forces, and the use of flora and fauna that facilitated healing, divination, and protection. Among others, the *calenda*, *chica*, *wangua*, and the Dahomean *vaudoux* and Kongolese *petro* rites were the predecessors to what would become the Haitian Vodou religion.[110] Initiation processes and vows of secrecy characterized several of these rites. Sacred practices often occurred when Africans and African descendants gathered in wooded areas after dark, in unused churches or burial processions, as these were protected places away from plantation authorities.[111] These assemblies were not merely spiritual in nature but were protected spaces for Africans and African descendants to express their intentionality for liberation.

Along with spiritual gatherings, individuals used ritual artifact technologies in their daily lives to mediate conflicts, to bring about good fortune, to heal sickness, or for protection from negative spirits. Ritual leaders who created these artifacts held privilege within the enslaved community but lived and worked alongside other laborers and runaways. Their esteem within the community was based on their efficacy in using spiritual power to make things happen in the natural realm. When leaders or their respective spirits were not efficacious, followers shifted their allegiance to more powerful rites. This would have been particularly true for newly arrived Africans whose traditions included the veneration of familial ancestors in sacred spaces such as burials or shrines. These Africans would not have had access to their familial spirits due to their forced migration to Saint-Domingue; therefore, they would have gravitated to spirits that were associated with universal forces, for example the Yoruba *orisha*. Given the ethnic pluralism of the colony, we can assume there was a rapidly changing spiritual landscape of shifting loyalties between competing sects and shared symbols between cooperative sects, all of which contributed to the forging of a collective consciousness and a cultural repository of ideas, histories, and practices.[112]

Vaudoux

Bight of Benin Africans were the most numerous group brought to Saint-Domingue in the early eighteenth century, and their cultural and religious influence seems to have set the mold for spiritual life in the colony. The most direct correlation between religion in the Bight of Benin and Saint-Domingue is the transfer of *vodun* spirits that appear on the other side of the Atlantic as the Haitian *lwa* spirits, such as Legba, Mawu-Lihsah, Azli, and several others.[113] The *vaudoux* refers to the most well-known and earliest documented ritual dance in Saint-Domingue; the term derives from a shorthand description of the dance of the *vodun*.[114] *Vaudoux* gatherings were highly secretive, guarded by levels of oaths and initiations, and presided over by a king and queen, reflecting the male–female leadership tradition of the Fon/Gbe-speaking region.[115] The snake spirit Dangbe/Danbala was the central deity of the *vaudoux* and was thought of as an all-knowing god. The priest and priestess administered the ritual oaths of secrecy within the group, and represented Danbala as members made appeals for money, healing from sickness, love, or influence over their owners. During the ceremony, the female leader stood on a box containing a snake and became mounted by the spirit. The woman issued directives and orders for the adherents to follow, or they risked misfortune or peril. After the spirit embodiment, offerings ensued, enhanced with dancing, a poultry-based meal, and alcohol consumption. Moreau de Saint-Méry considered these events to be benign, yet thought they could have subversive potential because of the willingness of adherents to assign ultimate power to the priest and priestess and the spirits they served.[116]

It was believed that the *vaudoux* was wildly popular in the colony; however, some observers mistook other ethnic groups' ritual activities for the *vaudoux*. For example, a Mozambican ritual in Cayes Saint-Louis in the southern department was described as *vaudoux* because it also involved "convulsions" of the spirit.[117] The presence of Mozambican captives increased after the Seven Years War when the French lost their Senegambian posts to the British. The French ventured south of Angola, a long-standing trade region of the Portuguese, along the East African shores, and significantly increased trade volume between 1769 and 1776.[118] Between the years 1750 and 1800, 3,713 Mozambicans disembarked at Saint-Domingue's western department ports Les Cayes, Léogâne, and Port-au-Prince.[119] It is plausible that the increased visibility of Mozambican's non-Islamic indigenous ritual practice involved similar elements like spirit reverence, possession, and herbalism that European observers were unable to distinguish.

Alternatively, Africans from other regions may have felt an affinity for the *vaudoux* and attempted to join Arada-led ceremonies. The *vaudoux* involved participants dancing in circular movements around the king and queen, and as Sterling Stuckey observed, the practice of circular dance – especially in the counterclockwise direction – was commonplace and held spiritual significance among several West and West Central African cultural groups. The dances, along with the singing and musical instruments, summoned ancestral spirits and other deities, which helped foster inter-ethnic contact and served as "the main context in which Africans recognized values common to them."[120] For example, Michel Descourtilz witnessed an enslaved Igbo man trying to join an Arada ceremony in Artibonite by offering rum, money, and a few chickens for sacrifice, but the man was refused entry.[121] The *vaudoux* gatherings were clandestine, and their participants were sworn to secrecy. Additionally, the Aradas and other Bight of Benin Africans were numerous enough in Saint-Domingue that they may not have felt inclined to welcome others to their assemblies. On the other hand, this account simultaneously supports and disproves claims that African ethnic groups self-segregated and held no regard for one another's gods.[122] African religions generally were not organized around a structured orthodoxy, allowing them to be welcoming of beliefs and practices that were compatible with their own worldview.[123]

The fact that an Igbo person willingly approached the Aradas and made an offering so his request would be taken more seriously shows that ethnic and/or racial differences did not prevent varying groups from interacting with each other in ritual spaces. Igbos were few in Saint-Domingue, so this Igbo man gravitated to Arada practices due to the reputation of *vaudoux* as having efficaciousness. Further, Igbos' spirituality was connected to reverence for their ancestral lands; therefore, alienation from their Bight of Biafra origins was especially disorienting, resulting in a reputation for suicidal tendencies. Igbos believed in the transmigration of spirits and that death would return them to their homeland.[124] The *vaudoux* was the primary religious and cultural influence in the colony due to their numerous presence at the beginning of the eighteenth century; participation in a *vaudoux* ceremony may have presented an opportunity to communicate with spirit beings who could provide insight into why the Igbo man had been expelled from his home and how he could remedy his predicament.

Islam

A scant but growing amount of archival data, in addition to what has already been uncovered and interpreted by Emilie Diouf (1998) and Michael Gomez (2005), further indicates there were a number of enslaved Muslims in Saint-Domingue. Slave trade records, as discussed in Chapter 1, indicate that captives from Senegambia and other Muslim areas on the Upper Guinea Coast were the third largest group brought to Saint-Domingue in the early eighteenth century. Though their numbers declined in the latter half of the century, a disproportionately high frequency of insurrections on ships leaving Senegambia headed to the Caribbean occurred in the years surrounding the Futa Jallon jihad and the short-lived Futa Tooro revolution that banned the slave trade. The influence of anti-slavery sentiments in Senegambian Islamic thought and practice may have influenced rebellion in Saint-Domingue. Accounts described maroon and famed poisoner François Mackandal as a Muslim from the Upper Guinea region, and several of his associates were Nagô/Yorubas also from the Bight of Benin. The notes from the prosecution trial against Mackandal include descriptions of his *gris-gris* sacred amulets, which contained written Qur'anic prayers. During his late seventeenth century religious movement, Nasir Al Din similarly instructed Senegambian soldiers of the Islamic faith to carry their talismans with them in battle to symbolize the power of the Qur'an.[125] Over one century later, Colonel Charles Malenfant reported finding African rebels during the Haitian Revolution in 1792 who carried *macoutes*, a type of basket or sack that enslaved people carried over their arms or chest, which contained Arabic writings believed to be prayers in text.[126] Swiss traveler Pierre Du Simitière visited Saint-Domingue, mainly Port-au-Prince and Léogâne, in the 1770s. In January 1773 at Léogâne, he recorded that an enslaved man of the Mandinga nation wrote a Qur'anic prayer in Arabic. A photograph of the text remains and appears in Figure 2.5.

Memorizing, reciting, and re-writing the Qur'an was an important way of proving oneself to be an upstanding Muslim.[127] Some enslaved Muslims in Artibonite attempted to fashion writing utensils using lemon juice, bamboo, wood tablets, and parts of palm trees.[128] Du Simitière found a second prayer that cast blessings on believers and castigated scandal mongers, back-biters, and those who piled up wealth.[129] This prayer was likely contained in a *macoute* ritual packet, and seemingly reflected a spiritual castigation of the type of unethical trading practices

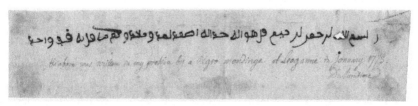

FIGURE 2.5. "Arabic fragment, a West African *gris-gris*, Library Company of Philadelphia"

that were rife during the height of the transAtlantic slave trade. The little evidence of these writings that exists further proves there were captives from Islamic regions of Africa who were taken to Saint-Domingue. A group of four runaways escaped a St. Marc plantation in 1768; possibly at least two of them were Muslim: Simon of the Tapa nation and Sultan *dit* or "the so-called" Alla, a 45–50-year-old *commandeur* of Aguia ethnicity.[130] Simon and Sultan's ethnic origins suggest they were from regions of the Bight of Benin that were influenced by Islam.[131] Given that Sultan, in particular, retained an Arabic name along with the nickname "Alla," meaning God, it is possible he had been targeted during the Futa Jallon jihad for being a Muslim cleric who was against slavery – presumably because he escaped his bondage. Sultan's spiritual power and leadership qualities may have been considered an asset to maintain order in the plantation economy, thus he was put in the position of a *commandeur*.

West Central African Beliefs and Practices

In West Central Africa among Kimbundu-speaking people, *zumbis* were ancestral otherworldy beings and *kilundas* were deities.[132] These terms, or their derivatives, appeared in the Saint-Domingue colonial context, although with slightly different meanings. The notion of a "zomby" existed in the colonial Kreyol lexicon as the appearance of a returning spirit, and descriptions of *calendas* in Saint-Domingue match aspects of *nganga*-led *kilundu* gatherings in seventeenth-century Angola and *calundu* ceremonies in Brazil.[133] At the *calendas*, a man or woman stood in the center of a group, including musicians and others who sang and shouted to call on a spirit being to occupy the body of the centered individual. The mounted person convulsed and spoke in the metaphoric language of the deceased spirit. Participants then consulted with the spirit about topics pertaining to the natural realm. West Central African *calenda* gatherings were not unlike the *vaudoux* rituals in that they both involved dance; alcohol consumption to heighten the senses of participants; and non-living spirits that occupied a living person, who was typically the assembly convener and communicated messages from the spirit world to advise, caution, or heal the living. Writing in the early eighteenth century, the priest Jean Baptiste Labat described the *calenda* as a dance gathering that had the potential to inspire rebellion because it brought blacks together in a state of "collective effervescence" induced by alcohol and the joy of time away from forced labor. Two drums regulated the dance movements: the three- to four-foot long *grand tambour* made from hollowed out wood and the shorter *bamboula* drum was made from bamboo. Performers played one drum rhythmically while playing the other drum more slowly; calabashes filled with small stones or grains of corn complemented the drumming sounds along with the *banza*, a hand-plucked four-string violin. Women and men danced in a counterclockwise circle, following the direction of the sun's movement to symbolize the beginning and end of the human life cycle and to invoke their ancestors, while clapping their hands and improvising songs in a call and response fashion.[134]

The gatherings in Saint-Domingue also centered around healing rituals to cure physical and spiritual ills through the removal of malevolent spirits.[135] Participants did not have access to the shrines that typically housed ancestral and territorial spirits; however, they captured spiritual power associated with respective spirits by carrying them in *nkisi* objects.[136] In West Central Africa, *nkisis* were public shrines that held regionally recognized spirits that supported good health and abundance. Without the freedom to construct such shrines in Saint-Domingue, Africans converted larger *nkisis* to smaller, individualized vessels that could allow users to clandestinely carry spirit energies. As such, *nkisis* in Saint-Domingue performed the same function as *gris-gris* or *macoutes* used by Muslims from Senegambia and the Bight of Benin – providing the wearer with spiritual protection. People could purchase *nkisis* and other sacred objects at *calendas*, which were also free spaces that enhanced oppositional consciousness. The participation of multiple ethnic groups in these gatherings may suggest that they were becoming "generically African" and contributed to the growth of solidarity around race and the most powerful spirit beings.[137] Though we cannot necessarily track each *calenda* occurrence, since they were held secretly, we can induce through primary and secondary sources that they were regularly occurring events, despite attempts to supress them.[138]

Some Africans from the Angolan coast south of the Congo River were already familiar with Christianity and had been combining their local traditions with Catholicism while still on the continent.[139] Other Africans seem to have passively accepted baptism and participated in church services but maintained their fundamental beliefs and practices. Catholic priests were responsible for baptizing newly arrived Africans, though they often found themselves understaffed and unprepared for the booming population increases. The Jesuit order bore the responsibility of reaching and converting the enslaved population, but the priests' efforts often appeared to colonial authorities as collusion with the slaves' maintenance of African practices and rebellious activity. In February 1761, there was a statement from the Council of Le Cap against the "abuses" of religion by free and enslaved people who conducted unsupervised and unauthorized church services for afternoon and night meetings with choir leaders, prayers, and lay preachers who promoted faith in the surrounding areas of Le Cap.[140]

In 1764, colonial authorities expelled the Jesuits from Saint-Domingue. Among other things, such as financial crimes, they were viewed as being complicit with rebellion by harboring runaways and discouraging an enslaved woman, Assam, from divulging the names of people involved in the Mackandal poison conspiracy.[141] The spiritual aspects of the Mackandal conspiracy and his network of followers, as well as other ritualists who represented leaders within the enslaved community and at times wielded that power to incite rebellion, will be explored in the next chapter. Though the Capuchin order took over Jesuit responsibilities, the volume of Africans brought to Saint-Domingue overwhelmed Catholic priests. The Kongolese routinely embraced healers and mediums to access spirits, therefore as enslaved people in Saint-Domingue they turned to priests for spiritual help and to perform rites. Catholic priests represented such a medium capable of reaching saints, who Africans would have interpreted as spirits local to either Central Africa or the Saint-Domingue context.[142] In the early 1770s, a priest revealed that enslaved Catholics, either those from the Kongo Kingdom or the recently baptized, would approach him to cast spells and to communicate with spirits. In the same decade, another priest claimed to have been walking with an elderly black Catholic woman who spotted a man carrying a staff with a garter snake. The woman immediately attacked the man, then knelt before the snake and prayed that Jesus and Mary protect it. The source described the snake as a symbol of the Dahomean Dangbe ritual sect present in Le Cap, of which the man with the staff may have been a member.[143]

CONCLUSION

Moreau de Saint-Méry's early observations of the enslaved population in Saint-Domingue indicated that Africans of different ethnicities did not interact and opposed one another for worshipping different gods, and that creoles overall dismissed continent-born Africans. The above examples of ritual life in Saint-Domingue, however, show that Africans of various ethnicities performed rites that typically are associated with other groups; for example, the Mozambicans who danced the *vaudoux*, or the Igbo man seeking entrance to an Arada ceremony. These cases suggest that white observers probably incorrectly labeled or misunderstood the ritual practice or the identity of the Africans themselves. This book uses primary source evidence to propose the idea that creoles and Africans of various extractions were not as self-segregating as previously assumed, since labor regimes largely dictated their social interactions. The newly arrived needed sources of human affirmation from a community of individuals sharing the same positionality, facilitating biological ties between creoles and their first-generation African kin. Recent plantation and slave trade studies have shown the demographic makeup of the enslaved population with a focus on ethnic dominance in particular geographic areas, for example the large numbers of West Central Africans on Saint-Domingue's northern coffee plantations. But these approaches neglect the existence of enslaved people of other ethnic identities and the ways in which they were enculturated into plantation-based communities during ritual practices and marronnage.

Due to the rigors of the plantation workday, it was not easy for enslaved Africans and African descendants to find time to engage in their sacred rituals. Field hands especially, who were overwhelmingly women and African, spent long days performing arduous labor under the strict supervision of the *commandeur* plantation driver. The *commandeur*, though usually an enslaved person, held a place of authority and was responsible for keeping order among the work gangs and doling out punishments with a whip. His authority in the fields often translated to authority in marronnage, which will be further explored in later chapters. The workday generally ended at sundown, although sugar plantations ran in 24-hour shifts, so there were only pockets of time when laborers were not heavily monitored, such as in their shared housing quarters, during assigned errands, or at the weekly Sunday market at the urban centers Cap Français and Port-au-Prince. Artisanal laborers, mostly males and creoles, such as carpenters, shoemakers, and hairdressers, had more flexibility to traverse the colony as part of their quotidian work duties. These everyday forms of mobility, along with slaves' escapes, allowed enslaved people to foster and maintain relationships, and to surreptitiously exchange sacred objects and organize ritual gatherings.

Ritual activity and marronnage were not only ways for enslaved people to gather and communicate, they were also vehicles through which long-standing traditions of resistance challenged the commodification, forced labor, and death that pervaded and shaped their lives in grotesque ways.

The following chapter will explore further the spiritual worlds of the enslaved who, in conjunction with and sometimes organized by maroons, used sacred objects and their sacred understandings of their social conditions to mediate the realities of enslavement in Saint-Domingue and castigate its most oppressive and exploitative dimensions.

II

CONSCIOUSNESS AND INTERACTION:
CULTURAL EXPRESSIONS, NETWORKS AND TIES,
GEOGRAPHIES AND SPACE

3

"God knows what I do": Ritual Free Spaces

Global African Diaspora communities experience overlapping forms of systemic oppression, economic exploitation, and marginalization such as physical and social segregation (Harris [1982] 1993; Hamilton 1988, 2007). The seemingly penetrating reach of plantation domination seems to have prevented scholarly exploration of the social world of enslaved people in Saint-Domingue, perhaps because they were considered "socially dead" – personae non-grata – in most social, economic, and political terms (Patterson 1982). The *Code Noir* intended to restrict enslaved people's everyday movements and activities, while the hierarchy of *commandeurs* and plantation managers readily used torture as punishment aimed to prevent rebellious behaviors. However, as agents of their own humanity, resistance, and social change, African Diaspora members formed social networks that used cultural and ideological tools in their collective liberation efforts (Hamilton 2007: 31–33). Enslaved people had one free day per week; and the population imbalance between them and plantation personnel inadvertently created social environments that were under the direction and control of blacks themselves, wherein they shared space and time without much European surveillance. Africans' ritual gatherings at burial sites, in churches, and at nighttime *calenda* assemblies served as free spaces where they could re-produce aspects of their religious cultures away from the observation of whites. Free spaces, or other monikers like communities of consciousness, safe havens, sequestered sites, or spatial reserves, are "small-scale settings within a community or movement that are removed from the direct control of dominant groups, are voluntarily participated in, and generate the cultural challenge that precedes or accompanies political mobilization" (Polletta 1999: 1).

These liberated sites allowed African descendants to transform existing social institutions into sites for collective struggle and social change, where they could freely articulate their understandings of self and cultivate shared oppositional consciousness, collective identities, cultural formations, and political agendas (Evans and Boyte 1986; Couto 1993; Fantasia and Hirsch 1995; Morris and Braine 2001). Various manifestations of African Diaspora communities' free spaces have been crucibles for participants to assert declarations of freedom and liberty (Evans and Boyte 1986); heighten awareness of unequal social conditions and invoke historical memory of past resistance strategies (Covin 1997); stake political claims for racial justice (Hayes 2008); and take part in civic activism, mutual aid, and community uplift (Hounmenou 2012).

This chapter argues that ritual free spaces in Saint-Domingue had several functions beyond cultivating an environment for cultural and spiritual expression, and that these gatherings allowed participants to: procure and employ sacred technologies to correct the imbalances of enslavement and reclaim personal and collective power; enhance oppositional consciousness through seditious speech; mobilize and establish social networks between enslaved people and maroons; revere women as important figures in ritual life; and build racial solidarity between African ethnic groups and enslaved and free blacks by binding each other to secrecy. Africa-inspired rituals flourished in free spaces over the course of two centuries, despite consistent repression from French Caribbean planters and failed attempts to Christianize newly arrived Africans (Peabody 2002). Africa-inspired rituals both reproduced and were the products of collective consciousness, identity construction, and participants' respective cultural and religious homeland practices (Durkheim 1912). Rituals are an often-repeated pattern of behavior set apart from other ways of acting, in such a way that aligns one with ultimate sources of power (Sewell 1996b: 252; Kane 2011: 10–12). Participants are aware that the focus of the activities concern ultimate power, and therefore feel solidarity through mutual connection to the power source and its symbolic representations. Symbolic meanings involve pre-existing concepts in the mind that are communicated via historical memory, images, and materials objects. They are historically constituted and transformed through intergenerational usage (Kane 2011: 10–12) – or, in the case of Saint-Domingue, through the constant replenishing of the Africa-born population through the transAtlantic slave trade. Though rituals are largely everyday occurrences, they can also punctuate major historical events and be incited by the collective excitement of revolutionary processes (Sewell 1996b), for example the Bwa Kayman ceremony that took place in August 1791 (see Chapter 8). In a non-sacred sense, rituals can be the hubs of forging political and cultural alliances that function as counterhegemonic structures. Through micro-level struggles common in colonial contact zones, disparate identity groups come together through identification with shared symbols, ideas, or goals that have a wider appeal to facilitate coordination and the exchange of ideas, strategies, and political goals, commitment to a cause, and identity development (Pratt 1992; Ansell 1997; Harris 2001; Kane 2011).

Cultural activities such as rituals use material artifacts, and participants perform symbolic representations that give actors access to shared knowledge, values, and power, and enhance solidarity and mutual connection (Johnston 2009; Kane 2011: 10–12). Africa-inspired ritual gatherings in Saint-Domingue may have been strictly coordinated on ethnic lines in the early eighteenth century,[1] but there was more than likely interethnic collaboration and exchange to meet the needs of Africans who were not part of the dominant Bight of Benin or West Central African ethnic groups. Africans and African descendants from varying backgrounds or statuses were aware of free space ritual gatherings and sought to participate in them to connect to something culturally familiar that affirmed their humanity. Though they were outlawed by the *Code Noir*, planters largely ignored secret night-time dances, burials, and all-black church services and thus they happened frequently. These were opportunities for people to perform the sacred rites associated with their religious and cultural background, encounter and network with maroons or other enslaved people from nearby parishes, buy and sell ritual artifacts, and be audience to lay-preachers, priests, and prophets to further comprehend the state of their collective existence and ways of seeking retribution. Therefore, I argue that participation in free space ritual gatherings and/ or using individualized sacred technologies produced and exchanged within those spaces not only helped mediate everyday issues, provide healing, and facilitate relationships with spirit beings, but also cultivated a growing oppositional consciousness aimed toward resisting enslavement and enacting collective rebellion.

Death was one of if not the leading everyday occurrence with which enslaved people contended using sacred means. Ritualists who had proficiency in healing, prophecy, assembling spiritual objects, and either inflicting death upon wrongdoers or protecting others from death were prominent figures within the enslaved community. Those believed to have supernatural powers traveled between plantations performing rituals and were mainly consulted by the enslaved, but in some instances even free people of color and whites utilized their services. These charismatic leaders claimed power from the non-material world, which in turn reinforced their power and influence within the plantation system. Similarly, African notions of political power and leadership, particularly in regions like the Bight of Benin and West Central Africa, were deeply connected to the spiritual realm. Rulers were ultimate sacred authorities with access to knowledge and power from the non-material world. As Chapter 1 discussed, kings and queens from the Bight of Benin and West Central Africa were keenly aware of their ability to wield spiritual power for political purposes. This provides a context for how enslaved people in Saint-Domingue would have conceptualized sacred ritual leaders like Pierre "Dom Pedro" or Jérôme Pôteau as fulfilling political roles that were of equal significance.

While most of the ritual leaders discussed in this chapter were men, it is important to note that women figured prominently in free space ritual practices as sacred authorities in keeping with West and West Central African gender roles. In the Dahomey Kingdom, women held important spiritual, political, and military positions as *vodun* ancestral deities, *kpojito* queen mothers who counseled kings, and "Amazon" soldiers who composed all-female regiments.[2] West Central African women like Queen Njinga and Dona Beatriz wielded political and spiritual power to marshal defenses against the slave trade and civil war.[3] On the other side of the Atlantic, gendered, racial, and class hierarchy relegated black women, especially those who were Africa-born, to the most labor-intensive work in the slavery-based political economy. Therefore, black women were marginally represented in spaces of formally recognized power in pre-revolutionary Saint-Domingue. However, ideas from Black/African Diaspora Studies, Sociology, and Anthropology help frame black women's social positionality as the springboard for "bridge" leadership activism that is most potent in culturally-driven free spaces, such as ritual gatherings, and that connects rank-and-file grassroots efforts to larger movement organizing (Terborg-Penn 1996; Robnett 1997; Kuumba 2002; Kuumba 2006; Perry 2009; Hounmenou 2012).

Bridge leaders occupy roles that defy components of traditionally recognized forms of leadership, such as holding titled positions within formal organizations. Instead, black women bridge leaders have mobility within non-hierarchical spaces and employ individualized interactive styles of mobilization and recruitment (Robnett 1997: 17–20). In the context of enslavement, women created social networks among themselves and others to ensure their survival (Terborg-Penn 1996: 223) and to coordinate liberatory actions. As Chapter 4 will show, adult women maroons in Saint-Domingue were more likely than men to have escaped with the assistance of a free person of color, a family member, or a relationship tie to another plantation, further indicating that women activated and maintained social networks beyond their immediate vicinity. This chapter will introduce readers to women like Brigitte Mackandal and Marie Catherine Kingué, whose skills with administering or healing poisonings made them highly regarded spiritual figures among enslaved people across several plantations. Later chapters of this book will highlight how enslaved women served as *vaudoux* queens, poison couriers, spies, protectors of sacred knowledge and secrets held by rebels, and mobilizers during the early Haitian Revolution insurgency. For example, Cécile Fatiman led the sacralizing ceremony for the August 1791 mass revolt, "Princess" Amethyste galvanized women fighters under the symbolism of *vaudoux* to help Boukman Dutty attack Le Cap, and other *vaudoux* queens discovered by Colonel Malenfant refused to identify their male rebel counterparts. Through the lens of black women's bridge leadership, we might think of Africa-inspired sacred rituals as a collection of localized idioms and practices that formed cultural resistance against the imposition of Western Christian values and were a vehicle for organizing mobilization networks (Kuumba and Ajanaku 1998).

This chapter follows the thesis put forward in previous chapters, that the insurrectionary activities of the enslaved that gave birth to the Black Radical Tradition were ontologically grounded in the non-physical, sacred realm and exemplified aspects of the non-material world that were beyond the reach of racial capitalism's early plantocractic manifestation. However, while Robinson argues that the violence that characterized the Black Radical Tradition was largely contained within enslaved black communities as a form of internal regulation – and this appears to be the case with some poisoning cases to be discussed below – much of the symbolic and physical violence perpetrated by enslaved people in Saint-Domingue targeted the owners and means of plantation production. More specifically, ritual practices helped to mediate and undermine the racialized subjugation of enslavement. African Diasporans' re-creation of rituals was rooted in their sacred understandings of the world, and they included participants and leaders from varying backgrounds and statuses: Africa-born, colony-born creole, mixed-race, free, enslaved, and runaways. Further, the Africa-inspired sacred ritual practitioners incorporated symbols, performances, and artifacts from diverse cultural groups to cultivate shared meanings, solidarity, and oppositional consciousness. For example, herbalist and poisoner François Mackandal used *calenda* gatherings as spaces to invoke the history of racial domination in Saint-Domingue and to prophesy the formation of a future black-led state. As we will see in Chapter 8, Boukman Dutty employed religious symbols from various ethnic groups in organizing the Bwa Kayman ceremony in the days before leading the August 1791 insurrection. Other ritualists escaped enslavement, used herbal packets as poison and for healing purposes, organized underground networks and cultivated large followings, and advocated for rebellion and independence. Over time, African Diasporans' collective consciousness became increasingly politicized and hostile toward their social conditions.

POISON

As Chapter 1 explains, many Africans in Saint-Domingue originated from societies in which imbalances, disharmonies, and disruptions in political, economic, and social spheres were managed and mediated through spiritual means. Conversely, the spiritual realm had the responsibility to serve as a check and balance against, and at times protector from, malevolent political and economic forces. African royal figures had the social and moral responsibility to rule with fairness, which their engagement in the slave trade directly countered. Especially in the Kongo lands, unethical behavior or the abuse of power could result in accusations of witchcraft, prompting ritualists to use *nkisis* as self-armaments and to conduct poison ordeals on order of the king. By the time African captives disembarked at Saint-Domingue's ports, they had already lost the social, spiritual, and military battles against the encroachments of the transAtlantic slave trade; they had not, however, lost the battle to gain their freedom from enslavement itself. While they did not have the necessary structures, such as shrines, to fully re-create their religious systems, African Diasporans relied on free space gatherings to piece together and exchange elements of their rituals such as the affinities to spirit beings and sacred technologies. These spaces, and the rituals themselves, then reinforced a sense of opposition to enslavement by enacting inter- and intra-racial justice against those deemed as witches or slave trade participants (Thornton 2003; Paton 2012). Poison was one tactic within enslaved people's repertoire of contention, a collection of resistance actions that also included marronnage, that was useful in the struggle against slavery. Repertoire tactics can change over time, or be discarded or appropriated, according to how participants assess its effectiveness (Tilly 1995; Traugott 1995; Taylor and Van Dyke 2004; Tilly 2006; Biggs 2013; della Porta 2013; Ring-Ramirez, Reynolds-Stenson, and Earl 2014). On the African continent, poison ordeals were associated with those in power, while in the Americas, the powerless adopted the poisoning tactic as a means of challenging inequality.

Enslaved ritualists used poison to disempower evildoers – members of the plantocracy and enslaved people suspected of cooperating with planters. When understood through the worldview of the enslaved population, spiritual activities like poisoning were not merely supernatural phenomena, they were critiques against the slave trade and racial slavery. The Atlantic slave trade was perhaps the most destructive force against African social, economic, and political formations (Rodney 1982); and enslavement in the Americas was deadliest in the sugar colonies, most prominently Saint-Domingue. One of the first recorded acts of using poison in *Ayiti*/Española against a slave owner was in 1530 when an enslaved woman was burned at the stake for attempting to kill her female enslaver.[4] In 1723, a runaway leader named Colas Jambes Coupées and several of his accomplices were arrested in Limonade and executed as "sorcerers" who poisoned other blacks, terrorized white planters, and conspired to abolish the colony.[5] Jambes Coupées, whose name suggests that one of his legs had been chopped off as punishment for repeated marronnage, was a predecessor to François Mackandal and other fugitive ritualists who cultivated a following of maroons and enslaved people. Chapter 7 will further explore the case of Jambes Coupées and marronnage in the early eighteenth century, an understudied period of Saint-Domingue's history. But as this chapter will show, marronnage, the convergence of spiritual and political leadership, and the fear of white death due to poison and slave rebellion in the late eighteenth century came to be synonymous with only one name: Mackandal.

The Mackandal Affair

Mackandal was formerly enslaved on a northern plantation owned by Sieur Tellier and he often worked for Lenormand de Mezy in the Limbé district.[6] Though one source identifies Mackandal as a Mesurade from the Windward Coast, an often-cited account from 1787, *Extrait du Mercure de France: Makandal, Histoire Véritable*, explains that Mackandal was brought to the colony at age 12 from the Upper Guinea region of West Africa, and that he was a "Mahommed," or a Muslim, who had at least some Arabic linguistic competency.[7] He was a distinctive character, with acquired skills and gifts in music, painting, sculpting, and herbal medicine. He attempted escape from enslavement several times before his final retreat into the mountains after losing a hand in a sugar mill and later tending to animals. Mackandal's 18-year escape into the Limbé mountains is where he developed a strong following as a charismatic leader. He claimed himself to be immortal and was considered a prophet who secretly traversed plantations spanning the northern plain, from Fort Dauphin to Port-de-Paix, to speak during night-time assemblies or in an "open school," as Moreau Saint-Méry described it. Early descriptions claim that Mackandal foretold the overthrow of enslavement, using different colored scarves as a metaphor to illustrate that the island once belonged to the "yellow" indigenous Americans, was under domination by white Europeans, but would soon be under the control of black Africans. Legend states that he aimed to rid the colony of whites by producing and distributing packets of poisonous mixtures that slaves could use to kill their owners and other enslaved people who were perceived as being in solidarity with whites.[8] Mackandal infiltrated plantation systems by recruiting an underground network of people who were willing to transport packets of poisons, potions, or remedies. The goal of this campaign, as he communicated at the evening religious gatherings, was to overthrow enslavement by poisoning the white colonials.

Court documents from the Mackandal case associated the *macandal* packets with *gris-gris* from the "langue mennade" – a direct reference to the Mende linguistic origins of *gris-gris* amulets produced by Muslim marabouts in the Upper Guinea region, which Pierre Du Simitière also observed in Léogâne (Figure 2.5). These amulets were leather pouches that contained written scriptures from the Qur'an for protective purposes. Clients ported *gris-gris* underneath head wraps; around their necks, arms, waists, ankles or knees; they could be mounted over doors or placed under beds.[9] In François' case, he wore his *gris-gris* or *macandal* under a hat. He combined other artifacts and prayed over the materials with what seemed to be an Islamic incantation of "Alla[h], Alla[h]," which he claimed invoked the power and blessing of Jesus. These sacks were composed of human bones, nails, roots, communion bread, small crucifixes, and incense that were bound together in holy-water soaked cloth and twine.[10] Individuals who had the expertise to compose the *macandals* and to invoke the spirits embedded in the sacks were considered to be of the first order, or the highest leadership rank among the community of ritualists. Each *macandal* was named after an individual who occupied a rank, which was delineated by knowing secret phrases or names of *macandal* producers. Those who gave the name of "Charlot" were of the first order, indicating women played indispensable roles within the network.[11] The *macandals* could be used for strength, to attract love, to protect a person from a slave owner's whip for committing marronnage, or to make the slave owner confused or the target of misfortune. After granting supplicants' requests, the *macandals* had to be "re-charged" with food left for them to eat, an antecedent to the ways that contemporary Haitian Vodou practitioners sacrificially "feed" the *lwa*, or spirits.

The anonymous letter *Relation d'une Conspiration Tramée par les Nègres* estimates that as many as 30–40 whites, including women and children, and about 200–300 other enslaved people and animals were killed in the Mackandal conspiracy. A man named l'Éveillé agreed to poison his first owner, an upholsterer named Labadie, as well as the wife of a slave owner, and a surgeon from Limonade. In Le Cap, a merchant named Mongoubert and Mme. Lespes were both poisoned by black women who were convicted and condemned to death. Several other cases emerged: Marianne, the "chief poisoner" at Le Cap was connected to Mackandal through his wife Brigitte. Marianne, Jolicoeur, and Michel poisoned a hairdresser named Vatin, because he would not allow them to partake in a Sabbath dinner in his kitchen. A woman who previously lived with Jolicoeur poisoned the wife of Rodet and wanted to kill Jolicoeur's enslaver, Millet. Henriette was accused and convicted of poisoning her female enslaver, Faveroles. Cupidon allegedly poisoned another black man named Apollon, as well as two Decourt women, and the owner himself. The following were also suspected of poison: black men and women belonging to M. Hiert, M. de la Cassaigne, Lady Paparet, Sieur Delan, and M. le Prieur. Thélémaque was condemned for poisoning with "vert-de-gris," or the green leaf that was the container for poison and synonymous with *macandals*, that he hid in a dish of sprouts, resulting in nearly all the houseguests becoming sick.[12] On April 8, 1758, three people, Samba, Colas, and Lafleur, were sentenced to death for their part in the poisonings that occurred in the northern department, and six slaves on a Limbé plantation were executed as punishment for allegations of poison.[13]

African-Atlantic Ethnic Solidarities

People associated with François Mackandal's poison network represented various ethnicities originating from Senegambia, the Bight of Benin, and West Central Africa, suggesting his prophesy of black rule was not merely rhetoric but was based on the lived experience of building a diverse network of Africans and creoles – even free people of color – who collaborated based on shared principles and common practices. Mackandal's speeches about restoring racial justice to the colony were particularly important in cultivating a sense of collective consciousness and solidarity among enslaved Africans of varying backgrounds. Solidarity can be thought of as a sense of loyalty, shared interest, and identification with a collective that enhances cohesion, and advances the idea that the well-being of a group is of such great importance that it will yield widespread participation in collective action (Fantasia 1988; Gamson 1992; Taylor and Whittier 1992; Hunt and Benford 2004). François Mackandal was probably indeed a Mende-speaker of Senegambian or Sierra Leonean origin from the widespread Guinea region, as early sources have suggested, and had some familiarity with Islam – which had been the driving force of the Futa Jallon and Futa Tooro anti-slavery movements in the seventeenth and eighteenth centuries.[14] Given the dire circumstances of enslavement, he collaborated with Africans of different ethnicities, such as his Kongolese associates Mayombé and Teyselo, whose fundamental worldviews were probably not incompatible with his own, particularly since Africans generally did not restrict their religious beliefs to fixed orthodoxies.[15]

Inter-cultural exchange within the sacred realm is a window through which we can begin to understand how collective consciousness and solidarity were forged within African descendants' ritual life, Mackandal's actions, and his network of Senegambian, Bight of Benin, and West Central African poisoners. The *calenda*, *vaudoux*, and other sects with which Mackandal was familiar shared commonalities of (1) levels of initiation, (2) herbal medicine practices, (3) spiritually charged objects, (4) divination and prophecy, and (5) anti-slavery sentiments. We might think of François Mackandal as an African-Atlantic "creole" from the Upper Guinea region whose early exposure to Islam in Africa, and later to West Central African practices in Saint-Domingue, provided him with socio-cultural and linguistic flexibility (Landers 2010) to interact with Africans of varying backgrounds and assert a racially themed prophesy of impending upheaval. Sugar plantations in the northern plain tended to have more ethnic diversity than coffee plantations, which West Central Africans increasingly dominated midway through the eighteenth century.[16] Some individuals, like Mackandal, would have participated in foreign rituals and had flexibility with sacred symbols from varying cultural groups, contributing to a wider appeal to the masses. Mackandal's main associates, Teyselo and Mayombé, like him, originated from a region that was dominated by or had ongoing contact with monotheistic, Abrahamic religions – Christianity in the Kongo Kingdom and Islam in the Senegambia region. For example, Mackandal incorporated small crucifixes into his *gris-gris* artifacts to invoke blessings from Jesus, which would have appealed to Africans from the Kongo Kingdom who either were already baptized before their arrival in Saint-Domingue or who later embraced Christianity.

Enslaved women who worked within the domestic sphere acted as bridge leaders, constituting the main poison transporters.[17] François Mackandal's wife Brigitte seems to have been his main courier and was knowledgeable in the ritual process involved in creating *macandals*, stating "God knows what I do, God opens the eyes to those who ask for eyes." Brigitte transported *macandals* between François and Marianne, a woman who was the "chief of the poisoners of Le Cap." A Poulard woman named Assam, a domestic on the LaPlaine plantation in Acul, admitted to witnessing a Bambara man named Jean transport poison between several plantations using other women as couriers. The two women, Marie-Jeanne and Madeleine, were Niamba and Nagô, respectively. In Petit Anse, a Yoruba man named Hauron was accused of giving poison to other slaves. Assam's testimony – combined with a spontaneous confession by an enslaved man named Medor in Fort Dauphin who admitted that the goal of the conspiracy was to collaborate with free people of color in destroying the colony so the enslaved could escape and be free – was what eventually exposed the network and led to François Mackandal's arrest in November 1757.[18] A number of women and three free people of color were among the 140 arrested for allegedly following Mackandal and providing arsenic to poison slave owners in support of slaves gaining manumission.

The Politics of Death

Those arrested in connection with the Mackandal affair were noted to have sung a song in Kreyol: "ouaïe, ouaïe, Mayangangué, zamis moir mourir, moi aller mourir, [... my friends are dying, I will die ...] ouaïe, ouaïe, Mayangangué."[19] The words of the song reveal a sense of shared fate, and perhaps hopelessness, in response to the overwhelming volume of deaths among enslaved people. It might be argued, however, that death was not necessarily viewed as a condemnation, but as a path to freedom from bondage, a return to the homeland "Guinea," and an entry into the spirit world where there was an opportunity to further influence the natural world. Mackandal's wife, Brigitte, may have transitioned into the world of the *lwa* as Maman Brigitte, who has authority over cemeteries.[20] Mackandal's claim that he was immortal, and the imminence of death reflected in the song were possibly more than spiritual messages – they could have been threats to unleash the power of the dead on the living. If we consider that Mackandal was a Mende speaker, as his familiarity with *gris-gris* would suggest, it appears that aspects of Mende cosmology fit Mackandal's profile. Within the Mende were decentralized structures, including societies based on ritual knowledge and the principles of justice, retribution, and secrecy. Mende leaders held the power of life and death and inflicted punishments on intruders or those who committed offenses against individuals or the whole community. Moreover, women were indispensable in Mende societies – even those that were male dominated – and were needed to mediate the human and spirit realm, which helps explain women's centrality in Mackandal's inner circle.[21]

After his initial arrest in November 1757, Mackandal escaped jail and was again free until he was later seized at a *calenda* ritual dance gathering at the Dufresne plantation in Limbé, then burned at the stake in Cap Français on January 20, 1758. Witnesses claimed that Mackandal's body evaporated before the flames engulfed him and converted him into a mosquito, a plague of which he had earlier prophesied would bring destruction to the whites. Several African belief systems include notions of an afterlife, the transmigration of spirits from one physical entity to another, or the elevation of a human into a pantheon of revered spirits.[22] Enslaved Africans' reaction to Mackandal's death, and the "ouaïe, ouaïe, Mayangangué" chant, can be considered part of a larger mortuary political stance, the "profound social meaning from the beliefs and practices associated with death ... employed ... [and] charged with cosmic importance – in struggles toward particular ends" (Brown 2008: 5). Death was ubiquitous in Saint-Domingue – nearly half of incoming Africans perished within five years – as were attempts to prevent it, symbolize and commemorate it, or inflict it. African Diasporans' belief in Mackandal's immortality was not merely a sense of mourning and reverence, but one that connected private emotions and conceptions of death and the afterlife with wider concerns about enslavement and freedom. Moreover, the *macandal* packets that he and others assembled and sold contained fragments of human bones, suggesting the dead carried sacred powers that were important and effective for navigating the natural world.

Mackandal's death supports the notion that funeral rituals involve both grieving and burying the dead, and provide time and space to address social, economic, and political issues (Tamason 1980). In pre-colonial African societies, especially those of the Bight of Benin and West Central Africa, spiritual leaders were revered and often held important political positions. Vincent Brown has argued that since enslaved ritualists "drew their most impressive power from the management of spirits and death, the prohibition [of ritual practices] amounted to a strategy to limit the prestige the enslaved could derive from association with the spirits of the dead, while maximizing the power of the colonial government's 'magic'" (Brown 2008: 151). The ability to communicate with or marshal the spiritual energy of the dead, to protect oneself or others from death, or to inflict death translated to a type of community-endorsed political power that transcended colonial authority and therefore was a threat to the social order. Mackandal – and as we will see with several poisoners who followed him, organizers and participants of *calenda* ritual gatherings, and later the midwife Marie Catherine Kingué – negotiated matters of life and death and at times relayed messages condemning racial slavery, which elevated them to the level of political significance. Mackandal's message regarding racial stratification, power, and control over land and resources infused into Africa-inspired rituals a politicized awareness of and oppositional attitude toward the oppressive colonial situation. This melding of the sacred and material worlds would not have been foreign to the bondspeople of Saint-Domingue, especially those of African origin from places like the Bight of Benin or the Loango Coast, where religion informed political and economic shifts and vice versa. The enslaved population likely would have welcomed such an articulation to facilitate comprehension of the new world into which they had been violently thrust, and as such revered Mackandal and his legacy.

Poison Post-Mackandal: 1760s–1780s

Mackandal's case inspired fear among the colonists and was a watershed event that altered the structures of the colonial order as the courts developed ordinances and divisions of police to further control and repress the enslaved population (Sewell 1996a). On April 7, 1758, the Council of Cap Français issued an ordinance regarding the policing of enslaved people in response to the Mackandal affair. Articles banned *affranchis* and enslaved people from making, selling, or distributing *garde-corps* or *macandals*, and issued a fine of 300 *livres* for any planter who allowed drumming or night gatherings on their property.[23] Yet, these codes were not fully enforced and therefore did not stop people from using Africa-inspired technologies to empower themselves to solve personal and public problems associated with their oppression. Enslaved people in the northern plain viewed poisoning as a successful repertoire tactic, given the political impact of the François Mackandal affair on the colonial order and on witnesses to his execution, and they adopted the tactic for themselves. After the execution, Mackandal's name became synonymous with certain religious leaders, dances, medicinal blends, and poisons most specifically.[24] Poisoning allegations continued in the wake of Mackandal's death, especially in northern Saint-Domingue, setting off a heightened repression of social and religious activities that were not explicitly Christian, such as using poisonous herbal blends and the *calenda* gatherings. Both enslaved and free black people were banned from practicing medicine in April 1764, which indicated a fear that free blacks with skills in medicinal practice and access to materials like arsenic used it to distribute to the enslaved and facilitate the poisoning of whites.[25] Repression did not hinder Africans and African descendants from partaking in sacred ritual artifacts or attending ritual gatherings. However, rather than hand over poisoners to the courts as in the Mackandal case, political authorities relinquished the responsibility for punishing poisoners to slave owners themselves. As poisoning accusations continued in the 1760s and 1780s, enslavers increasingly used torturous means to obtain confessions, while the colonial government abdicated its protection of the enslaved.[26]

Across the northern plain, enslaved people and maroons were implicated as poisoners between the 1760s and 1780s, suggesting a diffusion of collective consciousness about Mackandal, the acts of marronnage and poison, and solidarity with the political ideas he represented. On April 2, 1766, a Kongolese man named Eustache was reported missing from Mr. Boyveau's plantation in Dondon.[27] Not only had Eustache escaped, he had begun to assume the name "Makandal" in recent years, which can be attributed to a sense of connection, solidarity, or shared identity the former felt toward François Mackandal. Perhaps Eustache "Makandal" had been initiated in François Mackandal's network and was given his name before he escaped the Dondon plantation. Even if Eustache was not an initiate, he was more than likely aware of François Mackandal's life and influence given the proximity of Dondon to Limbé, less than 50 kilometers, where Mackandal was formerly enslaved.

In May 1771, a group of enslaved people went to Cap Français to complain that their owner was torturing accused poisoners, burning five women and men alive and killing two of them.[28] Another enslaved woman living with a white man, M. Beaufort, was accused of wanting to poison her owner, Madame Raulin, and going off as a maroon.[29] In 1774, a young man was arrested and arsenic was found in his bag; a black pharmacist was implicated but was dead by the time of the judgment.[30] Three enslaved domestics poisoned the manager at the Fleuriau plantation in Cul-de-Sac in 1776. A young boy warned the Fleuriau manager that his soup was poisoned, so they gave the soup to a dog and it died immediately. The three perpetrators admitted their actions and that they also poisoned M. Rasseteau, a former attorney; they were imprisoned and later burned alive.[31] In 1777, near Cul-de-Sac, a man named Jacques was arrested and burned alive for poisoning one hundred of his owner Corbieres' animals with arsenic over an eight-month span.[32] That same year, another police ruling was issued prohibiting enslaved people from meeting during the day or at night under the pretense of weddings or funerals. The ruling expressly forbade drumming and singing, and, in 1780, African descendants were again banned from making or selling any medicinal substances.[33] Colonists saw a connection between the ritual gatherings and poison, since these packets were often sold and distributed at the assemblies.

An alleged poisoner from Limonade, 33-year-old Marc Antoine Avalle, nicknamed "Kangal," was questioned on June 30, 1780, and jailed in Le Cap. Among other vices, Antoine and his accomplices Bayome, Palidore, and Pierre were accused of poisoning 25 black people and 49 animals, including mules, cattle, and horses in 1776, and were imprisoned in Le Cap.[34] Despite the 1780 ban on selling medicinal substances, a black apothecary was arrested in 1781 for selling a lethal drug to an enslaved person who used it to commit suicide – a common individualized response to the trauma of enslavement.[35] An overseer at Cul-de-Sac caught a washerwoman attempting to dump a poisonous powder into his water in 1782.[36] In 1784, a woman named Elizabeth "Zabeau" attempted to poison her owner with substances in his food and drink.[37] On May 8, 1781, an advertisement was placed for a *griffe* creole named Jean-Baptiste, born in Ouanaminthe. Fifteen days before the advertisement was placed, Jean-Baptiste escaped a plantation owned by M. Lejeune in Plaisance, a parish near Limbé, and was reported as a "thief" and a *macandal*.[38] In contrast to Eustache, the 1766 absconder who deliberately took the surname "Makandal," Lejeune described Jean-Baptiste as a *macandal* to indicate the more general crime of poisoning. Perhaps Jean-Baptiste had killed or attempted to kill someone on the Lejeune plantation, then escaped to avoid inevitable punishment. The advertisement details could have indicated the beginning of a real conspiracy, because two enslaved people on Lejeune's property allegedly killed his nephew later in 1783.[39] The advertisement also implies a long-standing paranoia about poison on the Lejeune property. Jean-Baptiste likely escaped from the same coffee plantation that became the center of controversy in March 1788, when the plantation owner's son, Nicolas Lejeune, nearly tortured to death two enslaved women named Zabeth and Marie Rose and executed four others. Lejeune accused the victims of poisoning nearly 500 bondspeople on the Plaisance plantation over the course of 25 years. Lejeune so brutally tortured the two women that 14 other enslaved Africans strategically used provisions of the 1784 *Code Noir* to file charges against him in Le Cap.[40] Laws to prevent assemblies and to keep black people from possessing medicinal and other ritual items were an ineffective means of repression against poisonings, however the torture of Zabeth and Marie Rose may have signaled to ritualists that poison as an individualized act of resistance was no longer an effective repertoire tactic. Enslaved and maroon ritualists continued to utilize sacred technologies for individual usage, but they also relied on organizing networks to inspire broader forms of insurgency.

COMMUNITIES OF REBELLION

In addition to Mackandal, rebels like Pierre "Dom Pedro," Télémaque, and Jérôme dit Pôteau communicated to their followers the injustice of enslavement and promoted ideas about freedom and independence. Ritual participants and leaders, suspected poisoners, and midwives escaped enslavement and used marronnage to organize other enslaved people. They preached liberation to audiences on plantation outskirts to address the unethical conventions of enslavement in Saint-Domingue, especially since West Central Africans and those who took part in their ritual technologies were keenly averse to exploitative, abusive practices, which they would have viewed as witchcraft. Seditious speech to incite or inspire rebellion against Saint-Domingue's racial conditions occurred within free spaces and served as a discourse of contention. It raised oppositional consciousness – which arises from a group's experiences with systems of domination, overlapping institutions, values, and ideas that support the exploitation and powerless of one group in favor of another – and enhanced critical comprehension about the social conditions enslaved people faced in order to develop the tools to combat those conditions while taking part in free space activities (Morris 1992; Morris and Braine 2001). As several cases will show, ritual rebels expressed sedition by encouraging other slaves to resist, challenging white authority, and even threatening whites – all verbal acts that disrupted the prevailing social interaction order that demanded black subservience (Tyler 2018) and that would have been met with dire punishments.

"Dom Pedro"

The contemporary *petwo* pantheon of spirits in Haitian Vodou is typically attributed to the *petro* dances observed by Moreau de Saint-Méry, who distinguished the *petro* from the *vaudoux* ritual dance, stating that the former was more dangerous, powerful, and had the potential to foment rebellion among the enslaved population. Nearly two centuries later, Haitian anthropologist Jean Price-Mars (1938) witnessed a *petwo* ceremony and linked it to the Lemba society of West Central Africa. Recently uncovered archival material about Pierre "Dom Pedro," the originator of the *petro* dance, seem to support Price-Mars' thesis that Dom Pedro and members of this spiritual sect were connected to the Lemba of the eighteenth century. The Lemba society was a closed but vast network of initiates and family members who regulated local markets in the region and practiced healing rituals to counterbalance the negative effects that the slave trade inflicted upon West Central African communities. The Lemba emphasized fairness and justice, and imposed harsh punishments on those who violated their peacekeeping code of ethics. As the transAtlantic slave trade weakened the power of coastal kingdoms and their justice systems, public *nkisi* shrines became increasingly "concerned with adjudicatory and retaliatory functions" to mediate societal imbalances.[41] In Saint-Domingue's colonial period, the *petro* sect was associated with thievery and other malevolent acts, which may have been the result of deported Lemba affiliates attempting to rectify the extreme level of exploitation and injustice they experienced as enslaved people.

Pierre "Dom Pedro" emerged as a leader among enslaved blacks living in and around Petit-Goâve by introducing them to a new dance, one that was similar to the established *vaudoux* dance but adhered to a faster and more intense drumbeat. Participants added crushed gunpowder to their rum to induce a highly intoxicated, frenzied state that was said to have killed some who drank it. As Chapter 1 indicated, items like rum and gunpowder were traded for African captives on the coasts of the continent and were assumed to hold the essence of slave trade victims, thus enhancing spiritual power of ritualists in Saint-Domingue. Pedro's followers quickly gained the reputation of being the most powerful and dangerous ritual community in the colony; members had the ability to see beyond the physical realm and used herbalism, poison, and secrecy to exact revenge on whites, uninitiated blacks, and animals. An account from an initiate describes a series of tests he had to undergo to prove loyalty to the group. Of importance was his ability to demonstrate strength under torture, discretion in keeping secrets, and willingness to do such oppositional acts as lying, stealing, or inflicting harm on humans or animals.[42] Another member was asked to hold a piece of hot coal in his hand, seemingly to test if his spirit was capable of absorbing rage, symbolized by the heat, until an appropriate time for it to be released was reached.[43] These acts required of initiates might also be seen as examples of Lemba ritual purifications to alleviate symptoms of the human-inflicted evils of slavery.[44] Authorities arrested 42 people, including some *mulâtres* and women, in connection with the Dom Pedro campaign. By 1773, several of them were still imprisoned in the jails of Petit Goâve, although it is possible that some escaped after an earthquake on June 3, 1770 destroyed much of the town and Port-au-Prince. In his wake, *Dom Pedro* became a title applied to any person who was known as a ritual leader who used sorcery to inflict harm and often carried a large stick and a whip.[45]

It was previously believed that Pierre had taken the name *Don* Pedro, suggesting he was a runaway from Spanish Santo Domingo, but recently discovered documents name him as *Dom* Pedro, a more common name from the Portuguese-influenced Kongo Kingdom. Between 1768 and 1769, Judge Joseph Ferrand de Beaudiere investigated Dom Pedro for traveling to several plantations in Petit Goâve, Jacmel, and Léogâne and spreading messages of freedom, rebellion, and independence from slave owners. Pedro's campaign for liberation would have amounted to sedition according to the high courts, and seems aligned with Lemba ethics that deemed slavery and the slave trade as a societal ill. Pedro's ritual performances, thought of as crude tricks by investigators, would have denoted spiritual efficacy that contributed to his growing following. De Beaudiere's notes indicate a small uprising of sorts, wherein Pedro subverted plantation power structures by assuring the enslaved that they would soon be free and encouraging them to turn the whip on *commandeurs* who attempted to uphold plantation violence. He then instructed the *commandeurs* to stop using the whip on the other enslaved people under their supervision and assured them that there would be no punishment from their owners. In advocating the use of the whip against *commandeurs* as retribution for their treatment of the enslaved, Pedro promoted a sense of reciprocal or "horizontal" justice and the exercise of force – these were hallmark principles of Lemba society. This type of contestation against existing power relations openly vocalized a sense of discontentment with the violent punishments associated with slavery that bondspeople typically could only have shared in private spaces. In exchange for spiritual and physical protection from slavers' retribution, Pedro imposed financial charges on his initiates. Similarly, clients customarily paid fees to Lemba priests for their ritual services of initiation, healing, or spiritual consecration.[46]

Pierre Dom Pedro, and his followers, would have understood enslavement in Saint-Domingue within the realm of greed, evil, and witchcraft – issues that needed to be rectified with both spiritual and material actions.[47] His Kongolese understanding of slavery could not abide the unjust practices that were so regular in Saint-Domingue. Dom Pedro's seditious resistance to the whip was both a literal repudiation of the non-ethical use of violence in slavery and served as symbol to instigate bondspeople's reclamation of power from those who sought to maintain slavery. Further, Pierre Dom Pedro's declarations of himself as "free" were probably not just in relation to slavery in Saint-Domingue; he may have been a freeborn Lemba priest or market trader who, in keeping with local custom, should have been protected from the slave trade. Indeed, in Portuguese Angola the honorific title "Dom" was usually reserved for the political elite, but was also used for freeborn commoners to indicate their status.[48] Pierre Dom Pedro's stance against slavery may indicate an association with longstanding Kongolese efforts to protect the local population from the encroaching transAtlantic slave trade and balanced practices related to enslaved laborers. These contributions were important antecedents to the early Haitian Revolution negotiations, when rebels sought more humane work conditions such as the abolition of the whip and modified work schedules.[49]

The Dom Pedro sect arrived in Saint-Domingue not long after the King of Kongo, Pedro V, failed to seize power from Alvaro XI, whose allegiance with local leaders who had large slave armies helps to explain the likely enslavement of Pedro V's supporters.[50] Though there is not yet clarity on Pedro V's relationship with the Lemba network, or his political and philosophical stances on the slave trade, further evidence from the other side of the Atlantic Ocean might shed light on the political implications of Pedro V's short reign. The actions of Pierre Dom Pedro and his followers critiqued the nature of enslavement and advocated for others to overturn the power imbalances embedded in everyday colonial life. Although these enslaved rebels could no longer alter social, economic, or political realities in their homelands, they attempted to affect change in Saint-Domingue by enacting their own brand of justice against the French colonial plantocracy through poisonings, theft, spiritual prophecy of impending revolt, and retributive violence. The Dom Pedro campaign may be a small window into the nature of the Kongo civil wars, as well as a new way to understand how African events and consciousness shaped anti-slavery positions and activities in the Atlantic world.

In December 1781, three months after Pedro V's remaining allies were driven out of São Salvador and the slave trade from West Central Africa increased, another "Dom Pedro" surfaced in Saint-Domingue and gained the attention of local authorities; this man was referred to as Sim dit Dompete.[51] Sim's name may indicate association with the Kongolese *simbi* nature spirits that controlled rain, and fertility, and that are recognized contemporarily as part of the Haitian *petwo* rite. In West Central Africa, the *simbi* spirits protected rocks, rivers, pools, and waterfalls, and were ruled by the mother spirit, Bunzi. The Bunzi priest had the critical responsibility for the spiritual installation of the King of Loango.[52] Sim Dompete was a runaway from Cayes and an alleged animal poisoner, perhaps using his ritual knowledge to enact poison ordeals. He was so well known in Nippes, southwest of Port-au-Prince, that members of the *maréchaussée* targeted him for capture as they were eager to demonstrate their disdain for Africans and African-based culture. During the expedition, the freemen hid in the woods for days until they saw Sim pass by carrying a sword, a white hat under his arm, and a *macoute*. Along the Loango coastlands, the *makute* was made of a piece of palm raffia cloth about the size of a large handkerchief; it was traded as currency and often used for ritual healing purposes.[53] As Sim appeared, the hunters attacked and they all fought for hours while Sim attempted to reach into the *macoute* to open its contents. The hunters believed he had a gun, and eventually shot and beheaded Sim then took his sword and bag. The *macoute* contained several small packets covered with red, blue, and white cloth and animal skin, with feathers, bones, and glass sticking from the bags. There were also black tree seeds and a small piece of white wax.[54] These contents match the description of the *garde-corps*, or "bodyguards" that Mackandal and ritualists in Marmelade created and distributed.[55] During the Haitian Revolution, Colonel Charles Malenfant also reported discovering *macoute* bags on the bodies of the few rebels he killed. The sacks contained writings in Arabic, which were probably Qur'anic prayers used in protective *gris-gris* amulets.[56]

West and West Central African ritualists like Mackandal, Dom Pedro, and Sim Dompete used their status as spiritual authorities to exercise political power among Saint-Domingue's enslaved communities and utilized a range of sacred practices, including poison, to bring about change in their immediate social world. Enslaved blacks and maroons produced and exchanged ritual artifacts clandestinely while people performed their work-related tasks – such as the female domestic laborers who delivered *macandals* – as well as in free spaces to arm and empower themselves against the everyday forms of violence embedded in the slave society. *Gris-gris*, *macandals*, *ouangas*, which were charms categorically close to *nkisis*, and *macoutes* were all small sacks containing varying materials that were prayed over and charged with comporting the spirits of non-human entities to grant the user's requests. These requests usually sought to alter slave owners' behavior – most commonly to prevent punishment for marronnage and for owners to grant emancipation after death from poison. Pouches of poison and other spiritual assemblages aided enslaved people, no matter their ethnicity of origin, in redressing power differentials in their everyday lives.

Not only did ritual leaders leverage sacred objects for individual usage, they also used marronnage to organize *calendas*, which were simultaneously spiritual and militaristic gatherings, and to propagate notions of liberation. *Mayombo* sticks empowered carriers, mostly men, to fight with enhanced spiritual power. Higher-ranking *calenda* fighters and organizers held more sacred power and were most associated with insubordination. The sacred packets, fighting sticks, and *garde-corps* were "popular" culture artifacts that represented the "raw materials" for free space ritual performances. Used by most enslaved people in the colony, sacred artifacts and those who produced them derived meaning from their African origins to shape individuals' responses to the colonial situation and guide social actions (Harris 2001; Johnston 2009).[57] Songs such as those sung by François Mackandal "ouaïe, ouaïe, Mayangangué" and the KiKongo "Eh! Eh! Bomba, hen! hen!" chant were other forms of cultural artifacts that operated as discourses of contention, or ways of communicating collective understandings and visions for social transformation through dialogue (Hall 1990; Steinberg 1999; Kane 2000; Pettinger 2012). The ritual songs and chants helped build solidarity by encoding information about the power of spirits to end slavery and, later, were part of the unfolding of the revolutionary process itself (Sewell 1996b; Johnston 2009).

Calendas

Enslaved Africans' collective and oppositional consciousness was already shaped and politicized by their experiences of war, capture, and commodification in Africa and during the Middle Passage. Rebels leveraged free spaces, such as *calenda* dances, designated for cultural and political practices as organizational structures to enhance the meanings enslaved people assigned to their conditions in a racially organized society and further develop insurgent potential. Maroons were central figures in cultivating these spaces and in recruiting participants from various plantations. Ritual gatherings were among the only social spaces under the control of enslaved people, making them what social movement scholars call indigenous organizational resources that draw on collective consciousness and do the micromobilization work of insurgency (McAdam [1982] 1999; Morris 1984; Morris and Mueller 1992). These free spaces were appropriated and politicized not merely due to the overlap of religion and politics in various African societies, but because of the powerful symbols invoked by connecting sacred understandings to wider issues (Harris 2001). Moments of acute social, economic, or political crisis, for example the Kongo civil wars in the case of Dom Pedro, can influence those affected and transform existing structures, cultural and religious practices, and identities into vehicles for change (Fantasia and Hirsch 1995). Saint-Domingue's black cultural "toolkit" included ritual objects, spirit embodiment, song, dance, and martial arts that were both sacred and political, and animated mobilization (Pattillo-McCoy 1998).

Calenda ritual gatherings held in the 1760s and 1780s were likely the product of an influx in the number of West Central Africans brought to Saint-Domingue's ports, which nearly doubled between 1781 and 1790 (Table 1.2) due to resumed fighting in the Kongo Kingdom between Pedro V, who attempted a coup in the early 1760s, and forces supporting his opponent Alvaro XI. Prisoners of war were sold through the Loango ports that were most used by the French. Former soldiers would have been trained in the sacred martial art tradition using *mayombo* sticks that Moreau de Saint-Méry described and which were seen in Cap Français in 1785. Kongolese fighters often preferred these types of personal weapons to larger bayonets for closer combat, which stood in contrast to European fighting styles. *Calendas* might then be considered training grounds that reinforced spiritual and military organizational knowledge that former Kongo civil war soldiers brought with them to Saint-Domingue.[58] Participants in the *calendas* imbued material culture artifacts with spiritual power to enhance their effectiveness as self-protective armaments. Further, training in combat combined with declarations of liberation and the power of Africans and African descendants indicated their anticipation of and preparation for events that would eventually lead to the dismantling of the enslavement system.

Sacred Martial Arts

In northern Saint-Domingue and other French Caribbean colonies, *kalendas*, or *calendas*, were not just ritual dances of enslaved people, they also included African martial art-styled stick fighting practices similar to West Central African *kilundus* or *kilombos*.[59] Stick and machete fighting traditions existed in the Bight of Biafra, West Central Africa, and the Bight of Benin, and they were used as mechanisms for warfare training, rites of passage, and, in the case of Dahomey, to train "Amazon" women fighters.[60] Enslaved women were not known to have participated in stick fighting, but T. J. Desch-Obi claims that "unarmed pugilism and head butts ... were gendered female in Saint-Domingue."[61] African kings and high-ranking soldiers commanded *kilombos*, militaristic communities that spread throughout West Central Africa in the seventeenth century, particularly in preparation for warfare. These fighters relied on hand-to-hand combat, and constantly performed mock battles, drills and other training exercises, and war dances to prepare for impending conflict. The war dances, as well as the movements associated with fighting styles during non-combative ritualistic gatherings, invoked spiritual meanings and reflected West Central African sacred understandings of the cosmos. Ancient ritual specialists performed specific movements like inverted kicks to invoke the power of ancestors who resided on the opposite side of the *kalunga*, the body of water that separated the worlds of the living and the dead.[62] With sacred power imbued in physical movements, the martial arts could be used to heal the living as well as "helping bondsmen's souls make return journeys across the kalunga." For example, the Mounsoundi (Musundi or Mousombe) of Kongo were noted for their association with stick fighting, as well as the belief in Africans' ability to fly away from enslavement back to their homeland.[63] A song that likely originates from the revolutionary era indicates the legacy of militaristic cultures of this West Central African ethnic group in Saint-Domingue:

> Mounsoundi, we will make war!
> Eya, eya, eya!
> We are war nations.
> Don't you hear the cannons fire?[64]

Overlap between sacred knowledge and military skills continued across the Atlantic via the collective memory of slave trade captives and resulted in similar practices emerging in pre-revolutionary Saint-Domingue.

Moreau de Saint-Méry described *calenda* stick fighting as serious conflicts, usually occurring over jealousy or an offense to one's sense of honor, self-image, or self-worth. It was not uncommon for combatants to strike each other with forceful head blows that drew blood. The fights began with a salute and an oath, wherein both participants wet their fingers with saliva then touched the ground, bringing their fingers back to their mouths, then pounding their chests while looking toward the skies. Saint-Méry was both impressed and entertained by the dexterity with which fighters handled their "murderous sticks," likening the fighting contest to fencing. Each delivered their blows quickly, using their sticks to defend against the other's and to issue offensive strikes. Possession of a fighting stick was a symbol of honor among participants, and the more decorated sticks were highly valued because of their spiritual power. The fighting sticks, called *mayombo*, were filled with a limestone-based powder, *maman-bila*, and were sold along with red and black seeds called *poto*. Nails inserted into the blunt end of the stick for additional force indicated one's position of leadership within the closed network of fighters. These materials match the description of elements used in West Central African *nkisi* bags and they were used to imbue the sticks with sacred power that would protect users against opponents who were not similarly armed.[65] In addition to *mayombo* sticks, other weapons, such as machetes and blunt metal-headed clubs, were used during the *calenda* gatherings. While Moreau de Saint-Méry described armed conflicts at *calenda* events as legitimate fights, he simultaneously dismissed them as a form of play associated with slave dances, void of any necessary training or potential usefulness in military combat.[66] The assemblies were not merely ritual performance activities; the sacred influence on expertise in hand-to-hand combat and non-firearm weapons gleaned from *calendas* was a significant contribution to success during the early phases of the Haitian Revolution uprisings.[67]

Police rulings prohibited assemblies of enslaved people during the day or night, and drum playing and singing were forbidden in the wake of the Mackandal affair, but *calendas* were continually held in the north especially around the dates of Catholic celebrations.[68] On August 5, 1758, a plantation manager in Bois l'Anse, a section of Limonade, was fined 300 *livres* for allowing a *calenda* to take place at Habitation Carbon on July 23.[69] This *calenda* was held three days before the Catholic recognition of Sainte Anne and Saint James the Greater on July 25–26 in Limonade. These dates correspond to a contemporary popular pilgrimage for Sèn Jak (Saint James), the Haitian Vodou-Catholic manifestation of Ogou Feray, in Plaine du

NÉGRES JOUANT AU BÂTON.

FIGURE 3.1. "Négres Jouant au Bâton, Archive Nationales d'Outre-Mer"

Nord just east of Limonade.[70] While Ogou (or Ogun) is the Yoruba god of war and iron, Saint James was the de facto patron saint of the Kongo Kingdom. Saint James celebrations in sixteenth-century Kongo included offerings and petitions to the saints, dancing and spirit embodiment, and decoration of the pilgrimage space. Ritual martial art performances were also witnessed in eighteenth-century Central Africa, and were often held to initiate newcomers on the Saint James feast day or prior to war.[71] We might then presume that activities at the 1758 *calenda* were militaristic in nature, revering spirits that presided over war – Ogou and Saint James – and creating solidarity among the participants by combining the spirits of the Nagô/Yorubas and the Kongolese.

A 1785 report from the Chamber of Agriculture described the *calenda* and *mayombo* sticks as a pervasive problem that encouraged the growing hostility among the enslaved population. Cap Français was deemed to be a troublesome environment where blacks openly displayed acts of insubordination and outright animosity toward whites:

many negroes in Le Cap never go out without a large stick, and on holidays you find 2,000 of them gathered at La Providence, La Fossette, and Petit Carénage all armed with sticks, drinking rum, and doing the *kalinda*. The police do nothing to prevent these parties and they never end without quarrels and fighting.[72]

That same source made several claims of acts of aggression – a group of blacks blocked a white couple from the sidewalk along Rue Espagnole, telling them "Motherfucker, if it was one hour later, you wouldn't dare say anything. You'd step aside yourself." Another man chastised a group of blacks for making too much noise in front of his home and was met with the response that "the streets belonged to the king" accompanied by a large rock being thrown at him, barely missing his face.[73] This verbal and potential physical assault against a white person was a clear violation of colonial codes and could have resulted in the execution of the agitator. Based on these reports and what is known about the nature of *calendas*, we can speculate that the *calendas* reinforced an awareness among enslaved people that they had the capability – politically, spiritually, and militarily – to overturn Saint-Domingue's racialized power dynamics at will. This account indicates that the open contempt toward whites from enslaved blacks in Le Cap stemmed from a sense that the city belonged to them given the population imbalance between blacks and whites, and especially at night and on the weekends when enslaved people from throughout the northern plain descended there for celebrations and to trade food at the weekly market. The diverse population of Le Cap, including the growing community of well-to-do *affranchis*, *gens du couleur*, as well as runaways from other parishes, may have signified to the enslaved that freedom, status, and power were fluid categories that could and did change quickly. The ability to congregate among themselves somewhat freely provided space to enhance oppositional consciousness and act on that consciousness in ways that countered common mores, behavioral expectations, and power structures. The ethos of these *calenda* gatherings involved sacred understandings of fighting and weaponry, which connected enslaved people to a range of African cultural symbols and emboldened them to disrupt the colonial order that rendered them powerless.

Maroons Mobilizing the Calenda

While most *calenda* participants were enslaved people, several were runaway maroons. Fugitive slaves could move about with more latitude than most enslaved laborers, which allowed them to visit different plantations or parishes and effectively recruit and mobilize participants for ritual gatherings. In 1765, a special division of the rural police was established with specific orders to eradicate marronnage and *calendas*, indicating authorities had some sense that the two forms of enslaved Africans' agency were interrelated, yet the implementation of this structural constraint on ritual life did not stymie their activities.[74] Several *calenda* attendees, dancers, and musicians appeared in *Les Affiches américaines (LAA)* runaway advertisements, exemplifying an intersection between ritualism and efforts to self-liberate. In April 1766, a 25-year-old *mulâtre* who claimed to be free, but was owned by the Pailleterie plantation, was witnessed going from plantation to plantation in Trou under the pretense of being invited to (or inviting people to) a *calenda*.[75] Though the advertisement does not provide enough information about the specific conversations and actions taken by this escapee during his eight days of marronnage, it is likely that he was engaging in some form of seditious speech against slavery given his proclamations of freedom and the political, spiritual, and militaristic nature of the *calendas*. While most of Saint-Domingue's mixed-race population were part of the landed *gens du couleur*, some were indeed enslaved, but used skin color to attempt to elevate their status in society. Conversely, this runaway used his skin color to pass as free, not to advance the political and economic interests of the *gens du couleur*, but to attempt to organize the bondspeople in his immediate vicinity. On September 16, 1767, an advertisement appeared for a 20–22-year-old Nagô male named Auguste with the branding "Lebon." Auguste was described as a merchant from Le Cap who enjoyed *calendas*, and who used his ability to travel as a merchant to his advantage in escaping.[76] Nagôs originated from the Bight of Benin region, so this example further counters accounts by early writers that African ethnic groups intentionally segregated themselves and antagonized each other. A Kongo man named Jolicoeur was described in a June 1768 advertisement after escaping Cassaigne Lanusse's plantation in Limbé. He was described as a good enough drummer, possibly meaning he was a key musician in ritual gatherings.[77] Another musician, named Pompée, who played the *banza* very well, escaped in November 1772 from Fort Dauphin and was seen near Ouanaminthe claiming to be free.[78]

In April 1782, an unnamed *commandeur* was accused of holding night-time assemblies and spreading superstition, for which he was condemned to a public whipping before being returned to his owner:

Declaration of the Council of Le Cap, confirming a Sentence of the Criminal Judge of the same Town, declaring a Negro, Commander, duly accomplished and convicted of having held nocturnal assemblies, and of having used superstitions and prestige to abuse the credulity of the other negroes, and to try to draw from them money; For the reparation of which he would have been condemned to the whip on the Place du Marche of Clugny; Then handed over to his master.

Commandeurs were responsible for maintaining productivity and order among the *atelier* work gangs. They also, at times, had to bear the weight of executing punishments for transgressions, which put them in a position of authority above the enslaved laborers. The announcement described the meetings as indulgent of the superstitions of the blacks, and as providing a way for this *commandeur* to use his position to swindle money from believers.[79] However, this is just one of several examples of *commandeurs* and other relatively privileged slaves operating in collusion with the field workers. *Commandeurs* like the one above had two faces, one for whites and one for blacks, and likely used their relative privilege among enslaved workers to invite people from different plantations and to organize rebellious activities.

In December 1784, an advertisement was published for an escaped coachman, who may have been a *calenda* organizer:

Cahouet, Mesurade, coachman, age 24 to 26 years, height of 5 feet 1 inch, fat face, stocky and hunched, great player of the bansa, singer, and coaxer of the blacks, always at each of the dances on the plantations belonging to M. Roquefort. Those who have knowledge give notice to M. Linas of Le Cap, to whom [the runaway] belongs, or to M. Phillippe. There is one portugaise for compensation.[80]

Like the unnamed *commandeur* who held night-time gatherings in 1782, Cahouet used his relative privilege within the slave community, and his role as a coachman, to contact people on several plantations and disseminate the word about the *calendas*. Cahouet's rank in the labor hierarchy may not have protected him from the typical ravages of slavery, meaning he may have sought freedom for the same reasons as other absconders. Alternatively, perhaps he felt he could be a more effective organizer if he were "underground" or off the plantation. Being of the Mesurade nation did not preclude Cahouet from taking part and having a leadership role in *calendas*. The evidence of ritual *calenda* gatherings persisted despite the May 1772 judgment banning free people of color from holding *calendas*, and the reiteration of this ordinance in March 1785.[81] A Kongolese cook named Zamore, who escaped in July 1789, was described as a full-time drummer for the dances since he was last seen in Port-de-Paix.[82] Jean-Pierre, a *mulâtre* drummer, was also a shoemaker in Le Cap used his French skills to pass as a free person of color in May 1790.[83]

These examples demonstrate that African descendants of varying statuses (free or enslaved), race (*mulâtre* or black creole), occupations within the slave hierarchy (merchants, *commandeurs*, cooks, and coachmen), and African ethnicities (Nagô/Yoruba, Mesurade, Kongo, Mondongue) participated in what were labeled as *calendas*. *Calenda* participants, and often the leaders of those gatherings, embodied a liberation ethos by liberating themselves from enslavement. Ritual work within spaces like *calenda* dance gatherings built racial solidarity through identification with several African symbols that were expressions of several cultural identities. Combined with the racial boundaries of colonial structures, Africa-inspired ritual participation, and other forms of collective action like marronnage, a collective racial identity began to emerge. Runaway advertisements indicate that *calendas* and other Africa-inspired ritual gatherings were a constant presence in the colony and provide piecemeal data that demonstrate ritualists were among the many who escaped enslavement and acted as micromobilizers, linking enslaved people from various plantations to free space ritual gatherings. We do not have a fully accurate account of how many *calendas* took place in Saint-Domingue, their exact locations, exactly how many people participated, or their identities. However, accounts of *calendas* in the few years leading to the Haitian Revolution might be a window through which we can understand ritual gatherings as politicized free spaces.

Ritual Rebels

Maroon-organized *calenda* ritual gatherings spread oppositional consciousness, through the invocation of *orishas*, saints, and the ancestral dead; the propagation of liberatory ideas; physical preparation for armed combat; and the inclusion of various enslaved people of varying ethnic groups and rank within the plantation regime. Colonists' fears that antagonistic sentiments among blacks would spread from cities like Le Cap into the rural areas came to fruition in 1786. On June 3, the Superior Council of Cap Français banned blacks and free people of color from participating in "mesmerism," a pseudo-scientific trend that had taken hold in Saint-Domingue. This ban was in response to several reports of *calendas* occurring in banana groves at the Tremais plantation in Marmelade, a northern district dominated by enslaved Kongolese Africans on newly formed coffee plantations. Four men: Jérôme *dit*, or "the so-called," Pôteau and Télémaque from M. Bellier's plantation at l'Ilet-à-Corne near Marmelade; Jean Lodot of Sieur Mollié's Souffriere plantation in Marmelade; and Julien, a Kongolese of the Lalanne plantation also in Marmelade, were charged with orchestrating secret assemblies that frequently drew as many as 200 participants. In addition to facing charges for organizing the outlawed gatherings, several witness testimonies asserted that the men were known for selling *nkisis* and performing other sacred rituals at meetings insiders called *mayombo* or *bila*.[84]

Jean Lodot was known as a runaway who frequented the Souffriere plantation work gangs in Marmelade, carrying a small sack containing a crucifix, pepper, garlic, gunpowder, and pebbles. Witnesses saw him leading at least two ceremonies, including one when an overseer saw him in his hut among a small gathering kneeling in front of a table covered with a cloth and holding two candles. Jean held up "fetishes," or unspecified ritual objects, in front of the table, which was an altar. Two machetes, crossed over each other, were laid on the ground in front of Jean. In a second meeting, participants drank a rum concoction containing pepper and garlic, which induced a sedative state from which Jean would raise them with the flat end of a machete, symbolizing participants' death and rebirth, and connecting machetes to Africans and African descendants' sacred world. Finally, a third witness, an enslaved man named Scipion, stated that Jean and his followers covered themselves with cane liquor, put gunpowder in their hands and lit themselves aflame.[85]

Witnesses testified that Jérôme and Jean were close associates who hosted these gatherings together. On several occasions, Jean disappeared from Molliers' plantation and sometimes he stayed on the land of Belier, who had enslaved Jérôme. Jean and Jérôme Pôteau, a man of mixed racial descent, were responsible for selling the *mayombo* sticks containing the *maman-bila* and the *poto* seeds – the possible source from where he assumed his surname, Pôteau. Jérôme performed demonstrations for audiences, and sold sacred objects based on demand. In his small sacks, he carried little stones, rum, a horn full of gunpowder, pieces of iron, and pieces of paper. Like Pierre Dom Pedro, Jérôme added gunpowder to the rum to stimulate participants and induce a state of excitement. For healing purposes, pepper and a white powder were combined with the rum to treat people with fevers. The red and black *poto* seeds helped to identify *macandal* poisoners and thieves.

Jérôme and Télémaque were also close associates; they had been in bondage on the same plantation from which they both eventually escaped. Belier's neighbor, Deplas, testified that numerous assemblies occurred on this property – one of which caused such alarm that Deplas went to disrupt the meeting. He stated that Télémaque was leading the ritual assembly and upon dispersal of that gathering, Télémaque threatened Deplas' servant saying, "you think you're still in Gonaïves, but you will soon know the negroes of l'Ilet-à-Corne!" Deplas claimed that the servant mysteriously died the next day from a violent colic, insinuating that Télémaque's supernatural abilities caused the death. Télémaque and Jérôme were also accused of preaching liberation and independence at the gatherings, attempting to instigate rebellion among the enslaved. A mass revolt would indeed occur five years later, but without any known contribution from the four men. In November, Jean was charged with disturbing the public and having been armed, during his marronnage, with a hunting knife, an iron stick, and a false passport so he could pass for free. His execution took place at the public market of Marmelade; the executioner strangled Jean until death ensued and exposed his body for 24 hours, then planted a small tree in the place where the body had lain. Julien was forced to attend and assist with Jean's execution, since the two had been arrested together in October; after this, he was returned to his owner. Télémaque and Jérôme were never captured but were ultimately hung in effigy.[86]

Women and Midwifery

Though there are few accounts detailing women's roles in ritual activities, it is highly improbable that they were *not* present and centrally engaged as significant contributors to enslaved people's sacred practices – especially given women's indispensability in West and West Central African religious systems. Similar to the queen mothers of Dahomey or West Central African women like Queen Njinga and Dona Beatriz, enslaved African and African-descendant women translated cultural and religious knowledge and practices into political power "to facilitate liberation from various forces of oppression" even as they experienced marginalization in patriarchal and racialized societies (Kuumba 2006: 120). Black midwives and *hospitalières*, or the lead medical practitioners among the enslaved population, deployed their sacred ritual skills and deeply embedded knowledge pools for medicinal purposes in ways that subverted plantation power structures. Men generally constituted the majority of the enslaved population, but women were increasingly targeted as slave trade captives in the years leading to the Haitian Revolution: West Central African men were 65.9 percent of French slave ship captives to Saint-Domingue in 1789, down from 74.9 percent in 1775.[87] Compared to creoles, and compared to men, Africa-born women were more likely to work in field gangs and did not have many opportunities for upward mobility. Mixed-race women were generally favored for domestic labor and other specialized positions.[88] However, women who were *hospitalières* relied on expertise in African and European healing methods to treat illnesses, injuries, and provide care for new mothers. As such, it is likely that Africa-born women with knowledge of healing methods practiced on the continent were primed for such a role. *Hospitalières* played a significant role on plantations that employed them; they were considered "trusted" slaves who had privilege and power.[89] Despite or perhaps due to these conditions, an Africa-born woman, Marie Catherine *dit* Kingué, came to be revered and feared as a powerful, dangerous threat in Saint-Domingue's northern department.

The case of Marie Catherine Kingué is found in the papers of François Neufchâteau, the attorney general of Cap Français in the late 1780s.[90] Kingué was likely a *hospitalière* who performed the duties of a midwife, healer, diviner, herbalist, and supposedly a *vaudoux* queen. Records identify her as being 36–40 years of age and as Kongolese, having two to three marks of her homeland on her cheek below her eye. She was known to claim to be free, and this was also signified by her use of an African name, suggesting that she renounced the forced naming practice that was part of the enslavement process. Her assumed name, Kingué, might indicate that she was from Kinguélé, the seat of the KaKongo Kingdom 35–40 miles inland from the Malemba port.[91] This renaming represented a self-fashioning of identity and a reclamation of personal power in a society where most African women were relegated to the lowest status; it also made her African origins – and the spirits with whom she was associated – recognizable to those who would become part of her following.[92] Inhabitants of the area north of the Congo River were not Christianized as scholars have previously believed, so it is possible that Kingué was a victim of judicial enslavement that targeted witchcraft or "fetisheurs."[93] When in Saint-Domingue, it is also possible that Marie Catherine attempted escape once; a December 1774 advertisement was placed in Le Cap for a woman named "Keingue" and a "nouveau" African man bearing a Maltese cross tattoo on his stomach and a tattoo of his country, Moinsa.[94] We do not yet have concrete evidence linking the runaway Keingue with the midwife Marie Catherine, but the possibility is compelling.

Nevertheless, by 1785 Marie Catherine Kingué was enslaved on a plantation owned by Sieur Caillon Belhumeur in Port Margot, near Le Cap, and she was known throughout Limbé and Plaisance for selling *garde-corps*, or *nkisis*. Kingue had a live-in partner and lieutenant named Polidor, also Kongolese, from the Labauche plantation in Pilate, Plaisance. Her following amassed quickly and to the extent that whites, including Belhumeur himself, were part of her clientele. Local planters sharply disparaged her in racialized and sexualized terms, describing her as a monster and a "hussy," and those who followed her as "weak-minded imbeciles." Several planters in Plaisance, writing to Neufchâteau in 1785, complained to Belhumeur about Marie's activities, even going to the high courts at Le Cap. They requested a special brigade to seize her, stating that the *maréchaussée* – the militia of free men of color responsible for chasing runaways in the colony – and whites could not be trusted because of their reverence toward her. Named in the letter were the Chailleaus; Mr. Marsan; Mr. Vazou; Saumice; Jean and Bernard Cherisse and Pironneau – three *mulâtre* planters of Plaisance; a surgeon named Pudemaine; as well as trusted enslaved *commandeurs* who all expressed concern about her "vagrancy, superstition, charlatanism, and other criminal and dangerous acts." Belhumeur promised to reprimand her, but planters bemoaned "il n'en a rien fait" – he did nothing. Apparently, he was paying her a monthly fee for her services.[95]

From as early as 1784, Marie Catherine established a reputation for her ability to identify and cure the effects of *macandal* poisonings, a valuable skill for any planter worried about his or her unpaid workforce dying from poison. Accounts from his neighbors claimed that Belhumeur had overworked his slaves, causing a few of them to die. Rather than accept overwork as the cause of death, he consulted Kingué to find out if the slaves had been poisoned and to locate the perpetrators. She "did a certain sleight of hand," or performed a ritual in front of Belhumeur and told him of an alleged conspiracy in his house. Documents also allege that Belhumeur proceeded to torture and kill the accused poisoners without a trial.[96] In another instance, Kingué was called to assist a pregnant woman who was sick and who had possibly had been poisoned; upon birthing, a dead snake emerged instead of a baby.[97] Other letters indicated that performances such as delivering a dead snake inspired Africans to revere Kingué as a god who had the power to kill and resurrect, and to heal all kinds of diseases. In addition to earning money by selling *garde-corps* or *nkisis* for 10 to 12 *gourdes*, Kingué amassed spiritual power and notoriety in the neighborhoods of Plaisance. One letter expressed anxiety that, "everyone wanted to consult her experience ... the fanaticism ... became to a point that the greatest disorder would arise in the work gangs."[98] A fourth anonymous letter, dated October 7, 1785, seems to suggest that Marie gathered one hundred men from a work gang and incited them to prepare to revolt against their owner. Marie Catherine also used her power to silence her detractors. When she performed rituals on the Marsan plantation, her former initiates Jean, Bernand Cherice, and

Pironneau were threatened from testifying against her. Another woman who was witness to Kingué was alledgedly tormented before she could speak out. On the Chailleau plantation, she had accused the first *commandeur* of being a poisoner.[99]

Though Marie's actions of helping Belhumeur to identify poisoners may have served to help maintain the workforce on plantations, her spiritual assistance to enslaved people aimed to provide them with health and care. Ultimately, Marie Kingué dealt directly with matters of life and death: childbirth, healing the afflicted from poison, and, if the accounts of her position as a *vaudoux* queen were true, summoning sacred power from the non-physical world. Her abilities and reputation raised her profile among the enslaved communities – and whites – of Port Margot, Limbé, and Plaisance. Planters felt that any such form of power exhibited by an enslaved person, especially a woman, would override white male authority and potentially lead to a revolt against the hierarchical nature of society. Despite enslavers' gender biases about black women's power, the enslaved people whom she served would have recognized Kingué's sacred authority as normative. Marie Kingué seems to have been either a Kongolese *nganga*, a *kitomi* of the Mbumba tradition, or part of the Mpemba midwifery movement originated by a woman with special techniques and powers.[100] One wonders what larger spiritual significance the snake would have for Kingué's Kongolese followers, since the snake spirit Mbumba was associated with Jesus Christ and "decentralized and democratized power."[101] The symbolism of these events hints at why Kingué was seen as a god who facilitated the birth of a Christ-like spirit which, to her followers, may have represented the coming of a new polity.

Women like Brigitte Mackandal and Marie Catherine Kingué demonstrated the "radical implications of black women's spiritual politics" by embracing acts of "woman-centered preservation," such as poison, healing, and midwifery, that fundamentally opposed racial capitalist exploitation of black women's bodies (Sweeney 2021: 56, 68). Midwives such as Kingué were seen as necessary evils that were required to help enslaved women reach their fullest reproductive capabilities in order to grow the enslaved population. They had some flexibility in the slave hierarchy, but were often demonized and accused of infanticide by using herbs to spread *mal de mâchoire*, a tetanus-like disease that locked a child's jaw and affected their ability to ingest food.[102] The hysteria may or may not have been valid, given that infanticide was a gendered form of resistance throughout the Americas – some women preferred not to see another child brought into the horrors of enslavement and therefore took matters into their own hands.[103] A midwife named Arada on the Fleuriau plantation in Cul-de-Sac, where poisonings occurred in 1776, was put in a rope collar with 70 knots representing the number of children she had been accused of killing. In 1786, a midwife owned by Madame Dumoranay was suspected to have been the source of high infant mortality, yet no concrete evidence against her was presented.[104]

Whether the midwives deliberately caused *mal de mâchoire* as a way of protesting forced breeding, or the disease was an unintentional result of unsanitary conditions, the women undoubtedly relied on African-based technologies and often gave counsel to European doctors.[105] Midwives' role in the plantation hierarchy made them valuable and privileged, but racial and gendered oppression (undoubtedly including sexual exploitation) made them a target. Several midwives escaped enslavement altogether, including a 55-year-old creole midwife named Zabeth who escaped from the Duconge plantation in Port-de-Paix. Zabeth fled on January 10, 1786 after being accused of killing over 30 infants and 11 other children who all suffered from the same disease.[106] In October 1778, a *mulâtresse* named Manon was announced to have escaped six weeks before. It was suspected that she left a Limonade plantation for the house of Dame Couttin in Le Cap where she trained in midwifery.[107] A Kongolese woman named Lise was the midwife for her plantation owner in Le Cap and escaped in 1784.[108] Though not a midwife, another Kongolese woman escaped from Saint Marc. In the colony, she was known as Diane, but her African name was Ougan-daga, which may be connected to the *ouangas* that were discovered in the Mackandal trial and became outlawed in post-revolution Saint-Domingue, suggesting that Diane was proficient in Kongolese ritual technologies.[109] As the gender imbalance came to parity approaching the Haitian Revolution, we begin to see women more prominently in gendered roles such as midwives and ritualists. The case of Marie Catherine Kingué and other maroon midwives establishes a precedent for understanding women like Cécile Fatiman – the *vaudoux* queen who presided over the Bwa Kayman ceremony just days before the Haitian Revolution uprising – and, more broadly, the ways black women leveraged their cultural and religious practices to advance liberation struggles.

CONCLUSION

Enslaved Africans and African descendants re-fashioned their spiritual spaces to cultivate their sacred understandings of their environment, oppositional consciousness, and social interactions and solidarities. Ritual free spaces in Saint-Domingue encouraged participants to empower themselves with sacred technologies, to seek retribution against enslavers using poison, and to rebel against slavery through marronnage and militaristic performances. These free spaces also allowed the enslaved to access and consult black women's sacred, cultural, and political power, which was essential within African and African descendants' worldviews but repressed by colonial society. African-inspired ritual technologies and practices; notions of freedom, slavery, rebellion, and militarism; and women's power were part of a counterhegemonic body politic that thrived within enslaved people's free spaces. Regardless of context, counterhegemonic ideas, practices that help to generate dissent, and free spaces are critical for organizing, planning, and orchestrating that dissent. Mobilizers can and do identify or create free spaces, even in the most repressive societies (Polletta and Kretschmer 2013), as evinced by the ritual rebels of colonial Saint-Domingue.

4

Mobilizing Marronnage: Race, Collective Identity, and Solidarity

Samson, Congo, about 25 years old, a height of five feet two inches, having red skin, very large and red eyes, very thick lips and filed teeth, stamped JOUSSAN, the said negro was a cart driver at Le Cap, where he has familiarity, there will be four *portugaises* to compensate for his capture; Sans-Souci, Mondongue, about 22 years old, a height of five feet, well constituted and marked from smallpox, stamped RAAR, having very black skin; Julien, creole, aged 16 years old, slender, having very black skin and scars on his legs, stamped RAAR; Kepel, creole, brother of Julien, age 12 years old, without a stamp, marked from smallpox, having very black skin and feet a little inside [pigeon-toed]; Ulysse, Mondongue, about 18 years old, of small height, stamped RAAR; Blaise, Arada, age 18 years old, of small height, having marks of his country on his cheeks, stamped RAAR; Mercis, Arada, about 20 years old, height of five feet three inches, reddish skin, pretty looking, having a scar on one leg from an old sickness, stamped RAAR; Nanette, of the nation Monbal, about 45 years old, of small height, without a stamp, a little marked from smallpox, having arched [bowed] legs; Marie, creole, daughter of Nanette, 18 years old, reddish skin, a little marked from smallpox, without a stamp, having arched [bowed] legs, she has given birth about a month ago to a girl, who she brought with her; Marinette, of the nation Moncamba, about 20 years old, of small height, having very black skin, her teeth filed and marks of her country on her face, stamped RAAR; Rose, of the nation Arada, about 20 years old, having very red skin and mark of her country on her face, stamped RAAR. The seven negroes and four nègressses coming from the divisions of Mrs. Raar and L'arouille, planters at Boucan Champagne of Borne, where the negroes have said, on the plantation of M. Millot, of Bas-Borgne and Corail, where they stayed for three months, have fled as maroons from the plantation of M. Jean Cochon at Riviere Laporte, quarter of Plaisance, since the 23rd of last month, with their booty, those who have knowledge are asked to give notice to M. Jean Cochon, owner of the said place, to whom the negroes and nègresses belong, or to Mrs. Milly and Cagnon, merchants at Le Cap. There will be compensation.[1]

Runaway slave advertisements such as the one transcribed above contain valuable information as well as critical silences about maroons and their intentions. The advertisements are a snapshot of a moment in time and reveal little about the maroons' past or future beyond the date of publication. This particular advertisement does not indicate what tasks most of the 12 bondspeople performed on the Raar plantation in Borne. It is unclear how and why they migrated to the Millot plantation, or how and why they ended up on the Cochon plantation in Plaisance, from where they left as maroons. Besides brothers Julien and Kepel, and Nanette, her daughter Marie, and Marie's one-month-old baby girl, the nature of relationships between the absconders is obscure. We do not know how and when they decided to escape together, nor can we elucidate more of their biographical details, such as for how long they had been enslaved in the colony or if they all spoke Kreyol. We cannot know their innermost thoughts, fears, or ambitions. It is not presently possible to find out what happened after their November 23 escape or what happened after the advertisement appeared in *Les Affiches américaines* on December 15, 1790. They may have been captured, jailed, and returned to Jean Cochon, or they could have remained at large and relocated to another existing maroon community.

Though we do not know for certain the circumstances of Raar plantation runaways' immediate past and future, the contents of this and similar advertisements reveal insights that help us speculate about enslaved people's racial and ethnic identities, their inner social world, and their inter-personal relationships. This unlikely group of 12 enslaved people escaped together on November 23, 1790, seemingly after having been sold or leased to a new owner, M. Jean Cochon. Most were branded RAAR, the name of their first owner. There were five women and girls, including Marie's baby, but most of the fugitives in this case – and those who took part in marronnage overall – were men. One was Kongolese and two were Mondongues of West Central Africa, three were Aradas from the Bight of Benin, four were creoles born in Saint-Domingue, and two were of lesser-known African origins, Monbal and Moncamba. There were two groups of biologically connected individuals. Some were survivors of smallpox and bore scars from other illnesses or injuries; others bore the distinctive cultural markings of their nations. Some were darker skinned, while others had a "reddish" complexion. One was described as having a specialized position, that of a cart driver, and was familiar with Le Cap, where he often worked. Yet, the differences between these bondspeople did not overshadow their shared social conditions and collective decision to engage in marronnage, despite the deadly obstacles they inevitably faced.

How can we understand this small but diverse maroon group as a type of network engaged in collective action? Maroons' identities and social network ties are lenses through which we can examine "the interaction mechanisms by which individual and sociocultural levels are brought together (Gamson 1992: 71)" during the act of escaping slavery. This chapter relies on protest event content analysis (Koopmans and Rucht 2002; Hutter 2014) of thousands of runaway slave advertisements placed in *Les Affiches américaines* and other colonial-era newspapers and focuses on two major aspects of how maroons' socio-cultural realities both shaped and were shaped by their social interactions. I argue in two parts that: (1) racially or ethnically *homogenous* group escapes reflected and maintained pre-existing collective identities, while racially or ethnically *heterogeneous* group escapes indicated and helped forge a sense of racial solidarity; and (2) wider networks of resistance were built from runaways' forms of human capital and their pre-existing social network ties to enslaved people, maroons, and free people of color. These patterns of interaction around identity and solidarity helped shape mobilizing structures during the Haitian Revolution. Moreover, they informed post-independence era modes of identity at the micro- and macro-levels: the formerly enslaved masses organized themselves socially, economically, and religiously around kinship and African ethnicity, while the Haitian state characterized citizenship in racial terms. The formation of these identity- and state-making processes can be traced to the colonial period as enslaved people navigated the boundaries of bondage using their social and human capital.

Micromobilization processes draw on aspects of individuals' identities and the social network ties that existed prior to mobilization, particularly during exceptionally high-risk collective actions such as marronnage. Network ties can influence multiple aspects of the social construction of mobilization, including an individual's decision to engage in collective action or not, their assessment of the nature and extent of that participation, their awareness of opportunities to participate, and critical comprehension of the reasons for mobilization (Fantasia 1988; McAdam 1988; Gamson 1992; Taylor and Whittier 1992; Hunt and Benford 2004; Ward 2015, 2016). Chapter 3 explored ritualist networks that, in enhancing collective consciousness about the unjust nature of racial slavery in

Saint-Domingue, used sacred technologies to rectify those imbalances. In addition to ritual spaces, linkages between enslaved people from various birth origins – Saint-Domingue, the Bight of Benin, or West Central Africa for example – were cultivated as people interacted with each other and learned to communicate in the Kreyol language within spheres of labor such as plantation work gangs, in housing quarters and family units, and at weekend markets. These settings foregrounded patterns of interaction in maroon groups by allowing enslaved people to safely query, discuss, plan, and strategize the dynamics of their efforts to self-liberate.

Marronnage was a dangerous endeavor – runaways rarely had access to food or clothing, were chased by hunting dogs and the *maréchaussée* fugitive slave police, and had to navigate the colony's complex terrain oftentimes alone. Those who were caught faced punishments such as having limbs cut off, whippings, or being chained or executed. Therefore, taking part in marronnage was not an easy decision, and choosing to do so with others in some ways only heightened the risk of capture. Enslaved people with knowledge of who had escaped, when, why, or where maroons were located could be tortured for that information, or they could be incentivized with money, their freedom, or other material goods to turn in maroons. Trust was of paramount importance when a runaway involved other people in their escape, and their sense of collective identities helped facilitate a "cognitive, moral, and emotional connection with a broader community, category, practice, or institution" (Polletta and Jasper 2001: 285). Collective identity in mobilization processes were especially complex in Saint-Domingue. Most of the enslaved population were Africa-born, so the most sensible option for strategizing escape within a group was to turn to one's "countrymen" who shared linguistic, religious, and cultural identities and affinities. The runaway advertisements' descriptions of African ethnicities are not much more precise than the labels that derive from slave trading records regarding the specific ethnonyms that Africans would have used, the exact geographic location of their birth, or even the correct port from which they embarked. Still, the ethnonyms in the advertisements give a sense that runaways who were described in similar terms were at most countrywomen and men who may have lived in close proximity or had real connections prior to capture. At a minimum, they were regional neighbors who shared linguistic, religious, or political commonalities, making it likely that these groups mobilized alongside members of their regional background. Findings from content analysis of the *Les Affiches* advertisements prove most runaway groups were racially or ethnically homogeneous, which further supports the salience of pre-existing collective identities among people of the same racial or ethnic designation in the practice of resistance to "New World" slavery (Thornton 1991; Reis 1993; Barcia 2014; Rucker 2015).

While ethnic identification can be an important organizing principle, racial formations can similarly play a role in African Diaspora collective actions (Butler 1998). Through geographic proximity, commercial networks, language, and other factors, the conditions of capture and enslavement explicated a "latent potential of ethnicity ... even among those who were not consciously so disposed prior to their capture" (Gomez 1998: 7), adding a secondary layer of solidarity building that was at work through heterogeneous group escapes. Constructing a collective identity around Africanness may have been a primary step toward developing a broader sense of blackness. This chapter also aims to make sense of heterogeneous group escapes such as the Raar plantation maroons who were described as Kongo, Mondongue, Monbal, Moncamba, Arada, and Saint-Domingue creole, and explains the broader implications of these types of network formations. New identities and social network ties can form during, and because of, mobilizations like marronnage as disparately identified insurgents developed a sense of solidarity, or shared identification with and loyalty toward each other and a common fate or destiny (Melucci 1989; Gamson 1992; Taylor and Whittier 1992; Diani 1997; Kuumba and Ajanaku 1998; Hunt and Benford 2004). The transAtlantic slave trade, the *Code Noir* policy on French Caribbean slavery, and colonial plantation regimes forcefully imposed a "flattened" black identity onto the masses of enslaved Africans (Robinson 1983: 99–100; Bennett 2018). However, I argue that maroons and their enslaved or free co-conspirators autonomously socially constructed racial consciousness and racial solidarity through mobilization.

For example, Senegambians and Kongolese captives probably never would have come into contact on the African continent because of the distance between the two regions, thus their only commonalities were their shared survival of the Middle Passage and the status of being enslaved in a foreign environment. As these groups endured colonial structures in the Americas that categorized and exploited people because of their *blackness* rather than their ethnic, religious, or political origins, inter-ethnic solidarity between enslaved Africans and African descendants became increasingly important (Gomez 1998; Borucki 2015). Moreover, given the sheer size of the Africa-born population in the colony – two-thirds of the enslaved – it is fair to assume that most creoles and mixed-race individuals had direct parentage or other kinship ties to an African, despite claims from early sources that Africans and colony-born creoles were socially distant from each other. There were instances where it was more advantageous for runaways to compose groups that were racially and ethnically heterogenous – such as the Raar maroons. The racial and ethnic groups represented by the Raar maroons might have been able to marshal a wide range of knowledge pools, techniques, and tactics to better strategize escape. But to overcome the boundaries of their birth origins, cultures, religions, and languages, heterogeneous groups of absconders had to develop a certain level of depth in their relationships to establish trust and solidarity. They would have had to cultivate some understanding of their shared positionality of experiencing enslavement based on their blackness, rather than their respective heritages or other aspects of fragmentation among the enslaved population, making racialized experiences the basis for their marronnage.

The colonial newspapers *Les Affiches américaines*, *Gazette de Saint Domingue*, and the *Courrier Nationale de Saint Domingue* published the runaway slave advertisements. *Les Affiches* (hereafter *LAA*) was published in Cap Français (Le Cap) and Port-au-Prince beginning in 1766, three years after widespread printing operations were introduced to Saint-Domingue, until 1791, the year the Haitian Revolution uprisings began.[2] In the weekly papers, planters advertised sales or rentals of their goods, land, animals, as well as enslaved women and men. Separate listings of advertisements were placed for runaways who escaped enslavement, some for as short as three days, others for over ten years. Planters' sole intention for placing runaway advertisements was to locate and re-capture fugitives to restore the economic losses of the enslaved people – who as chattel slaves were one of the colony's foremost forms of capital – and the value of their labor productivity. It was not in planters' immediate financial interest to provide full narrative accounts of fugitive escapes, since the advertisements themselves cost money to publish; nor was it within the realm of their ontological reality to consider runaways as strategic thinkers who planned their escape. The advertisements contain the implicit and explicit biases of slave owners who viewed enslaved people's agency as an impossibility, and therefore inscribed into the advertisement texts the impossibility of accessing the full scope of the runaways' lives. Despite the omissions, deliberate silences, violence, and virulently racist language that are embedded in the texts, there are also elements of enslaved people's lived reality that can help expand our understanding of their inter-personal relationship dynamics and collective intentionality.

To identify and relocate slaves and recoup their lost funds, planters had to provide some modicum of accurate information – however speculative – when placing the advertisements, making them a strong source for demographic representations of the escapee population.

The advertisements present general information including the escapee's name, age, gender, and birth origin. It was also important for the planter, or plantation lawyer or manager, to identify themselves and provide contact information for where they could be reached and the bounty they were willing to pay as a reward for capture. Typically, the advertisements also included distinctive characteristics such as bodily scarring, the owner's brand and other physical traits, personality disposition, or the person's labor skills as a means of locating the escapee. Frequently, the advertisements contain an indication of the duration of time the self-liberated person had been missing, the area from which they had escaped and with whom they fled, and where or with whom they were suspected of hiding. These and other characteristics, such as the maroons' linguistic skills, are helpful for studying the role of race and ethnicity, gender, and social ties in marronnage. The following section revisits the question of stratification among the enslaved and maroon populations with discussion of the demographics of the 12,857 runaways described in the *Les Affiches* advertisements.

FRAGMENTATION: RACE, ETHNICITY, AND GENDER

Gender

One of the widest imbalances among the maroon population was that of gender. Men over the age of 16 were the majority of runaways, accounting for nearly 80 percent of the 12,857 individuals described in the newspaper advertisements as shown in Table 4.1. Men were the largest proportion of the early transAtlantic slave trade captives and the enslaved population of the French colonies, but sex ratios were almost even leading up to the Haitian Revolution.[3] Still, men were slightly over-represented in the distribution of the enslaved population, accounting for their high proportion among runaways. Men were also more likely to occupy artisanal labor positions that allowed them a certain amount of latitude during the workday. As will be discussed below, coopers, carpenters, shoemakers, fishermen, and other artisans ran errands, apprenticed and were leased by their owner to other plantations, or hired themselves out to earn their own money. As such, men could take advantage of quotidian labor-related tasks to escape without immediate detection. African men

TABLE 4.1. *Frequency Distribution of Gender and Age (N = 12,857)*

Gender	Frequency	Percent	Cumulative
Women	1,858	14.45%	14.45
Men	10,271	79.9%	94.35
Girls (16 and under)	216	1.68%	96.03
Boys (16 and under)	512	3.98%	100

probably adapted to acquiring these proto-industrial work skills since, in several African societies, particularly the Loango and Angola coast regions, women performed agricultural work. For example, male captives in Portuguese-controlled Angola rejected agriculture-based slavery – seeing it as demeaning to their masculinity – and fled in response.[4] Therefore, it is possible that African men who were field workers in Saint-Domingue were more likely to escape as a masculinist rejection of "women's work."

Conversely, enslaved African women in Saint-Domingue were over-represented as field workers and performed the most physically taxing jobs. While creole and mixed-race enslaved women were likely to be artisanal laborers or were found in the domestic sphere, most Africa-born women were under strict surveillance throughout the workday and therefore did not have as much flexibility to travel beyond the plantation.[5] There is a disproportionately low number of women reflected in the runaway advertisements, with women representing only 14.45 percent of the reported runaways. Some historians (Gautier 1985; Fick 1990; Moitt 2001; Thompson 2006; Blackburn 2011) postulate that women were more likely to commit *petit* marronnage, and though planters did not report these missing cases, women acted as bridges between plantations and communities of escaped people and helped to create the mobilization structures necessary for organizing the Haitian Revolution. Conventional ideas about women's marronnage also suggest that child-rearing responsibilities precluded many of them from taking the risk involved with escape on a permanent basis. Additionally, creole women were more likely than their male counterparts to receive legal manumission, often resulting from bearing a child biologically connected to white slavers due to mostly involuntary sexual relations. But, when we explore women's resistance and look at their escape strategies, we see that some women did commit marronnage and at times did so with their children in tow. Some women who took flight were accompanied by young children, and 30 women escaped while with child.

We do not know much about the experience of childhood in Saint-Domingue, however it is important to note that black children below the age of 16 were enslaved and escaped bondage, either with a parent or another adult but sometimes alone. Gender patterns in marronnage among children generally mirrored those of adults (Table 4.1). Male children escaped over twice as often as female children: 3.98 percent compared to 1.68 percent, respectively. Plantation inventories show that boys tended to begin work around age eight, tending animals, working as domestics, or working in the field. Girls worked as nurses, domestics, and field hands.[6] But Moreau de Saint-Méry observed that creole girls tended to have children at an early age, as young as 11 or 13, which temporarily delayed their entry into the workforce until after their first child was born.[7] Adult women were slightly more likely than men to run away in a heterogeneous maroon group – 16.5 percent compared to 14.7 percent respectively – (Table 4.3) and this is probably because of those who escaped with their children such as the case of Nanette, a Monbal woman, her creole daughter Marie, and one-month old grand-daughter from the Raar plantation.

Thinking about women and children, and the ways in which enslaved women's reproductive capabilities birthed hereditary racial slavery and hierarchies of racial capitalism (Morgan 2018) can give us an indication of the familial ties that existed between Africans and creoles, including bi-racial *mulâtres*. When African women's children fathered by African or creole men were born in the colony, the children were called creole *nègres*, or blacks, which automatically inserted racial difference between mothers and children where there may have otherwise been a previously existing ethnic similarity. Creole women's children were similarly black, but when an African or creole woman's child was a product of coerced sexual encounters with white men, the children were born bi-racial *mulâtres*. If a creole black woman had a child with a *mulâtre*, then the child was a two-thirds black *griffe*. Less common were *quarterons*, those who were one-quarter black. Therefore, when enslaved women reproduced, their children usually were described as being of a different race. For example, Genevieve, a *mulâtresse*, who escaped with her daughter Bonne, a *quarteronne* in March 1786, were categorized differently based on phenotype and parentage.[8] Different ethnic or racial identifiers did not inherently signify separation between enslaved people, who were likely related to an African person, given their overwhelming representation among bondspeople. Though women and girls were not highly represented as maroons, their rates of social network ties to family, a plantation-based relationship, or contact with other runaways or free people of color during marronnage were slightly higher than their male counterparts. Thus, enslaved women were indeed deeply connected within the landscape of the enslaved, marooned, and freed people of African descent (Table 4.11). Analysis of marronnage, as this chapter will show, is a way to highlight the nature of those interactions that can begin to complicate the ways we understand how race, ethnicity, and solidarity functioned at the micro-level in a colonial society that was stratified and fragmented by race, gender, occupation, and status, then became an independent nation where blackness was the primary qualifier for citizenship.

Race and Ethnicity

A significant intervention that this chapter, and this book, seeks to make is to disrupt not only the idea that enslaved people were "socially dead" without meaningful interpersonal relationships among other things, but the notion that differentiation and contention characterized and overdetermined the relationships that indeed existed among people of African descent. Early observers and subsequent scholarship regard maroons, slaves, Africans, creoles, mixed-race people, and free people of color as disparate categories of actors who were singularly self-interested and self-segregated. They also describe an internal hierarchy in which creoles occupied a higher status and carried an attitude of superiority toward recently arrived Africans, even though many creoles and mixed-race people shared kinship with older Africans. Moreau de Saint-Méry's accounts, as well as those from the priest Jean-Baptiste Labat in the early eighteenth century, describe the enslaved population as a group divided by labor tasks and according to skin color, ethnicity, language, and religion. Indeed, the runaway advertisements themselves attest to the vast diversity of the enslaved population, over half of which were adults born in Africa representing over 100 "ethnicities."[9] These ethnic delineations were usually specified in the advertisements, but may not have been entirely historically accurate due to the imprecise nature of European–American slave trading documents. Some African captives were labeled based on the port from which they were shipped like the Capelaous (Cape Lahou), while others were based on broad coastal regions like the "Congos."[10] However inaccurate these labels might be, they represent the closest identifiers presently available to help us understand African origins.

There were 3,122 black creole runaways in the advertisements, so they comprised 24.3 percent of the runaway population (Table 4.2). This is a

TABLE 4.2. *Frequency Distribution of Saint-Domingue-born*
"Creoles" (N = 12,857)

Racial Category	Total	Percent
Nègre	3,122	24.3%
Mulâtre	540	4.2%
Griffe	136	1.1%
Quarteron	43	0.3%
Indien/indigenous	53	0.4%
Total	3,894	30.3%

slight under-representation with respect to their number among enslaved people, which was closer to 33 percent (one-third), likely due to the possibility of gaining freedom through other means. Though a relatively rare occurrence, enslaved creoles could purchase manumission with their labor, and men could join the military and *maréchaussée* fugitive slave police. Duty in the armed forces was a way for colonial authorities to co-opt marronnage, creating an option for legal emancipation. Similarly, mixed-race people described as *mulâtres, griffes,* and *quarterons* were few in number among runaways, since as a group they were more likely to be *gens du couleur libres* rather than enslaved. However, these findings nuance understandings of Saint-Domingue's free population of color by demonstrating that not all mixed-race people were privileged by their white fathers' wealth. The sample was comprised of 4.2 percent *mulâtres,* 1.1 percent *griffes,* and 0.3 percent *quarterons,* meaning over 5 percent of runaways had some degree of white admixture in their lineage. Several advertisements do not describe the runaway's race or ethnicity at all, but only include the person's name and the name of the planter. Though we can assume that the runaway was a person of African descent, it is not entirely possible to accurately gauge the person's racial category – or their geographic origins in Africa – without this information.

Continent-born Africans comprised approximately 62 percent of the runaway population and well over half of these were West Central Africans, which corroborates other historical data that indicate they were the majority regional group in late eighteenth-century Saint-Domingue. The most numerous of these were generally labelled as "Congo" (hereafter Kongo) without further specification.[11] Most French slave trading in this region was at the ports of Malemba and Cabinda on the Loango Coast, while Kongolese captives from Angola, where the Portuguese had long-standing relations and control, were filtered north by the Vili traders.[12] But, since the region was comprised of several independently operating kingdoms, such as Loango and KaKongo, there are yet unanswered questions as to the true origins of those described as "Congo" in Saint-Domingue. Despite the mislabeling of most Kongos, there were also significant numbers of West Central Africans like the Mondongues, Mayombés, and Mossoundis from the Loango Coast interior. Only eight 'Angoles' and sixteen Congo-Francs were listed, both groups that originated from Angola, providing evidence, albeit thin, of the small presence of Kongo Kingdom captives.[13]

Although they were the ethnic majority of the enslaved population in the early eighteenth century, by mid-century Bight of Benin natives were a distant second-place African group in Saint-Domingue, comprising 8.9 percent of runaways. Both Nagôs and Aradas were groups conquered by the Dahomey Kingdom, which actively captured and traded slaves along what was referred to as the "Slave Coast." Though some members of the Dahomey Kingdom did become enslaved due to warfare, only three runaways were described with terminology specifically referencing the kingdom – Dahomet or Dahomey. Nagôs, also referred to as Yorubas in other parts of the Atlantic world, were the largest number of Bight of Benin Africans, with 432 people in the sample. Aradas were the next largest Bight of Benin group, accounting for 372 runaway persons; they were also called by their linguistic grouping of "Fon," but only 27 Fon absconders appear in the advertisements. There were more Tiambas/Chambas than Fon – 119 – making them an important but less considered component of the Slave Coast population.[14] Natives of the Senegambian/Upper Guinea region were the third largest regional group, totalling 5.2 percent of reported runaways. The Mandingues were the highest number of Senegambians, with 212 runaways, followed by 179 Bambaras and 143 Wolofs. Biafrans comprised 3.1 percent of the sample, and most of these were Igbos. The much smaller numbers of Bibi and Moco were Bantu-language speakers who were exported from Biafran ports.[15] Most southeastern Africans were from Mozambique, where the French had begun trading in the 1770s.[16]

Africans from the Gold Coast, Windward Coast, and Sierra Leone were the least represented among runaways – even fewer than southeastern Africans from Madagascar and Mozambique, who numbered 1.3 percent of reported runaways. There were 153 Minas in the sample, making them the largest group of Gold Coast Africans. One hundred and two Cangas were in the sample, making them half of the number of

Windward Coast natives. Sierra Leoneans, from a neighboring region to Senegambia, included Sosos, Mendes, and Timbous. Together, Sierra Leoneans made up 0.5 percent of the sample, the smallest number of runaways. Newly imported Africans, whose ethnicity was not yet logged, routinely escaped from ports or plantations before they underwent "seasoning." Since they were not fully integrated into the plantation system, these runaways were simply referred to as *nouveau* in the advertisements. *Nouveau* fugitives would have been conspicuous, having just disembarked a slave ship – perhaps without clothing but with chains binding their necks, feet, and wrists. Still, they made up 3.1 percent of the runaway population, the same as the number of Biafrans represented in the sample.

Saint-Domingue's enslaved population was diverse according to the ways slave traders and colonial social norms categorized individuals in terms of race, ethnicity, and birthplace. However, these markers of identity were not discrete categories that separated people from one another – for example, one could simultaneously be a mixed-race person or creole born in the Americas to an Africa-born woman. The categories that whites imposed were often unstable and an imprecise reflection of captives' self-defined identities or their interpersonal relationships. The claims of writers like Moreau de Saint-Méry and Jean-Baptiste Labat, that enslaved creoles segregated themselves from Africans, harken to the false distinctions that late fifteenth- and early sixteenth-century Spanish colonists made between *ladinos* and *bozales* to attempt to predict and control one group's propensity to escape and rebel over the other. These efforts to reify the differences between enslaved creoles and Africans were not based on actual cultural, linguistic, regional, political, or religious differences, but were mechanisms of obfuscating the conditions of enslavement and bondspeople's inherent opposition to it. As the Spanish colonists found, and as the analysis of runaway advertisements below demonstrates, colony-born bondspeople were not significantly more or less likely to rebel than were Africans of various backgrounds, and in many cases they did so in concert.

INDIVIDUAL AND GROUP ESCAPES

Most escapees ran away by themselves, accounting for 60.5 percent of runaways, while a total of nearly 40 percent escaped in a group of two or more people (Table 4.3 and Figure 4.1). Though most fugitives escaped

TABLE 4.3. *Frequency of group escapes (N = 12,857)*

	Total	Percent
Individual escape	7,773	60.5%
Homogeneous racial/ethnic group escape	3,132	24.4%
Heterogeneous racial/ethnic group escape	1,952	15.2%
Total group escapes	5,084	39.6%
Total	12,857	100%

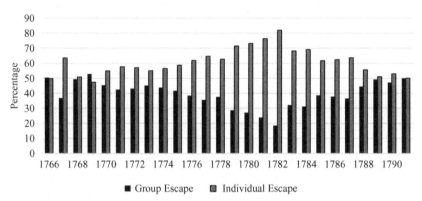

FIGURE 4.1. Rates of group and individual escapes over time (N = 12,857)

alone, focusing on group escapes helps us understand how oppositional consciousness was operationalized beyond one person's pursuit of freedom and extended to small-scale groups and bands. Not only were they family units, runaway groups were comprised of shipmates bound together by chains and regional origin, artisanal laborers and members of the same work gangs who fled together, and even strangers with a shared goal of freedom in mind. Homogeneous group escapes, meaning each runaway in the advertisement was described in the same racial or ethnic terms, indicated that a collective identity existed among the cohort; and heterogeneous group escapes, or escapes among runaways from different racial or ethnic backgrounds, demonstrated some sense of racial solidarity between individuals. Cultural and linguistic similarities made it easier for people of similar African heritage to collaborate and escape together, thus homogeneous group escape accounts for 24.4 percent of the sample. It was more difficult for groups comprised of different races and ethnicities to escape together because of cultural and linguistic differences. This can help account for why heterogeneous group escapes were less common, at 15.2 percent.

TABLE 4.4. *Chi-square test, group escapes by gender (N = 12,857)*

	Individual escape	Homogeneous group escape	Heterogeneous group escape	Total
Men	6,013 (58.5%)	2,751 (26.8%)	1,507 (14.7%)	10,271 (100%)
Women	1,273 (68.5%)	279 (15.0%)	306 (16.5%)	1,858 (100%)
Boys	382 (74.6%)	63 (12.3%)	67 (13.1%)	512 (100%)
Girls	105 (48.6%)	39 (18.1%)	72 (33.3%)	216 (100%)
Total	7,773 (60.5%)	3,132 (24.4%)	1,952 (15.2%)	12,857 (100%)

Note: p = 0.000.

At a rate of 74.6 percent individual escapes, boys were more likely than girls and adults of both sexes to flee by themselves (Table 4.4). Girls, on the other hand, ran away by themselves less often than anyone else at a 48.6 percent rate of individual escapes; therefore, they fled in groups at the highest rate. More specifically, girls escaped in a homogeneous group 6 percent more often than boys and 3 percent more often than adult women. Girls fled in a heterogeneous group 33 percent of the time, which was more often than anyone else. Since African girls were the minority group in the slave trade and the colony, they would have had a harder time finding someone of a similar background to join in absconding. For example, an eight or nine year old Arada girl named Félicité seems to have fled from Le Cap without an adult in 1768.[17] Men were more likely than women or children to escape in homogeneous groups, suggesting men had an easier time identifying and forging relationships with men of a similar background. This is probably because men were the majority in both the slave trade and the colony; indeed, adult women escaped by themselves more than adult men (Table 4.4).

Saint-Domingue-born and other Atlantic creoles were more likely to escape individually, averaging 78.8 percent and 81.98 percent respectively, while Africans overall had higher levels of group escapes (see Tables 4.4 and 4.9). Few African ethnic groups escaped individually at the same rates as creoles – only "Miserables" (which was possibly an aspersion cast either by their neighbors or French traders),[18] Taquas, Capelaous, Cramenties, and Mesurades escaped by themselves over 75 percent of the time (Table 4.6). I have argued elsewhere that Africans were more likely to collaborate in marronnage because they needed to work together to navigate an unfamiliar landscape during their escapes.[19] When people did escape in groups, they were more likely to do so with a cohort composed of a cohesive language, culture, race, or

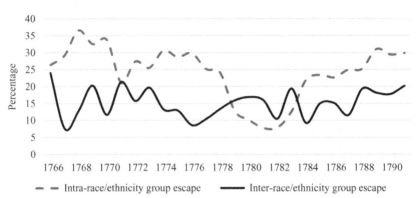

FIGURE 4.2. Homogeneous and heterogeneous group escape rates over time
(N = 12,857)

ethnicity. However, with time spent in the colony, acquisition of the
Kreyol language, and participation in shared rituals, African and creole
runaways could form alliances around their shared blackness and
enslaved status.

Analysis of homogeneous and heterogeneous group escapes over time
helps to reveal observable changes that might indicate growing solidarity
among Africans and creoles of diverse backgrounds around a sense of
racial identity or whether people clung to their disparate racial or ethnic
identities of origin. Homogeneous groups were predominant over heterogeneous groups, reaching their height in 1768, representing 36.5 percent of
all escapes then decreasing until the lowest point of 7.7 percent in
1781 and then increasing steadily until 1791 (Figure 4.2). Heterogeneous
group escapes were less prevalent overall and were at their highest point in
1766 with 23.9 percent; however, they did outpace homogeneous escapes
between the years 1779 and 1784. These years coincide with the decline of
group marronnage overall (Figure 4.1), and the American independence-
era British blockade on Saint-Domingue's ports that prevented new slave
ships from arriving. Therefore, enslaved people were forced to either
escape alone or build new relationships with people of diverse backgrounds due to the lack of newly imported Africans. From 1784, heterogeneous group escapes increased steadily, albeit at a slower pace than
homogenous group escapes, until 1791. While shared African ethnicity
remained a significant aspect of group escapes, it was also becoming
common for runaways to take flight in a group of people from diverse
backgrounds. This indicates that a growing sense of racial solidarity was
forming within rebellious activities during the pre-revolutionary period.

Collective Identity: Homogeneous Group Escapes

Homogeneous group escapes among Africans were more common than not. Homogeneous escapes were significantly more common among West Central Africans, especially those labeled with the generic "Kongo" identity – at 31.87 percent – since they were the largest African ethnic group in the colony. Other ethnicities similarly escaped with their kith and kin, probably because they were freshly arrived from the slave ports and were most familiar with each other. Hausas escaped with each other at a high rate as well: 33.72 percent. Nearly 39 percent of Côte d'Or, or Gold Coast, Africans escaped together. Sosos also escaped together at a rate of 29.8 percent; and 27.45 percent of Cangas group escapes were homogenous. This type of identity cohesion may have contributed to developing effective means for escaping, such as: six Nagô men and three Nagô women who escaped in 1786; six "new" Aradas – Hillas, Alexandre, Antoine, Content, Colas, and Tu Me Quitteras – who fled on January 17, 1776; eight "new" Mondongues, who were reported missing for several months in October 1769; the seven Soso (Sierra Leone) runaways in 1787; or the five Igbo absconders in 1788.[20]

The label of "new" was also used in cases where the runaways' ethnicity was not yet known because the captives had not yet been fully integrated into the plantation system. The two women and six men described as "new" who escaped the Defontaine plantation at Gonaïves were not assigned names nor were their ethnicities detailed, but we can assume that they were from the same background.[21] Runaways whose ethnic identity was unknown because they were new to the colony were most likely to escape together, since they escaped immediately after arrival. Sixty-seven per cent of group escapes among *nouveau* Africans were with other *nouveaus*, further demonstrating that shipmate relationships were sustained beyond the ports.

Black creoles had the easiest time finding other creoles to escape with, since 21 percent of creoles' group escapes were homogeneous. In September 1775, a group of three creole women, Judith, Marie-Jeanne, and Nannette, and six creole men, Apollon, Jerome, Tony, Hercule, Achille, and Polydor, escaped the Fillion plantation at Boucan-Richard in Gros Morne.[22] Sully, Thelemaque, Jean-Pierre, Manuel, and Therese were all creoles who left Haut du Cap in February 1786.[23] Among Saint-Domingue-born enslaved people, black creole runaways were most numerous, and thus took advantage of those numbers and their cultural dexterity (if they were born to African parents) to escape with other creoles, Africans, or mixed-race individuals (see Tables 4.5 and 4.6).

TABLE 4.5. *Chi-square test, group escapes among Saint-Domingue-born "Creoles" (N = 12,857)*

	Individual escape	Homogeneous group escape	Heterogeneous group escape	Total
Nègres	1,989 (63.7%)	656 (21.0%)	477 (15.3%)	3,122 (100%)
Mulâtre	441 (81.7%)	21 (3.9%)	78 (14.4%)	540 (100%)
Griffe	110 (80.8%)	9 (6.6%)	17 (12.5%)	136 (100%)
Quarteron	34 (79.1%)	5 (11.6%)	4 (9.3%)	43 (100%)
Indien/ Indigenous	47 (88.7%)	2 (3.8%)	4 (7.5%)	53 (100%)
Total	2,621 (20.4%)	693 (5.4%)	580 (4.5%)	3,894 (30.3%)

Note: p = 0.000.

Racial Solidarity: Heterogeneous Group Escapes

One of the largest group escapes was a heterogeneous band of 22 Africans who escaped the Duquesné plantation at Borgne in October 1789. Three of the 22 were Mondongues: Rampour, Barraquette, and Pantin; eight were Kongos: Abraham, Midi, Nicolas, Theodore, Emeron, Telemaque, and two women named Printemps and Catherine; three were Minas: Pyrame and two women Thisbe and Henriette; five were Igbos: Alexandre, Victor, Hipolite, Agenor, and Luron; one was a Senegambian woman named Agathe; one was a Bambara man named La Garde; and one was a creole woman named Poussiniere.[24] Another large group of 19 Africans fled Petite Anse in 1773. Their group included three Kongolese people: Tobie, Lubin, and a woman named Barbe; four Aradas: Blaise, Jean-Baptiste, Timba, and a woman named Grand-Agnes; a Nagô man named Toussaint; and eleven creoles: three women named Louison, Fanchette, and Catherine, and eight men named Foelician, Laurent, Christophe, Jean-Jacques, Joseph, Hubert, Baptiste and Louis.[25] These types of heterogeneous group escape were particularly diverse, considering that they were composed of people from vastly different regions. African runaways usually formed groups based on shared regional background, language, or religion. For example, Kongos and Mondongues seem to have been a common combination since they both were KiKongo speakers; as were Nagôs and Aradas, who shared religious commonalities and a common enemy, the Dahomeans. Similarly, Bambaras and "Senegalais" (Senegambians) were a common pairing, such as the group of a group of two Bambaras and

TABLE 4.6. *Chi-square test, group escapes among continent-born Africans (N = 12,857)*

Broad African region	Ethnic label	Individual escape	Homo-geneous	Hetero-geneous
West Central Africa & St. Helena	Congo, Kongo	2,236 (55.5%)	1,283 (31.87%)	507 (12.59)
	Mondongue, Mondongo	507 (51.49%)	110 (25.29%)	101 (23.22%)
	Baliba, Bariba	5 (71.43%)	2 (28.57%)	0 (0)
	Massangi, Mazangui	2 (20%)	7 (70%)	1 (10%)
	Moussondy, Mousombe	7 (63.64%)	2 (18.18%)	2 (18.18%)
	Missi-Congo	1 (50%)	0	1 (50%)
	Congo-Monteque	2 (100%)	0	0
	Congo-Franc	10 (62.5%)	5 (31.25%)	1 (6.25%)
	Mayombé, Mayembau	9 (60%)	5 (33.33%)	1 (6.67%)
	Mazonga-Congo	1 (100%)	0	0
	Gabonne	1 (100%)	0	0
	Angole	1 (12.5%)	7 (87.5%)	0
	Baassa, Abaffa	2 (25%)	6 (75%)	0
Senegambia	Bambara, Barba	99 (55.31%)	32 (17.88%)	48 (26.82%)
	Senegalaise, Wolof, Yolof	98 (68.53%)	13 (9.09%)	32 (22.38%)
	Malez, Mâle	2 (18.18%)	9 (81.82%)	0
	Poulard, Fulbe, Foule, Poule	23 (60.53%)	2 (5.26%)	13 (34.21%)
	Mandingue, Mandingo	132 (62.26%)	49 (23.11%)	31 (14.62%)
	Hausa, Aoussa, Haoussa,	38 (44.19%)	29 (33.72%)	19 (22.09%)
Bight of Benin	Mina, Mine, Amina, Amine	101 (66.01%)	9 (5.88%)	43 (28.10%)
	Arada, Aja, Adja, Juda, Adia	233 (62.63%)	80 (21.51%)	59 (15.86%)
	Nagô	245 (56.71%)	103 (23.84%)	84 (19.44%)
	Fon, Fond	19 (70.37%)	0	8 (29.63%)
	Tiamba, Thiamba, Chamba, Quiamba	84 (70.59%)	4 (3.36%)	31 (26.05%)
	Taqua, Attapa, Tapa, Taquoua, Tapaye	24 (77.42%)	1 (3.23%)	6 (19.35%)

(continued)

TABLE 4.6. (*continued*)

Broad African region	Ethnic label	Individual escape	Homo-geneous	Hetero-geneous
	Cotocoli, Cotocoly,	31 (68.89)	6 (13.33)	8 (17.78)
	Aguia, Yaguia	12 (50%)	2 (8.33%)	10 (41.67%)
	Damba, Lamba	1 (100%)	0	0
	Gambery, Gamberi	4 (80%)	0	1 (20%)
	Guinee	1 (7.14%)	11 (78.57%)	2 (14.29%)
	Daomet, Dahomey	3 (100%)	0	0
	Miserable	34 (79.07%)	2 (4.65%)	7 (16.28%)
Bight of Biafra	Ibo, Igbo	243 (62.63%)	80 (21.51%)	65 (18.31%)
	Bibi	21 (53.85%)	8 (20.51%)	10 (25.64%)
	Moco	3 (75%)	0	1 (25%)
	Gimba	1 (100%)	0	0
Gold Coast	Cramenty, Caramenty	19 (82.61%)	0	4 (17.39%)
	Bandia, Banguia	2 (40%)	0	3 (60%)
	Cote d'Or	24 (42.11%)	22 (38.6%)	11 (19.3%)
	Quincy, Kissi, Quissi, Quicy	4 (33.33%)	2 (16.67%)	6 (50%)
Windward Coast	Canga, Kanga	54 (52.94%)	28 (27.45%)	20 (19.61%)
	Mesurade	40 (76.92)	3 (5.77)	9 (17.31)
	Capelaou	33 (75)	6 (13.64)	5 (11.36)
Sierra Leone	Soso, Sosso, Zozeau, Sofo	25 (43.86)	17 (29.82)	15 (26.32)
	Timbou, Thimbou, Thimbo	7 (70%)	2 (20%)	1 (10%)
	Mende	0	0	0
Southeast Africa & Indian Ocean	Madagascar	3 (60%)	2 (40%)	0
	Mozambique, Mozamby	66 (40.24%)	82 (50%)	16 (9.76%)
"Nouveau"		106 (26.57%)	270 (67.67%)	23 (5.76%)
Total		4,619 (36%)	2,301 (17.9%)	1,206 (9.4%)

Note: p = 0.000.

two Senegambians who escaped together in December 1783, since they originated from a similar region in Africa and perhaps also shared the Islamic faith.[26]

Overall, heterogeneous group escapes were more frequent among Africans than African descendant creoles. Bambaras' heterogeneous escape rate was 26.82 percent, for Poulards (Fulbe or Fulani) it was 34.21 percent, Minas had heterogeneous group escapes 28.1 percent of the time, Thiambas escaped 26.05 percent of the time with others, and Aguias had the highest rates of heterogeneous escapes with 41.67 percent (Table 4.6). None of these groups had substantial numbers, and therefore may have collaborated with others out of necessity, since comrades from the same ethnicity were not readily available. But, black creoles absconded in heterogeneous groups more than other Saint-Domingue-born people at 15.3 percent (Table 4.5). An example of an heterogeneous group escape of Saint-Domingue-born runaways comprised three *mulâtre* men – François, Baptiste, and Catherine – and six creole counterparts: Haphie, Zabeth, and Cecile, all women, and three men Codio, Gracia, Hypolite.[27] In a separate case, three young women, Marguerite, aged 17, Barbe, aged 15, and Marie-Jeanne, aged 16 were all creoles who brought a four-month-old *griffe* baby with them during their escape from Gros-Morne.[28] Another group was composed of two *mulâtresses* named Marinette and Labonne, two creole women, Marie-Noel and Lalue, and a creole man, S. Pierre, who escaped the Piis property in Dondon in November 1785.[29] A fourth example in 1789 shows that a group of 16 absconders was composed of creole women, men, and children, and one Nagô woman.[30] *Mulâtres* had the second-lowest homogeneous group escape rate, at 3.9 percent, and the second-highest heterogeneous group escape, at 14.4 percent. This is likely because *mulâtre* children were taken with their Africa-born or colony-born creole mothers, or other family members. Similarly, *griffes* probably had immediate family members of a different race, making their group escapes inherently multi-racial at a rate of 12.5 percent. *Quarterons* were not very numerous as enslaved people or as runaways, resulting in them escaping by themselves 79.1 percent of the time and in either heterogeneous or homogeneous groups less frequently. "West" and "East" Indians had the highest level of individual escape, at 88.7 percent, and the lowest group escape rates, 11.3 percent altogether, due to their low population numbers.

INTRA-AMERICAN SLAVE TRADE CAPTIVES
IN SAINT-DOMINGUE

When discussing the notion of an emerging racial solidarity, it is also important to consider the presence of African descendants who were enslaved on other islands within the circum-Caribbean and then re-sold to Saint-Domingue. Julius Scott's (2018) renowned *The Common Wind: Afro-American Communication in the Age of the Haitian Revolution* brings attention to the intricate interconnectedness of the Caribbean by way of trade and communication networks. Enslaved and free African descendants who worked as sailors, soldiers, and traders traveled the high seas and transported with them news of events from across the islands. Similar to figures like Olaudah Equiano and Denmark Vesey, exposure to and experience with different imperial structures, plantation regimes, and African ethnic groups helped to cultivate a sense that blackness, not ethnicity, was the basis for enslavement across the Americas. The vast experiences of these "Atlantic creoles" and their observations of black people's shared circumstances across the Caribbean gave them leadership qualities that could bring together masses from disparate groups. Henry Christophe, who had been part of the siege of Savannah during the American War of Independence and who later became King of northern Haiti in the post-independence era, is said to have been born in either Grenada or Saint Christopher; and "Zamba" Boukman Dutty was brought from Jamaica on an illegal ship in the years before the Revolution. Indeed, English-speakers from Jamaica seem to be the largest enslaved Caribbean group brought to Saint-Domingue. The *Trans-Atlantic Slave Trade Database* has recently included findings from the intra-American trade, displayed in Table 4.7.

The French royal government banned most of these intra-American trades, so there is an incomplete picture of the full population of enslaved

TABLE 4.7. *Disembarkations of enslaved people to Saint-Domingue from the circum-Caribbean, all years*[31]

Year Range	Dutch Caribbean	Dominica	Jamaica	Totals
1701–1725	102	0	0	102
1726–1750	224	0	0	224
1751–1775	18	0	0	18
1776–1800	41	396	10,176	10,613
Totals	385	396	10,176	10,957

people from across the Caribbean. However, the runaway slave advertisements help to fill in those gaps and demonstrate that captives arrived not only from Jamaica, Dominica, or the Dutch Caribbean, there were also many from Spanish colonies, other French colonies, and North America. Enslaved people brought to Saint-Domingue through the circum-Caribbean trade had experiential knowledge and consciousness that they brought from their perspective locations. They spoke several languages, most commonly English, Spanish, Dutch (and the Dutch creole Papiamento), and French, and some were reading and writing proficiently in those languages. These "creoles" had exposure to information that circulated the Atlantic world via news reporting and interactions at major ports. Not only would they have known of events related to European-Americans, they also would have known about enslaved people's rebellions that occurred throughout the Caribbean. The largest number of Atlantic-zone runaways were those brought from other French colonies, especially Martinique and Guadeloupe. This is closely followed by the 1.7 percent of escapees who were formerly enslaved in colonies under English rule, mostly Jamaica and including some from Mississippi. At 1.1 percent, the third largest group of Caribbean-born runaways were from Dutch-speaking locations, mainly Curaçao, and a smaller number from Surinam (Table 4.8).

There also were AmerIndians and East Indians enslaved in Saint-Domingue, making it additionally difficult to ascribe identity in instances of missing data, which accounts for 5 percent of the sample. Fifty-three runaways were described as indigenous Caraïbes or *Indiens*. These included Joseph, a Caraïbe with "black, straight hair, the face elongated, a fierce look," who escaped in December 1788; or Jean-Louis, a Caraïbe who escaped with two Nagôs, Jean *dit* Grand Gozier and Venus, in July 1769.[32] An *Indien* named Andre, a 30-year-old cook who spoke many

TABLE 4.8. *Frequency distribution of "Atlantic Creoles"* (N = 12,857)

Colony of origin	Total	Percent
Anglais/English (Jamaica, Mississippi)	219	1.7%
Espagnol/Spanish (Cuba, Puerto Rico, Santo Domingo)	41	0.3%
Hollandais/Dutch (Curaçao, Surinam)	139	1.1%
Portugais/Portuguese	26	0.2%
Other French colony (Martinique, Guadeloupe, St. Christopher)	274	2.1%
Total	699	5.4%

languages, escaped Le Cap in July 1778; and another named Zephyr, aged 16–17, escaped the same area in late August or early September of 1780.[33] Caraïbes were native to the Lesser Antilles and perhaps were captured and enslaved in Saint-Domingue as part of the inter-Caribbean trade.[34] The origin of other *Indiens*, however, is less straightforward. Scholars generally believe that the Taíno population had completely disappeared by the eighteenth century, but this may not be entirely true. Recent developments indicate the Spanish underestimated sixteenth-century census data due to the numbers of Taíno who escaped, oftentimes with Africans, and those who were of mixed heritage.[35] Moreau de Saint-Méry witnessed indigenous people's ritual ceremonies and saw their remains and artistic artifacts throughout the north. However, he used "Indiens Occidentaux" to describe Caraïbes and other indigenous peoples brought from Canada, Louisiana, and Mississippi. Other *Indiens* were black or dark-skinned sub-continental Asian Indians, or what he called "Indiens Orientaux."[36] For example, there was Zamor, a "nègre indien … creole of Bengale … having freshly cut hair," who at age 25 escaped the Aubergiste plantation in Mirebalais in August 1783.[37] Moreau de Saint-Méry distinguished two types of East Indians: one he perceived as similar to Europeans, with straighter hair and narrow noses. The other he likened to Africans, stating they had shorter, curlier hair and were closer in relation to blacks in Saint-Domingue. Further research is needed on the enslavement of non-Africans in the French colonies, and the possible connections to the African presence in India and the Middle East.[38]

Spanish-speaking runaways escaped by themselves most often; this is perhaps an indication of their small numbers in the colony and lack of contact with others from their language group (Table 4.9). The fugitive migration trail typically tended to go from west to east, so very few escaped from the Spanish colony of Santo Domingo into Saint-Domingue. Yet, in October 1789, the commandant of St. Raphael in Santo Domingo Montenegro reported nine Kongolese men and four women missing.[39] Several other "Espagnols" listed in the advertisements were fugitives who were brought from Puerto Rico and Cuba. Small numbers and language barriers did not necessarily preclude non-Saint Dominguans from escaping with others. "Portuguese" (probably Brazilian) captives escaped in heterogeneous groups more often than in homogeneous groups, as did fugitives from Dutch, French, and English colonies. At a rate of 12.2 percent for heterogeneous group escapes, Dutch-speakers were much more likely to run away in a diverse group

TABLE 4.9. *Chi-square test, group escapes among "Atlantic Creoles"* (N = 12,857)

	Individual escape	Homogeneous group escape	Heterogeneous group escape	Total
English	150 (68.5%)	32 (14.6%)	37 (16.9%)	219 (100%)
Spanish	37 (90.2%)	0	4 (9.76%)	41 (100%)
Dutch	118 (84.9%)	4 (2.88%)	17 (12.2%)	139 (100%)
Portuguese	20 (76.9%)	2 (7.7%)	4 (15.4%)	26 (100%)
French	245 (89.4%)	7 (2.55%)	22 (8.0%)	274 (100%)
Total	570 (4.4%)	45 (.35%)	84 (.65%)	699 (5.4%)

Note: p = 0.000.

than a homogenous one. In 1770, a group of six escaped the island in a boat – they were Basile, a *mulâtre* from Curaçao; Tam, a Kongolese who spoke the Curaçaoan patois "Papimento"; Louis, a creole from Guadeloupe; François from Curaçao; Jean-Baptiste *dit* Manuel from Curaçao, and Baptiste from Curaçao.[40] English colony-born absconders had the highest rate of heterogeneous group escape. On the other hand, English-speaking runaways also escaped with each other the most. French colony runaways escaped alone at the second-highest rate, 89.4 percent, even though they had the linguistic benefit of being able to escape with Saint-Domingue-born runaways. Their French- language skills may also have been to their advantage in passing as free or cultivating relationships with free people of color.

SOCIAL NETWORK TIES AND DESTINATIONS

Alberto Melucci's *Nomads of the Present* (1989) clarifies tensions that exist between individuals and groups as they contend with one another, everyday life, and the processes of identity-making within submerged networks. He defines a "submerged network" as a system of small groups, where information and people circulate freely within the network. These networks operate in public view and are transitory, as members may have multiple memberships with limited or temporary involvement. Like ritual free spaces, submerged networks bring to light the importance of shielding these social spaces and relationships from dominating forces within society in order to maneuver with flexibility. The web of maroons, enslaved people, and free people of color that made up submerged networks created new understandings of social circumstances and circulated

TABLE 4.10. *Frequency distribution of social ties and destinations*
(N = 12,857)

Social ties and destinations	Total	Percent
Family tie	130	1.0%
Labor-/skill-related	1,632	12.7%
Plantation/area of birth	153	1.2%
Spanish territory	80	0.62%
Other runaways and free people	80	0.62%
Total	2,075	16.1%

ideas, resources, as well as strategies and tactics for collective action. An important part of the knowledge shared among the submerged networks of runaways was where one could hide once leaving the plantation. Sunday markets in the major towns like Cap Français were opportunities for blacks – free, enslaved, and runaways alike – to converge and interact, buying and selling food, exchanging services, and sharing information about issues pertinent to their lives, such as achieving freedom. Planters' advertisements often speculated about where the runaway was going, based on the enslaved person's known familial ties or the places they were known to frequent to give further alert to other whites in the areas where a runaway might be hiding. These types of location-based relationship ties from formal and informal social spheres like neighborhoods, work, or family are an influential factor in cultivating collective action participation (McAdam 1986; Gould 1995; Diani 2003). The current section analyzes five types of social ties and destinations that maroons deployed in their freedom journeys (Table 4.10).

Besides running away in small-to-large groups, fugitives used their human and social capital to flee from bondage. When possible, enslaved people attempted to connect with family members or other known associates on various plantations. Over time, the enslaved cultivated and established relationships – biological or chosen – with other enslaved people or free people of color. I coded *familial ties* if the advertisement specifically describes the runaway as having a family member in another location. A second common destination for runaways who were sold and taken elsewhere, but who sought to re-connect with social familiars, was the *plantation or parish of their birth*. Artisanal labor skills were also an important avenue for escape. Most enslaved Africans and African descendants performed hard labor in the fields of sugar, coffee, and indigo plantations – tilling land, cutting cane, tending to animals, etc. However, larger-scale operations, especially sugar plantations, had a wider array of specialized tasks and positions that men mostly occupied, allowing them more daily flexibility than field hands. Sometimes, owners leased these artisanal laborers to other planters, or the artisans leased themselves out to earn money or their freedom. In these instances, quotidian work patterns of unmonitored travel from one plantation to another, or even between different buildings on the same plantation, would have provided narrow but existing windows of opportunity to slip away without immediate detection. I coded *labor- and skill-related destinations* if the runaway had access to individuals or spaces beyond the location of their captivity because of their specialized occupation. Another common destination that emerged from the advertisements was the sparsely populated *Spanish territory*, Santo Domingo, to the east of Saint-Domingue. The imaginary border was the cause of friction between the two colonies, which runaways exploited to their benefit. The ongoing tension over the border will be discussed further in Chapter 6. Finally, I coded *free communities* to include other maroons and free people of color. In Chapters 6 through 8, I discuss in more depth the small-scale communities of runaways interspersed throughout Saint-Domingue's numerous mountain chains in hard-to-reach areas, living quietly but at times raiding nearby plantations for provisions. Enslaved people knew of these communities – and sometimes neighborhoods designated for free people of color – and were attracted to these spaces, seeking safe haven.

Gender and Birth Origin

Compared to Africans, Saint-Domingue-born African descendants were more than 10 percent likely to use family ties, and more than three times as likely to seek old plantation connections to aid their escape (Table 4.11). Creoles were born and socialized in the colony, had more familial relationships, and had more knowledge of the colony's landscape. Conventional notions that labor hierarchies followed the logic of the colony's racial stratum leads many to believe that Saint-Domingue-born creoles were preferred over Africans for artisanal labor positions. However, Africans and Atlantic creoles were more likely to have an artisanal trade than Saint-Dominguans; were more than twice as likely to flee to Santo Domingo; and were more than twice as likely to have been harbored by other maroons or free people of color. Perhaps constant movement and migration were normalized among those who were foreign to Saint-Domingue, having been brought from either Africa or other parts of the Caribbean.

TABLE 4.11. *Social ties and destinations by birth origin (1,978 observations)*

Birth origin	Family tie	Labor/skill	Plantation/area of birth	Spanish territory	Runaways/free people	Total
Saint-Domingue	103 (12.7%)	599 (70.8%)	103 (12.2%)	19 (2.3%)	22 (2.6%)	846 (100%)
Africans & Atlantic creoles	21 (1.86%)	956 (84.5%)	42 (3.7%)	57 (5.0%)	56 (4.95%)	1,132 (100%)

Note: p = 0.000

The relationship between gender and social network ties does not prove that women escaped in all-female groups as has been suggested;[41] however, it does demonstrate that social networks and mutual aid more generally were an important aspect in women's patterns of escape (Table 4.12). For example, an Ibo woman named Dauphine escaped as a maroon, taking with her a 13-year-old bi-racial girl named Gabrielle in order to return the child to her mother and siblings.[42] When adult women runaways who had some sort of destination in mind stole away from plantations, they were more likely than men to have either a family relationship, a plantation-based relationship, or contact with other runaways or free people of color. Twenty-three year old Reine escaped Port-au-Prince, possibly heading to Grande-Rivière where she had a sister who was free.[43] Women fugitives were slightly less likely than men to escape to Santo Domingo, since women relied more on their social capital and relationships to abscond.[44] In keeping with plantations' gendered divisions of labor, men were more likely to use their artisanal labor as an exit strategy, exploiting travel for errands, market days, or going to other plantations as leased labor as a window of opportunity for escape.

Labor

Enslaved people performed a variety of tasks associated with the sugar, coffee, and indigo plantation regimes, and they experienced varying levels of physical exertion, punishment, position, and privilege. The vast majority were field hands, but a select few were artisanal trade laborers or otherwise domestic workers who performed tasks that were specialized, which often allowed them to travel beyond their immediate plantation to run errands, or at times even learn to read and/or write a European language. These differentials within the enslaved labor pool might indicate a stratification by occupation that would preclude cooperation between field hands and artisanal laborers or incentivize enslaved artisans from escaping at all. However, over 1,600 maroons, or 12.7 percent of the sample (Table 4.9), were described as having a labor-related skill, and according to the *Marronnage dans le Monde Atlantique* database, 683 distinct *métiers* or jobs are found in the advertisements. Seamstresses, midwives, fishermen, hairdressers, shoemakers, carpenters, valets, coopers, sugar boilers, coaches, and *commandeurs* were just a few of occupations that were considered to have a higher rank in the enslaved labor force. These people would have had relative flexibility in their everyday lives compared to bondspeople, whose labor was confined to the plantation

TABLE 4.12. *Chi-square test, social ties and destinations by gender and age (2,075 observations)*

Gender	Family tie	Labor/skill	Plantation/area of birth	Spanish territory	Runaways/ free people	Total
Men	99 (5.66%)	1,423 (81.4%)	96 (5.5%)	68 (3.9 %)	62 (3.6%)	1,748 (100%)
Women	24 (9.6%)	158 (63.5%)	46 (18.5%)	8 (3.2 %)	13 (5.2%)	249 (100%)
Boys	5 (7.6%)	43 (65.2%)	10 (15.2%)	4 (6.1%)	4 (6.1%)	66 (100%)
Girls	2 (16.7%)	8 (66.7%)	1 (8.33%)	0	1 (8.33%)	12 (100%)
Total	130 (6.3%)	1,632 (78.7%)	153 (7.4%)	80 (3.9%)	80 (3.9%)	2,075 (100%)

Note: p = 0.000.

fields (Table 4.9). Though they were still enslaved, artisanal bondspeople in more populated urban areas had contact with people of varying walks of life and saw parts of the colony they may not have otherwise seen. Women tended to be seamstresses, hairdressers, and vendors. Merancienne, a creole woman from Martinique, was a seamstress and laundress who fled Le Cap in September of 1767, and was last seen selling eggs and poultry.[45] Another female vendor was 18-year-old Isidore of Kongo, who sold herbs and flowers on the streets of Le Cap and escaped repeatedly in 1770 and 1772.[46] Baptiste, a creole man, was both a hairdresser and a violin player who wore a blue vest and black culottes, signifying his relative privilege.[47] Even *commandeurs*, members of the enslaved labor force responsible for maintaining order among the work gangs, escaped their bondage. Scipion, an Arada bondsman, also served as a mason for his owner and ran away for the second time in the fall of 1779.[48]

Literacy in European languages dominant in the Atlantic world was another skill and form of human capital that facilitated escape. Reading and writing capabilities would have allowed fugitives to legibly forge free papers. Spoken fluency could allow runaways to present themselves to others as free persons of color whose native home was either Saint-Domingue or another colony. For example, runaways speaking Dutch or English could potentially head to a nearby port to board a ship. Thom, a *quarteron* from Saint Christopher, escaped in July 1788 and was believed to have "liaisons with the English."[49] Marie-Rose, a 14- to 16-year-old girl, spoke very good Dutch and was suspected of hiding out at the coast of Le Cap with a cook who used various alias names.[50] An unnamed *mulâtre* from Guadeloupe spoke French very well and used this knowledge to pass for free in Léogâne.[51] Simon, a creole, spoke both French and Spanish, indicating that he may have passed for free in Saint-Domingue or crossed the border into Santo Domingo.[52] Besides artisanal labor positions, linguistic skills were one of the only forms of human capital afforded to enslaved people, since most did not have access to formal education or other tools that could be translated to economic or political power. Therefore, runaways made use of the resources most readily available to them in the colonial context, including language and their social relationships.

Family and Plantation Ties

Altogether, runaways who sought out known family ties and old plantations comprised 2.2 percent of the sample (Table 4.9). It was not uncommon for enslaved people to have immediate family members who offered them refuge. Though some women attained manumission through their owners, children of these relationships were not always freed. For example, a mixed-race woman named Magdelaine sought out her free mother, Suzanne, in Cap Français.[53] Jean-Baptiste was a creole runaway who had escaped for 15 months, possibly reaching his family of free people of color living in Port-de-Paix, where he was born.[54] Other instances show that family members who were still enslaved also provided shelter, even if only for a temporary visit, for their kin. The parents of Phaëton were based on a plantation in Trou when he absconded to find them; and Venus was suspected to have found her mother, who lived in Port-Margot.[55] Plantations, especially larger ones with several housing units, could be places of refuge for runaways who were either temporary absentees or lying in wait for a fellow absconder. Père Labat claimed there was a sense of loyalty and cooperation between enslaved people and runaways, detailing the double closets slaves constructed in their cabins to conceal a friend or to hide stolen goods.[56] Desirée, a Mondongue, belonged to the Charron plantation in Acul, yet it was suspected that for some time she had been staying at the Caignet plantation, also in Acul.[57] Jean-Baptiste, a dark-skinned creole "having traits of a white" had escaped for more than 15 months, and the advertisement states he was born in Port-de-Paix, where nearly all of his family was free.[58]

Chosen kin ties were also strong, perhaps forged during the Middle Passage, and prompted people to seek out comrades from whom they had been separated. Isidore, a 22-year-old Kongolese stamped T. MILLET and G. ANSE, representing Sieur Millet of the Grand Anse region in the south, stole a canoe that was later found in Petite-Anse in the north. Millet had sold several slaves to the Balan plantation and it was suspected that Isidore was trying to rejoin them.[59] For some, being sold to an especially punitive planter could be reason enough to seek out a previous owner who was relatively benevolent. Such "master exchanges" existed in the Loango Coast areas, when mistreated enslaved people offered themselves to new owners.[60] As James Sweet has pointed out, a 16- or 17-year-old Kongolese boy named Cupidon had been missing from his owner for six months, and it was believed he was in his old master's neighborhood; another 17-year-old boy from the Kongo, Julien, escaped heading to Fort Dauphin, hoping to be reclaimed by his first owner.[61] Godparentage was another example of fictive kin relationships that supported marronnage, such as the case of Marie-Louise, also called Marie-Magdeleine, who left Eaux de Boynes and may have reached Le Cap where her godmother lived at the women's religious house.[62] Enslaved people used their family relationships to facilitate marronnage; conversely it also stands to reason that they used marronnage to sustain their familial relationships. Despite the practice of slaveowners selling bondspeople to plantations across the colony and away from their familiars, enslaved people and maroons risked their lives to actively nurture their kin relationships and to aid each other in their attempts to self-liberate. Another potential advantage for escapees was having a connection to free people of color or an established maroon community, since these groups could offer protection, housing, and resources like food, clothing, or arms.

Santo Domingo and Free Communities

Interestingly, escaping to Spanish Santo Domingo and seeking out other communities of runaways or free people of color were the least common destinations – each accounting for only 0.62 percent of the sample observations (Table 4.9). The low reporting of runaways fleeing to Santo Domingo and to self-liberated encampments contrasts with several complaints from planters and accounts by former *maréchaussée* leaders that attest to the presence of absconders both in Saint-Domingue and across the eastern border. Military sources also indicated that Saint-Dominguan runaways settled in Santo Domingo and married locals.[63] This could have been the case with Cupidon and Bernard, both Kongolese men who had disappeared ten years before 1787; Jacques, a Mondongue, who was missing for five years; and l'Eveille, an Igbo man missing for two years. The advertisement speculates that they were in Santo Domingo because the four men had not been seen at all since they escaped.[64] Others traversed into Santo Domingo to trade with or work for the Spanish, such as Gillot, who was considered very dangerous because he stole horses and mules, then sold them to the Spanish.[65] A Mondongue woman named Franchette had been at large for three years and was known for her business dealings with the Spanish.[66] French planters' concerns about runaways to Santo Domingo will be discussed in more depth in Chapter 6.

Free people of color provided refuge to runaways as well, although they risked losing their freedom for doing so, such as Hercule who was sold to the king of France in March 1768.[67] The neighborhood of Petit Guinée in Cap Français was a regular destination for runaways to find housing, lease themselves out for pay, and blend in with the growing population of free people of color. While many free people of color were wealthy slave owners themselves, manumitted slaves of the *affranchi* class maintained biological and social ties to enslaved people and at times offered them shelter, food, clothing, or work. In June 1786, an absconder named Toussaint, along with a group of slaves and free blacks, was accused of theft. Toussaint was flogged and hanged in the public square of Le Cap, and the others were whipped and sentenced to the chain gang for forging free passes and taking up rental rooms for a freeman named Larose.[68] Marie-Jeanne, a creole woman who disguised herself as a man, escaped from Petit Saint-Louis on March 5, 1788 and was presumed to have been sheltered by free people of color; and in 1771, eight men and two women from the Fessard plantation in the Black mountains were suspected of hiding with free people of color.[69] Four runaways of the Nagô nation – a man named Jean and three women named Rosalie, Jeanneton, and Marie – fled a Petite-Anse plantation with their work tools and other essential items and were suspected of being concealed by other slaves or free people of color.[70] A Kongo woman named Zaire was suspected of escaping with a woman from another plantation, as they had escaped around the same time. Zaïre was believed to have been staying in either Limonade, Trou, or Terrier Rouge, where free people of color may have been hiding her.[71] These examples not only indicate the existence of collaboration between enslaved people and maroons, they also highlight the role of some free people of color in aiding efforts for liberation – even at the expense of their own interests.

CONCLUSION

Group escape was one vehicle through which runaways exhibited or cultivated relationships and trust – people decided to escape with familiars from slave ships, living quarters, or work gangs, individuals who were willing to take a life-threatening risk, or were otherwise in their immediate proximity. Over time, group escapes did become more frequent, although not as frequent as individual escapes, and the average group size slightly increased each year. Generally, it was easiest to build ties for marronnage with members of the same ethnic, religious, linguistic, or regional background. This explains why homogeneity remained a prevalent characteristic of most group escapes. These racially/ethnically cohesive mobilization network patterns mirrored those that appeared among rebel bands that were organized by nation during the early years of the Haitian Revolution, such as the Nagô, Gold Coast, Moco (Igbo), or the Kongolese fighters led by Macaya.[72]

However, by recruiting and mobilizing people of a different racial or ethnic backgrounds, runaways exhibited the growing importance of racial solidarity. Heterogeneous group marronnage increased slowly after 1784, and though the rate was still less than homogeneous group escapes, it was closely associated with longer lengths of escape, which I discuss in Chapter 5. Moreover, longer lengths of escape were reported before the Revolution. Therefore, heterogeneous marronnage has interesting implications for understanding the importance of "weak ties" in successful marronnage leading to the Haitian Revolution. Although previously existing relationships have long been acknowledged as important resources in building one's social capital, there is also value in transient, "weak" relationships with those outside the scope of one's immediate trust networks. While homogeneity in a personal network can help foster confidence, trustworthiness, and a sense of cohesion, heterogeneity exposes people to new knowledge, information, resources, and opportunities (Granovetter 1973). Social ties can lead to participation in mobilization (McAdam 1988), but heterogeneity in those collective action networks also contributes to shared affinity with a cause and the production of a singular identity over time (Melucci 1985, 1989; Taylor and Whittier 1992; Diani 1997). Diversity of skills and knowledge was beneficial for a dangerous venture such as marronnage, because a mistake or gap in timing, resources, or information could be life-threatening. Though it required a considerable amount of trust among participants, a diverse composition of marronnage groups was a successful strategy for escape.

It is true that colony-born creoles were more likely to escape alone or in homogeneous groups, while Africans escaped in groups more often than did creoles. Also, overall, creoles did not have more social ties and destinations than Africans, except for plantation- and kin-based connections. Women especially used their relationships with family, plantation-based connections, other runaways, and free people of color to facilitate escape. This sheds empirical light on previous speculations that personal networks shaped women's marronnage. Conversely, Africans were more likely to head to Santo Domingo, to other runaways, and used their labor skills to escape. Chapter 5 will demonstrate that while conventional wisdom suggests that creoles were more "successful" at marronnage because of the social capital afforded by previously existing connections, this may not have been completely true because refuge in Santo Domingo and inter-ethnic group escapes were two of the most effective means of achieving longer lengths of self-liberation. Saint-Dominguan creoles were more likely to pass for free, which was another effective way of staying free. Still, it seems that in marronnage, building weaker ties through reaching out to people from other backgrounds and seeking unfamiliar lands to the east had more pay-off in terms of duration of escape.

Micromobilization theory suggests that temporal stages of participation are important when considering who joins collective action efforts, why they join and when, and what their participation qualitatively looks like (Ward 2015, 2016). At times, it may not necessarily look like participation at all, particularly if the overall movement is in abeyance. However, awareness of and sympathies for a cause can indirectly or directly contribute to action, given the right timing and circumstances, available resources, and linkages to people who are already involved. Runaways and slaves were not necessarily discrete categories of social actors, they represented different stages of human activity that may or may not have transformed into collective action. We will see repeat absconders discussed in Chapter 5, and in Chapter 8, enslaved people who escaped, were re-captured or returned voluntarily, then escaped again only to bring along others or to become part of a wider uprising. The linkages created or exemplified by runaway groups, and their ongoing contact with plantations – via raids, hideouts, recruiting, or kidnapping – fostered an oppositional consciousness that may not necessarily have manifested itself in an immediate sense, but unfolded over time. Chapter 7 will further engage micro-level and aggregate patterns of marronnage within the historical context to identify factors that contributed to, or hindered, escapes.

5

Marronnage as Reclamation

Marronnage, in many ways, was about enslaved people reclaiming possession of themselves and other intangible and tangible resources that enslavers stole from them. Colonial society aimed to nullify enslaved Africans' identities and sever ties to their cultural heritages. Enslavers commodified enslaved people, extracted their labor power for no compensation, dominated enslaved people's time, and denied them access to any form of capital. Maroons upended these conditions through various acts to reclaim themselves, their time, and their resources, representing a "dialectical response to the capitalist plantation system whose imperative was to reduce them to units of labor power – to dehumanize them," as Sylvia Wynter has argued (n.d.: 73–74). Maroons' actions reflected their oppositional consciousness, which is defined as a "set of insurgent ideas and beliefs constructed and developed by an oppressed group for the purpose of guiding its struggle to undermine, reform, or overthrow a system of domination" (Morris 1992: 363). In reversing the conditions of dispossession, maroons' acts of reclamation at the micro-level were foundational for revolutionary tactics and eventually expanded to the larger project of socio-political reclamation of the nation *Ayiti*/Haiti (Roberts 2015). The current chapter attempts to detect an oppositional consciousness among enslaved African descendants and maroons in the years before the Haitian Revolution. Social scientists do not often consider the Haitian Revolution, and its antecedent forms of resistance, to be part of the revolutionary processes that constituted the making of the modern era (Bhambra 2016). However, through their oppositional actions during marronnage, runaways embodied their own social, economic, and political projects by reclaiming personal sovereignty, asserting themselves as free and equal citizens, and building solidarity through their social networks. While colonists' definitions of freedom and liberty meant having the right to engage in the "free trade" and enslaving of human flesh, maroons enacted opposing forms of modernity, giving meaning to the revolutionary slogan *"liberté, égalité, fraternité"* well before the 1789 Declaration of the Rights of Man.

In Saint-Domingue and other French colonies, the *Code Noir* outlined royal dictates for enslaved people's behavior and the status of their condition. The *Code Noir* articulated the economic, social, and political apparatuses that bolstered the subjugation and enslavement of African people while justifying the brute force violence of the colonial plantation enterprise. Though the *Code Noir* was in part written with the intention to "protect" the enslaved with guidelines for punishments, enslavers in Saint-Domingue generally disregarded top-down policies from the French crown and exerted physical punishments that exceeded regulations issued by the king. The *Code Noir* implemented strict rules that were designed to constrain black people's everyday behaviors and movements, with the assumption that access to freedom of movement, time, material resources and forms of capital, political power, and the ability to bear arms would contribute to rebellion. The *Code Noir* barred enslaved people from congregating with others from different plantations for any purpose without the written permission of their owner, riding horses, or walking on the roads after dark; it prohibited them from carrying weapons in public, and in the aftermath of the Mackandal case, any enslaved person carrying a sword or a machete could face three months in prison. According to Articles XVIII, XIX, and XXIV of the *Code Noir*, the enslaved could not sell any sugarcane under any circumstances, could not profit from the sale of commodities or foodstuffs at markets without the slave owner's permission, and were not allowed to earn income for the trade of subsistence food on their days off. Particularly in the aftermath of the Seven Years War, eighteenth-century Saint-Domingue was an increasingly repressive society where philosophies and scientific ideologies of white supremacy took root and further shaped constrictions on the enslaved and even free people of color. For example, black people were not allowed to bear the names of their white patrons, or even wear clothing items or hairstyles that might convey similarity to French culture; free people of color were banned from practicing medicine and eventually were banned from mainland France altogether.[1]

Plantation owners and members of the management class benefitted from the power dynamics created by the *Code Noir*, which authorized them to exert control and surveillance upon all areas of enslaved people's lives. Drawing on the likes of Paulo Freire and Frantz Fanon, John Gaventa has argued that such stark imbalances rely on three dimensions of power: brute force tactics; social, economic, and political apparatuses that preclude the subordinated from seeking or obtaining power; and, most notably found in colonial situations, the hegemonic "shaping of wants, values, roles, and beliefs of the colonized (Gaventa 1980: 32)." This combination of tripartite power dynamics, when they are fully exercised, can make rebellion even more difficult to observe. In such extreme conditions of structural powerlessness — accompanied by hegemonic cultures and ideologies that legitimate social, economic, and political disparities — some might assume that the lack of major enslaved people's rebellions in Saint-Domingue, such as those that occurred in places like Jamaica and Brazil, would point to a general quiescence to domination and injustice. Enslavers often assumed that bondspeople accepted their status and desired to mimic the behaviors of whites, such as adopting styles of dress or dance movements from France, for instance. It was not uncommon for plantation owners to incentivize docility and deference with trinkets or money. For example, Fort Dauphin planter Louis Tousard incorrectly thought it wise to pacify a rebellious enslaved *commandeur* named Pierre Loulou with a new coat.[2] However, Tousard's attempt was a response to the "onstage" face that enslaved people like Pierre Loulou had to present in order to avoid violent punishments and to prevent suspicion of their "offstage" actions, or behaviors that occurred beyond the immediate sight or understanding of power-holders and opposed control of the dominant class (Scott 1990).

It is the contention of this book that the enslaved of Saint-Domingue never fully internalized the logic of their subordination into their collective consciousness, evinced by the perpetuation of African-based rituals and militaristic ideas, and the island's *longue-durée* tradition of marronnage. Individual and collective actions that violated either parts or entire systems of oppression and the hegemonic ideologies or cultures of ruling classes are a window through which to see oppositional consciousness. The enslaved regularly transgressed colonial restrictions; for example, enslaved people bought and sold goods, or leased themselves out as laborers at the *nègre marche* in Port-au-Prince and Le Cap. However, other actions – especially those undertaken by maroons when they fled – not only speak to enslaved people's desires for economic autonomy, but point toward conceptions of themselves as 'free' with the right and liberty to define their identities, to self-protect, and to determine the course of their own lives. When enslaved people escaped, they knew that they were risking their own death, and that of loved ones, and needed protection and resources to enhance the probability of a successful escape. To do this, they had to violate the colony's policies and assume certain specific oppositional actions to ensure their survival.

This chapter brings attention to how maroons reclaimed their humanity by reimagining their status and identity, taking possession of forms of capital and raw materials that upheld and sustained plantations' divisions of labor, adopting tactics of self-arming and militancy, and reclaiming their time. The fugitive advertisements placed in *Les Affiches américaines* give some insight into the minds of runaways by speculating on the actions they took in the minutes or days before or after they fled. Rather than interpret these actions through the lens of enslavers' foreshadowing of maroons' movements for the purposes of surveillance and re-enslavement, this chapter employs subaltern analysis of maroon actions as they are linked to a broader sense of collective consciousness regarding freedom and liberation. Subversive reading of the advertisements highlights maroons' *hidden* transcripts, their oppositional actions, gestures, and practices that "confirm, contradict, or inflect" the narratives that plantation personnel sought to convey within the *public* transcript – the very same advertisement deployed to re-establish and reaffirm control over the enslaved (Scott 1990: 2–5). While Chapter 7 will bring attention to macro-level economic, political, and environmental changes that affected trends of marronnage as a repertoire of contention, the current chapter narrows down to the micro-level actions that were influenced by shared consciousness and that constituted the tactics of marronnage. Repertoire tactics can include a wide range of activities such as civil disobedience, confrontations with police, consciousness raising, strikes, bodily assault and murder, throwing objects, looting, singing, arson, and many other actions (Taylor and Van Dyke 2004). Macro-historical contexts shape the types of tactics that can be used within a particular setting; enslaved people's "toolkit" of resistance tactics was generally narrow, including mostly individualized and embodied resistance actions such as suicide, work tool sabotage, or feigning illness, as well as other actions that were most immediately feasible.

Verta Taylor and Nella Van Dyke identify three characteristics of repertoire tactics, "contestation, intentionality, and the construction of collective identity (2004: 268)," that can make claims-making during marronnage more easily identifiable. Maroons' repertoire tactics relied on embodied acts of contestation to pursue changes in structural power relations (see Tables 5.1–5.3), and to help develop oppositional

TABLE 5.1. *Frequency distribution of oppositional actions, (N = 12,857)*

Oppositional actions	Total	Percent
Passing as free	576	4.5%
Appropriation of goods	410	3.2%
Bearing arms	64	0.5%
Repeat escape	58	0.45%
Total	1,108	8.6%

TABLE 5.2. *Chi-square test, oppositional actions by gender and age (N = 12,857)*

Gender	Passing as free	Appropriation of goods	Bearing arms	Repeat escape	Total
Men	429 (48.6%)	350 (39.7%)	58 (6.6%)	45 (5.1%)	882 (100%)
Women	129 (72.9%)	34 (19.2%)	2 (1.1%)	12 (6.7%)	177 (100%)
Boys	11 (31.4%)	19 (54.3%)	4 (11.4%)	1 (2.86%)	35 (100%)
Girls	7 (50%)	7 (50%)	0	0	14 (100%)
Total	576 (52%)	410 (37%)	64 (5.8%)	58 (5.2%)	1,108 (%100)

Note: $p = 0.000$.

TABLE 5.3. *Chi-square test, oppositional actions by birth origin (1,068 observations)*

Birth origins	Passing as free	Appropriation of goods	Bearing arms	Repeat escape	Total
Saint-Domingue	301 (58.9%)	168 (32.88%)	22 (4.31%)	20 (3.91%)	511 (100%)
Africans & Atlantic creoles	259 (46.5%)	223 (40.04%)	40 (7.18%)	35 (6.28%)	557 (100%)

Note: $p = 0.000$.

consciousness and collective identity. One way runaways reimagined their status and identity was by passing as free. Before retreating from plantations, some runaways who could read or write in French or other European languages – a form of human capital that was valued in the Americas – replicated documents to declare themselves free. Others found "fancy" clothing or otherwise disguised themselves to be considered as part of the population of free people of color. Maroons also enacted intentionality through strategic decision-making and conscious intentions to create lasting change for themselves. They appropriated material goods and technologies through looting horses, mules, or canoes to reach their chosen hideout quickly, or they took money, clothing, or food to consume or to exchange at a market. They empowered themselves with militant actions by bearing arms such as guns, sabers, sickles, and other work tools as they prepared to endure the high-risk action of living in marronnage. Finally, maroons reclaimed themselves and their time by repeatedly escaping or remaining at-large for longer periods of time. Those who escaped repeatedly faced increasingly violent repercussions with each return, yet fear of brutal punishment was not enough to dissuade the most resolute fugitives. By fleeing, maroons denied the plantocracy access to their knowledge pools they had garnered as enslaved laborers and marshalled those resources toward the creation of self-freed social networks and independent living zones. The time that maroons appropriated not only allowed them to live on self-defined terms, it also facilitated the space to recruit others into marronnage. The diffusion of oppositional ideas and tactics, through the repertoire tactic of marronnage, helped to spread collective consciousness and solidarity as the Haitian Revolution approached.

REIMAGINING STATUS AND IDENTITY

Passing as Free

Though the *Code Noir* allowed unmarried slave owners to marry bondswomen and manumit them and their resulting children, most enslaved people in Saint-Domingue had few options for formal emancipation from slavery – even when the law was on their side. For example, a group of six *mulâtres* were scheduled for manumission by their owner, and soon after his death they parted from the plantation. Unbeknownst to them, he had not actually freed them and they were still considered fugitives. Four of the men were returned, but one woman and her children remained at large. She won her freedom in court, but it was later revoked and the women were re-enslaved.[3] For many, freedom dreams could only be fulfilled through marronnage – even though Saint-Domingue's intendent declared in 1767 that maroons would never be formally recognized as free – maroons embodied liberated identities regardless of legal recognition.[4] Henriette, a Kongolese woman around 30 years old, escaped her owner in Le Cap during the night in mid-November 1771. Henriette was described as a thin woman with an elongated chin and was noted for her work as a good seamstress, laundress, and ironer. The advertisement placed for her return could not definitively state whether she left as a maroon on the 14th or 15th, meaning that Henriette had effectively slipped away without her absence being detected for at least two days. However, by the time the advertisement was published in *Les Affiches américaines* two weeks later on November 30, the contact person on the advertisement – Sieur Trutou, a hat maker from Le Cap – had begun to speculate that Henriette was presenting herself as a free woman of color.[5] Given her expertise in sewing and cleaning clothes, Henriette indeed may have been able to create outfits to adorn herself in a similar style to Saint-Domingue's free women of color, who were famed for their fashion sense, and to blend into that group as she set out as a self-liberated woman.

The repertoire tactics of marronnage were actions that people knew how use and were feasible given the confines of the context in which they lived. Enslaved people's awareness of the free population, and its political, economic, and social influence in Saint-Domingue, was part of the societal context within which maroons inserted themselves as liberated people. The most common way fugitives embodied oppositional consciousness and countered colonial era codes was to blend into the population of free people of color, at times by replicating documents or verbally attesting to their non-slave status. Of the total runaway population, 576 people, nearly 5 percent of runaways, either replicated or took free papers, disguised themselves as a free person of color, or took extended liberties with their *billets* or "tickets," which were written slips that allowed an individual enslaved person to travel with their enslaver's permission (Table 5.1). Many advertisements used the phrase "se disant libre" – calls themselves free – to indicate that fugitives were self-presenting or telling people that they were a free person of color. Any enslaved person who pretended to be free but could not produce an eyewitness to verify their emancipation could be fined 3,000 *livres* and punished by a sentence of three months in prison; and anyone caught in public after eleven o'clock at night would receive 15 whip lashes.[6] Yet these punishments did not deter maroons from reimagining their status in order to reinforce a sense of dignity, self-respect, and liberation.

Enslaved women like Henriette were much more likely than men to choose attempting to pass as free as a marronnage tactic (Table 5.2). David Geggus attributes the differences in gender and birth origin in passing for free as linked to free people of color and the notion that lighter-skinned women had an easier time blending with free women. Creole women, especially those who were domestic laborers, may have had better access to writing materials and the plantation owners' files to replicate or take tickets or passes. For example, a creole woman named Rosette had already been missing for three months when an advertisement for her disappearance was published on November 23, 1771. Rosette had lived in France with her owner for ten years and, upon returning to Saint-Domingue, decided to free herself and to articulate her status as such.[7] The economic power of free women of color in Le Cap and Port-au-Prince would have been an attractive and attainable achievement for a woman like Rosette, whose long-term residence in France would have deepened her cultural competency and language skills, which would have allowed her to become a member, on her own terms, of the *gens du couleur*. On the other hand, Africanity bore its own relation to freedom pursuits. Clarice, a 45-year-old Arada woman, took her ten-year-old creole daughter as she fled their owner in Port-au-Prince during the winter of 1790. The advertisement announcing their marronnage specified that Clarice had "the marks of her country," or cultural scarifications, and that her unnamed daughter also had a scar on her upper eyelids. Neither of them had been stamped by their owner in Saint-Domingue, but Clarice did bear the stamp of the ship that transported her from the Bight of Benin to the Caribbean.[8] The advertisement's composer highlighted Clarice and her daughter's scars not just to identify them, but to differentiate them as African, which presumably put them at a disadvantage in the French colony. However, we might consider Clarice's scars as part of a Fon-based cultural heritage that would have informed her self-declared freedom. If Clarice was born around 1745, the Dahomean-Oyo conflicts were likely part of the context of her adulthood and increasingly shaped her worldview as she and others faced the instability of freedom at the Bight of Benin.

The gendered dimension of passing for free in marronnage, combined with the fact that enslaved women were more likely to be manumitted by their owners than enslaved men, means that even as enslaved women reclaimed their freedom, they in some ways conceptualized freedom within the boundaries of the colony's legal frameworks. The constrained possibilities for freedom shaped the imagination of what could be actualized. However, enslaved men were also structurally privy to avenues to emancipation through service to the *maréchaussée* – the police force primarily composed of freemen of color tasked with chasing fugitive runaways – and through self-purchase using funds saved from artisanal trade work. Despite the prominence of free women of color in the port cities, for women passing as free at times meant traversing gender identity and assuming masculinity. For example, a creole woman named Helene from the Paterson plantation called herself free and was described as "disguising herself often as a man," as did a Kongo woman named Esther who fled disguised as a man.[9] Similarly, an advertisement posted on August 15, 1789 announced the escape of a creole woman named Victoire, who fled as a maroon from a Grande-Riviere de Jacmel plantation three years earlier and was often seen frequenting the areas between Jacmel and Léogâne. Victoire was described as a beautiful 40-year-old – which may be part of the reason she chose to belie her attractiveness by disguising herself as a man and wearing the uniform of the *maréchaussée*.[10] For Victoire, the audaciousness of marronnage not only meant assuming the appearance of a member of the free people of color class; it also entailed performing militarized maleness, which was seemingly effective since she was able to avoid capture for three years.

Saint-Domingue-born creoles were more likely (though not considerably so) than Africans and other Atlantic creoles to pass as free (Table 5.3). This is probably because enslaved people from Saint-Domingue were likely to have had closer proximity to the necessary tools to accomplish this aim – such as European language literacy, a trade, or household wares like clothing and writing materials. However, though other Atlantic creoles may not have been fully accustomed to the French language and Saint-Domingue's landscape, several Caribbean-born runaways seem to have had the advantage of speaking, reading, or writing the dominant languages of the Atlantic world and they used these capabilities to move fluidly from enslavement to self-fashioned freedom. Marc, a bi-racial creole man from Martinique, was a cook who escaped wearing a blue frock coat and his hair in a ponytail. The advertisement stated that Marc was very "clever" and was perhaps carrying a fake ticket to attest to his freedom.[11] Emmanuel was a maroon described as a "creole of the Spanish islands," who had a slim figure, was missing two of his front teeth, and wore a short beard. Emmanuel had escaped his owner in Le Cap on more than one occasion. The first time, he was arrested with several others from the same plantation and they were placed in the jail at Saint Marc. The second time Emmanuel escaped, between the end of October and the first of November 1779, seems to have been the last time he was officially seen: he took his clothes and was passing as free near Fort Dauphin. Emmanuel was also described as speaking English, Dutch, and Spanish, which would have allowed him to traverse into Santo Domingo undetected as a free black man. Language seems to have facilitated his passage into freedom – two years after the first advertisement was published, he had still not been found.[12]

Other cases problematize the question of who had access to self-fashioned freedom that was legible in Saint-Domingue; those born in the Caribbean were not the only ones who were exposed to a wide array of cultural, religious, and linguistic practices. Catherine was a laundress born in the Kongo, who may have experienced relations with Portuguese colonists, traders, and enslavers while in her homeland. When she escaped her owner in Dondon, she set out "calling herself Portuguese, or sometimes Swedish, knowing how to speak Spanish."[13] We do not know the nature of Catherine's familiarity with the Portuguese and the Spanish – it is possible that she was transported to the Caribbean on ships owned by either country – but what is clear is that she used her experiences from the Middle Passage to her advantage. Similarly, Jean, a wigmaker by trade who also was born in the Kongo, was described as calling himself creole since his good French and little Spanish made him "able to play the role of a free negro by his intelligence." His owners also suspected that Jean had taken several pieces of gold with him as he escaped.[14]

Appropriating Material Goods and Technologies

Not only was enslaved labor exploited for no compensation, enslaved people were prohibited from financially benefitting from other types of economic activity such as trading food, sugarcane, or other commodities. To counter being dispossessed of any economic autonomy, maroons gravitated to cities and town markets to participate in "market marronnage" (Sweeney 2019). Enslaved people in the areas surrounding Cap Français were exposed to many of the luxuries available in the city, which attracted people from all walks of life, especially during the weekend markets. Urban slaves, African, and mixed-race individuals alike purchased their own freedom and in some instances went on to own businesses and real estate. The Petit Guinée ("Little Africa") neighborhood was composed of *gens du couleur* and *affranchis* and was a magnet for runaways, enabling them to socialize and rent rooms as they re-fashioned their lives as free people. During a search of Petit Guinée in the early 1780s, police found over 200 runaways.[15] Le Cap was a rowdy city of 20,000, patrolled by fewer than 20 police officers – leading to the 1785 Chamber of Agriculture report about *calendas* and other gatherings of slaves (see Chapter 3).[16] In June 1786, colonial authorities flogged and hanged a group of maroons, enslaved people, and free blacks accused of theft in the public square of Le Cap; they whipped and sentenced others to the chain gang for forging free passes and renting rooms from a freeman named Larose.[17] On the night of January 15, 1785, the group had entered the room of a free *mulâtress* named Catherine and stole furniture and other effects. Included in the court statement were François, an enslaved man who belonged to a free woman named Jeannette; Colas, a slave; Bijou; Alexandre; Jean-Louis, an enslaved Kongolese; Versailles; Jean Louis, an enslaved Mondongue; Anne; Sieur Masse; Hypolite; Cesar, an enslaved mattress maker; Toussaint, a maroon who formerly was enslaved by the free widow Jupiter; and Jean-Louis, a creole wigmaker.[18]

The complex strata of race, color, status, and class in Le Cap made these kinds of informal economic activities possible. The population density of the city and the ongoing interactions between enslaved people, free people of color, and runaways facilitated connections between them to circumvent colonial structures through rebellions, conspiracies, and other forms of resistance. Both enslaved people and maroons took part in informal trading of wares and illicit expropriation of resources to bolster a sense of economic independence and freedom. People of African descent attempted to demonstrate economic autonomy and accumulate various amounts of capital, even when it cost them their lives to do so. In January 1775, three men in Le Cap – Joseph Lacroix, who worked as clerk for Sieur Foäche, and two enslaved men named Jolicœur and David – were arrested for breaking into Foäche's safe and stealing 70,000 *livres*. While Jolicœur and David were returned to their enslavers, Lacroix received a harsher sentence, death by hanging in the marketplace, since he used his key to enter Foäche's house.[19] Mardy, a Kongo man, was convicted in 1784 of burglarizing and assassinating his enslaver, for which he was disemboweled on the breaking wheel torture device and decapitated. The authorities exposed his head on a pike at Fossette, outside Le Cap, where enslaved people typically performed their burial rites.[20] Two enslaved men and one woman sawed a hole in a white man's home in Limbé and stole merchandise, an offense for which they were executed in 1786.[21] A creole man named Cezar, owned by a Capuchin priest, was accused of trafficking enslaved women and men from Gonaïves and attempting to make money from the sales, which was a violation of the 1758 Le Cap ruling. After the discovery of Cezar's plan, he was condemned to death by hanging; also prosecuted were the proprietor who rented him a room and the free people of color who replicated Cezar's free papers.[22]

Maroons also appropriated resources that could be considered forms of capital that could allow them to participate in the market for trade, or enable them to use materials for subsistence farming and consumption within self-liberated communities. Although many enslaved people attempted to escape spontaneously when they viewed an immediate window of opportunity, others planned their journey as carefully as possible. Careful deliberation was necessary to avoid capture and to reach a chosen destination. Food, money, clothing, or horses – which the enslaved were prohibited from riding – were necessary for survival or to expedite the escape, and over 400 runaways appropriated such items during marronnage. Africans and other Atlantic creoles were over 7 percent more likely to steal items and provisions in order to escape than those born in Saint-Domingue (Table 5.3). In addition to taking flight in boats and canoes to navigate Saint-Domingue's waterways, maroons also took horses as either a means of transportation or to sell as livestock. Marie-Louise, a 'Sénégaloise woman,' and Prince, a Bambara man, fled as maroons from Terrier-Rouge and stole a red horse from a plantation in Trou as they made their escape.[23] Another couple, an unnamed woman and man, escaped Le Cap on a horse as they headed to Jean Rabel.[24]

A work gang *commandeur* named Petit-Jean fled a Port-à-Piment plantation on horseback after taking possession of three to four thousand *livres* worth of gold and clothing that allowed him to pass as free.[25] Twenty-five-year-old Azor of the Mondongue nation was a maroon suspected of conspiring with other blacks to steal a chest full of silver, jewelry, handkerchiefs and other articles, and a wallet containing various papers.[26] Some runaways seized opportunities to take items that were not necessarily directly needed for survival but may have served a purpose that was more significant – though difficult to discern. Free papers and replicated passes may not have been the only documents of interest to fugitives: for example, a creole man named Andre escaped with an unnamed woman who had been charged with fleeing the prison of Le Cap, taking with them papers belonging to the manager of the Damare plantation.[27] Many runaways embodied more than one oppositional action, appropriating plantation materials and arming themselves. For example, Pierre, a creole of Gros-Morne, left as a maroon with a horse, 600 *livres*, guns, a machete, and was wearing the jacket of his owner Adam Courier.[28] Several advertisements were published over the course of four years for a Mozambican runaway named Nérestan, who escaped more than once between 1786 and 1790 and was seen wielding a large machete and claiming to be free. Nérestan had taken refuge among enslaved people from several sugar plantations around Matheux, who brought him stolen goods in exchange for rum that he bought from local drink stands.[29]

MILITANCY

Repertoire tactics that involve some level of militancy, such as violence, and other forms of public disruption are considered effective means of creating change because they require actors to assume an increased commitment to the actions, and because of the level of uncertainty such actions engender among power-holders (Taylor and Van Dyke 2004: 280). Planters rightly feared violent uprisings of the enslaved, as violence represented not only clear discontent with the conditions of enslavement but a direct reciprocation of the violence that planters inflicted on the enslaved. Enslavers used violence to extract labor power, conversely in some cases "to kill the owner of the slaves' labor power was the only way in which to regain ownership of that labor power" (Wynter n.d.: 134). Even at the risk of sure execution mandated by the *Code Noir* as punishment for killing or even physically assaulting a white person, bondspeople's arming of themselves and uprisings against their owners became more frequent as the enslaved population increased.

In August 1758, 13 men and two women armed with guns, machetes, and billhooks attacked Thomas Bouchet of the southern Nippes district.[30] In 1775, a runaway named Francisque killed a plantation accountant.[31] The following year, a group of seven killed their owner named Poncet, a planter in Trou, who may have been some of the slaves' father. Sannon, a *quarteron*, and Guillaume were sentenced to death and public exposure of their corpses. Several others were charged for their role in Poncet's murder: a *commandeur* named Saintonge and a miller and coachman named Boussole were sentenced to death by being broken on the wheel; a *quarteron* woman named Sannite or Gogo was sentenced to death by strangulation after the birth of her child; and two "negres *nouveaux*," Paul and Etienne, were sentenced to assist with the execution of the others and to serve in the chain gang in perpetuity.[32] A black woman named Rosalie killed her owner, Gautarel, with a knife in 1779, for which she was sentenced to having her hands cut off, and to be hanged and burned.[33] Also in 1779, runaways from the plantation La Ferronaye at Grand Rivière du Nord set fire to the sugarcane and poisoned the plantation steward and the overseer.[34] In April 1784, an Igbo man named Saint-Eloy was sentenced to death by strangulation for just hitting a white man.[35] Lafortune killed his owner at Dondon in May 1786 by stabbing him in the chest and side, and he was sentenced to death at the breaking wheel.[36]

Bearing Arms

Enslaved people were barred from carrying weapons in the colony but did so routinely, for instance, carrying *mayombo* fighting sticks at *calenda* ritual gatherings or when they were attempting to free themselves. They used work tools such as machetes and sickles, or stole pistols, hunting rifles, and swords as they faced the imminent danger of their journey. This type of hardware was familiar, or at least suitable, to Africans from regions where hand-to-hand combat was most common in warfare. Africans used swords, battleaxes, spears, firearms like muskets, and poison-laced arrows in their fighting styles and would have made effective use of available tools and weapons as maroons and rebels (Thornton 1999). Sixty-four absconders, mostly Africans and other Atlantic creoles, prepared themselves by illegally carrying some sort of weapon like a gun or a machete, and were considered armed and dangerous (Tables 5.1 and 5.3). La Fortune, an Arada *commandeur*, was believed to be armed with a machete when he escaped a Marmelade plantation in on July 1, 1790.[37] In May 1790, four African men from the "Maquoua" nation, Alerte, Adonis, Azor, and Polite, escaped the Mongirard plantation at l'Islet-a-Pierre-Joseph with guns, pistols, gunpowder, lead and other materials.[38] Two creoles, Cambray and Charlot, escaped carrying a sword and a machete.[39] Jannitte, a creole man, had escaped for two months in 1767 with a gun, a machete, and other effects.[40] Pierre Baillard escaped in January 1775 with a machete and two knives.[41] In February 1773, an entire group of armed runaways escaped Quarter Morin in the north: four men, Joseph, Belair, l'Africain, Theodore, and three women, Catherine, Colette, and Leonore; they were all Aradas and each took with them their sickles and hatchets.[42]

RECLAMATION OF TIME

One of the more critical – or perhaps even the "ultimate resource for collective action" that runaways appropriated and could use for the purpose of organizing other maroons and potential rebels was time. Time is not abstract nor is it infinite, which limits certain social actors from feasibly performing certain tasks in the work of collective action

(Oliver and Marwell 1992: 257). Enslaved people were structurally dis-advantaged in organizing themselves for revolt because their time was almost entirely monopolized by the demands of rigorous plantation labor regimes. Labor was highly regimented and in between tasks, there was little time for rest, recreation, or social connectivity until nightfall or Sundays. Some sugar plantations were 24-hour operations where laborers were separated by shifts, getting as little as four hours of sleep per night. *Commandeurs*, other plantation personnel, and the *maréchaussée* closely monitored enslaved people's time that was not spent directly on work to instill social control and prevent escape or any other type of resistance action. Time was socially constructed within a context of extreme inequality and relations of dominance and subordination to reinforce the economic, social, and political power of white slave owners.

Time was racialized and was a valuable form of capital; enslavers accumulated labor and financial capital through the extraction of enslaved people's time (Mills 2014). Racial time – meaning the temporal inequality that emerged from unequal power relations between racially dominant and subaltern groups (Hanchard 1999) – was the very structure that maroons challenged as they struggled for autonomy by appropriating time, for shorter periods as *petit* maroons or for longer periods as *grand* maroons. Just as time was not innocuous for enslavers, we can assume maroons similarly used their appropriated time to advance their own personal, social, economic, and political interests. As Neil Roberts (2015) has argued, marronnage was not just an act of flight, it engendered liminal spaces of liberation where maroons could garner and use time and other resources at their discretion. In the years preceding the Haitian Revolution, marronnage was an increasingly common tactic to accumulate time (Figure 5.1) and to do the mobilizing labor of establishing and expanding connections with potential rebel recruits and making key decisions regarding the impending revolt.

There were several ways enslaved people appropriated or manipulated time to facilitate marronnage: by remaining at-large for longer periods of time; escaping repeatedly; and aligning their escape according to holidays and changes in season.

Long-Term Escapes

An important insight the advertisements provide is the approximate length of time the runaways had been missing, which allows us to deter-mine runaways' relative success at absconding. Out of the 12,857

TABLE 5.4. *Maroons' length of escape in weeks (9,888 observations)*

Mean	Median	75% Percentile	90% Percentile	95% Percentile	99% Percentile	Range	Standard deviation
9.03	3	8	17	30	104	780	28.7

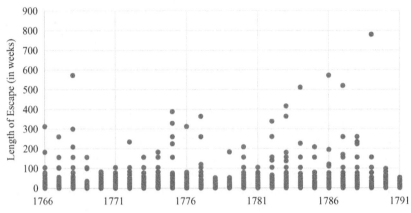

FIGURE 5.1. Length of escape (in weeks) over time

runaways listed in *Les Affiches*, 9,888 of them were described as having evaded escape for a particular period of time, which I measured in weeks, without being captured and jailed then returned to the plantation (Table 5.4). The average escape length was nine weeks, or approximately two months. The median was only three weeks, meaning most advertisements were placed less than one month after a person's disappearance; some advertisements were posted as soon as within the same week. Still, these figures help to distinguish *petit* marronnage – or temporary truancy from *grand* marronnage – the intent to permanently escape. The other half of runaways observed escaped for more than one month, which is longer than the few days of absenteeism typically associated with *petit* marronnage. Five percent of the observations, or 494 runaways, had been missing for 30 weeks, or over six months. Of these, 99 runaways had been missing for over two years. Genevieve, a 30-year-old creole woman, and her two *griffe* sons Françoise and Paule, had the longest reported escapes – 780 weeks or 15 years.[43] Longer lengths of escape clearly indicated a desire to live as a free person, however defined, away from plantation enslavement. Some of these escapees fled to Santo Domingo and intermarried, some found maroon communities in the mountains, and others passed for free in Saint-Domingue's urban towns.

In addition to openly assaulting their owners and taking their property, the enslaved increasingly sought permanent refuge from the plantation system altogether. The histogram in Figure 5.1 shows a gradual increase in escape lengths over time, proving an escalation of *grand* marronnage leading up to the Haitian Revolution. The rapid increase of the enslaved population after 1783 also signaled a steady increase of length of runaways' escapes reported in *Les Affiches américaines*; more runaways were reported missing for months and sometimes years. People were becoming knowledgeable about how to escape and were applying that knowledge to their freedom treks. A limitation to our understanding of *grand* marronnage and runaways' length of escapes is the issue of underreporting. Plantation managers often failed to mention issues of marronnage to planters who lived abroad, likely to avoid questions about mishandling of the enslaved workforce.[44] While private inventories and other records may indicate that plantations were missing laborers, these runaways do not always show up in *Les Affiches* advertisements.

For example, a 1775 inventory of the largest of the Galliffet sugar plantations, Grande Place, indicates there were seven people at large: François, a *mulâtre* missing since 1749; Augustin, age 57, Samuel, 60, and Andre Igbo, 53, all missing for "a very long time;" Mingo age 54; and Mathieu age 53 and Neptune *dit* Anga, 35, were both missing for four years. Eight years later, a 1783 inventory of the same plantation shows that Samuel, Andre, Mingo, François, Mathieu, and Neptune were still fugitives, or at most they may have been de facto *affranchis* who were colloquially referred to as *libres de savanne*. Others mentioned in this list had also committed *grand* marronnage: Paul, age 33, was missing since September 9, 1775 and Marie-Françoise, *griffe*, since 1749. The 1783 inventory for Habitation Desplantes, another Galliffet property, shows that Michel, a 45-year-old Kongolese man, had been "en marronnage" for a long time, as well as Alexandre, 26, who escaped in 1778. In the 1786 inventory for Grand Place, Blaise was added to the list of maroons. He was 32 and escaped on September 10, 1784, during a trip to the hospital. It seems that he was probably subsequently captured because, with the exception of Blaise, the original ten Grande Place and Desplantes runaways were still listed as maroons in January 1791.[45] This case serves as an example of the fact that some plantation managers and owners simply gave up looking for runaways with any real earnest, allowing fugitives to make out on their own for years at a time, potentially having children and reproducing, and forming self-contained maroon communities or passing for free in nearby towns.

Besides plantation managers' negligence, other factors like group escapes, maroons' destinations, and their oppositional actions contributed to the ability of individuals to successfully escape. The differences in average lengths of escape between individual maroons and homogeneous and heterogeneous group escapes were not that large (Table 5.5). However, heterogeneous group escapes yielded a slightly longer length of escape of 9.8 weeks. This shows that racial solidarity and the various skills and forms of knowledge runaways carried with them were important resources that contributed to a slightly above-average length of escape. When looking at the average length of escape between runaways using neighborhood ties or journeys to other destinations – family, labor sites, former plantations, Spanish territory, and other fugitives – there was only a statistically significant difference in escape durations between labor/skills and the Spanish territory in facilitating escape (Table 5.6). The difference between them was 21 weeks: labor/skills contributed to an average of 10.6 weeks of escape, whereas those who escaped to Santo Domingo had an average of 31.86 weeks of escape. Thus, on average, runaways who decided to flee Saint-Domingue altogether, though a rarity, were the most "successful" runaways. The second most successful plan was to be harbored at other plantations, runaways hiding at plantations in the living quarters of their comrades had an average of 15.68 weeks of escape. Having family connections and linkages to other runaways had similar success rates of contributing to an average of approximately 14.3 weeks of escape.

The duration of escape for runaways who were passing for free was well above the average for the entire sample, which was 9.03 weeks (Table 5.4), meaning that passing as free was the most successful

TABLE 5.5. *Kwallis one-way tests of variance, groups' average lengths of escape (in weeks)*

	Mean	Standard deviation	Frequency
Individual escapes	9.19	24.81	6,154
Homogeneous group escape	8.18	37.01	2,432
Heterogeneous group escape	9.81	28.04	1,302
Total observations			9,888

Note: p = 0.0001.

TABLE 5.6. *Kwallis one-way tests of variance, length of escape (in weeks)*
by social ties and destinations

	Mean	Standard deviation	Frequency
Family	14.28	31.43	105
Labor/skills	10.56	35.79	1,268
Former plantations	15.68	44.73	118
Spanish territory	31.86	95.47	65
Other maroons	14.26	25.24	65
Total observations			1,621

Note: p = 0.0498.

TABLE 5.7. *Kwallis one-way tests of variance, length in escape (in weeks)*
by oppositional actions

	Mean	Standard deviation	Frequency
Passing as free	22.81	59.10	434
Appropriation of goods	3.1	4.63	320
Bearing arms	5.23	6.1	56
Repeat escape	8.74	16.36	42
Total observations			852

Note: p = 0.000.

oppositional action that contributed to a longer length of escape – 22.8 weeks (Table 5.7). This is a testament to the existence of the modicum of social fluidity in Saint-Domingue that allowed a minority of enslaved people, particularly Saint-Domingue-born creoles, to change their social status from maroon to de facto free person of color. A distant second most influential oppositional action was repeated escape, which led to an average of 8.74 weeks of relative freedom. Though enslaved people who attempted to free themselves repeatedly probably learned new tactics with each unsuccessful escape, their durations of escape were still below average for the entire sample. Similarly, the appropriation of goods and bearing of arms – actions that Africans, Atlantic creoles, and young boys most commonly took – did not result in an above-average duration of escape, which suggests they were less than effective means of escape.

While most runaways were reported within a short window of time, fugitives were slowly beginning to find ways to be more successful at escape. Increasingly, enslaved people were leaving plantations for months and years, rather than days or weeks, at a time. There was a steady increase in the number of outlier durations between the years 1783 and 1786, with advertisements for 416 and 572-week long escapes appearing. Additionally, heterogeneous group escapes were also becoming more frequent, showing that there was a slowly increasing sense of racial solidarity among the enslaved population. The skills, information, and experience shared by individuals from diverse backgrounds was valuable knowledge to add to their marronnage repertoire toolkit. The longest recorded length of maroon escape, 780 weeks or 15 years, was advertised in the year 1789, the same year that saw the largest group escape, composed of 22 runaways who were from widely different birth origins – Kongo, Igbo, Senegambian, Bambara, and creole. This supports the finding that heterogeneous group escapes contributed to a slightly above-average duration of escape (Table 5.5). Before the colonial situation, these groups probably would never have encountered each other on the African continent, but conditions in Saint-Domingue prompted them to interact in work arrangements, living quarters, familial units, and ritual gatherings, forging relationships across cultural, geographic, and linguistic boundaries. For example, Chapter 8 discusses another group of Kongolese, Mina, and creole maroons established an independent living zone on a coffee plantation in Cayes de Jacmel, hiding in plain sight for more than three years without detection.

Repeat Escapes

Fifty-eight runaways were noted to have escaped then were returned on more than one occasion – an offense that could have resulted in whipping, branding with the fleur-de-lys, mutilation of ears or other body parts, or execution. Advertisements were placed for perpetual maroons – people who were captured after an initial escape then ran away again. For example, A Kongolese man escaped in October of 1774 and was quickly captured by the *maréchaussée*, but then escaped again the following December.[46] Another Kongolese man named Chaudiere escaped, then was imprisoned for one month, then escaped again after being taken back to Jérémie.[47] Although repeat escapees constituted only 0.45 percent of the sample, women were more likely than men to be repeat runaways. Other examples of repeat runaways come from plantation records, including a creole woman named Zabeth, who in 1768, left a Léogâne sugar plantation manager exasperated at her constant escapes. Zabeth took every opportunity to sneak away – she feigned illness and promptly attempted to steal another woman's clothes so she could run away. After being caught in the act, she promised not to take flight again, but did shortly thereafter. When it was realized that she was legitimately sick, Zabeth was sent to a plantation infirmary; yet she took off again once the manager sent her another change of clothes. She fled twice more, both times after having been chained up and and becoming ill nearly to the point of death.

In May 1774, the same planter who owned Zabeth, Madame du Fort, sent a group from a sugar plantation in Léogâne to her coffee plantation in Abricots. During the exchange, the coffee plantation manager wrote to her indicating that three people escaped – Jasmin Barbe-Blanche, his wife Nanette, and a younger man named Marquis. It was suspected that they went to Cayemittes and advertisements were placed for them at Jérémie and Tiburon. A month after their escape, all three were discovered to be in jail in Jérémie. Soon after being returned to du Fort's manager, Jasmin ran away again. This time he did not make it far, due to starvation and sickness. Before Jasmin died in late September, he admitted that he was familiar with the Grande Anse area and planned to pay another black man with a silver cufflink to take him across a river. Despite the hardship Jasmin endured, Marquis still ventured to run away again in October. He had stolen chickens belonging to other blacks and used for subsistence, presumably to sell them for himself.[48]

Some runaway advertisements were published multiple times and across different publications. The *Gazette de Saint Domingue* and *Courrier Nationale de Saint Domingue* carried a small number of the same notices that were placed in *Les Affiches américaines*. Repeated advertisements were not counted in the current dataset for quantitative analysis; however, their frequency has qualitative implications regarding the length of time runaways escaped, or those who were captured then escaped again after their return. For example, Jasmin, a 25- to 26-year-old Kongo man was reported as a runaway on January 18, 1783, one week later on January 25, then again four weeks later on February 22, suggesting that he avoided capture for at least one month.[49] Advertisements for Victoire, a creole woman, ran on July 15, 1789, July 22, and July 29.[50] Over time, *Les Affiches* runaway advertisements seem to have run repeatedly with increasing frequency, especially as the Haitian Revolution drew nearer. Out of 798 advertisements placed in the year 1790, over 300 of them had been repeats of previously published advertisements. On the other hand, there were only 11 repeated advertisements for the years 1766 through 1768 combined. It seems that reporting became more negligent because the number of repeated advertisements increased alongside the growing number of Africans imported to Saint-Domingue.

The Timing of Marronnage

Part of runaways' strategy in escaping was to deliberately time their flight to align with windows of opportunity when there would be less attention paid to the goings on of the enslaved population. Weekends, holidays, and natural disasters created enough distractions for absconders to slip away without detection. Colonial planters allowed enslaved people to have leave from work to attend parties on Christmas, Easter, New Year, and other Catholic celebrations. Temporary absenteeism after these events was expected, either due to dalliances with romantic partners or a long weekend stay at a different plantation's party. Planters kept track of who was missing at their end-of-year account books but were measured in giving out punishments for escapes during the holiday seasons. Analysis of the runaway advertisements shows that escapes were most frequent during high summer months and least frequent at the end of the year. Overall, the 25th, 29th, and 30th weeks of the year saw the highest numbers of reported runaways, overlapping with June 20–26, July 18–24, and July 25–July 31, respectively. Higher productivity on plantations may have contributed to an uptick in marronnage during the summer, since harsh weather made hard labor unbearable. Other Catholic festivities during those weeks were for Saint Jean-Baptiste in Trou and Jean-Rabel (June 24); Sainte Marguerite in Port-Margot (July 20); Saint James the Greater (July 25); Sainte Anne in l'Anse-a-Veau (July 26); Saint Pierre in Limbé (July 29); and Sainte Marthe in Marmelade (July 29). In addition to being moments of distraction for plantation personnel, these locally celebrated holidays would also have been gathering times for enslaved people to partake in their sacred rituals and, as I argued in Chapter 3, to enhance oppositional consciousness and influence marronnage through seditious speech about freedom and liberation.

CONCLUSION

Maroons' micro-level repertoire actions reflected their politicized, oppositional consciousness that directly countered the dispossession and oppression of slavery. Maroons reimagined their status and identities, appropriated goods and technologies, exhibited militancy, and reclaimed their time – demonstrating their intentions to be free, and to assert ownership of themselves, their human capital, and other resources. The current and previous chapters have shown that maroons leveraged their cultural and ritual spaces, knowledge pools and labor skills, social networks, and other tangible and intangible resources within their immediate vicinity to facilitate their escape. The following chapter will examine maroons' understanding of Saint-Domingue's geography as part of their repertoire of knowledge and action. Examination of the locations from where maroons escaped and the destinations they had in mind can help us better understand the colony itself and the ways enslaved people and maroons carved out their own geographies of subversion, even in the shadows of slavery.

6

Geographies of Subversion: Maroons, Borders, and Empire

In 1725, an enslaved man named Capois of Gros Morne was searching the savannahs of northern Port-à-Piment for his owner's missing cattle when his horse became stuck in the mud. After noticing the extreme heat of the water beneath his feet, Capois assessed that he had found a hot spring. He recalled hearing stories of bathhouses in France and decided to dig a six-by-four-foot hole and build a small hut on top. Capois found two fellow bondsmen who the springs could potentially heal, one suffering from extensive rheumatism and another in Jean Rabel whose ailment was thought to have been incurable. Both men were successfully cured. Within a few years, the spring gained a reputation for miraculous healing and became a site of pilgrimage as a shrine had been constructed around it, with old crutches and written testimonies decorating nearby trees. By the end of the century, what became known as Eaux de Boynes was instituted as a formal government-sponsored health spa. Capois was offered his own personal slave as reward for his discovery, an offer he declined.[1] He was not a maroon, but in being obligated to search for his owner's missing property, he was able to explore the land beyond his plantation of origin. In so doing, not only had Capois identified a previously undiscovered natural resource, but he demonstrated an awareness of its inherent value and usefulness as a healing mechanism.

Enslaved people like Capois were, at times, at the front lines of exploring geographic spaces that European colonizers had not yet explored or exploited. Drawing on insights from historical and postcolonial geographies, this chapter is concerned with enslaved Africans' geographic knowledge as part of their collective consciousness that aided the pursuit of freedom. The story of Capois and the Eaux de Boynes hot springs demonstrates that black people learned the land on an intimate level and figured out ways to generate life-sustaining elements and processes from it. Whether it was physically tending to the land on sugar, coffee, indigo, or cotton plantations, laboring on public works irrigation projects, cultivating crops on personal small land plots, locating specific plants and herbs to assemble ritual packets, discovering pathways and riverways to quicken escape routes across the plains or mountain ranges, or finding caverns or densely forested mountains to hide in as maroons – the colony's environmental landscape was itself a form of cultural knowledge with which Africans and African descendants needed to become familiarized in order to survive. Armed with this knowledge, they found nooks and crannies within and external to the system, carving into and subverting social and geographic spaces intended for the financial benefit of the plantocracy, creating maroon spaces amid a wildly prosperous slave society. This chapter looks at the physical environment of Saint-Domingue and how maroons leveraged their knowledge of it in their freedom journeys. *Les Affiches* advertisements oftentimes indicate from where the maroon had escaped and, in at least 1,000 cases, speculate about where that person may have been trying to flee. This information, and data from other sources, helps to foreground the spatiality of marronnage, allowing us to read beyond what is present in texts or maps to find out the natural and topographical realities maroons faced and grappled with in reconstituting colonial landscapes as geographies of subversion.

As this chapter is concerned with viewing marronnage as a contestation of colonial geographic formations, it becomes important to highlight the micro-, meso-, and macro-levels of power, plantation economies, and empire as well as the limitations of each. The first part of the chapter explores how maroons forged possibilities of freedom within immediate locales that were dominated by plantation slavery. Saint-Domingue's diverse environment contained nearly 500,000 enslaved people and an untold number of maroon individuals and family units who hid both in plain sight and in areas previously believed to be uninhabitable. They constructed what Sylviane Diouf (2014: 8–9) calls a "maroon landscape" at the intersection of three worlds: maroon refuge, white-dominated spaces, and physical and social territories carved out by enslaved people. This maroon landscape constituted geographies of subversion, as maroons sought refuge and community, and built solidarities across Saint-Domingue, from its urban centers to its mountains and forests – the very landscape that French planters and authorities had exploited slave labor to in turn exploit and profit from – and beyond, into Santo Domingo. Maroons built huts in the mountains and forests using mud and leaves, and constructed booby-traps with the same flora and fauna. They lurked on the outskirts of large plantations, and drank from the rivers, and cultivated their own gardens. They retreated to urban centers where there were enough free people of color that the *maréchaussée* fugitive slave police would not be able to easily identify a maroon who was living as a free person. Or they defected to Santo Domingo, becoming a source of tension between the Spanish colony and Saint-Domingue and presenting a need for diplomacy between the two colonies around the issue of marronnage. The second part of the chapter examines the relationship between empire and marronnage, and how, for well over a century, enslaved Africans had knowledge of and exploited the geopolitical conflicts between the French and Spanish crowns by traversing the border between Saint-Domingue and Santo Domingo and establishing liberated zones on their own terms.

By committing marronnage within and against the French colonial enterprise of Saint-Domingue, runaways forced authorities to reckon with questions of imperial reach and power. European imperialistic pursuits in the Caribbean can be described as an "act of geographical violence through which space was explored, reconstructed, re-named and controlled" (Crush 1994: 337). The island that Saint-Domingue and Santo Domingo shared was the first location in the Americas to encounter Christopher Columbus and accompanying Spaniards' violent imperial ventures. Initially called *Ayiti* by the Taíno-Arawak indigenous inhabitants, Columbus re-named the entire island *La Española* when he arrived and wrested control of the island's southern areas. Upon the beginning of French rule over the western third of Española in 1697, they renamed the region Saint-Domingue and each city and town was given recognizably French names. This symbolic dominance over the landscape through naming processes was combined with the terroristic violence that Taínos and Africans encountered, and environmental violence against the land itself.

Included in the conquered physical spaces was "nature" itself, which was converted into "natural resources" that colonists extracted, processed, and imported into Europe, such as sugarcane, coffee, gold, and other minerals. (Mignolo 2011). French colonization of western Española, Saint-Domingue, spread much farther and faster than the attempts of Spanish predecessors, exploiting high-quality, moisture-rich lands and razing the forests to create space for hundreds of sugar planta-tions.[2] Colonial conquest therefore involved processes of deforestation and reforestation – the transfer of plants, trees, and crops from one space to another to construct a desired arboreal landscape and to attach new social and economic meanings to environmental formations (Sheller 2012: 187–188). As early as the 1690s, the French royal government recognized the detrimental effects of plantation expansion on Saint-Domingue's woods and implemented legislation to protect and preserve vegetation and other natural resources. The *Code Noir* made it illegal to sell firewood, and the king banned the felling of the Gayac tree that was used for ship construction. These policies were ignored, leading to increased importation of wood for hospitals and shop building. In 1712, plantation owners were required to clear land plots within a year of purchase, a rule that inadvertently helped to further stimulate the slave trade, since planters relied on enslaved people to do the clearing. Plantation owners near Le Cap also forced slaves to steal wood from the hospital, where it would then be sold at the city's market.[3] Colonists' destruction of Saint-Domingue's physical environment made room for more plantations and thus more enslaved laborers, who were then coerced into performing geologically harmful labor.

Colonialism also spatialized slavery itself, in that the institution of racialized forced labor was intended to exist singularly in the colonies, not the French mainland. France was thought to have been an entirely free nation regardless of one's racial identity. However, even this belief was challenged when in 1777 free people of color from the colonies were banned from entering the home country and claiming citizenship.[4] Generally speaking, France was a geographical space meant for free whites, and Saint-Domingue was a space designated for enslaved blacks. By the end of the eighteenth century, the spread of sugar increasingly dominated Saint-Domingue's landscape in the lowlands and valleys, and coffee plantations in the mountainous highlands. In 1789, there were nearly 800 sugar plantations, over 3,000 coffee plantations, over 3,000 indigo plantations, and nearly 800 cotton plantations.[5] Sugar plantation sizes were quite large and could cover between 580 and over 900 acres of land.[6] But while sugar was produced in the plains, and the plantation presence expanded horizontally, coffee plantations in the mountains added a vertical dimension to sites of oppression. The looming presence of these plantations and the *maréchaussée* fugitive slave police operated in a panopticon-like fashion where enslaved people were under seemingly constant surveillance. In France, punishment for serious crimes was increasingly peripheralized to prisons, but in Saint-Domingue, authorities centralized demonstrations of colonial punishment, executing known maroons and other rebels in town squares, thus creating a symbolic association between rebellion, death, and humiliation in public spaces (Foucault 1977).

The enterprise of European colonialism exerted power over the land to gain the surplus value of the agricultural products that enslaved Africans physically extracted; therefore, coercive authority extended to Saint-Domingue's enslaved inhabitants, whose physical movements and actions were restricted to activities related to productivity – specifically for French profits. As Stephanie Camp (2004: 6) explained, "places, boundaries, and movement were central to how slavery was organized and to how it was resisted." She argues that enslaved people lived within a "geography of containment," where, through law and custom, plantation personnel patrolled slave grounds, determined and enforced work schedules, and required passes to account for slaves' comings and goings. The *Code Noir* had several provisions that dictated the terms of how, when, and where black people could move and for what reasons, and the *maréchaussée* fugitive slave police were responsible for imposing the boundaries of the geography of containment. Slaves belonging to different owners could not congregate for any reason lest they face the whip as a minimum punishment or death at most, since frequent violations would constitute *grand* marronnage. Owners were prevented from allowing assemblies of slaves and would be fined if held in violation. The *Code Noir's* limitations on enslaved people's physical movement were also linked to disempowering them economically: slaves were not supposed hold *marché de nègres* or *nègre* markets and could not sell sugarcane, fruit, vegetables, firewood, herbs, or any other type of commodity. Their goods could be confiscated and returned to their owner unless they had a ticket from that owner. But given the overwhelming population of Africans and African descendants in Saint-Domingue, these rules were not always upheld or were outright ignored. For example, the *marché de nègres* were prominent features of city life in both Port-au-Prince and Cap Français. As discussed in Chapter 3, enslaved people were known to congregate in churches, at burial grounds, or on the outskirts of plantations to perform their sacred rituals and other cultural practices. Chapter 4 highlighted maroons' social ties to other maroons, free and enslaved people, and how their skills and experience in selling goods at the markets allowed them to traverse the colony.

The connections constructed by enslaved people and maroons in living quarters, ritual spaces, markets, mountains, caves, and other unmonitored areas were part of a "rival geography," which Camp (2004: 7) defined as an "alternative way of knowing and using space that conflicted with planters' ideals and demands." Maroons cultivated rival geographies beginning with the early Spanish colonial period. Late Haitian anthropologist Rachel Beauvoir-Dominique (2009) argued that petroglyphs and archaeological remains found in several cave systems indicated that the collaborations between Taínos and Africans during Cacique Enriquillo's early sixteenth-century revolt against the Spanish and the rebels' collective retreat to mountain chains – such as the Baoruco west of the city of Santo Domingo – facilitated the exchange of cosmological beliefs about the world and practical knowledge of the island's topography, plant usage, and resistance tactics. Within West African and West Central African cosmologies, elements of the natural environment – bodies of water, flora and fauna, rocks, the wind, lightning, and thunder – were associated with the deities and other spirit entities. The sacrality of the land itself informed enslaved and marooned Africans' ways of interacting with the environment, redefining space, and reclaiming power. For example, the Bwa Kayman ceremony that ushered in the August 1791 uprising occurred under the canopy of the sacred *mapou* silk cotton tree, which holds spiritual meanings and functions as a social space for ancestor reverence. The *mapou* marks important crossroads for public gatherings in contemporary Haitian Vodou and other African and indigenous-based cultures of the Caribbean like Jamaica, Trinidad, and Guyana (Sheller 2012: 137–139, 201–204). The existence of such modes of thinking suggests Africans not only held alternate conceptions of spatial orders, but they struggled in the material realm to create rival geographies – or geographies of subversion – by staking claim to "resources, land, and livelihood" in contest with the rapidly expanding plantation regime (ibid.: 190). Rival geographies are similar to, or can constitute, free spaces that accompany or foment collective resistance and other forms of prefigurative politics by providing safe, protected zones where actors can interact, freely communicate, express emotion and thought, and share information and other valuable resources. Networks of resistance actors, and the networks of physical spaces they occupy and frequent, are part of an ongoing process of building insurgent "scenes" (Creasap 2012) where enslaved people and maroons could have "reimagined their lives as free people within the very geography in which they were intended to be enslaved" (Miki 2012: 503).

Another example of maroons' usage of rival geography included their contentious occupation of mountainous zones that sat along the Saint-Domingue–Santo Domingo border, and their entanglement in geopolitical fights between the French and Spanish. The second part of this chapter treats the imperial border as part of Saint-Domingue's geographic land-scape that had a critical relationship to marronnage. The Saint-Domingue–Santo Domingo border changed over time and proximity to it enticed runaways to attempt escape; moreover, the presence and value of black people as a form of capital, as potential laborers, and as rebels shaped the border itself as an ongoing political project. Though the island was the first in the Americas to receive European explorers and colonists, by the end of the seventeenth century it had become a backwater colony, effectively leaving the western lands open to settlement by maroons, pirates, and *boucaneers*. After several decades of fighting, the Spanish finally ceded Saint-Domingue to the French in 1697 with the Treaty of Ryswick and maintained rulership over the island's eastern two-thirds – the colony of Santo Domingo. Yet the agreement did little to quell rivalry between the French and Spanish crowns, nor struggles over property ownership at the border itself. These localized spats were reflections of inter-imperial competition for control and dominance over the slave trade, the enslaved, sugar production, and territory. For over a century, beginning in the late 1600s, enslaved Africans and maroons leveraged the conflict between the French and the Spanish to their benefit, turning on one empire or the other until the boundary between Saint-Domingue and Santo Domingo was finalized with the 1777 Treaty of Aranjuez.

Enslaved people perceived several incentives for pledging allegiance to the Spanish. Since Santo Domingo had not developed a plantation system at the same pace or depth as Saint-Domingue, and there was more geo-graphic space in the east for runaways to inhabit, farm, and start a new life. The Spanish Empire based its policies on slavery on the medieval *Siete Partidas*, which affirmed the innate humanity of enslaved people. Spanish codes were widely considered to have been more amenable to sustaining human life – while the reverse was true of Saint-Domingue. Throughout the Spanish Empire, it was not uncommon for entire towns to be built for free people of color. Moreover, interactions and collaborative rebellion among Africans and indigenous Taínos began in the Baoruco mountains near the city of Santo Domingo, creating a long-lasting legacy of resistance and freedom that was known to even newly-arrived Africans, as gener-ations of enslaved people made their way to the growing maroon settle-ment. Several formerly enslaved people of Saint-Domingue were aware of the geopolitical stakes and at times wagered on marronnage in Santo Domingo as an alternative route to freedom. As these fugitives disap-peared behind the border, they implicitly denied French planters' access to their labor value and therefore caused financial loss. Additionally, once on Spanish lands and having assurances of Spanish loyalty, some maroons took up arms against the French or raided nearby plantations. Besides the runaway advertisements, primary sources such as letters from planters and military officials help to highlight cases of runaways who fled Saint-Domingue for Santo Domingo and explore several instances of the Spanish co-opting African Saint-Dominguans by arming them and/or implicitly and explicitly promising freedom from enslavement or better treatment and a better quality of life.

THE SPATIALITY OF MARRONNAGE

Information about the geographic dimensions of marronnage was a key component of *Les Affiches américaines* advertisements. Planters who placed advertisements for the public to help locate and recover a fugitive needed to identify themselves and the location of their plantations so that readers could associate the bondsperson with a particular parish or neighborhood. Planters often had to travel from rural areas to reach the major towns to publish the advertisements, but in cases where the slave owner's location of origin was not specified, this information can be inferred from the name of the plantation owner, lawyer, or manager listed in the advertisements. Slave owners needed to include as many details as possible, however speculative, about where a runaway might have absconded. Geographic data gleaned from *Les Affiches* advertisements provides insights into how many advertisements were placed or distributed in the major urban centers, either Cap Français, Port-au-Prince, or Saint Marc, the location where the planter was based, and the runaways' suspected whereabouts. Of the over 10,000 runaway advertisements, the majority – 6,874 – were placed in the newspaper that was circulated from Cap Français (Table 6.1). Based on the volume of advertisements placed at Le Cap, the city and its surrounding region experienced the highest volume of marronnage over time, since it was the colony's oldest and most populated urban center, followed by Port-Prince and Saint Marc. Besides the three cities, plantations at Léogâne, Gonaïves, Arcahaye, Artibonite, and Dondon reported the highest numbers of maroons.

In over 1,000 cases, advertisements included speculative information about where the runaway(s) hid. As previous chapters have clarified, enslaved people were far from socially dead figures who lacked meaningful relationships to kith and kin. Planters were aware of bondspeople's intimate relationships and used this information to surmise that some

TABLE 6.1. *Frequency of runaways' locations*

Newspaper publication location	Parishes	Location of runaways' escape	Runaways' suspected locations
North (Cap Français) – 6,874 runaways	Ouanaminthe	70 (0.69%)	22 (1.85%)
	Fort Dauphin	274 (2.71%)	52 (4.37%)
	Terrier Rouge	95 (0.94%)	36 (3.02%)
	Trou	191 (1.89%)	48 (4.03%)
	Valière	30 (0.30%)	2 (0.17%)
	Limonade	227 (2.25%)	40 (3.36%)
	Quartier Morin	134 (1.33%	22 (1.85%)
	Grande Rivière	278 (2.75%)	40 (3.36%)
	Dondon	348 (3.44%)	30 (2.52%)
	Marmelade	127 (1.26%)	11 (0.92%)
	Petite Anse	187 (1.85%)	22 (1.85%)
	Cap Français	1,287 (12.73%)	122 (10.24%
	Plaine du Nord	58 (0.57%)	27 (2.27%)
	Acul	158 (1.56%)	25 (2.1%)
	Limbé	263 (2.6%)	48 (4.03%)
	Port Margot	158 (1.56%)	31 (2.6%)
	Borgne	263 (2.6%)	24 (2.02%)
	Plaisance	270 (2.67%)	25 (2.1%)
	St. Louis du Nord	118 (1.17%)	9 (0.76%)
	Port-de-Paix	210 (2.08%)	24 (2.02%)
	Gros Morne	104 (1.03%)	32 (2.69%)
	Jean Rabel	102 (1.1%)	8 (0.67%)
	Môle Saint Nicolas	84 (0.83%)	7 (0.59%)
	Morne Rouge	108 (1.07%)	23 (1.93%)
West (Saint Marc) – 577 runaways	Saint Marc	500 (4.95%)	30 (2.52%)
	Gonaïves	384 (3.8%)	29 (2.43%)
	Artibonite	305 (3.02%)	59 (4.95%)
West-South (Port-au-Prince) – 4,402 runaways	Bombarde	2 (0.02%)	0
	Port-à-Piment	15 (0.15%)	4 (0.34%)
	Ile de la Tortue	6 (0.06%)	0
	Petite Riviere	15 (0.15%)	2 (0.17%)
	Verettes	28 (0.28%)	4 (0.34%)
	Mirebalais	169 (1.67%)	16 (1.34%)
	Arcahaye	346 (3.42%)	16 (1.34%)
	Croix-des-Bouquets	219 (2.17%)	27 (2.27%)
	Port-au-Prince	647 (6.4%)	45 (3.78%)
	Léogâne	427 (4.22%)	47 (3.95%)
	Grand Goâve	73 (0.72%)	7 (0.59%)
	Baynet	27 (0.27%)	0
	Jacmel	161 (1.59%)	15 (1.26%)
	Cayes de Jacmel	19 (0.9%)	1 (0.08%)

TABLE 6.1. *(continued)*

Newspaper publication location	Parishes	Location of runaways' escape	Runaways' suspected locations
	Cul-de-Sac	212 (2.12%)	43 (3.61%)
	Isle Gonâve	5 (0.05%)	6 (0.5%)
	Petit Goâve	133 (1.32%)	25 (2.1%)
	Fond des Nègres	73 (0.72%)	6 (0.5%)
	Anse à Veau	217 (2.15%)	8 (0.67%)
	Petit Trou	74 (0.73%)	4 (0.34%)
	Jérémie	341 (3.37%)	13 (1.09%)
	Cap Dame Marie	37 (0.37%)	1 (0.08%)
	Cap Tiburon	26 (0.26%)	2 (0.17%)
	Coteaux	27 (0.27%)	2 (0.17%)
	Port Salut	56 (0.55%)	0
	Torbeck	7 (0.07%)	1 (0.08%)
	Cayes	237 (2.34%)	11 (0.92%)
	Cavaillon	61 (0.60%)	6 (0.5%)
	St. Louis du Sud	21 (0.21%)	1 (0.08%)
	Aquin	89 (0.88%)	14 (1.18%)
	Santo Domingo	24 (0.24%)	16 (1.34%)
Total observations		10,107	1,191

who embarked on marronnage were actively seeking to reconnect with friends and family members on other plantations, in different neighborhoods or different parishes of the colony. Other aspects of maroons' identities that gave clues to their whereabouts included their labor-related skills or a reputation for past rebelliousness. Ultimately, only the individual who decided to become a maroon knew definitively the reasons behind their escape and the destination they had in mind as they escaped. As Saint-Domingue's economic development escalated in the eighteenth century, plantations increasingly covered the rural landscape and cities grew, multiplying the enslaved population and leaving fewer unoccupied areas for maroons to claim and settle. Maroons left urban areas heading for the mountains or other desolate areas, others left rural regions for the cities, and still others lingered near familiar surroundings or were captured before they were able to venture afar (see Figures 6.1 and 6.2). The movement of maroons between plantations and between urban and rural areas meant that they subverted places dominated by plantation expansion and created autonomous spaces in the absence of slave-based economies.

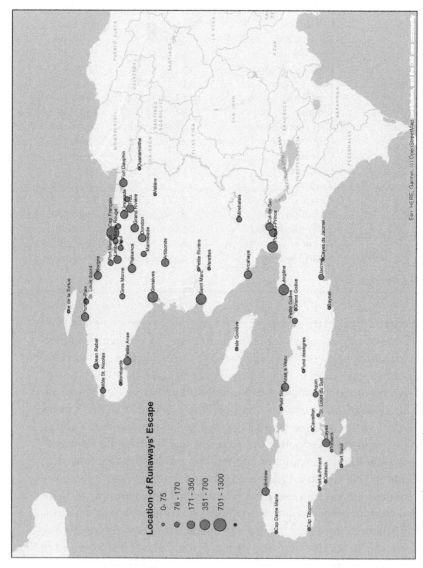

FIGURE 6.1. Runaways' locations of escape, map created by Reese Manceaux and Crystal Eddins

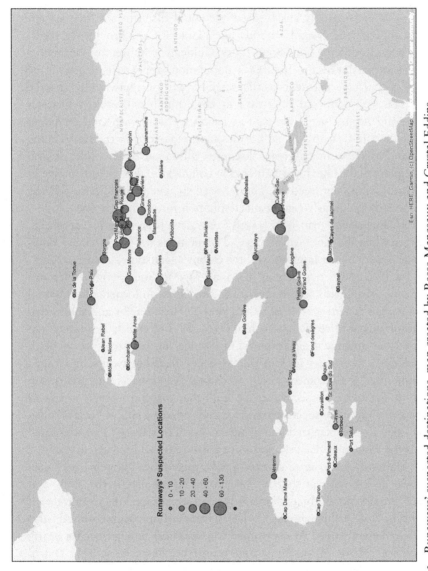

FIGURE 6.2. Runaways' suspected destinations, map created by Reese Manceaux and Crystal Eddins

Hiding in Plain Sight

Many runaways were attracted to the bustling city of Cap Français, in part because the significant presence of free people of color created social spaces where formerly enslaved people could blend in and live as self-freed individuals. Neighborhoods like Haut-du-Cap, Providence, Petit-Carenage, and Petite-Guinée or "Little Guinea," a section of town with a significant enslaved and free black population, appear frequently in the *Les Affiches* advertisements as suspected havens for runaways living in Le Cap. Le Cap attracted runaways in large numbers: between October 1790 and August 1791 alone, 122 runaways were suspected of hiding somewhere in Le Cap, and authorities captured over 500 runaways in the city and its surrounding areas.[7] Escapees with an artisanal trade, or who were perceived as having a lighter skin complexion, had an advantage in self-fashioning their freedom. Though men escaped to Le Cap as well, the city was the singularly significant destination for maroon women.

Unlike enslaved men who traveled as valets, fishermen, or carpenters, women often did not venture beyond plantations for work-related tasks. Women were not as familiar with the colony's landscape, in part accounting for their lower numbers as maroons. Instead, some women maroons fled into urban areas where they could participate in formal and informal commercial activities as "market maroons." They bought and sold provisions, goods, and services, which allowed them economic autonomy and "their own insurgent geographies, fashioning an infrastructure of black freedom ... where they took up public space, created networks, and forged community." Free women of color were already known as entrepreneurs in Port-au-Prince and especially in Le Cap; that maroon women sought to assimilate into these social, geographic and economic spaces "was an open challenge to the racialized and gendered logics of slavery" that mandated enslaved women exclusively perform agricultural and reproductive labor.[8] For example, Marianne, a 23-year-old mixed-race woman, was well known as a vendor at the Le Cap market selling fish, herbs, milk, and fruit.[9] An unnamed Mina woman was often seen around the plantations of Haut-du-Cap selling bread.[10] The Haut-du-Cap neighborhood also harbored an unnamed Arada woman who had been hiding there for nearly a month.[11] Rosie of the Aguia nation used her language skills in Dutch, English, and Spanish to pass as a free woman and possibly marketed herself as a broker or trader alongside other free women of color at Le Cap.[12]

Maroons also fled their enslavers from within Cap Français at a high rate, meaning there was a circulation of people to and from the city to the mountainous rural districts. Men especially gravitated to areas like Artibonite, Léogâne, and Fort Dauphin, less-populated areas that were connected to waterways, mountains, and caverns, and could facilitate escape and informal economic activity. Places like Fort Dauphin were especially considered dangerous and difficult to access; however, these characteristics would have made for the creation of insurgent geographies as maroons organized themselves and laid claim to lands and rights. Léogâne was the home base of the rebel ritualist Dom Pedro in the 1760s, Fort Dauphin saw several conflicts between armed maroons and the *maréchaussée*, and Artibonite was home to smaller, self-liberated communities. Where colonists saw inaccessibility, maroons saw geographies of freedom.

Reaching the Inaccessible

Through forced labor tasks or their self-initiated journeys, Saint-Domingue's enslaved people and runaway fugitives traversed the colony and were exposed to its vastly diverse topography, including its several mountain chains. The Taíno moniker *Ayiti*, and the most literal interpretation of the well-known Haitian proverb "behind the mountains are more mountains," derived from the fact that mountain ranges cover three-fourths of the 10,714 square miles of what became Saint-Domingue-Haiti. In addition to several smaller mountain ranges in the north, in the west there are the Cahos and Montagnes Noires, and the southern mountains of Pic la Selle, the Matheux, and the Baoruco – all of which were hiding places for maroons.[13] Two of these mountain chains exceed heights of 1,000 meters above sea level, including one in the westward-jutting southern peninsula where maroons later established the Platons Kingdom during the Haitian Revolution. The other 1,000-plus-meter mountain range occupies the island's south-central region, Pic la Selle, sitting southeast of Port-au-Prince.[14] Semi-arid savannas, lush rainforests, sinkholes and deep cave systems also characterized Saint-Domingue's landscape. The caves were locations for Taíno ritual practice, transculturation and exchange between Taínos and Africans, and served as protective zones for runaways in transit toward maroon communities.[15] Some of these sites included what is now called the Voûte à Minguet of Dondon and Bassin Zim in Hinche, Central Plateau; the Bohoc/Colladère at Pignon and St. Francique at St. Michel de l'Attalaye, both in the Central Plateau; Dubedou near Gonaïves in Artibonite; the caves of Tortuga Island; Grotte Dufour in Marmelade; the Morne Deux-Têtes

Meillac at Limbé; caves at Camp-Perrin; the Moreau Cave at Port-Salut; the Grotte aux Indes at Pestel; the Grande Grotte at Port-à-Piment; and the Grotte nan Baryè in Grand Anse.[16]

Among the identified destinations for runaways, areas in the northern department were the most common. Besides those who went to more populated towns like Le Cap or Port-au-Prince, many runaways were last seen in Fort Dauphin, Trou, Limbé, Limonade, and Grand Rivière. With its mountain ranges and savannahs, and immediate access to both the northern coast and two major roads leading to the interior of Santo Domingo, Fort Dauphin had been the second most important city in the north and was the first to receive influxes of inhabitants when the town was known as Bayaha under Spanish rule.[17] But by the eighteenth century, the French found Fort Dauphin less than optimal for a viable naval base and it was sparsely populated, apart from five potteries, rendering it a "useless" port.[18] Moreau de Saint-Méry similarly described Fort Dauphin in less than flattering terms: as a "pesthole" that was dangerous and difficult to access due to overflows of river water.[19] However, it was a porous site of the Saint-Domingue–Santo Domingo border, operating as an entrepôt for illegal smuggling between Monte Cristo and Le Cap, especially during the Seven Years War.[20] The informal economic activities of French, Spanish, Dutch, and North American traders made Fort Dauphin an attractive place for some runaways to peddle items or sell their services and find some financial independence. For example, a creole man named Étienne had passed for free for ten years since 1756 – he was not branded, spoke strong French, and had pierced ears, though his legs were scarred. Étienne was known to frequent Maribaroux and Fort Dauphin, working as a *pacotille*, or a vendor of various wares.[21] A 20-year-old Kongolese woman named Zaire was described as a trader and left her owner in Le Cap, a *mûlatre* woman named Zabeau, headed for Fort Dauphin.[22]

In the early eighteenth century, the mountainous towns east of Le Cap were renowned for the threatening presence of armed maroon bands who were known to rob and kill whites and attack plantations. According to Moreau de Saint-Méry, places with names like Piton des Nègres, Piton des Flambeaux, Piton des Ténèbres, Tête des Nègres at Môle Saint Nicolas, and Crete à Congo signified the dominance of fugitives who had occupied inaccessible places. At Trou, just south of Fort Dauphin, the name of notorious maroon rebel Polydor evoked memories of his band, murders, and the intensive effort to capture him.[23] Later, a section of Trou called Écrevisses, along with Fort Dauphin, became a popular destination for runaways and was the place where Thélémaque Canga, Noël Barochin, and Bœuf pillaged plantations and fought the *maréchaussée*. The mountains of Morne à Mantegre, between Grande Rivière and Limonade, had a reputation as a maroon haven since Colas Jambes Coupée's campaigns in the early 1720s.[24] In the southern peninsula, the section of Grand Anse bears the name Plymouth after the maroon Plymouth who, along with his followers, destroyed plantations throughout the region and was captured in 1730.[25]

While the northern plain was more densely populated and sprawling with closely connected plantations, the western and southern departments were less developed. Outside of Port-au-Prince, the western parishes of Artibonite, Léogâne, and Cul-de-Sac attracted the most runaways, probably because plantations were spread farther apart, and parishes sat adjacent to mountains like the Cahos and Montagnes Noires. The priest Jean-Baptiste Labat reported in the 1720s that 700 heavily armed maroons were occupying the Montagnes Noires northeast of Port-au-Prince.[26] *Les Affiches* advertisements also indicate that these mountains were places of retreat for runaways in the latter half of the century. Two men and a woman of the Ganga and Mina nations all marooned to the Montagnes Noires near Port-au-Prince.[27] A group of four Kongolese and one Mondongue men took haven in the Montagnes Noires – Houan (Juan) or Jean, Jean-Louis, and Jupiter escaped to join with Cesar and Louis who had already been there for some time.[28] Pierre-Louis, a *griffe* and a carpenter, hid for two months in the Grand Bois mountains in Croix-des-Bouquets, which was a site of conflict between maroons and the *maréchaussée*.[29] Above Port-au-Prince, a group of 17 unnamed maroons, described as mostly creoles, escaped a Gonaïves plantation in May 1769 and were presumed to have been hiding at Artibonite.[30] One unnamed Kongolese woman and ten Kongo men escaped from Artibonite and were suspected of finding haven with "other black maroons."[31] Télémaque, a creole from Jamaica who spoke English and "the language ordinary to the *nègres*," had been in flight for nine months and was thought to be either in the Cahos mountains around Saint Marc or on the Santo Domingo side of the hills.[32]

The southern parishes that most maroons fled from were Jérémie, Les Cayes, and Anse-a-Veau. Though these southern districts did not report as many runaways' suspected destinations as northern parishes, this does not mean there were no maroon hideouts in those areas. Maroon activity was reported in Grand Anse as early as the seventeenth century prior to French rule, and bands like those led by Plymouth were hunted in the

1720s and 1730s. Since the southern department developed much more slowly than either the northern or western departments, maroons in these regions probably lived among themselves in relative peace until the rise of the mixed-race coffee planter class during the mid- to late eighteenth century. Planter Laborde learned in September 1780 that three bondsmen, Jean, Cupidon, and Jupiter, had been captured or killed during the pursuit of a maroon band residing in the mountains of Aquin.[33] Neron, an Arada man, and Cipryen, a Kongolese, had escaped for six months and were suspected to be hiding with a black man from Corail Guerineau and "several others" – other maroons presumably – in the southern Baynet mountains that separated Grande Rivière from Gris-Gris.[34] Just before Christmas of 1788, a Bambara woman named Françoise escaped from her owner in Cap-Tiberon and was suspected of attempting to reach an armed community near Jérémie:

Françoise, Bambara, stamped on the breast [MARAIS], age around 30 years, of tall height, red skinned, having marks of her country on the face and body, the middle finger of the right hand cut, speaking French and English; people have seen this nègress in the heights of the Riviere des Anglais, called Baumanoir, with a negro who carried a bundle of linen and a sickle, they have taken the road from the Source-Chaude [Hot Springs], opposite Jérémie, north and south, from the Anses, at that spring there are many maroon negroes; there is another negro who left as a maroon at the same time and from the same quarter, and who has carried off a gun with around six [units] of powder and lead. Give notice to M. Marias Lamothe, at Cap-Tiburon.[35]

The fact that Françoise spoke English suggests that she was either brought to Saint-Domingue through the intra-American slave trade from Jamaica or North America, or perhaps she learned English from ongoing interactions with English-speaking Jamaican slaves and traders near Jérémie. In any case, she was seen with a man carrying a package of linens and a sickle near Riviere des Anglais, the northern end of which heads toward the mountains between Cap Tiberon and Jérémie. A third man escaped around the same time as Françoise, but was carrying a gun and six units of gunpowder. Françoise and her unnamed companion took the road of the Hot Springs near the coves of Jérémie, where many runaways were residing. The hot spring coves in which runaways would have sought refuge may have been either the Port-Salut Moreau Cave or the Grotte nan Barye of the Grand Anse.[36]

Letters sent in 1775 described marronnage as a pervasive problem that had the capacity to undo the colony; one contributing factor cited was the dense, nearly impenetrable mountain ranges into which the *maréchaussée* and other hunters attempted and often failed to pursue fugitives.[37] Though Saint-Domingue's mountains were increasingly occupied by coffee plantations by the mid-eighteenth century, maroons were adept to finding locations that were isolated and difficult to access enough to avoid capture. West Central African runaways especially would have been inclined to turn to the mountains, since the highlands north and south of the Congo River were more densely populated due to the hospitable climate for farming and fishing.[38] Spaces that were supposed to be unreachable and uninhabitable were the very places where maroons were able to find refuge away from the reach of the plantocracy. Waterscapes were also a space that, in Europeans' imagination, provided the means of transportation associated with trade and slaving. However, enslaved people utilized Saint Domingue's rivers and sea-adjacent ports as routes to free themselves.

Waterways: Routes of Un/slaving

Kevin Dawson's (2018) work, *Undercurrents of Power: Aquatic Culture in the African Diaspora*, provides a unique lens through which we can view Africans' and African descendants' relationship to, knowledge of, and uses of waterways that were part of their cultural geographies. Contrary to beliefs widely purported by Europeans that Africans had water phobias or that their bones were too dense to float, continental Africans who lived along the coasts or on riverways were equipped with technical abilities to navigate waters, build and operate boats, deep dive and even surf — oftentimes with stronger proficiency than Europeans themselves. West Central Africa, the zone where most of Saint-Domingue's African population originated, was a rainforest ecology that experienced heavy rains and had major river systems that flowed for miles from the interior to the coast, such as the Congo and Kwanza rivers. High waterfalls, whirlpools, and swamp wildlife made these rivers and their tributaries difficult for Europeans to navigate, while locals fashioned small canoes and arrows that allowed for easier fishing and hunting.[39] African children learned to swim, surf, and canoe at an early age, and various water sports provided opportunities for men to exhibit their bravery and masculinity. Water-based activities were not only recreational and cultural in nature; familiarity with waterscapes allowed Africans to resist the slave trade in ways other than suicide by drowning as an act of spiritual self-preservation, as associated with the Igbo.[40] In 1544, a marooned community of Angolan shipwreck survivors formed on the southern coast of São Tomé, and at the Bight of Benin, the lacustrine community Tofinuland originated from migrations of Aja-Fon speaking peoples fleeing the prolific slave trading Dahomey Kingdom's imperial conquests of the early eighteenth century.[41]

By the eighteenth century, transoceanic travel from Africa was associated with slaving activities. Few examples of Africans' voluntary movement across the Atlantic exist; most of the millions who involuntarily voyaged on ships were captives whose collective experience constituted the Middle Passage. Over the course of three centuries, European nations refined their slave trading processes to a bureaucratic science, leveraging capital funds and insurance from privatized and state-sponsored companies, using ledger books to account for their cargo, employing a range of personnel – including sailors, surgeons, and brokers – to complete each voyage, and maintaining trading relationships at ports of each point of the "triangular trade" between Europe, Africa, and the Americas. The systematic nature of the racialized slave trade nearly ensured that any black person crossing the Atlantic was destined to be enslaved in the Americas, making the ocean and other smaller waterways sites where freedom was impossible (Mustakeem 2016). Canoes and canoe-makers were critical components of fishing communities and were the fundamental means of transport that helped form commercial networks between African coastal ports and the hinterlands. Economic enterprise and cultural, social, and political developments associated with the slave trade were heavily dependent on these boatmen and their knowledge of waterways to establish trade relationships. Traveling along rivers allowed European slave traders and their African intermediaries to have greater access to communities deep in Africa's interior, where violent raids resulted in boatloads of captives being taken to the coastal ports where they would then wait for weeks or months at a time to board a slave ship. The crisscrossing oceanic travel and commerce of European-owned slave ships made them "living, microcultural, micropolitical system[s] in motion" (Gilroy 1992: 4) that transported African worldviews, mores, sensibilities, behaviors, and practices.

Less frequently, enslaved Africans were not only made into cargo occupying the bellies of slave ships, they were owned by naval and other government officers, fishermen, and large-scale traders, and spent long periods of time on the vessels' top decks, performing a variety of tasks associated with the maintenance of the vessel. Aquatic skills gained on the continent and at sea were part of the cultural legacy enslaved Africans brought to the Americas, which was useful in a water-bound colony like

Saint-Domingue. The difficulty of crossing the colony's many mountains meant that coastal shipping and water-based movement were primary modes of transportation.[42] Over 30 identified rivers flowed from the mountains to the coastlines, and with a wet climate and natural disasters, flooding was a common and dangerous occurrence. Some of the major river routes included Trois Rivières, which flowed south from Port-de-Paix and the Artibonite River, often referred to as Saint-Domingue's "Nile," that flowed nearly 60 miles east into central Santo Domingo. The colony was made up of over 800 miles of coastline, which meant that every region of Saint-Domingue touched or was close to the sea.[43]

Having access to a body of water, such as women who bathed or washed clothing in rivers (Figure 6.3) would have made boating or swimming away from slavery a tempting possibility; runaways who were skilled swimmers had an advantage in marronnage. For example, an unnamed Mondongue man threw himself from a schooner three leagues, or about ten miles, from land and was suspected of reaching Môle Saint Nicolas, since his comrades attested that he was an excellent swimmer.[44] Enslaved people who inhabited plantations with proximity to waterways had access to small boats and canoes that they used to escape – even if they

FIGURE 6.3. "Propriété sucrière des familles Thiverny et Fresquet à Saint-Domingue, aquarelle anonymeArchives Bordeaux Métropole, Bordeaux Fi Saint-Domingue 1"

were not particularly noted for having maritime experience. Dozens of runaways listed in *Les Affiches américaines* and other runway advertisements were suspected of taking flight in a *canot* or canoe. The *Gazette de Saint Domingue* reported that four men and two *nouveaux* women of the Nagô and Arada nations banded together to escape their owner Jarossay in a fishing boat in June 1791.[45] While long-distance trade in Africa was largely conducted by men, women similarly had canoeing skills and used them to conduct local trade. Two unnamed women, one of whom was breastfeeding a two-month-old child, may have already had boating experience when they left Cayes in a canoe in December of 1767.[46]

Several runaways in Saint Domingue were canoe-makers or masons, fishermen, swimmers, or were part of the colony's naval forces. Fugitives with maritime knowledge and experience, even those from different regional or ethnic backgrounds, could find common ground and escape together through the rivers or ports. For example, three sailors – Pierrit, a Kongolese man described as the captain, an English-speaking Nagô man named Louis, and Azor, who was also Nagô – fled Le Cap in a stolen boat over 30 feet long. It was believed they were headed to the Jacquezy neighborhood in Le Trou, a common maroon destination and hotbed for armed band activity.[47] Some maroon sailors were enslaved people sold to Saint-Domingue from other Caribbean islands, which gave them a wider understanding of inter-imperial waters. Saint-Marc, who claimed to be a freeman from Jamaica, and Jacob, who also spoke a little English, were two sailors who left in a Danish boat called *The Iris*.[48] Two other sailors from the Anglophone Atlantic, Robin and Guillaume, escaped Fort Dauphin in a small fishing boat, and may have taken another enslaved person with them.[49]

For Europeans, waterways were highways for the commercial buying and selling of captive slaves. But for Africans, water and water-based activity facilitated trade and leisure, and in the colonial context their acquired recreational and practical skills also contributed to efforts to liberate themselves. Self-directed mobility was a scarcity for enslaved people, as were windows of opportunity to escape. Yet the vastness of Saint-Domingue's topography, its mountains, rivers, plains, ports, sink-holes, and caves offered a number of options for seeking refuge in the act of marronnage. Also, part of this landscape was the ever-changing boundary between French Saint-Domingue and Spanish Santo Domingo. The border not only drew the political distinction between two European empires, it represented a nearly 400-mile gate to a new geographic, social, economic, and cultural scene. The contention between the two colonies and their respective royal administrators made the border more than just an imaginary line in the earth; it became a literal site of grappling between French, Spanish, African and indigenous peoples through trade, competition for land and slaves, and collaboration and resistance. The next part of this chapter will explore relations between the Spanish and the French, and the ways in which people of African descent took advantage of inter-imperial conflict and carved out social and geographic spaces for themselves as maroons.

SITES OF CONTENTION: THE SAINT-DOMINGUE–SANTO DOMINGO BORDER

Spatial structures, like social, economic, and political structures, shape material conditions and humans' lived experiences; conversely, human activity in the form of sustained collective action can impact or transform those structures. Mimi Sheller (2012: 191) argues that "despite the existence of dominant social orderings of space and legal systems to uphold that ordering, in practice other social productions of space nevertheless emerge alongside or are directly superimposed on hegemonic space." The border between Saint-Domingue and Santo Domingo operated as a spatial structure that delineated the nature of the colonial social order and slavery in Saint-Domingue. It also proved to be a structure – much like the colony's urban areas, mountains, and waterways – that, through the conscious and sustained collective action of black people, could be manipulated and mobilized as a subversive rival geography. Two late seventeenth-century policies delineated the legal and geographical boundaries of French slavery: the 1685 *Code Noir* formalized regulations about slavery in Saint-Domingue and other French Caribbean islands, and the 1697 Treaty of Ryswick established French control of western Española. In the months leading up the *Code Noir's* ratification in 1685, the governor of Saint-Domingue sought specific directives to limit the number of enslaved Africans in the colony. He also expressed concern about the numerous Africans, indigenous people, and *mûlatres* escaping to the Spanish territory after the French military captured 100 fugitives and returned them to Saint-Domingue. The governor alleged not only that runaways had learned the meaning of freedom during their escapes but that 24 of them were responsible for killing white colonists. These concerns influenced the *Code Noir's* aim to maintain royal control of the colonies through the regulation of "crimes" committed by the enslaved – especially marronnage.[50] The inauguration of this repressive legal mechanism to extend and institutionalize the powers of plantation regimes, colonial authorities, and the French monarchy was in part a response to Africans' ongoing collective agency, which certainly did not cease in 1685. Enslaved Africans also disregarded the Treaty of Ryswick by subverting and exploiting the artificial border between Saint-Domingue and Santo Domingo, as conflicts between the French and Spanish provided Africans with geographic leverage to negotiate their freedom through marronnage. But more importantly, the ever-shifting geopolitical border *itself* was constituted by inter-imperial competition for land, resources, and laborers, as well as Africans' collective acts of agency for their freedom.

From the earliest moments of enslaved Africans' presence on the island of Española, runaways and rebels regularly resisted forced labor under the Spanish *encomienda* and *repartimiento* systems by reconstituting sections of the landscape as liberated zones. The first Africans and remaining Taíno escaped Spanish mines, ranches, and plantations, finding refuge in the Baoruco mountains or the western region that the French later occupied. Rebels in the northwest traded goods with French and Dutch settlers in the late sixteenth- and early seventeenth-centuries. Runaways joined up with Dutch raiders as early as 1625, but the formal onset of French colonization of Saint-Domingue in 1697 and its aggressive sugar-based plantation economy essentially reversed the directional flow of African runaways from east–west to west–east.[51] Africans brought to Saint-Domingue encountered a slavery regime that was much more relentless, violent, and industrialized than anything developed on the continent of Africa or in Santo Domingo, especially after the Spanish redirected their energies to mining on the South American continent. For over a century, conflicts between the Spanish and French over land, resources, and slaves had an immediate impact on the enslaved people of Saint-Domingue and their perception of options for freedom. Not only did Spanish colonists raid French plantations and kidnap enslaved people in Saint-Domingue, but open warfare between the two royal governments created windows of opportunity for enslaved people to disavow their French owners and see what life in Santo Domingo had to offer.

Slave codes, existing in both the French and Spanish colonies, attempted to delineate the social boundaries of bondage as it related to enslaved people's freedom statuses, family, and rights to humane treatment. A major distinction between the two codes was that the Spanish system was based on the medieval *Siete Partidas* code, which stated that though slaves had no civil rights, they did have innate human rights.

This is not to suggest that enslavement itself was easier in the Spanish Empire than elsewhere in the Americas, but in contrast to officials in slave-holding French Caribbean colonies, Spanish officials actualized aspects of their policy to ameliorate the basic living conditions for enslaved people. Assimilation into Christianity and the Spanish language and culture, as well as marriage rights, were important avenues for enslaved blacks to create extensive social networks. Narrow paths of manumission were also available and served as a form of social control to discourage rebellion. Courts in the Spanish Empire reinforced enslaved people's human rights by allowing them to seek prosecution of abusive owners using a court-appointed defender. They also sued for their freedom, the right to marry, and the right to keep their families together. The Catholic Church had traditions of charitable works that created social institutions which benefitted enslaved people, such as the *cofradias* or confraternities, hospitals that served slaves and free people of color, and service in local militias, which could lead to mobility or emancipation.[52]

The willingness to arm blacks through militia participation and other means to fight enemy forces was a feature of slavery in Santo Domingo from as early as 1600–1650, when Spanish planters armed slaves against their local sugar-planting competitors.[53] Not only could blacks be armed in Santo Domingo, but some freemen occupied their own town, symbolizing a possibility of freedom and mobility that would never have been officially sanctioned by the French colonial state. After nearly two centuries of fighting rebels during the Christmas Day Wolof uprising and maroons like "Captain" Sebastian Lemba, Diego Guzman, and "the cowboy" Juan Vaquero, the Spanish established a town near Santo Domingo for self-freed runways called San Lorenzo de los Negros de Minas. The town was self-governing and captains from each major ethnic group – Minas, Aradas, Kongos, and Brans from the Gold Coast – held authoritative control over their respective group. Garcia Congo was the sergeant of the town militia, while his lieutenant was Mina and the captain was of the Bran nation. The groups operated independently but collaborated when necessary.[54]

In 1679, the same year as San Lorenzo's founding, a man named Padre Jean led an insurgency in the north aiming to kill all the white colonists between Port-de-Paix and Port Margot. Padre Jean killed his Spanish owner then headed toward Tortuga for refuge; the small island had been the site of rebellion of white planters desiring independence from France.[55] From there, he crossed over to Petit Saint Louis, where he recruited 25 enslaved Africans, some of whom had been kidnapped by the French from Spanish owners. As they travelled east, nearly reaching Port Margot, they mobilized others and killed any Frenchmen with whom they crossed paths, with hopes of gaining a pardon from the Spanish. The insurgents were blocked at the Borgne parish while raiding plantations for additional arms and supplies. *Boucaneers* commissioned by the governor eventually sought out the insurgents who then retreated to the mountains near Port-de-Paix and were found by French settlers' defensive units who were initially reluctant to engage. Padre Jean and six associates were killed, but many others fought their way back into Spanish territory, where they were received with impunity. Other runaways from French plantations in the west began running east to claim religious asylum.[56]

Ongoing inter-imperial warfare fostered the seeds of rebellion among the enslaved. In 1689, the French fought against Spain, England, and parts of the Holy Roman Empire in a conflict known as the Nine Years War, and Española's western lands became a local scene as the Spanish and French embarked on a near-century-long struggle for control of the territory.[57] The French attacked the Spanish city of Santiago in 1690; and the next year, the Spanish retaliated by pillaging what would become Cap-Français and reinstating it into their territory. Between 1691 and 1695, Spanish and English forces penetrated as far west as Port-de-Paix, burning towns, capturing enslaved Africans, and taking them to San Lorenzo de los Negros de Minas.[58] Bondspeople owned by the French took advantage of the conflict and planned to rebel: in 1691, around Léogâne, 200 were implicated in a conspiracy to kill their owners and take over their plantations. Authorities executed two of the men involved on the breaking wheel and three others had their legs cut off.[59] November of 1691 saw another conspiracy in Port-de-Paix organized by Janot Marin and an 18-year-old Senegambian named George Dollo "Pierrot," who planned to rally others to leave the colony and go to war against their owners. With Marin at the head of seven, their plan was to assemble in Limonade and head to the Spanish territory. Once they left, the remaining slaves at Port-de-Paix would kill all the white men, women, and children of the parish and the rebels would be granted power over the district by the Spanish. Marin and Pierrot were assisted by a young white indentured servant, who later revealed the plot, and a bilingual, bi-racial man from the Spanish territory. The "*mûlatre* Espagnol," named Espion, was a spy who had been in communication with Marin and Pierrot for three months. Espion instructed the men to try to take over Port-de-Paix by convincing the blacks to leave, and, once the masses agreed, Marin and Pierrot would send a black lieutenant named Congre to Gonâve so the

Spanish could receive the news then descend on Cap Français. Upon arrival, the Spanish would relinquish control over Port-de-Paix to the black rebels. However, once the French learned of the impending Spanish attack, military aid was sent to galvanize troops from the northern districts who were then informed of the conspiracy to join the Spanish. Although it was nearly a successful attempt to exploit the fighting between French and Spanish forces during the Nine Years War, the plot failed, and a military tribunal sentenced Marin and Pierrot to be burned alive.[60]

Others were more successful at using Spanish aggression to their benefit and they escaped to San Lorenzo de los Negros de Minas or other small towns near the capital city, Santo Domingo. Over 100 escaped in 1692, and 20 years later approximately 500 former enslaved Saint-Dominguans were still living in the Spanish lands. In May 1697, 300 enslaved people in Quartier Morin and Petite Anse organized an insurrection but were quickly disassembled, though it is not clear if this was another attempt by the Spanish to undermine French control of enslaved Africans in order to gain the upper hand in combat.[61] Still, the Treaty of Ryswick was ratified in November 1697, ending the Nine Years War – but it would not be the last time enslaved people's uprisings and escapes were timed to exploit the ongoing French–Spanish conflict that created vacuums of power in Española's northeastern regions.

Another plot was uncovered in 1704, when M. de Charritte proclaimed that Africans near Le Cap were again planning to kill the local whites at the behest of Spanish agents.[62] This conspiracy may have been connected to a maroon camp that formed in the mountains outside of Cap Français, where entire family units resided and organized incursions until 1704.[63] Acknowledging that rates of marronnage into Santo Domingo tended to be excessive during wartime, the Council of Léogâne issued a bounty for the government to pay 25 *piastres* for any person in Santo Domingo who could return a runaway, but this restitution was rarely paid. In February 1711, the king of France overruled the Council of Léogâne, stating that each planter had an individual responsibility to re-locate fugitives.[64] Still, government funds were used to help planters recoup costs associated with chasing runaways. Later, in May 1711, two runaways – Houx and Moussac – were killed, and their owners were compensated with six hundred *livres* each for their losses.[65] Even after the war ended, early eighteenth-century Saint Domingue had not yet fully formed into the proto-industrial sugar-producing powerhouse it would soon become and maroons seemed to have free rein of the colony, prompting the creation of the *maréchaussée* fugitive slave police in 1721.[66] M. Dubois, the colonel commandant of Cul-de-Sac, reported mass desertions, to which militias were organized to capture the deserters in 1715 and 1717.[67] In July 1715, Dubois sent a convoy to Santo Domingo to re-capture runaways, but this search came up empty handed because the Spanish warned the escapees of the convoy's arrival.[68] The 1717 dispatch did discover a settlement that had a well that was 40 feet deep, presumably constructed by the fugitives to meet their needs for fresh water.[69]

Runaways to the Spanish territory remained an issue and attempts to control them resulted in mixed outcomes. In 1718, the Spanish king gave an order to return to the French all the blacks who had taken refuge in Santo Domingo.[70] The French moved into Azua, with the commandant of Azua leading the charge. An expedition into the Baoruco mountains in 1719 resulted in the capture of a band leader and ritual healer named Michel, as well as other leaders in Maribaroux.[71] In another case, runaways in Santo Domingo were rounded up for return to Saint-Domingue in 1719, but local Spaniards forcefully opposed this ruling and instead took the captives to San Lorenzo. By the late eighteenth century, San Lorenzo held some 300 free black inhabitants, all descendants of either kidnapped or runaway African Saint-Dominguans.[72] Between 1721 and 1723, tensions between the Spanish king and his colonial officials were again exacerbated when the governor of Santo Domingo declared that he would no longer return French runaways to Saint-Domingue. In somewhat of a ploy, he wrote to French administrators that he had captured 128 runaways and that the colonists could come and retrieve them, so the French colonists sent a ship to the bay of Ocoa with two representatives onboard. The two agents went to Santo Domingo, but as the fugitives approached the boat the Spaniards changed their minds and gave arms to the Africans, who then revolted in a declaration that they were free. The two agents only narrowly escaped but later attempted to charge the Spanish crown for the sunk costs.[73] Aggression between the French and Spanish continued into the 1730s; in 1727, 15 Spaniards destroyed two French settlements in Trou-de-Jean-de-Nantes, Ouanminthe, and took with them some enslaved Africans.[74] Later, a group of Africans stole a boat and went to Santo Domingo, where they intermarried with members of the local population, and a colonial officer, LaGrange, was tasked with finding them and returning them to Saint-Domingue.[75] Despite the Treaty of Ryswick establishing the west as French territory in 1697, the presence and value of black people cast a stark relief onto the distinctions between life, society, and slavery in the two colonies, making the border a hotly contested, politicized entity. Spanish incursions from the east continued until the 1770s, when a formal agreement in December 1777 finalized the final geographical boundaries between the two European colonies.[76]

Maroons Making the Border

Geopolitical contestations between the French and Spanish starting in mainland Europe continued to spill across the Atlantic to the island of Española and caused conflicts between colonists, as well as rifts and misunderstandings between colonists and their respective royal governments. These struggles centered on competition for land, resources, and enslaved people, whose very presence and collective actions to self-liberate further ignited and shaped inter-imperial contestations over the border, and shaped the border itself. The decrease of sugar production in Santo Domingo did not stem the desire for outputs like those occurring in Saint-Domingue, leading envious Spanish planters to take advantage of Saint-Domingue's deadly labor regimes and harsh punishments for maroons by luring or kidnapping enslaved people from plantations during raids from the east. Spaniards attempted to drive away several planters from Bassin-Cayman, Dondon in 1741, and in 1747 they kidnapped five blacks and a plantation overseer from Marre-a-la-Roche, Dondon.[77] When Port-au-Prince was founded in 1749 and sugar production increasingly spread in its suburban areas, economic development in the areas surrounding the city and the Cul-de-Sac region pushed Saint-Domingue's boundaries eastward, and maroons who had been in these border regions found themselves at the center of conflicts between French and Spanish authorities.[78] As in previous decades, a major concern of Saint-Domingue colonists was that enslaved Africans were continuing to take advantage of geographic proximity to the Spanish territory as a channel for escape. African Saint-Dominguans had an incentive to do so since Spanish codes held several provisions that allowed for manumission from enslavement and, at times, the establishment of free black towns such as San Lorenzo de los Negros de Minas.

In October 1751, the militia commander of Mirebalais received a substantial budget from colonial authorities to chase runaways into Santo Domingo. The commander, Bremond, had at his disposal 300 *livres* for every captured runaway, a high-ranking militia officer, and as many *maréchaussée* archers as he could pay himself.[79] According to Spanish officials, some 3,000 runaways from Saint-Domingue had escaped to

Santo Domingo, or the Baoruco mountains more specifically, in 1751 alone.[80] A good number of these perhaps escaped after the earthquake on November 21 of that year that almost destroyed Port-au-Prince.[81] Spanish planters likely welcomed these refugees to provide additional labor due to the lack of plantation-based economic growth in the island's eastern regions. While Saint-Domingue's enslaved population grew exponentially in the eighteenth century, Santo Domingo's reached a maximum of 15,000 in 1789, a far cry from its neighbor to the west. Though there was growing industry toward the end of the century, Santo Domingo had essentially become a sparsely populated "backwater" colony of the Spanish empire.[82] Spanish colonists' desires for land and black workers continued to manifest as aggression over the border – they burned four plantations in Ravines-a-Mûlatres in Valière in 1757 after warning the planters to abandon the settlements.[83]

While island-dwelling Spanish colonists irritated relations with their French neighbors, during the 1760s, the Spanish crown offered collaborative support regarding Saint-Domingue's problem of runaways. A letter from the king of Spain on October 18, 1760, revealed that the primary cause for marronnage was the harsh treatment enacted by French planters, who had not held to their agreement to stop punishing deserters.[84] Yet, Spanish colonists again undermined Saint-Domingue's attempts to regulate its runaway problem when on May 22, 1764, the governor of Santo Domingo, Don Manuel d'Azlor, proposed that Saint-Domingue model San Lorenzo de los Negros de Minas and build its own free settlements to house runaways.[85] Spanish attitudes toward re-settling fugitives may have incentivized more runaways from Saint Domingue, resulting in another expedition in pursuit of fugitives into the Spanish territory on August 21, 1764.[86] In February 1765, the Saint-Domingue colonial governor, Comte d'Estaing, declared a state of alert, mandating that all colonists were required to be armed at all times with guns, bayonets, gunpowder, sabers, and machetes or swords. Further, he ordered that fugitive-chasing militias would be comprised of *gens du couleur* and free black *affranchis*.[87] One year later, a treaty was established between d'Azlor and Rohan, general governor of Saint-Domingue, to return all maroons, thieves, and absent-without-leave soldiers, and to stop the sale of goods by merchants who passed through Bete à Cornes without legal right.[88] The 1766 treaty also stated that any Santo Domingo planter would be fined 50 *livres* for harboring fugitives or kidnapped Africans. The two colonial forces also decided to cooperate to chase maroons in the mountains.[89] This agreement suggests that despite ongoing negotiations between the two royal representatives, Spanish planters continued use Saint-Dominguan runaways as labor and as trading partners – meaning that maroons played an active role in orchestrating relations between the two colonies as they attempted to concretize and manage the border.

The Spanish and French royal and colonial governments were conjoined by shared interests in enslaving and preventing maroons from dominating areas that bordered the two colonies. Yet, their common goals did not reach the local level, where planters from Santo Domingo continued to antagonize Saint-Domingue planters over land and slaves. In 1769, Don Nicholas de Montenegro, commander of St. Raphael in Santo Domingo, renewed aggression against Saint-Domingue when he kidnapped a Dondon planter and four black captives and took them to Santo Domingo until 1771, when the planter paid a ransom to the king of Spain. Spanish planters continued to violate the 1766 agreement and stake claim to French lands in Saint-Domingue, again in the parish of Dondon. Montenegro gave a French *mûlatre* permission to settle in Dondon in March 1771, but 50 Spanish men arrived in May, kidnapping the plantation overseer and a black woman, then burning down several plantations. In retaliation, an armed force went into Santo Domingo and kidnapped nine blacks and an overseer without damaging any property. Negotiations to return each set of hostages ensued, and the French agreed to return portions of Dondon to the Spaniards.[90] Interestingly, over twenty years later, on the night of October 10 or 11 in 1789, nine men and four women, all Kongolese, escaped to Saint-Domingue from their owner, Montenegro, the commander of St. Raphael.[91] These maroons may have been the kidnapped slaves who chose to return to Saint-Domingue, perhaps due to its familiarity or kinship ties they may have formed. In either case, these maroons and people enslaved along the border were both subjects and agents of the border's creation.

Despite these local spats, Spanish colonial forces adhered to their earlier agreements and sent convoys into the border region to search for runaways, and the French continued to establish militias to retrieve the numerous maroons from the Spanish territory.[92] In 1770, a group of 13 runaways from Saint Domingue were captured in the countryside along the border and then interrogated in the city of Santo Domingo. Six were from the Loango Coast, identifying as Kongo and Mondongo. Several knew their French owners, while others were recently arrived and could not speak Spanish or French. An unbranded African named Bucu did not know how long he had been in the colony because he had escaped toward the east immediately after leaving the slave ship. This indicates that the political strife over the Spanish–French border was not lost on even the most recently arrived Africans, who used the contestation to their benefit.[93] By 1775, some 15,000 maroons were believed to be in Santo Domingo.[94] Africans' knowledge of the eastward haven did not go unnoticed; the French government created a commission in January 1776 to search for runaways "who passed daily into Spanish Santo Domingo," providing compensation per fugitive recovered.[95]

Some maroons who fled Saint-Domingue for Santo Domingo blended into colonial society, either farming, working for local Spanish planters, or residing in San Lorenzo de los Negros de Minas. Others joined established maroon communities who operated outside the sphere of both colonial societies and antagonized plantations in Saint-Domingue and Santo Domingo. In Saint-Domingue's western department at Béate – a small island that forms a sound with Baoruco and Anse-a-Pitre in Cayes de Jacmel – maroon bands' attacks on plantations in the 1770s prompted a renewed struggle between the French and Spanish to defeat the maroons. The Council of Léogâne had already increased *maréchaussée* presence in the south in 1705, 1729, and 1741. Yet as the numbers of troops increased, so did the number of runaways. Administrators sent a detachment to Fond-Parisien in Croix-des-Bouquets on February 19, 1771, and another group was sent to Grands-Bois in Mirebalais on May 19, 1774. On February 8, 1775, there was an ordinance to build a town in Croix-des-Bouquets and a sheriff with several mounted police were assigned to Fond-Parisien, Roche-Blance, and Grand-Bois. These troops were ineffective in preventing raids from runaway bands, and on October 13, 1776, another dispatch arrived at Boucan Patate because the maroons destroyed a newly built guardhouse. Though this offensive was somewhat successful, resulting in rebel deaths between Fond-Parisien and Grand-Bois as far south as Sale Trou, maroon militaristic strategy bewildered Spanish and French forces. The colonial militias were not as adept at navigating the mountains as the maroons, who for generations had deployed the mountains as part of their geography of subversion.

Two months later, in December 1776, a full-scale collaborative offensive between the French and Spanish – numbering 180 men and costing 80,000 *livres* – launched from Croix-des-Bouquets against the maroons in the Baoruco mountains. But by January 1777, the expedition was struggling to enter the dense forest and was running out of energy, food, drink, and supplies; troops were even reduced to drinking their own urine in order to survive. While some retreated to Port-au-Prince for provisions, the rest went south to Cayes and sent a boat of 100 men to Béate, where Spanish guides suggested there were maroon settlements based in the caves. When the boat arrived, the maroons had temporarily disappeared. That spring, the maroons re-appeared, initiating a counter-attack at Fond-Parisien – back in Croix-des-Bouquets where the expedition had begun. The rebel bands attacked Boucan-Greffin in May 1777 and again in November 1778, this time kidnapping an enslaved domestic worker named Anne from the Coupe property. On December 15, 1778, another detachment was sent to Boucan-Greffin in Croix-des-Bouquets, where a brigade of eight archers and two corporals were lodged at Sieur Coupe's property to protect him. While in the hands of her captives, Anne was coerced into marrying a rebel leader named Kebinda, perhaps a BaKongo man named after the port city Cabinda. However, before the nuptials started, she convinced Kebinda to take her to a church where she was recovered by Spanish officials.[96]

Once divided by maroons who took up arms for the Spanish against the French, collaborations on expeditions in pursuit of maroons united the two colonial forces and pushed them to an agreement on the contours of the geopolitical landscape and the treatment of future maroons. After a year of negotiation, on June 3, 1777, Saint-Domingue and Santo Domingo ratified the Treaty of Aranjuez to finally settle the geographical limits of the boundary between the two colonies. One of the central parts of that treaty concerned the treatment of maroons who abandoned Saint-Domingue for the Spanish countryside and mountain ranges. The two nations again agreed to collaborate on pursuits, since maroons were considered a threat to both colonies, and that the French would give compensation of 12 *livres* for returning runaways.[97] But, Saint-Dominguan runaways, and perhaps also kidnapped enslaved people, continued to disregard the agreements between the French and Spanish authorities by making new lives for themselves in Santo Domingo. In January 1778, the Intendant of Saint-Domingue suggested that there needed to be concern and consensus about the price of return for runaways who were married and living in the Spanish territory, and in the rare case that Spanish blacks were caught in Saint-Domingue as runaways, they would not be sold in the cities but kept in jails separate from other absconders.[98] Colonists' fear of maroons from Saint-Domingue and Santo Domingo possibly co-mingling indicates their conscious awareness that maroons collaborated in manipulating inter-imperial relations and persuaded each other to rebel. Over the course of three centuries, maroons forced French and Spanish colonists to expend energy, time, and resources toward finalizing the border between Saint-Domingue and Santo Domingo. Colonists were ineffective at using the border to maintain separate societal spheres and control over the respective enslaved populations, and therefore turned to other policies that they hoped, incorrectly, would placate the enslaved and prevent further rebellion.

While the Spanish actively sought to expand the slave trade in its Caribbean and South American territories, they aimed to do so according to customs and codes that governed the treatment of enslaved people throughout the empire. The *Code Noir* was the envy of the Spanish Empire and was perceived as an important source of Saint-Domingue's economic prosperity. In 1785, a year after the French king issued a royal decree aimed to ameliorate conditions in Saint-Domingue, the Spanish similarly issued the Carolinian Slave Code for Santo Domingo. Included the Code were provisions for learning Catholicism, the right to a small plot of land for personal cultivation, several conditions for slaves to earn their freedom, and the right to marry. In response to this new code, it seems that the number of runaways from Saint-Domingue into the east was increasing. Moreau de Saint-Méry, writing from Cayes de Jacmel, claimed that raids in this area stopped after 1785, but as Chapter 8 will explain, later incursions and conflicts with the Maniel maroons would prove this to be false.[99] In 1788, the Marquis de Najac wrote to a former governor of Saint-Domingue essentially accusing the governor of allowing the maroon problem to grow: "during your administration, over four thousand slaves fled into Spanish territory; since your departure, the Spanish hardly returned any of them, and I am convinced that there are now six thousand in the Spanish colony."[100] Saint-Dominguan planters and traveling merchants also attested to growing unrest among their slaves in October 1789 because of circulating rumors that the Spanish were again giving refuge to runaways.[101] This may reflect local interpretations of the 1789 Spanish code Royal Instructors for the Education, Trade, and Work of Slaves, which limited punishments to no more than 25 strokes of the whip and threatened punishments to owners who caused serious injury, blood loss, or mutilation.[102] However, these policies were not qualitatively distinct from those that existed in Saint-Domingue, and the 1789 *Real Cedula* was not actually promulgated in Santo Domingo.[103] Whereas there once may have been a perception among runaways that Santo Domingo was a safer space due to its underdeveloped plantation economy, the changing circumstances in which Spain now aimed to reinvigorate its agricultural production and slave-holding practices meant that the Bourbon colony might no longer be considered a haven for Saint-Domingue's maroons. After centuries of exploiting the border as a geography of subversion, new Spanish policies attempted to bolster Santo Domingo as a geography of containment.

CONCLUSION

Geographic proximity to what was perceived as a less-hostile colony, Santo Domingo, was a critical component of Saint-Domingue's context. Though *Les Affiches américaines* advertisements only indicate 80 runaways headed east over the 26-year publication span, other primary sources paint a very different picture: one in which, for several decades, streams of Saint-Domingue's enslaved labor force made their way to Santo Domingo with the implicit and explicit welcome of the Spanish. On the other hand, it would not be unlikely that planters exaggerated their losses to obtain financial compensation from the royal or colonial governments. Further, the overwhelming majority black population in Saint-Domingue kept white residents at a heightened level of anxiety about a possible revolt – especially when the colony was most vulnerable during periods of war. Whites feared a looming maroon presence and often requested reinforcements to protect plantations from fugitives who returned to steal goods, food, weapons, tools, or to bring others to freedom. It is difficult, if not impossible, to quantify the actual number of runaways in the colony due to the failure of some plantation managers to report fugitive advertisements. Additionally, we do not know the numbers of children that maroon women birthed while living in self-liberated zones – though it is highly likely that they had more children than enslaved women.[104] Therefore, it is a challenging task to determine how much of planters' anxieties were justified. On the other hand, corroborating contemporary sources about rogue fugitive bands can help fill in the picture about the nature and scope of marronnage in Saint-Domingue.

When considering the complex geographic and geopolitical history of marronnage in Saint-Domingue and its neighbor Santo Domingo, it is no mystery why the Spanish were eager to support the revolutionary forces of 1791 led by Georges Biassou and Jean-François Papillon, himself a maroon. African collective action through marronnage had long helped shape Saint Domingue's colonial landscape and inter-imperial relations well before 1791. In the same way that structures of domination and counterhegemonic practices co-exist and grapple with each other in ongoing dialectal processes, the maroon presence was equally as pervasive as the reach of the plantocracy. Maroons hid in plain sight in urban areas and created spaces for themselves in geographically difficult areas. Not only was their presence a reality, but their collective impact on the colonial order was undeniable. Maroon domination and agency marked locations that were re-named to reflect histories of rebellion. Moreover, marronnage pushed the boundaries of empire by forcing French colonists to reckon with their Spanish neighbors, giving insight to the ways in which subaltern intentionality impacts social and the spatial structural processes.

III

COLLECTIVE ACTION AND REVOLUTION

7

"We Must Stop the Progress of Marronnage": Repertoires and Repression

The mutinies were put down; since then the colony had steadily gained in wealth and importance. This development failed to stamp out the spirit of insubordination at the foundation of the social system.

Anna Julia Cooper ([1925] 1988: 50–51)

Enslaved people asserted themselves in their everyday lives, navigating and responding to the shifting social and environmental conditions that shaped their existence while disrupting colonial structures through marronnage and other oppositional actions. Saint-Domingue was an economically booming colony with rapidly growing sugar- and coffee-producing sectors. Enslaved people saw little to no fruits of their labor value – in fact, despite its famed wealth, the colony often faced food shortages because of mismanagement during inter-imperial conflicts, which only bolstered discontent. The greed of the plantocracy and the demand for sugar in Europe further inflamed the slave trade and the growth of the enslaved population, inadvertently causing the colony to buckle under the pressure of its own weight during the latter years of the eighteenth century. In France, the migration of citizens from rural to urban areas caused increasing economic distress, furthering societal strain and contributing to revolutionary outcomes (Goldstone 1991); similarly, enslaved Africans' forced migration to Saint-Domingue deepened their discontent with commodification and the dire conditions they faced in the colony. Howard Winant (2001: 52–53) argues that, "as capitalism, empire, and communication all experienced substantial growth, this growth also fueled emancipatory aspirations and potentialities." Colonial economies expanded due to the rise of global sugar prices, precipitating the demand for sugar plantation laborers and the rapid population growth of enslaved Africans. Influxes of enslaved people, some of whom were experienced in war either as captives or soldiers, contributed to increasingly larger and more frequent acts of marronnage and insurrection in the Americas.

European colonizers' late seventeenth- and early eighteenth-century economic aspirations transformed previously unexploited lands into full-fledged plantation societies founded on enslaved African labor (Scott [1986] 2018: 1–4). Between the 1670s and 1750s, significantly larger numbers of captive Africans disembarked at Jamaica and Brazil than Saint-Domingue (Table 7.1).[1] Within the same time period, both colonies saw the rise of large-scale fugitive settlements that staged revolts against their respective colonial powers and threatened to upend local plantation economies: the Leeward and Windward Jamaican maroons and the Brazilian Palmares Kingdom. These self-liberated zones were organized settlements where runaways' patterns of interactions and social network relationships produced distinct cultural, religious, political, and militaristic expressions. The maroon communities were highly populated, armed, and their insurrections challenged colonial authorities – in some instances with such vigor that they commanded and negotiated treaties with respective colonial governments. Other runaway communities – including

TABLE 7.1. *African disembarkations to Haiti, Jamaica, and Brazil, all years*

Year Range	Haiti (Saint-Domingue and Santo Domingo)	Jamaica	Brazil
1501–1525	287	0	0
1526–1550	2,408	0	0
1551–1575	6,033	0	332
1576–1600	8,406	150	536
1601–1625	6,413	2955	1,412
1626–1650	2,046	0	32,144
1651–1675	1,107	8,806	6,680
1676–1700	2,954	56,635	72,423
1701–1725	39,459	117,172	209,571
1726–1750	120,663	170,642	370,634
1751–1775	222,850	218,848	320,921
1776–1800	310,792	289,625	417,812
1801–1825	1,048	66,835	937,518
1826–1850	0	2,557	791,045
1851–1875	0	362	7,900

numerous *quilombos* in Brazil, maroons in Suriname and Jamaica, and *palenques* in Cuba and Colombia — existed and thrived during the seventeenth and eighteenth centuries (Price [1973] 1996; Genovese 1979; Heuman 1986; Thompson 2006; Moomou 2015).

In contrast to the rapid population growth and armed revolt in Jamaica and Brazil at the end of the seventeenth century, *Ayiti/Española/Saint-Domingue* was sparsely populated after sixteenth-century maroon resistance contributed to the fall of sugar production and the Spanish withdrew to pursue mining on mainland South America, leaving the island to be ruled by the "masterless" class of free blacks, maroons, and pirates. As Chapter 6 explained, the island had become a backwater of the Spanish empire; disputes over land, enslaved labor, and the border between the Spanish and the newly formed French territories marked the first half of the eighteenth century. The relatively slow growth of Saint-Domingue's enslaved population between the late seventeenth and early eighteenth centuries meant that most fugitive communities were likely small-scale geographic nodes composed of a family or several families. These maroons were likely either Spanish colonial-era inhabitants or escaped enslaved peoples who created new "maroon landscapes" in the borderlands, hinterlands, and the more immediate shadows of plantations (Miki 2012; Diouf 2014). The most well-known and only officially recognized maroon community from Saint-Domingue was the Maniel, who established free and independent living spaces through their negotiations with the French and the Spanish. Though these maroons were considered to be agitators due to their attacks on plantations, they did not mount the same military threat as their contemporaries in other colonies.

Since seventeenth-century "masterless" emancipated blacks and maroons were the island's population majority – including in regions that later became Saint-Domingue – when the French arrived, they expanded structures of repression against marronnage, and the black population writ large, to create a plantation regime that would enslave as many people as possible to generate wealth primarily for French colonists and owners in the metropole. Violent repression facilitated the French colonial sugar revolution, as the enslaved population exploded in the early to late eighteenth century due to political changes, warfare, and instability on the African continent. Yet, it was this population growth, combined with the window of opportunity presented by the French Revolution and the prevalence of maroon organizing tactics, that helps explain why the 1791 Saint-Domingue uprising went further than the Jamaican and Brazilian maroon rebellions in overturning slavery and colonialism. This chapter focuses on how maroons navigated state-sponsored repression, strategic-ally responded to local and international socio-political events, and developed the means of communicating ideas of liberation between them-selves and enslaved people that helped propel the Haitian Revolution.

We can think of marronnage as a tactic within enslaved people's repertoire of contention (see also Chapter 5), a collection of distinctive combinations of organically developed resistance actions that endure, evolve, are reinvented or readopted if participants deem them feasible, legitimate, and effective (Tilly 1995; Traugott 1995; Taylor and Van Dyke 2004; Tilly 2006; Biggs 2013; della Porta 2013; Ring-Ramirez, Reynolds-Stenson and Earl 2014). Historically constituted forms of consciousness allow individuals to make sense of their circumstances and develop the tactics suitable for initiating historical transformations (Swidler 1986; Fantasia 1988; Hall 1990; Kane 2000). As Chapter 2 demonstrated, marronnage had been the core dimension of anti-colonial, anti-slavery resistance since the first black *ladinos* and African *bozales* disembarked on the island and took up rebellion with the Taíno, and their legacies of struggle influenced future generations of rebels. Established repertoire tactics, like marronnage or poisoning (Chapter 3), were then taught to subsequent generations of actors, whose awareness of changing social, economic, and political conditions allowed them to adapt their disruptive performances to effectively con-test power structures. Newly arrived enslaved people and maroons who remained from the Spanish colonial period had to strategically assess the rapidly changing landscape of Saint-Domingue – growing numbers of sugar and coffee and plantations, an increasing bonded population monitored by the *maréchaussée* fugitive slave police, and a complex topography – to make careful decisions about when, how, and with whom to escape and where to hide. Repertoires, and the combinations of tactics of which they are comprised, are therefore historically specific and bound by time and space, meaning that choices about how to engage in marronnage varied depending on the period and place in which one lived, and where plantations were located in relation to urban centers or geographically desolate regions.

Repression or reaction from antagonists was one of the most signifi-cant contextual factors with which enslaved rebels had to contend. Repression constrains the number of available repertoire tactics by deter-ring people from taking action, incapacitating those who represent a threat to repressive agents, and utilizing forms of surveillance to gain information and disrupt action. Private agents like plantation owners and personnel, colonial government agents like town councils and courts or members of the *maréchaussée* fugitive slave police, and royal authorities all participated in repression, albeit to varying degrees and using different tactics. Repressive actions toward the enslaved population and potential maroons at times involved "channeling" or making offers to dissuade or encourage certain types of behavior, such as financially incentivizing the capture of runaways and major maroon leaders; but repression was mostly coercive, involving acts of violence and brutality that oftentimes occurred in public (Earl 2003, 2006, 2011). French colonial authorities were particularly creative in their methods of torture. While the popularity of public execution was declining in mainland France (Foucault 1977), in the colonies it served not only to punish overt resistance but was also a symbolic deterrent to prevent others from absconding and disrupting labor productivity. Some maroons were sentenced to the breaking wheel, a gruesome torture apparatus that disemboweled its victims and simultaneously broke all of their bones. These executions also gave maroon band leaders notoriety within slave communities, elevating them to the status of local heroes whose deaths were not only mourned but would have been revered based on Africa-inspired cosmologies. Maroon leaders like Noël Barochin commanded armed bands, and at times enslaved people, who re-grouped in response to repression and to avenge their fallen comrades.

Repertoire tactics like marronnage also shifted according to economic, political, and environmental trends. These macro-level trends included transAtlantic slave trade patterns that show the growth of the enslaved population due to the influx of newly arrived Africans to labor in the expanding sugar and coffee industries; environmental factors like natural disasters, floods, and dry seasons; and political factors like inter-imperial warfare, or royal declarations that attempted to ameliorate social conditions for enslaved people. Repertoires and mobilization more broadly are particularly efficacious when regimes experience periods of economic or political crisis (Skocpol 1979; Goldstone 1991; Tilly 2006), such as, for example, Atlantic world conflicts between the French, Spanish, and English that created economic strain and food shortages in Saint-Domingue. These external factors provided moments of opportunity for maroons to flee without fear of retribution from an already weakened state. While enslaved people did not escape frequently during periods of worsened food insecurity, armed maroon band activity appears to have heightened. However, enslaved people took advantage of amelioration policies to advocate for better conditions on plantations, participating, for example, in marronnage as a form of labor strike. As Julius Scott ([1986] 2018) has argued, enslaved people were conscious of, and helped propel forward, socio-political events within the Atlantic World that contributed to new definitions of freedom, citizenship, and liberty.

Enslaved people's awareness of the changing economic, political, environmental, and social landscape was not limited to events occurring within Saint-Domingue. Knowledge of North American, Caribbean, and South American maroon communities and rebellions would have spread to Saint-Domingue through increased inter-imperial slave trading, sailors, and the press (Scott [1986] 2018), perhaps influencing and validating the long-standing tradition of marronnage as an appropriate repertoire of contention tactic. This shared geo-political consciousness lent itself to forming effective repertoire tactics through the identity-work of social ties, such as those explored in Chapter 4, which are the organizational forms that constitute everyday life and produce collective action (Tilly 2006: 42). The exchange of knowledge, information, and ideas not only flowed between black people internationally, but we can also speculate that there was a local "common wind" of liberatory notions circulating among the enslaved and maroons through their secret interactions, practices of naming landspaces after famed maroons like Plymouth and Polydor, or even rumor and second-hand storytelling. Maroons themselves circulated across plantations when they were captured, jailed, and sold to a new owner, taking with them first-hand experiential knowledge of marronnage. The sale of rebellious bondspeople to new plantations generated a local "common wind" that helped facilitate more connections between runaways, plantation slaves and small-scale uprisings, which occurred increasingly before the Haitian Revolution began.

REPRESSION IN THE EARLY EIGHTEENTH CENTURY

By the very end of the seventeenth century, just after the formal commencement of French rule in Saint-Domingue, settlements such as the Maniel maroon community continued to form in the Baoruco mountains of the island's south-central section. Some of these maroons may have descended from, or were inspired by, the first waves of maroons who fled from and fought against the Spanish in the sixteenth century. Spain's abandonment of the island (in part a capitulation to ongoing insurrections) in search of silver elsewhere left behind a backwater colony where a growing population of free blacks – descendants of maroons and those who were emancipated – became the majority who raised cattle and farmed. The French seized on the loosening of Spanish colonial control of the island and quickly organized the local bureaucracy to outfit the land-space for sugar, cacao, and indigo production, which meant forcibly clearing the land of maroons who either remained from the Spanish period or escaped after having disembarked from French slave trading ships. Small slave rebellions, as well as large-scale and loosely organized settlements of self-liberated women, men, and children, were a constant presence in Saint-Domingue in the early eighteenth century. These communities depended on access to food, clothing, work tools, and weaponry to survive, none of which were easily obtained. Maroons gathered in the woods and selected leaders from among themselves. While at large, they robbed travelers, found food at various plantations, and hid in the quarters of other enslaved people still on plantations.[2] Armed, self-liberated bands often attacked nearby towns or plantations to gather needed resources. These raids were reported as "disturbances," to which several iterations of colonial constabularies – usually comprised of free men of color – were galvanized to respond. With the founding of the *maréchaussée* fugitive slave police, the colonial state expanded in the 1720s and 1730s in order to repress black uprisings and maintain the labor force within the rapidly growing sugar industry.

Though Saint-Domingue and other slave societies were known for their deadly material conditions, most repression research focuses on democratic or authoritarian regimes rather than colonial settings, or the ways repression functions as a tool of racial capitalism. However, portions of Jennifer Earl's (2003) typology categorizes repressive actors and the types and nature of repressive actions and are broad enough to help clarify the current case (Table 7.2). State agents loosely connected to national political elites (Saint-Domingue's colonial regime) or private agents (plantation personnel) generally enacted repression in two forms: as coercion, involving "shows and/or uses of force and other forms of standard police and military action ... e.g. intimidation and direct violence," and "channeling," which included indirect attempts to deter protests (Earl 2003: 48). Royal authorities, colonial agents, and enslavers sanctioned and enacted repression, relying almost exclusively on highly visible acts of coercion in the form of "hunting" maroons, public executions and other acts of violence, and incarceration. Maroon leaders' militaristic abilities, bolstered by the influx of enslaved soldiers and war captives in the wake of West and West Central African conflicts, stoked fears of potential widespread rebellion and prompted harsh punishments toward maroons and their collaborators. Such repression can have varied

TABLE 7.2. *Repression against marronnage*

Repressive actors	Coercion	Channeling
State agents tightly connected to elites: *royal authorities*	Public executions; Financing coercion by subsidizing *maréchaussée* "chases" and offering monetary bounties for maroons; incarceration and forced chain gang labor	1784 amelioration policy; restricting punishments for marronnage
State agents loosely connected to elites: *colonial regime*		Manumitting enslaved cooperators; restricting enslaved people's movements and activities; using print media as maroon surveillance
Private agents: *plantation personnel*	Killings, beatings, torture	

impact on collective action: repression hampers mobilization in some cases or inspires mobilization in others. However, scholarship on repression shows that insurgent actions, especially those considered more threatening, are almost always met with heightened repression (Earl 2003; Davenport 2005; Earl 2011). These insights suggest that some form of repression indeed followed threats of black insurgency, which is instructive in the absence of archival data that could reveal the inner workings of armed maroon bands who left behind no records of their own. Repressive actions against maroons, which often used public funds, tell us that these rebels indeed existed and were considered a valid threat to the social order.

Coercion

To purge lands of maroons in the south and central plain at the beginning of the eighteenth century, troops under the command of Saint-Domingue's governor Galliffet responded to various reports of runaways. Maroons were known to have elected leaders from within their groups and collaborated with enslaved people who fed them information on how to organize plantation raids for food and other resources. In June 1700, a letter was sent to Brach d'Elbos complaining that the number of runaways that resided in the mountains was still considerable, despite efforts to hunt them – indeed, houses and crops belonging to approximately 50 maroons were found in the countryside surrounding Léogâne. Then, in August, other complaints from Petit Goâve stated that runaways were escaping to the mountains in dyads and triads, then eventually in larger groups. A planter in Nippes claimed to have lost ten slaves and only recaptured three; five out of seven slaves slipped away from a plantation manager named Castera; and an official named Bricot lamented that six to eight people fled from his property. For the next two years, Galliffet continued to pursue runaways in the Baoruco mountains, at Jacmel, and at Cayes de Jacmel, but had little success extracting them from the caverns, caves, and tunnels. Later, in 1703, four blacks ran away from a Galliffet plantation, prompting him to report their escape. In the west, Galliffet and a crew of 15 men spent over two months in the woods – at times going for days without water – pursuing a runaway band. On the expedition, Galliffet destroyed the maroons' food resources and plantations; he killed three fugitives and captured eleven, while 30 others escaped.[3]

Defections from plantations and plots to overthrow enslavers further inflamed efforts to repress rebellion and to punish maroons. For example, in 1717 the Council of Le Cap issued a bounty for a runaway from Port-de-Paix named Joseph, who was accused of stealing, attempting to form a rebel band, and conspiring to kill his owners.[4] Reports of a large assembly of nearly 1,000 gathered in Ouanaminthe and Cul-de-Sac, and 600–700 heavily armed women and men living at the Montagnes Noires northeast of Port-au-Prince, prompted the formation of the *maréchaussée* fugitive slave police force in March 1721 in order to chase maroons and other rebels.[5] Mass desertions of enslaved people were becoming more and more common, and, in July 1721, colonists expressed their fears of financial ruin in the event of awaking to hundreds of laborers having escaped overnight.[6] These fears may not have been unfounded, as three months later the court of Le Cap condemned twenty-one people for organizing a revolt at Saint-Louis, charging five of the conspirators with being armed. The others had taken arms with them to desert to Santo Domingo. The court identified Alexandre, César, Bozat, Jasmin, Francœur, Louis, Marion, and Thérese as the major conspirators of the rebellion. Colonial officials executed Alexandre and César – the primary leaders – by strangulation, and then decapitated them and displayed their heads at their owner's plantation as an example to others. They also forced Bozat, Jasmin, Francœur, Louis, Marion, and Thérese to watch Alexandre and César's execution before sending them back to the Saint-Louis prison, where, on their first day, prison officials flogged then branded them with a hot iron in the shape of the fleur-de-lys to prevent them from escaping again.[7]

Enslaved people who managed to repeatedly escape their owners were seen as particularly threatening, such as a runaway named Claude, who colonial officials imprisoned in Léogâne in September 1724 for repeated marronnage.[8] Other maroons who remained at-large and accumulated followers became infamous in their neighboring communities, making them targets. One notable figure in this regard was Colas Jambes Coupées, who officials captured and executed in 1723 at Bois-de-Lance, between Grande Rivière and Limonade. For four to five years, Colas was known for attacking whites throughout Bois-de- Lance and Morne à Mantègre in Limonade, the home base of a known runaway settlement. The courts of Le Cap deemed him the "chief of the cabales," or conspirators, who was

known for his marronage to the Spanish, seducing and carrying off other slaves; leader of an armed band, highway robber in broad daylight as well as at night . . . attacking even whites; having several intelligences and secret correspondences to abolish the Colonies; instigator or accomplice in the gangs of Cézar, Jupiter, Louis, and Chéri, all of whom were punished with extreme torture and death; accused, furthermore, of sorcery and magic for having, a number of times, escaped from irons and prisons, and having poisoned several Negroes. And since all his crimes and his life are known all over the area, and by everyone in the most minute detail . . .[9]

From the above passage, it seems possible that Colas collaborated with the same Cézar and Louis who were part of the 1721 conspiracy and later escaped the Saint-Louis prison. Colas' capture was not without resistance, as the newly formed free colored corps refused to pursue him.[10] His group is another example of a submerged network with plans to overthrow the social order of enslavement using poison and serves as an interesting predecessor to Mackandal, who is often thought of as the first runaway leader who also was a ritualist (see Chapter 3).[11]

In response to the rash of maroon activity, the French royal government supported and institutionalized the repressive actions of enslavers and colonial officials to strengthen local efforts in the central plain and the south. The colonial state expanded by order of the king, who, in 1722, appointed Jean-Baptiste Duclos, Sorel, and Montholon as lieutenants of Petit-Goâve specifically to fight against marronnage.[12] The royal and colonial governments aligned in a coercive measure to assign chiefs to lead new branches of the *maréchaussée* to pursue maroons, especially in the south. On June 7, 1726, maroons in Grand Goâve had caused enough disorder, through killing and thievery the previous February, to warrant a request for the *maréchaussée* to disperse them.[13] In 1728, officers at

Jacmel were sent into the Baoruco mountains, where they captured 46 runaways; then in 1730, they caught 33. Authorities sentenced this group to the chain gang. This band was particularly mobile, using horses to sack plantations in Saint-Domingue and toward the southern coasts. Along the way, they recruited other runaways by offering to give asylum to those who wanted to join.[14] Areas of the Grand Anse southern peninsula, such as Nippes, had been a stronghold for marronnage since a group of runaways fled there in 1681, because it was sparsely populated and surrounded by mountains and small patches of forest.[15] Plymouth was the leader of a band of runaways from Nippes who destroyed portions of Grand Anse. *Mulâtre* soldiers captured 30 of his followers, and killed several others, including Plymouth himself in 1730. After his capture, a section of Grand Anse became widely referred to as Plymouth in memory of the maroon.[16] The *maréchaussée* were re-established in January 1733 to attack the runaway communities who lived in the mountains, and, in October 1733, a fugitive police force, composed of ten men under the leadership of Fayet and Duclos, captured 32 of the many runaways who had taken refuge in the southern quarter of Nippes.[17]

While the royal government seemingly supported the colonial regime by appointing new personnel to lead the charge against marronnage, the crown at times seemed to undermine those efforts by withholding funds to compensate for losses incurred during maroon chases. On September 30, 1726, the king cancelled a declaration of Petite-Goâve's Conseil Superieur from the previous May, which promised a reward of 300 *livres* for the head of each runaway and the freedom of any enslaved person who helped with chasing the fugitives.[18] On the other hand, offering a financial bounty became a measure used to solicit the help of private actors in capturing well-known and deeply feared maroons, such as Polydor. Five white workers from the Carbon plantation, whom the Conseil du Cap later compensated with 1,000 *livres*, found Polydor and mostly destroyed his band in 1734 after he and another runaway named Joseph led several incursions in the northern Trou district. Trou, like Fort Dauphin, was a vulnerable area due to its proximity to the Spanish border.[19] Polydor's capture was a challenge, and was in part facilitated by an enslaved man named Laurent *dit* Cezar, whom administrators rewarded with his freedom on June 28, 1734.[20] Well after his capture, authorities and the enslaved alike remembered Polydor's exploits – the death toll (presumably of whites) and robbery of plantations – by naming a savanna after him.[21] Polydor and his considerable following were deemed such a menace to the colony that authorities at Le Cap celebrated François

Narp, a planter and militia captain of Le Cap who fought and captured Polydor, as a hero by granting his children an honor in his name some 40 years after the revolt.[22] Three years after Polydor, another leader named Chocolat emerged in Limonade. He was described as more skillful and bold than Polydor, plundering white planters' lands for 12 years.[23] In February 1735, the Conseil du Cap reimbursed a group of private actors responsible for chasing, capturing, and killing three more unnamed rebel leaders.[24]

After Polydor was captured, the colonial state financially incentivized maroon repression, adding a third layer to the colonial state's commodification of black people – first their initial capture and enslavement, second their labor value, and third their surveillance and re-capture – to preserve them as property. Racial dynamics shaped repression: free people of color were afforded an avenue for employment and status at the expense of enslaved blacks; and though the freemen were co-opted, they were simultaneously repressed in other ways. For example, a 1705 ordinance threatened to return to slavery any free person of color who helped or traded with fugitives.[25] The *maréchaussée* fugitive slave police were predominantly composed of free people of color, whose service provided them access to social network ties that aided socioeconomic mobility; they, and plantation owners, were the primary financial beneficiaries of maroon "hunting." In 1739, the *maréchaussée* were re-organized and paid extra for any maroon they could capture in rural places rather than cities (see Table 7.2). Remote places like Dondon, Borgne, or Plaisance demanded riskier expeditions, and thus the colonial regime paid *maréchaussée* members 48 *livres* for their work there. They paid 100 *livres* to those who engaged in challenging chases or joined brigades with training in mountain chases to capture a runaway. Officials later expanded the geographic area in which this 100-*livre* bounty applied to include the island of Tortuga, just north of the coast of Port-de-Paix.[26] Officials recognized that maroon chases in these areas were more dangerous because they were strongholds of runaway communities and thus rewarded private actors to scale. The institutionalization of the *maréchaussée* as a coercive deterrent to escape was accompanied by violent measures to entrench the domination of enslavement and prevent marronnage altogether. As early as March 1726, the court of Léogâne decided that the punishment for a first offense of repeated marronnage was to cute the maroon's ears off, and to brand her or him with the fleur-de-lys.[27] This policy expanded to other parts of the colony in March 1741, when facial branding and sentencing to chain gangs replaced the

TABLE 7.3. *Maréchaussée pay scale by location*

Jurisdiction	Parish	Maréchaussée pay
Cap Français jurisdiction	the city of Cap Français	6 *livres*
	in the Mornes and Balieue of Cap	12 *livres*
	Petite-Anse, Quartier Morin and Plaine du Nord	15 *livres*
	Limonade and Acul	18 *livres*
	Limbé, Grande-Rivière, the Sainte-Suzanne dependency of Limonade	21 *livres*
	Port-Margot and Dondon	30 *livres*
	Quartier Vazeux, dependence of Dondon	48 *livres*
Fort-Dauphin	the city of Fort Dauphin	6 *livres*
	the quartier Dauphin	12 *livres*
	Terrier-Rouge and Ouanaminthe	18 *livres*
	Trou	21 *livres*
	quartiers of Ouanaminthe, Trou de Jean-de-Nantes, Capotille and others	36 *livres*
Port-de-Paix	the city of Port-de-Paix	6 *livres*
	quartier of Port-de-Paix	12 *livres*
	quartier of Saint-Louis near the point of Icaque and Bas de Saint-Anne	18 *livres*
	between the point of Icaque and Borgne	48 *livres*
	Jean-Rabel and Gros-Morne	30 *livres*
	Pilatte and Plaisance	48 *livres*

death penalty as punishments for repeat runaways. The new punishment regulations reflected the needs of a growing sugar economy that could make more effective use of captured runaways than those who had been sentenced to death.[28]

Sugar prices doubled between 1730 and 1740 and tripled by 1750, yet prices for enslaved people grew much more slowly, meaning that the actual life values of enslaved people was rapidly decreasing during this time (see Chapter 2).[29] But, the demands of sugar production required a labor force that was alive – rather than dead after being executed as maroons – and healthy enough to work long hours on little nourishment. Still, conditions for Saint-Domingue's enslaved population and maroons remained poor, and even worsened with the expansion of the coffee market. As coffee cultivation expanded to the mountains surrounding the urban plains of Cap Français and Port-au-Prince and the *maréchaussée's* reach grew, living in marronnage became a more difficult endeavor. The expansion of plantations toward the colony's border zones and areas surrounding the Cul-de-Sac plain ignited several conflicts between settlers and the runaways who had staked claim to those lands. Near Dondon, in Port-Margot, the Council of Le Cap compensated a man named Ancel with 1,000 *livres* after he was crippled during a maroon chase.[30] The *maréchaussée* provost attacked 22 maroons in 1740 at Mirebalais, killing seven, arresting 14, and failing to capture one – all had been born in the forest, attesting to the ongoing presence of maroons possibly from before French colonial rule. The 14 who survived the attack stated that there were still 23 others who had escaped. They appeared later in 1742 at Anses-a-Pitre of Cayes de Jacmel and in 1746 in Jacmel; and 12 maroons were captured again in Jacmel in 1757.[31] Tensions between enslaved people and cruel enslavers boiled over in 1744, when 66 bondspeople fled a Cul-de-Sac plain plantation in protest, demanding the removal of an overseer who later killed an pregnant woman. After her murder, the maroon group returned to the plantation and kidnapped and killed the overseer. Though they were condemned to death, the governor of Saint-Domingue advocated on their behalf, stating that the overseer's brutal practices justified the maroons' actions.[32] A royal decree seemed to have supported the governor's decision by issuing a ban on using public monies to reimburse planters for the death of maroons or other enslaved people sentenced to execution for any reason.[33] While violent coercion was still used, the expansion of the sugar and coffee economies was accompanied by the increased use of channeling repression methods to prevent indiscriminate killings of enslaved people and maroons.

Channeling

Violent repression of maroons and other rebels was costly: the royal and colonial governments spent a significant sum of money sponsoring the *maréchaussée* and reimbursing enslavers for dead or injured runaways, and enslavers themselves lost the monetary value associated with the fugitive and their surplus value from labor. As the sugar and coffee economies expanded, colonists implemented new measures to suppress marronnage in less violent ways. Though violent, coercive repression undoubtedly continued, rather than rely singularly on brutality, Saint-Domingue introduced forms of "channeling," which "involves more indirect repression, which is meant to affect the forms of protest available, the timing of protests, and/or flows to resources of movements" (Earl 2003: 48). To prevent or restrict marronnage, limits were placed on the types of punishments given to runaways, enslaved people who cooperated with maroon chases were offered manumission, ordinances were passed to restrict enslaved people's movements and activities, and print media were used as maroon surveillance.

The François Mackandal trial resulted in an April 1758 ruling of the Council of Cap Français that not only targeted Africa-inspired ritual practice but also attempted to limit slaves' everyday movements in order to prevent marronnage. The articles of the ruling banned enslaved people from carrying any offensive weapons except for when they participated in a maroon chase with the permission of their owners. The ruling also prohibited the enslaved from carrying iron sticks on roads in the cities or parish towns and mandated that they had to have their owner's written permission to ride horses or mules. Neither could free people of color carry swords, machetes, or sabers unless they were members of the military or the *maréchaussée*. They also risked losing their freedom for harboring runaways, and after a shoot-out between maroons and the *maréchaussée* in 1767, free people of color were prohibited from purchasing arms and gunpowder in order to prevent any possible further collaboration with the rebels.[34] The ordinance may have been effective at reducing runaways' ability to obtain weaponry and remain at large for longer periods of time (see Chapter 5). The king of France also gave colonial planters permission to commute death sentences for fugitives in September of 1763, offering cheek branding or perpetual chaining as alternative methods of punishment.[35] While the king suggested that these lesser punishments would "conserve" the enslaved workforce, planters rarely adhered to regulations from above and usually dismissed the king's suggestions. Yet, Africans may have perceived these changes as incentive to escape without fear of deadly consequences.

To further stem the flow of runaways, Saint-Domingue and slave societies throughout the Americas used newly developing print media to publish runaway slave advertisements and parish jail lists, which were among the earliest forms of surveillance technology that continue to inform racialized techniques of social control (Browne 2015). On February 8, 1764, the Intendant of Le Cap decided that *La Gazette de Saint Domingue* would begin to include lists of captive runaways by parish jail. These lists included the name, nation, brand, and age of each runaway, and their respective owners to be subsequently contacted.[36] The lists of runaways captured and jailed also provide some insight into the number of people in flight and their destinations. A sample of Saint-Domingue's two newspapers, *La Gazette* and *Avis divers et Affiches américaines*, shows 371 runaways from February to August 1764.

Two hundred and five were found in the jail of Le Cap, and 91 came from Fort Dauphin because of its proximity to the Spanish border. Other common destinations were the area surrounding Saint Marc, particularly the frontier behind the mountains, and Port-au-Prince.[37]

Royal and colonial authorities aimed to repress marronnage through media and policing, and economically benefitted from criminalizing, capturing, and imprisoning maroons. If jailed runaways were not claimed by owners who could show evidence of ownership, the maroons were then sentenced to work on public chain gangs in either Le Cap, Port-au-Prince, or Cayes de Saint Louis. This created both a free source of labor for the state to complete public works projects, such as building galleys, and a means to earn extra revenue by fining negligent owners. Owners who came to reclaim runaways had to repay the jail for providing a month's worth of food. After a month, if a fugitive was still unclaimed, they would be re-sold as "damaged" in the town centers.[38] Later, in November 1767, the king issued an ordinance overturning a previous colonial ruling so that, rather than selling captives after one month, unclaimed runaways would be housed in jail for three months before they were sold, allowing a larger window of time for jailers to expropriate labor from the prisoners.[39] These measures may also have subsidized local planters, since Saint-Domingue's economy suffered during the Seven Years War. The state, rather than the planters themselves, was absorbing the costs of housing, feeding, and providing care, albeit minimal, to enslaved people so they could perform chain gang construction labor. Once the coffee industry expanded and Saint-Domingue's post-war economy rebounded, the Council of Cap officially released the control of maroon chases and costs associated with deaths of runaways to individual jurisdictions on March 20, 1773. This allowed local parishes to manage the policing of marronnage and to respond to disturbances.[40]

As the policing of runaways became more pronounced at the local level, it seems that enslavers had become reliant on local jails to rid their plantations of rebels. In response, the court of Le Cap made a ruling in July 1774 that prisons would no longer incorporate enslaved people into chain gangs without confirmation from slave owners. Owners were then charged 120 *livres* for an enslaved person who was on the chain gang without their owner's authorization. In 1780, planters were sending sick bondspeople to prison, not as discipline for marronnage but to avoid healthcare-related expenditure. Courts decided in May that any new entry to the chain gang had to receive a clean bill of health and readiness for work by a medical examiner.[41] While this measure aimed to keep excessive numbers of enslaved people who were not runaways out of jails and chain gangs, it did not have any measurable impact on marronnage overall. However, the measure may have contributed to the re-cycling of captured runaways into the plantation system rather than their isolation in jail. It was common practice for fugitives to be returned to their plantation of origin, or to a new plantation, taking with them their knowledge, skills, and past experiences of forging a path to freedom. This local "common wind" will be explored further below.

MAROON INSURGENCY AGAINST REPRESSION

The 1770s and 1780s saw an increase in the coercive repression of armed maroon bands in response to what must have been an increase in their activities. While the colonial regime monetized the capture of runaway slaves, perhaps no other entity profited more from efforts to repress marronnage than those who had the most contact with fugitive rebels – and perhaps the most insight about them – such as members of the *maréchaussée*. Bernard Olivier du Bourgneuf, a planter and former provost of the *maréchaussée*, wrote a memo in 1770 to the naval department on the topic of marronnage. Du Bourgneuf boasted of his experience of regularly hunting fugitives and his ability to force runaways back to their owners within six months. Per his past experiences with robberies and incursions by maroons near Fort Dauphin, du Bourgneuf estimated that there were approximately 80,000 runaways in different parts of the colony. He assessed that the disparate *maréchaussée* troops were poorly organized, and their respective provosts had no real understanding of the complexities of the colony. As such, du Bourgneuf suggested the appointment of an inspector – presumably referring to himself – to monitor all the *maréchaussée*, who would then be better equipped to restore tranquility to the colony.[42] While Du Bourgneuf's estimate of 80,000 fugitives in the colony was most likely an exaggeration aimed at creating a stream of revenue for himself, there were indeed attacks on plantations by maroons at Fort Dauphin, a popular runaway destination (Table 6.1), during the 1770s and 1780s.

Writing in October 1791, Claude Milscent, a planter, former *maréchaussée* lieutenant, and later an advocate for the rights of free people of color and slavery abolitionist, described his first-hand experiences with and knowledge of the history of marronnage in Saint-Domingue.[43] One of his first militia expeditions was at the Montagnes Noires, outside of Port-au-Prince, where a band of nearly 100 runaways had established a base and were stealing food from frontier plantations. Maroons had occupied this mountain since the early eighteenth century, when Père Labat claimed 700 armed runaways lived there. Milscent recounted that the rebels put up a vigorous resistance during the confrontation, but the *maréchaussée* killed their leader, Toussaint, in the conflict and injured or captured several others, who colonial officials later beheaded. After dispersing this group and returning survivors to their owners in 1774, officials sent Milscent into the rural areas surrounding Cap Français: Fort Dauphin, Ecrevisse in Trou, and Valière. Fort Dauphin and Trou were among the most popular runaway destinations; 4.37 percent and 4.03 percent of absconders were suspected of escaping to the two parishes (Table 6.1). There, Milscent was to chase three rebel bands led by Noël Barochin, Thélémaque Canga, and Bœuf. These groups operated separately, but collaborated when one of them was under attack, inciting fear of revolt in the border towns.[44] Milscent's appointment in the region was likely a response to planters' complaints, including a letter dated November 21, 1774, from the minister of Valière petitioning for an organized pursuit of runaways to "destroy the black marrons" and to "stop the progress of marronnage." The writer suggested appointing a Provost General over all the parishes who would only answer to the colony governor specifically relating to the chase, capture, and destruction of marronnage. The governor could then request that the king provide an order to put together a *maréchaussée* of free blacks and *mulâtres* to take the chase into the mountains. It was also suggested that chain gangs should be formed as public deterrents to other potential runaways.[45] These measures had already been in place for some time, but they were ineffective at keeping people from escaping plantations then returning to pillage them.

Another coercive tactic to repress rebel maroons was to offer a bounty on the heads of leaders, such as the case of Laurent *dit* Cezar, who was emancipated for helping capture the maroon Polydor.[46] In March 1775, a price was set for the capture of Noël, formerly belonging to Barochin of Terrier Rouge, who was accused of disorder and robbery in Fort Dauphin. He had assembled a considerable number of bondspeople around him, including *commandeurs* from different plantation work gangs. Noël's network may have included Paul, a Spanish-speaking *commandeur* from the Narp plantation in Terrier Rouge, who fled in November 1775.[47] Noël exerted power and authority over the plantations of Fort Dauphin through the *commndeurs*, so enslaved people would have known his identity. He even managed to scare the *maréchaussée* so much that they would not dare to approach him. Part of the declaration of Mr. Vincent, lieutenant of the king in Fort Dauphin, stated that he felt there was no other way to stop Noël and his band other than to offer a financial reward or freedom to enslaved laborers who would help the *maréchaussée*. Vincent insisted that danger was imminent, and that the entire parish of Fort Dauphin was afraid and in need of public safety since the procurer-general had retired. The court decided to provide funds from the colonial bank to offer 4,500 *livres* to a free person who could turn in Noël alive; 3,000 *livres* to someone who could bring his head and his brand so he could be accurately identified as belonging to Barochin; 1,000 *livres* to an enslaved person who could capture Noël alive; and 600 *livres* to a bondsperson who could bring his head and his brand. If an enslaved person captured Noël, an estimated value of the slave would be paid to the owner in compensation for their freedom.[48] The maximum reward of 4,500 *livres* was a hefty sum to pay, equivalent to price of some of the most valued enslaved men who were young, healthy, and had an artisanal trade.[49] The use of a bounty to capture maroon leaders apparently worked: Milscent recounted that a member of Noël's band betrayed him and cooperated with authorities to facilitate a *maréchaussée* soldier killing him.[50]

Armed maroons in the northeastern corner of Saint-Domingue responded to repression by aligning themselves into a single unit. Milscent claimed that after Noël died, his followers merged with maroon leaders Canga and Bœuf, whose collective band grew to over 1,500 individuals. The two factions also grew more embittered and pillaged more plantations in retaliation. While some maroons were loosely organized groups of fugitives who struggled to survival in the woods, other marronnage bands relied on guerilla warfare skills inherited from African militarist cultures and long-term repertoire tactics learned over time in the colony. They armed themselves, built their camps behind fortified ditches, and worked in collaboration with enslaved people to strategically decide which plantations to attack and when.[51] Under Saint-Domingue's governor, d'Ennery, several militia detachments pursued the rebels after they were reported to have plundered one plantation, but they quickly disappeared and re-appeared to plunder another.[52] This description of maroon's offensive strategy is reminiscent of the West Central African fighting styles that befuddled French soldiers in the early days of the Haitian Revolution.[53] The stealth demonstrated by the rebels helped to create an illusion that they were ever-present and larger in number than they actually were. According to Milscent, whites near Fort Dauphin were petrified of what they believed to be over 10,000 runaways in Canga and Bœuf's bands alone. While Milscent admits that this figure was exaggerated, as Bernard Bourgneuf's estimation also was, the potential scope of marronnage and black revolt was a consistent topic of conversation that invoked much fear in the colony.

In the early 1770s, marronnage was a major concern, at least according to planters and former military officials near Fort Dauphin, who were "terrorized" by bands like those headed up by Noël Barochin, Thélémaque Canga, and Bœuf. In response to these rebels, the mid- to late 1770s saw an increase of coercive and channeling repression against marronnage in the form of *maréchaussée* expansion. The *gens du couleur* and *affranchis* were increasingly viewed as key components of the ongoing struggle to rid the colony of marronnage. A 1775 ordinance was issued to stem marronnage by co-opting enslaved men who might possibly try to free themselves through their own means, and allowing planters to manumit enslaved men in exchange for service to the *maréchaussée*. One man who eventually became a supernumerary in the *maréchaussée* had been a maroon himself: Pierre escaped his owner, Jean-Baptiste Coutaux *dit* Herve – a free *mulâtre* in Port-au-Paix – in 1786, and found work in the fugitive slave police in Le Cap. When Herve tracked down Pierre, he intended to take him back to Port-au-Paix, but two free *mulâtres* in Le Cap offered to give Herve another young male slave and over 1,000 *livres* in exchange for Pierre's manumission. Pierre's experience highlights the type of social mobility that was accessible through free black military networks.[54] In cases of those who were less fortunate than Pierre, new participants in the *maréchaussée* found service to be a burden, since a condition of the provision was that a person was still technically enslaved until the end of their service.[55] For example, one freeman of color named Antoine was threatened with losing his freedom and being sent back to servitude for abandoning a maroon chase before its completion.[56] Despite some individuals viewing *maréchaussée* membership unfavorably, the expanded militarization to eradicate marronnage impacted runaways by providing more human resources to the fugitive police and by offering an alternative path to manumission for potential male rebels.[57] The expansion of the *maréchaussée* seems to have been an effective measure: data from *Les Affiches* advertisements show that the frequency of marronnage decreased from 514 runaways in 1775 to 426 in 1777, eventually reaching its lowest point of 290 runaways in 1779 (Figure 7.1).

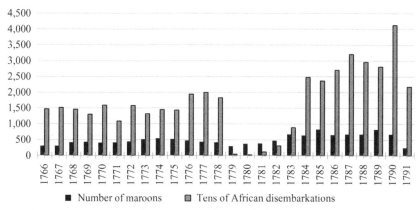

FIGURE 7.1. Frequency of runaways and tens of african disembarkations over time (N = 12,857)

Three years after former lieutenant Claude Milscent went to northeast Saint-Domingue and the *maréchaussée* killed Noël, Thélémaque Canga was finally captured. Milscent, along with 26 mixed-race and six white officers, located and confronted Canga's army of 300 rebels, whom Milscent again extolled for their brave defense. Canga's army injured three of Milscent's men during the conflict and one later died. Fatalities among the rebels were more numerous, perhaps because they fought with machetes rather than guns. Milscent's *mulâtres* killed 19 blacks, wounded and captured eight and chased away 23. Canga himself was shot in the head but somehow survived and escaped, only to be captured again. Few of the survivors made off again and Milscent returned nearly 80 to their owners.[58] On October 2, 1777, the Council of Cap Français announced that Thélémaque Canga and several survivors of his band had been captured, tried, and sentenced to death for destroying several plantations at Ecrevisses and Fond-bleus in Fort Dauphin, the same location where Noël had been active. Canga was charged with defending himself against a white man. His second in command, Isaac, was described as enslaved and accused of the same things; and the third, Pirrhus *dit* Candide, was also convicted of injuring a white person. The three were sentenced to being broken alive on the wheel until death and then having their heads placed on poles on the road from Fort Dauphin to Ecrevilles. Six other men and women were also to be hanged, flogged, and branded.[59] It is difficult to know when and from where these rebels escaped, but it is possible that Thélémaque, as the leader, spent the longest time as a maroon. Though further evidence is needed to confirm Thélémaque's identity, *Les Affiches* advertisements may provide a hint: an advertisement appeared on August 29, 1768, announcing the escape of a Kongolese, Thélémaque, from M. Franciosi's plantation in Fort Dauphin.[60]

Another request for a select few *mulâtres* and free blacks to organize a "maroon chase" was submitted in September 1778, claiming that many enslaved people from Limonade had escaped from the habitation Heritiers and were "devastating" the plantation community. There was concern that the runaways were armed with machetes and other sabres, or blunt-ended sticks, and would put up a resistance.[61] In December 1778, in order to address the issue in Limonade, the *maréchaussée* were given license to arrest any enslaved person without a pass from their owner at the market, on plantations, or other public places.[62] A response letter from the governor was sent to Limonade later in 1779, stating that at least one runaway was killed during a chase.[63] The maroon camp could have evaded capture again due to its proximity to mountainous cave systems. The Bois de Lance mountain chain in Limonade had been Colas Jambes Coupées' hideout for four to five years; and according to Moreau de Saint-Méry, these mountains continued to be a refuge for runaways.[64] Data from *Les Affiches* advertisements indicate that 3.36 percent of runaways whose destinations were known were headed to Limonade, which was just west of Trou. Another common runaway hiding place in the north was Grand Rivière, which harbored the third highest number of absconders after Fort Dauphin and Trou (Table 6.1).

Small-scale rebellion in the north continued, evidenced by an advertisement posted on January 18, 1780, describing a group of three escapees from the Rogery plantation of Morne Rouge: Blaise, Noelle, and Jean-François, all creoles. They met with Jean-Baptiste and Colas of the Delaye plantation and were reported to be causing disorder on several sugar plantations, and their owners requested that neighboring planters send *commandeurs* as reinforcements to help put down the rebels.[65] It is possible that Blaise, along with maroon band leaders Joseph Mabiala and Pierre, was later captured and sentenced in 1786 by the High Court of Cap Français to be broken alive and have their bodies exposed at La Fossette following the execution.[66] Fossette was a common meeting place for bondspeople to hold *calendas* and burials, so the public execution at this location would have served as a visible deterrent against rebellion.

Public executions were not the only danger to potential runaways; the *maréchaussée* often killed fugitives during a "hunt." Planters sought compensation from the government for these deaths, since the fugitive could no longer be counted as a productive member of the enslaved workforce. For example, in February 1780 the heirs to the Butler properties filed a claim for 3,000 *livres* against the commander of the fugitive chase that killed one of their bondspeople named Achille. The case was revisited in 1782 and the family was reimbursed with 1,200 *livres*.[67] The same year, a colonist was whipped, branded, and sent to the galleys for unnecessarily slitting the throats of two runaways he had arrested.[68] The Bergondy brothers, planters at Fort Dauphin, reported several runaways from their property, for whom a chase was organized in 1781. The *maréchaussée* shot an enslaved woman named Zabeth to death during this chase, and her owners were repaid 1,200 *livres*.[69] In 1785, a *maréchaussée* officer killed a man named François, who was not running away; François' owner demanded a repayment of 1,200 *livres* for the murder.[70]

The *maréchaussée* hunts and public executions were only temporarily effective measures against marronnage, yet planters had few alternatives for eliminating rebellion. Another letter from Jacmel emerged in August 1780, suggesting it would be beneficial to work with the Spanish to eradicate marronnage.[71] This request may not have been honored, since another letter later was sent to bring attention to the "ravages" being done by maroon bands at Cayes de Jacmel, Salle Trou, and Boynes in late 1781 and 1782.[72] A hunt was organized in March 1781, but it was unsuccessful and the *maréchaussée* had to return to Anse-à-Pitre for more water. In 1781, planters resorted to hiring hunters that were not *maréchaussée*, perhaps indicating dissatisfaction with the specialized police force; they used a black man named Remy and paid him 1,200 *livres* per runaway he found.[73] Despite the use of cash rewards to assuage and co-opt the enslaved population, marronnage and rebellion remained an issue, though those decades also saw harsh weather conditions that either prompted or dissuaded enslaved people from committing marronnage. Over the course of the 1760s and 1770s, Saint-Domingue became an increasingly repressive society that relied on coercive violence and methods to channel insurrection in other directions. Combined with the rapidly growing enslaved population and the exploding production of sugar and coffee that exploited painstaking labor and wartime economic strain, Saint-Domingue was a powder keg awaiting ignition. Moreover, in the 1780s, policies to ameliorate the material conditions for the enslaved and to lighten their punishments for insubordination, since they were more valuable as workers than dead, meant there was more room to rebel with less fear of retribution.

OPPORTUNITIES TO REBEL

Inter-Imperial Dynamics and the Environment

There was a flurry of activity among armed maroon bands in the mid-1770s and early 1780s, yet the frequency of marronnage reported in the advertisements declined during this same period. The cause for this seeming contradiction may not lie in repression, but with the environmental and economic difficulties the colony faced, which undoubtedly adversely impacted the enslaved population and their decisions about whether or not to escape. People adjust their repertoire tactics in response to the socio-economic, geopolitical, and environmental factors that make up their material conditions (McAdam [1982] 1999; Traugott 1995; Tilly 2006). Those who were participating in or who considered participating in marronnage as a repertoire tactic had to be aware of the conditions they faced in order to best avoid violent repression or death. Conversely, dire conditions may have incited already existing maroon bands to increase their raids on plantations for provisions. During these years, Saint-Domingue was a precarious regime (Boudreau 2005) that was vulnerable to inter-imperial conflict and natural disasters; this was opportunity ripe for maroon bands to take advantage. Moreover, the need to resort to violent repression in the face of maroon insurgency further signaled to the enslaved population the illegitimacy of white rule (Oliver 2008), which some protested by striking or opposing plantation personnel. Reports of fugitives increased between the years 1766 and 1791, though at a slower pace proportionate the growing enslaved population (Figure 7.1). The lowest frequency of marronnage occurred in the year 1779, when only 290 runaways were reported. The rate of marronnage increased most dramatically between 1779 and 1783, doubling from 290 to 666 yearly runaways. The frequency of marronnage continued to increase to its highest level of 820 and 817 runaways during the years 1785 and 1789, respectively. By 1791, only 238 runaways were reported, however this is likely due to the uprising in the north that ended the publication of *Les Affiches américaines*. The section that follows introduces social, economic, environmental, and Atlantic world political events, alongside repression at the local level, to contextualize micro-level marronnage trends and highlight the ways in which black resistance shaped and was shaped by the geopolitics of the day.

Although some scholars have argued that hunger was a primary cause for marronnage, the number of runaways did not increase during the droughts in 1775 and 1776 that killed thousands of enslaved people.[74] Rather, the frequency of marronnage slightly decreased during those years and continued to do so in part because weakness and starvation prevented people from venturing into an even more precarious situation as a runaway (Figure 7.1). Cul-de-Sac officials issued an ordinance forcing planters to grow a certain number of bananas, manioc, or potatoes per slave to prevent further deaths. But food shortages arose when prices for provisions increased again in 1777 under the British blockade. In 1776, North American allies of France declared independence from Britain, and in February 1778, British naval ships anchored in Saint-Domingue's ports, blocking imports. When France signed the Treaty of Amity and Commerce, sugar prices dropped rapidly, which may have caused harsher work regimes on plantations in order to produce more and generate more revenue – even under conditions of famine and starvation.[75] Hunger and fatigue from being overworked in order to meet pre-blockade-level profits may have deterred all enslaved people from facing the uncertainty of life outside the plantation where food rations, however meager, were guaranteed. Additionally, the stark reduction of newly arrived Africans during the blockade contributed to the overall reduction of runaways. The British naval presence at Saint-Domingue's ports had a direct impact on French traders' abilities to transport more enslaved Africans to the colony, and those already in the colony would bear the weight of compensating for French losses of labor power and decreasing sugar prices. Between 1779 and 1782, less than ten French slave ships arrived at Saint-Domingue.[76] The frequency of marronnage was at its lowest in 1779 – 290 runaways reported – because continent-born Africans made up the largest proportion of runaways, as they dominated the enslaved population itself. The lack of incoming Africans forced people to forge relationships across linguistic and cultural boundaries as they sought refuge from bondage, evidenced by higher rates of heterogeneous group escapes during the blockade (Figure 4.1).

The British blockade on Saint-Domingue's ports during the North American War for Independence had a devastating impact on everyone in the colony. Food was scarce and expensive, exacerbating the malnutrition enslaved people already experienced. Extreme weather conditions, like the droughts of 1775 and 1776, also contributed to a lack of access to locally grown foodstuffs. The dry seasons were followed by flooding four years later when the Artibonite River flooded on October 16–17, 1780, then a hurricane hit in November, sweeping away several plantations and destroying important crops.[77] Harsh living conditions in the colony kept enslaved people from venturing away from plantations, but those who had already successfully escaped faced an equally dire situation. Maroon bands increased their plantations attacks, in part as retaliation against the *maréchaussée* and to expropriate food, weapons, tools, and even women during the colony-wide, 18-month dry season and period of widespread malnutrition in 1779 and 1780.[78] Some individual maroons took the wartime strain as an opportunity to secure their own freedom through military service. In the early 1780s, several runaways attempted to join the ranks of Comte Charles d'Estaing, the former governor of Saint-Domingue and French naval officer who led the siege on Savannah, Georgia in September 1779 with troops of freemen of color including Henry Christophe and Andre Rigaud.[79] In late July 1781, Jean-Pierre, an 18-year-old creole man, was suspected of having taken refuge in the French king's ships at harbor after already having attempted to join d'Estaing's squadron in August 1779. Similarly, Silvain, a 19-year-old Kongolese man, and Michel, a 45-year-old captive from a Dutch colony, escaped their owner on July 25, 1781 wearing iron neck collars, and attempted to embark on the ships of Comte d'Estaing at Le Cap.[80] Finally, two *mulâtre* brothers, Jean and Jean-Baptiste Lefevre, escaped Port-au-Prince in July 1783 under the false pretense of having been freed by Comte d'Estaing after serving in the campaign in Savannah.[81]

After the North American War of Independence ended, African wars intensified – likely in part because French slave trading resumed to full swing by 1783. Between the years 1781–1785 and 1786–1790, the number of captives shipped to Saint-Domingue nearly tripled (Table 1.2). Conflicts between the Dahomey Kingdom and its neighbors persisted in the 1770s and 1780s, funneling losers on both sides into the slave trade. On the West Central African coasts, former soldiers in the Kingdom of Kongo civil wars of the 1780s also fed the French slave trade thousands of captives. These captives, as well as Africans from other regions, were transported to Saint-Domingue in record numbers, bringing with them cultural, religious, economic, and militaristic knowledge and skills.[82] As the enslaved population swelled, the frequency of marronnage increased, reaching the highest rates in 1785 and 1789, 820 and 817 respectively (Figure 7.1). Runaways sought out life beyond plantation properties, forming organized settlements, and taking up arms to defend those communities. Additionally, a French royal ordinance of 1784 may have further inspired maroon communities to take on characteristics that indicated organized tactical planning of independent living zones and revised labor practices.

Maroon plunder during wartime had some effect on royal policies. Rebellion, in addition to the food shortages, dry seasons, and flooding, prompted the king of France to impart an ordinance in December 1784 to improve the quality of enslavement in the French colonies. Part of the ordinance also aimed to sever ties between enslaved people and maroons who hid on plantations and joined "fêtes, assemblies, and dances," implying that maroon agency had some effectiveness in altering the structural ordering of enslavement. Though enslavers largely ignored its requirements, the 1784 ordinance prevented planters from forcing slaves to work on Sundays and during fêtes, or Catholic holidays; it restricted punishments; and it provided enslaved people with the ability to legally denounce abuse by owners. Pregnant women and wet nurses were supposed to receive a midday break from work, and additional clothing was demanded for each enslaved person. Another provision aimed to prevent malnutrition and starvation, and to deter marronnage by urging owners to provide enslaved people with land plots for cultivation.[83]

But these revised conditions of enslavement not only failed to prevent marronnage, they incentivized demands for better conditions and escape without fear of excessively harsh punishment. Enslaved people at the Foäche merchant house in Le Cap, and on other northern plantations, used marronnage to reclaim their time and labor to protest plantation personnel who were too harsh or whom they did not like. "All of the slaves of the Lombard plantation have marooned, claiming the decree allowed them to choose their manager," bemoaned the wealthy Galliffet sugar plantation owner. Galliffet's notes from 1785 and 1789 described several acts of insolence, insubordination, complaints, and marronnage on northern plantations such as the Chastenoy, Montaigue, Choiseuil, and Galliffet's own La Gossette, as he railed: "the 1784 decree is fatal to discipline and causes insurrections in part of our province."[84] The frequency of marronnage reached its peak in 1785 after the ordinance was issued, with 820 runaways reported in *Les Affiches américaines* (Figure 7.1). Runaways could appropriate food in their newly emerging gardens to trade and sell, and steal weapons and work tools to cultivate production on their isolated plots of land. As Chapter 8 will explain, self-contained maroon settlements emerged in the south, where established maroon settlements pillaged neighboring plantations and outfitted abandoned plantations for crop production.

Still, other maroons did not wait for the 1784 ordinance before striking out on their own; and maroons remained active in the colony's central regions. In 1784, another proposal was put forward to eradicate maroons in and around Mirebalais, Port-au-Prince, Grand Bois, and Jacmel. This plan included the recruitment of 800 *gens du couleur* to be divided into 16 units.[85] Grand Bois was a section of Mirebalais formed by a series of bluffs, rivers, and hills, making it difficult to access from Saint-Domingue but easier to reach from Santo Domingo.[86] Additionally, there was proximity to runaways in the rural or mountainous areas in the south, such as the Montagnes Noires outside of Port-au-Prince. In the north in 1785, colonists reported that the maroons' audaciousness was increasing by the day, and they requested reinforcements to chase several maroons that were gathered at Limbé. Though the new governor claimed in September 1786 and August 1787 that marronnage overall was decreasing, rebel activities in Port Margot were reported at the end of 1786 and the number of maroons listed in *Les Affiches* remained relatively high in the latter years of the 1780s in comparison to the previous decade (Figure 7.1).[87] As late as 1789, there was a maroon group operating outside Le Cap led by François, who Lieutenant Milscent described as very intelligent and capable of the greatest feats. Milscent, who commanded forces against Noël Barochin and Thélémaque Canga, claimed to have captured 50 rebels and killed 20, including the leader François, after the maroons had killed several French and Spanish planters and plundered their dwellings.[88]

A Local and International "Common Wind"

Political and environmental opportunities were not the only times enslaved people developed consciousness about the possibilities of employing marronnage as a repertoire tactic to seize and define freedom on their own terms. Julius Scott ([1986] 2018) has provided a framework for understanding the international "common wind" of circulating ideas, knowledge, information, and rumors; however, there also was a local common wind of stories, rumors, or even lore upon which enslaved people and maroons relied. These deeply cultural insights, social networks, and daily interactions constitute the field of action from which repertoires tactics develop (Tilly 2006). Runaway communities did not completely disappear due to encroaching deforestation for sugar and coffee plantations, but became more creative in locating hiding spots. For example, Morne Bleu, a hill located east of Cavaillon, contained several caves where the maroon Pompey hid until he was arrested in 1747. The cave also held evidence of Taíno presence, noted by their ritual artifacts, supporting Rachel Beauvoir-Dominique's findings that cave systems provided shelter for Africans and Taínos to collaborate spiritually and in revolt.[89] An account from a December 1761 expedition exemplifies the creativity maroons used to protect their settlements, and simultaneously shows the nature of ongoing antagonism between them and the *maréchaussée*. When the *maréchaussée* encountered the maroons during the search, they were probably perplexed and irritated when the fugitives began to dance as a means of taunting their enemies. When the *maréchaussée* launched to attack, however, many of them fell into a large ditch that had been dug and filled with pine wood stakes and liana plants. As I argued in Chapter 6, familiarity with the landscape was a key component of enslaved people's cultural knowledge, and maroons were adept at using their surroundings and flora and fauna to protect their chosen living spaces. Fourteen of the *maréchaussée* were left maimed after falling into the ditch; however, the maroons were not without casualities and many of them were also killed.[90]

Newly arrived Africans may have encountered these well-hidden maroons and remaining indigenous peoples, or heard stories of them from those who were more knowledgeable about the landscape and the history of maroon presence in the mountains. For example, after François Mackandal was brought to Saint-Domingue in the 1730s where he lived as a fugitive for 18 years, he would have learned about Colas Jambes Coupée, Polydor, Chocolat, and other rebels in the north through word of mouth. Additionally, some locations bore the name of fugitive communities, such as Piton des Nègres, Piton des Flambeaux, Piton des Tenebres, Crete a Congo, Fond des Nègres, and the area named after Polydor. Moreau de Saint-Méry also confirmed that there were free blacks living in Acul de Samedi in Valière.[91] Some of these remote locations appear in *Les Affiches* advertisements as runaway's locations of escape or their suspected destinations. Therefore, collective memory of maroon rebels was part of enslaved people's consciousness, and likely influenced their own desires for freedom and inspired the continuation of marronnage as a repertoire tactic.

It is logical to surmise that enslaved people were just as preoccupied with marronnage as their owners; in fact, they were probably *more* knowledgeable about maroon leaders and their exploits (Scott [1986] 2018).

Rather than retreat to the mountains, some fugitives camped out at nearby plantations where friends, family members, or lovers protected them. From *Les Affiches* advertisements, 153 runaways sought out familiar plantations, allowing them to be in marronnage for an average of 15.68 weeks (Tables 4.10 and 5.6). Alternatively, former members of rebel bands were returned to their respective plantations.[92] Additionally, captured and jailed runaways sometimes did not know or divulge the names of their owners, therefore they remained in jail unclaimed. In such cases, they were advertised in newspapers like *Gazette de Saint Domingue*, *Les Affiches américaines*, and the *Courrier Nationale de Saint Domingue* as "damaged" or abandoned, then re-sold to planters in the city centers – a convenient way for local jailers to generate revenue, since slave prices increased in the 1760s.[93] Fugitives who were captured and re-located to new plantations likely shared their experiences with bondspeople, introducing them to successful and unsuccessful tactics for escape. This internal trade of rebellious enslaved people would have been just as important in raising collective consciousness about marronnage as the rumors about the armed conflicts occurring in the colony's northeast corner. While individual members of the enslaved population at times took advantage of financial rewards offered to capture rebels, further research on the internal trade of rebels might suggest that mutual support and collusion among Africans and African descendants, enslaved and maroon, was more common than previously understood.

While planters seemed to have had no problem incorporating captured runaways into their workforces, they did worry about the negative influence of factors external to Saint-Domingue. A letter surfaced in 1775 framing marronnage as a pervasive problem that had the capacity to undo the colony. The letter identified several factors that contributed to the unchecked rule of maroons: (1) the Spanish, who provided a safe harbor for Saint-Domingue's runaways and potentially politicized them against the French; (2) the dense, nearly impenetrable mountains into which the *maréchaussée* and other hunters attempted and often failed to pursue fugitives; (3) runaways' propensity to reproduce while at large; and (4) their constant attacks on plantation. These issues exasperated planters who – judging by the number and tone of their letters – were desperate for reinforcements. The combination of these factors also led this writer to compare the problem to those of Jamaica and Surinam, suggesting imminent revolt if marronnage was not contained and eradicated.[94] Even in Martinique, a priest named Charles-François de Coutances cited the 80,000 maroons in Surinam, troubles in Jamaica, and the "greatest danger" in Saint-Domingue six years earlier – during the Mackandal poisoning scare – as presenting a threat to the Lesser Antilles island.[95]

It is telling that these writers cited two major Caribbean uprisings as legitimation for their fear of marronnage in Saint-Domingue, implying that runaways were inherently ripe for rebellious uprising especially during periods of international conflict like the Seven Years War. In Surinam, failed treaties with the Ndjukas, Saramakas, Matawais, and Boni maroons marked the beginning of a series of wars between them and the Dutch colonists.[96] Additionally, in 1763, there was a revolution in Berbice (present-day Guyana), directly neighboring Surinam, where Governor Coffij and Captain Accarra led a seven-month hostile takeover of the government by other Gold Coast and Kongolese Africans. Word spread about the Berbice uprising, perhaps from disaffected French mercenaries based in Surinam who fought with the Berbice rebels. Information circulating throughout the Caribbean via sailors, military men, and traders carried the news of rebellions in the Guianas and Jamaica to Saint-Domingue. Edward Long's *History of Jamaica*, published in 1774, described the 1760 revolt in Jamaica as an island-wide attempt of Gold Coast Coromantee Africans to overthrow the colonial government.[97] Long's account provided awareness of, and insight to, the Jamaican revolt, to which both colonial Europeans and Africans would have paid attention.[98]

Knowledge of these events would not have been isolated to Saint-Domingue's white planter population; in fact, bondspeople may have learned of the rebellions before their owners. Captives from English-, Spanish-, Portuguese-, and Dutch-speaking colonies were routinely brought to Saint-Domingue through legal and illicit intra-American trade (Tables 4.7 and 4.8; Scott [1986] 2018). For example, in 1781 a ship carrying 390 captives sailed from St. Thomas to Le Cap. One of the bondspeople on that ship was a 14-year-old boy known as Télémaque, sometimes called Denmark, who upon being sold in Saint-Domingue began feigning epileptic fits until his previous owner, Captain Joseph Vesey, was forced to take the boy back with him to Charleston, South Carolina. Forty-one years later, Denmark Vesey was a free man who was executed for organizing one of the largest slave conspiracies in North American history, which aimed to return to the free state of Haiti.[99] Just as Saint-Domingue and the Haitian Revolution directly influenced other Atlantic world rebellions, it follows that during the pre-revolution period, Dutch-speaking maroons in Saint-Domingue perhaps would have been familiar with the Berbice and Surinam rebellions of the 1760s; African-Jamaicans and other English speakers probably knew about Queen Nanny's Maroon Wars, Tacky's Revolt, and the black Carib Wars on Saint Vincent island; and before the Haitian Revolution, African-Martiniquans probably knew of the 1789 revolt on the tiny French island. Conversations during Sunday markets, clandestine night-time gatherings in living quarters, and marronnage networks would have informed the local populace about goings on in nearby colonies, heightening their awareness of and strivings for liberation.[100]

CONCLUSION

Despite, or perhaps because of, eighteenth-century capitalist development through the expansion of Saint-Domingue's sugar and coffee industries, maroon rebellion erupted at various levels of scale and intensity and persisted well into the revolutionary era. Some planters may have exaggerated the nature and scope of the presence of maroons; the extent of the damage from maroon raids on plantations remains unclear. Planters commonly requested compensation from the state for enslaved people whom the *maréchaussée* unjustifiably killed, but it does not appear that any planter asked to be reimbursed for damage to their property. Still, planters' fear of maroon attacks prompted increased militarization via the *maréchaussée*. There were no more than 300 *maréchaussée* soldiers throughout the colony, a seriously limited number compared to the enslaved population – and the maroon bands led by Noël Barochin, Thélémaque Canga, and Bœuf – meaning the *maréchaussée* were outnumbered.[101] Therefore, the *maréchaussée* continually received funds to conduct "hunts" that at times resulted in casualties on both sides. The need for land – especially in previously unexploited areas where maroons resided – and for enslaved labor, required planters, the colonial state, and the royal government to rein in the "masterless" using various methods of repression. Repression was a critical factor that attempted, albeit at times unsuccessfully, to respond to the seemingly constant threat of marronnage and aimed to constrain its spread. The *maréchaussée* and other militias hunted maroons, and torturous public executions of prominent rebels temporarily deterred others from escaping. The 1770s and 1780s was a time of heightened aggression from maroon bands in Saint-Domingue's northeastern corner and the especially in the south. In the case of the Fort Dauphin maroons, repression inspired solidarity and further rebellion when the death of Noël Barochin at the hands of

Milscent's troops united Thélémaque Canga and Bœuf's bands. The militarized fugitive slave police had to contend with a massively growing African population whose survival and fighting skills were rooted in their continental experiences.

Rebels adapted to repression and their social, political, and environmental conditions, developed collective consciousness through their geopolitical awareness, and persisted in their attacks on plantations. *Longue durée* analysis of marronnage from the sixteenth century shows that rebels had a keen sense of geopolitics and adapted to or took advantage of political and economic cleavages. Marronnage can be considered a consistent repertoire tactic that, at the macro-level, was characterized by the exploitation of economic difficulties caused by international warfare, and the population growth of enslaved people in Saint-Domingue. Though African wars increased the numbers of captives to Saint-Domingue, European conflicts like Seven Years War and the North American War of Independence halted the slave trade and fostered political strife and the breaking down of Saint-Domingue's societal inner workings, which armed maroon bands exploited for their benefit with aggressive attacks on plantations. Conversely, enslaved people adapted to environmental circumstances like drought and food shortages by staying on plantations until blockades withdrew and everyday material conditions improved. They also forged inter-ethnic relationships in order to escape in heterogeneous maroon groups when their countrywomen and men were not accessible.

At the micro-level, social ties between maroons and the enslaved also played a significant role in cultivating consciousness. Examples such as Noël heading a network of *commandeurs* demonstrate that runaways used marronnage strategically to communicate with and recruit enslaved people, giving insight to the dynamics of leadership in the relationship between maroon bands and enslaved people. To that end, more research is also needed to track the circulation of "damaged" runaways from within the colony and those who were re-captured from Spanish Santo Domingo, who were sold to new plantations and who took with them their knowledge, experiences, and leadership skills as maroons.[102] Enslaved people gained knowledge about successful and unsuccessful strategies for rebellion and marronnage from several sources: their African experiences; rumors of revolt in other Caribbean colonies; the legacies of well-known maroon leaders; and runaways who were captured and returned to plantations. This knowledge accumulated over time and proved to be particularly effective when rebels took advantage of strain and breakdowns in social, economic, and political spheres. As the *gens du couleur* agitated for their liberties in the late eighteenth century, Africans increasingly took advantage of social, economic, and political crises to assert freedom on their own terms. Enslaved people's interrelationships and the spread of consciousness between urban and rural plantations was in part based on the increased forced migration and "urbanizing" of the slave population, which some scholars have observed are factors that can produce actors – such as the early revolutionists – who can organize contentious political action and gain access to legitimated channels of power (James [1938] 1989; Scott [1986] 2018; Goldstone 1991; Tilly 2006). For example, accounts of marronnage on the outskirts of Cap Français in 1790 provide evidence of some secret meetings that occurred before the Haitian Revolution began. The possible relationship between the revolutionaries Jean-François Papillon and Pierre Loulou could be a compelling revelation that sheds new light on the types of allegiances and relationships that were forged in the colonial period.

8

Voices of Liberty: The Haitian Revolution Begins

The god who created the sun which gives us light, who rouses the waves and rules the storm, though hidden in the clouds, he watches us. He sees all that the white man does. The god of the white man inspires him with crime, but our god calls upon us to do good works. Our god who is good to us orders us to revenge our wrongs. He will direct our arms and aid us. Throw away the symbol of the god of the whites who has often caused us to weep, and listen to the voice of liberty, which speaks in the hearts of us all.[1]

Boukman Dutty, August 1791

This prayer is said to have been spoken by Boukman Dutty at the Bwa Kayman (Bois Caïman) ceremony of August 1791 when he, the *mambo* priestess Cécile Fatiman, and delegates representing the enslaved masses from plantations across the northern plain plotted the demise of the sugar plantation economy and outlined the terms of their liberation. The ritual component of the gathering drew on a combination of Bight of Benin and West Central African spiritual practices and deities, which ideologically and militarily cemented solidarity between Saint-Domingue's ethnic groups. There has been some scholarly debate about the date and location of the ceremony, whether or not Boukman was present, and if this prayer was actually said; however, historical validity aside, the prayer articulates a distinctive difference between the worldviews of the insurgents and those of their oppressors, and in so doing it issues a derisive critique of Western modernity. This contrast in worldviews is instructive for approaching an understanding of the insurgents' perspective on the material conditions in which they lived and the rationale for their rebellion. Indeed, the Christian "god of the white man" – more pointedly represented by members of the

Catholic Church, missionaries, priests, and slave owners eager to convert their human chattel – provided the ideological foundation that ushered in the racialization of non-Christians and non-whites, facilitated and christened the transAtlantic slave trade, and actively supported the slavery-based economic regime in the Americas. Surely the role that the Catholic Church played in weaponizing Christianity against people of African descent was not lost on Boukman Dutty and the Bwa Kayman participants. The prayer, fabled or factual, speaks to racialized spheres of collective consciousness and diverging ontological understandings about the nature of God *and* the character of God-inspired human action. What would it have meant for the god of enslaved people to "direct ... and aid" them, for the masses of Saint-Domingue to "revenge wrongs" and to actualize listening to "the voice of liberty"? Whether divinely inspired or not, they took steps, small and large, to reverse the conditions of their enslavement based on their ontological understanding of themselves as free and of the plantation system's nature as unjust. By rebelling against the plantation system, the revolutionaries of 1791 and maroons who largely functioned outside of system subverted the mode of Western modernity in which they lived – which functioned through racism, violence, forced religious indoctrination, and economic exploitation. Their actions opposed Saint-Domingue's systems of domination and expressed an alternative understanding of their humanity.

As I argued in Chapter 1, enslaved people's collective consciousness emerged from their common experiences as victims of the transAtlantic slave trade and survivors of the Middle Passage. Centralized political and economic power was increasingly associated with slaving, greed, injustice, and witchcraft, spawning forms of resistance that critiqued social, economic, and spiritual imbalances. Marronnage, open warfare, and religious consolidation proved to be effective means of resisting the slave trade in West Central Africa, Senegambia, and the Bight of Benin. Africans carried these socio-political critiques and tactics with them across the Atlantic Ocean to Saint-Domingue, where African political thought, warfare strategies, marronnage, and the early coalescence of Haitian Vodou informed the revolutionary struggles of 1791. This chapter focuses on the masses of formerly enslaved people who embodied ideals that pushed forward even those who were considered most radically progressive at the time, such as Toussaint Louverture and other leaders of the Haitian Revolution. At various stages, leaders who became part of the military elite either failed to advocate for abolition, continued to rely on harsh plantation regimes to maintain Saint-Domingue's economic prowess, or repressed the masses of African rebels, maroons, and ritualists. This continued until it became clear that racial equality, full emancipation, and national independence hinged on the mobilization of the former slaves and the solidarity between them, black military officers, and free people of color.

Marronnage was not just an act of escaping slavery, it was a process of reclamation, an organizing structure, and a socio-political critique of the plantation system that, over time, "would converge with the volatile political climate of the time and with the opening of a revolution."[2] It entailed individuals not only removing themselves from plantations, but various levels of actions and behaviors that either directly countered the logic of the plantation system or stood in contradistinction to it (Casimir 2001, 2015). Though most enslaved people did not participate in marronnage, the tactics and strategies they employed before and during the Haitian Revolution reflect characteristics of marronnage presented in the current and previous chapters. I have developed a framework of actions and patterns of behaviors associated with marronnage that inform how enslaved people operationalized oppositional consciousness based on Black Studies and social movements' theoretical insights and analysis of archival findings. What follows is theoretically and empirically informed, yet broad enough to perhaps be considered a framework for a more general understanding of how the structural positionality of African descendants under racial capitalism shapes Black mobilization at the micro-level. The tenets of marronnage include:

- reclamation of the Black self as a commodified source of capital, and reclaiming and redirecting time, energy, and effort toward individual, familial, or collective needs and interests;
- creation of networks composed of maroons, free, and enslaved people who share social positions and/or liberatory goals;
- networks often characterized by movement or transience, having network nodes that are linked by women;
- appropriation and subversion of material goods and technologies that are typically used as apparatuses of racial capitalism;
- experiencing geographic, social, economic, and political marginalization, and disempowerment and disenfranchisement from centers of power and capital, yet creating spaces organized around communal principles;
- drawing on intimate knowledge of land, space, and ecologies for immediate or long-term survival;

- using coded forms of communication and systems of protection to enhance solidarity and to avoid surveillance or betrayal by racialized or non-racialized beings whose socio-economic mobility hinges on figurative or literal forms of re-enslavement;
- developing rituals to orient collective ontology, to affirm collective identity, and to build community;
- reimagining, subverting or rejecting, and traversing hegemonic identities, gender norms, and socio-political borders;
- developing self-defense or direct-action fighting techniques and tactics, such as martial arts, bearing arms, or adopting militaristic strategies to contest repression;
- disruption of capital accumulation processes that seek to and do extract resources from Black spaces.

These dimensions of marronnage help to clarify dynamics of mobilization during the early days of the Haitian Revolution uprising. Most participants of the massive revolutionary insurgency, especially its women fighters, did not leave behind records attesting to their thoughts, motivations, strategies, or inner workings. But it is possible to link pre-revolutionary rebellion to the August 1791 uprising through the lens of marronnage and by tracing social and spatial ties. I follow recent shifts in the sociology of revolutions that move from macro-level analyses absent of micro-level theorizing (Tilly 1978; Skocpol 1979; Goldstone 1991; Skocpol 1994; Beck 2017) toward emphases on networks, individuals' and small groups' agency, ideologies, and cultures to highlight the means of action (Foran 1993; Selbin 1997; Goldstone 2001; Sohrabi 2005; Selbin 2010). Rather than center rebels' actions taking place in the north as the origins of the mass revolt, as is typical historiographical practice, the chapter instead follows the processes related to marronnage as a socio-political critique and a form of collective action that were simultaneously localized in the colony's southern, western, then northern departments. This geographic re-adjustment of the narrative surrounding rebellion in the years before the Haitian Revolution lends to the understanding of insurgency as a practice that is grounded in social networks and place-based politics (Gould 1995; Creasap 2012). I am not suggesting that the Haitian Revolution started, historically speaking, in a specific place and time (i.e. the colony's southern department on a specific date) and then moved to the west and then north; but that it started, sociologically speaking, within the social, economic, cultural, religious, geographic, and political processes and formations that black people in

Saint-Domingue constructed and re-constructed over the course of several centuries since the first *Ayitian* Revolution. In each of the southern, western, and northern departments, I detail evidence of the connections between enslaved people, maroons, and free people of color during revolts and ritual gatherings that helped the beginnings of the Revolution. I recount mobilizations that occurred in Saint Domingue's southern, western, and northern departments and attempt to identify evidence of racial, gender, and labor politics that would inform post-independence refusals to be enslaved or exploited by either Europeans or the creole elite.

RUNAWAY AND PLANTATION REBELS

The South

Though some from the Bight of Benin and West Central Africa who were taken to Saint-Domingue were former soldiers, military slaves, and war captives, the vast majority of slave trade victims were distanced from spheres of economic, political, and military power. Fishermen, gold and salt miners, agriculturalists who cultivated crops that would later become slave society staples, pastoralists, priests, merchants, and textile producers made up a large proportion of Saint-Domingue's enslaved population. Having access to land through marronnage allowed runaways of African ancestry to reclaim those labor skills – as well as the skills they were forced to acquire on plantations – and use them for subsistence farming and other forms of self-directed work. Maroon communities in the south took up space on abandoned plantations, on the outskirts of larger estates, or on unsettled lands that were largely inaccessible to colonists and enslavers where they enacted their own sense of work, trade, and division of labor. Even a planter named Friedmont acknowledged in 1767 that land ownership for enslaved people would end marronnage by restoring a sense of dignity to enslaved people. He indicated that enslaved people had an attachment to the land and the idea of proprietorship, which led them to escape in search of autonomy.[3] For the enslaved, freedom and independence did not necessarily mean a life without labor, but rather subverting colonial enslavement's violent, involuntary, and unremunerative nature by appropriating oppressive technologies as tools for their sustenance on their own terms. Runaways in Cayes de Jacmel formed their own economic mode of production based on the technologies previously used for their oppression. It is possible that the Cayes de

Jacmel maroons sold their products to the Spanish – or to the remaining Neybe maroons nearby – for provisions. Moreau de Saint-Méry claimed that between Cayes de Jacmel, the Baoruco, and Pointe Beate, there were two tracts of land appropriate for cultivation – one measuring over 170 square miles and the other over 270 square miles. He suggested that these lands, both plain and mountainous, could potentially hold several sugar and coffee plantations.[4] It was in these areas that enslaved Africans from Saint-Domingue organized self-sufficient work regimes away from the domination of white planters.

A group of seven runaways from the Vedel plantation in Sale-Trou, a neighborhood of Cayes de Jacmel bordering the Spanish territory and the Baoruco mountains, escaped in early spring 1787. The fugitives included Valentin, creole; Paul, creole, 26; Jupiter, Kongo, 35; Coacou/Coucou, creole; Lafortune, Kongo, 22; and Andre, a Mina man, and Marianne of Kongo, both aged 55 and in chains. Instructions in the *LAA* advertisement directed that Lamothe Vedel should be notified if any of the runaways were identified or located.[5] Four of these fugitives – Paul, Coucou, LaFortune, and Andre – were either captured or returned to Vedel voluntarily; however, they did not remain at his plantation for long. They were part of another group of 16 runaways who escaped Vedel's plantation on August 16, 1788, during a hurricane: Andre, a Mina; Paul, Coffi, Coucou, Jacob, and Tranquillin, all creoles; Cabi, Valeri, Sans-Nom, Casimir, LaFortune, Basile, Phanor, Hilaire, Catin, and Urgele, all Kongos; and Justine, a creole *mulâtresse*.[6] The second group of escapees fled to the heights of Pic de la Selle, one of Saint Domingue's steepest mountains in the parish of Cayes de Jacmel. Based on what we know about African inter-ethnic solidarity in runaway communities of the Americas, runaways tended to elect representatives from their respective ethnic group who then collaborated on strategies of rebellion. The composition of the Vedel maroons indicates that Paul, Coucou, and Lafortune, part of the 1787 contingency of runaways, acted as representatives who recruited members of their ethnic group to escape again in 1788. Paul and Coucou were both creoles and they brought more creoles with them; and Lafortune was a Kongolese man who mobilized others who also were from the Kongo. The absence of the 16 maroons from the Vedel plantation was causing a delay in productivity; and since the runaways were armed, they posed a threat to Vedel and other planters in Selle and Sal-Trou.

A Kongolese woman named Rose was found on the Lillancourt property after having recently left the runaways led by Andre, Coucou,

Lafortune, and Paul. Rose admitted to working with two other women, one named Nangout, under the direction of a black man named Lafoucault at Lillancourt, where she planted coffee, cotton, corn, and other crops. Rose's testimony confirmed previous suspicions that other enslaved people on the Lillancourt coffee plantation were sheltering the Vedel runaways, but Vedel's previous attempts to pinpoint their location and return had them somehow failed. The fugitives were growing coffee and cotton, which had become Saint-Domingue's fourth agricultural crop. Cotton was often illegally sold to Jamaicans, who had begun "free trading" at the ports of Jérémie and Cap Tiburon.[7] The day after Rose was questioned, Justine was also captured at Lillancourt but quickly escaped again. Another woman, named Heneriette, a maroon for three years, was found during a search of the Lillancourt property; a valet named Zephir had given her shelter. After Henriette was questioned, undoubtedly under duress, and after hearing her statements, Vedel and M. Noel, provost of the *maréchaussée*, marched off to Lillancourt. The rebel band was angered at the news of Henriette's capture and prepared themselves for a confrontation with Vedel and Noel. When the two men arrived, they encountered Andre – the Mina man who escaped in the spring of 1787 and again in summer 1788 – armed with a machete and a gun, raising his gun to shoot at Vedel. Unarmed, Vedel called for Noel to retrieve his gun. By the time Noel returned, Andre was already out of sight.[8]

Not far from the mountains where the Vedel maroons settled, the Maniel maroons occupied the Baoruco mountains between the southern and western departments of Saint-Domingue, and leveraged geopolitical tensions between French and Spanish colonists to make their own demands for land, freedom, and independence. After years of negotiations with colonial officials and priests, over 130 members of the Maniel maroons came to a treaty agreement with the French and Spanish to cease their plantation raids and settle on cultivable land in Saint-Domingue. Despite the terms of the agreement, many of the maroons hesitated or outright refused to claim their property due to mistrust of the French and better relations with the Spanish.[9] Several letters surfaced claiming that these maroons were still problematic; not only were they not cultivating the lands distributed to them, but they were carrying out raids on plantations that required joint military action to address.[10] They spied on and plundered plantations, and other enslaved people, such as in the case of Kebinda and Anne (Chapter 6), were included in the bounty by being held in captivity and subjectivity to the maroons.[11] Despite the treaty with the smaller group labelled the "Maniel," it was reported in August 1786 that there were still maroons living in the Baoruco mountains near Neybe. There were an estimated 1,500 at another site called Christophe, which was outside of Port-au-Prince between the mountains and under Spanish control; Moreau de Saint-Méry also suggested that the number of Maniel maroons was thought to be as high as 1,800.[12] That same month, two other letters – one apparently addressed to the royal government seat in Versailles – appeared, similarly complaining about the maroon problem and stating that fugitives from the Spanish territory were still invading Saint-Domingue.[13] The Maniel finally agreed to settle at the town of Neybe, just north of the Baoruco mountains, where they would be governed by the Spanish and baptized as Catholics.

The theme of land rights and self-initiated, self-organized work continued to shape revolt, especially in the south, well into the years of the Haitian Revolution and the immediate post-independence era. For example, a maroon-styled insurgency led by Jean-Baptise "Goman" DuPerrier continued at Jérémie until his death in 1820. The Grand Anse region was a base of maroon organizing for livable work conditions and land ownership during the Haitian Revolution. Port-Salut, just southeast of Jérémie, became the site of a large revolt conspiracy in January 1791 when rebels armed with guns, machetes, sticks, and other handheld weapons galvanized forces in the area, and neighboring Les Cayes, to join them. Led by representatives from each plantation, they decided on the night of January 24 to collectively demand the three free days per week they believed the French king promised based on a rumor that had spread through the colony. To further their cause, they kidnapped a *commandeur* and three other enslaved people from one plantation. This revolt conspiracy was discovered and the leaders were captured and sentenced. One of the leaders, Dominique Duhard, was arrested, whipped, branded, and sent to the galleys for life; but he somehow escaped and went on to become part of the Platons maroon kingdom the following year.[14]

Soon after the conspiracy at Les Cayes, hundreds and eventually thousands of enslaved people fled southwestern plantations and formed the Platons Kingdom maroon settlement in the mountains in the summer of 1792. Many enslaved people in the south received arms from free people of color who were fighting for political equality, but after the April 4, 1792, decree granted those rights, the enslaved and maroons continued to take up arms in their own defense. Maroons negotiated with André Rigaud in July 1792, making demands that echoed those of the

Port Salut rebels: three free days per week and the abolition of the whip as a means of social control and punishment. Though some members of the Platons community negotiated their own emancipation, many did not accept the terms of manumission and continued to follow Armand, Bernard, Marechal, Formon, Gilles Benech, and Jacques, who led the defensive fight against advances by governor Blanchlande's troops. The maroons withstood incursions for several months, with the help of plantation slaves, raiding plantations for provisions. Though the vast majority of those at Platons were eventually defeated or gained their freedom through negotiation, maroon leadership outlined terms that predated those issued by the general emancipation in 1793, therefore providing a lens through which we can better understand the ways that rebellion among maroons and their enslaved co-conspirators pushed forward their own notions of freedom in ways the French had not yet conceptualized.[15] Veteran rebels of the Platons Kingdom, like Gilles Benech, Nicolas Regnier, and Jean-Baptise "Goman" DuPerrier, went on to mount the pivotal southern resistance to the 1802 LeClerc expedition, helping to pave the way for Haitian independence from France.[16]

The West

In the western department, politics around race led to pre-revolutionary solidarities between free people of color, enslaved people, and maroons. The repeal of the rights and privileges of *gens du couleur* to hold *calendas*, to practice law or medicine, to have French citizenship, or even to visit France contributed to an overall sense of dissatisfaction and frustration about discrimination and tightening restrictions on their social mobility and rights in the colony and the metropole.[17] Free people of color traveled to the National Assembly in France in October 1789 to agitate for citizenship, and their ideas were thought to be spreading among the enslaved population; rumors of the "rights of man" swirled the Atlantic world, foreshadowing impending revolt.[18] Some colonists even went so far as to attempt to incite a rebellion in order to justify maintaining enslavement and the colonial order, while another colonial official stated in July 1789 that the denial of legal freedom would contribute to a swell of runaways.[19] Indeed, 1789 saw the highest numbers of marronnage overall and the longest duration of escapes from plantations (Figures 7.1 and 5.1). While some freemen in the north were sympathetic and in favor of abolition, *gens du couleur* of the west generally sought to protect their interests – which largely included slavery, since many mixed-race individuals were landowners and owned and traded slaves as property. Though most free people of color did not identify with the enslaved population or their African cultures, they were not opposed to mobilizing (and, during the revolution, coercing) slaves for their own benefit.

In early 1791, 35 free people of color – led by Buisson Desmarres, Renaud Robin, the Poissons, and the Bauges, and several of their slaves and family members – were charged and sentenced for the death of three white men.[20] Buisson Desmarres and his white neighbor got into an argument about Desmarres' animals crossing over onto the man's property and when confronted, Desmarres lost his temper and physically attacked him – a grave mistake for a freeman of color. The white man furiously left for Port-au-Prince and recruited 20 other whites to assail Desmarres for daring to raise his hand to a white person. Knowing that he would soon need to defend himself, Desmarres called his in-laws the Bauges, Renaud Robin, Jean Poisson, several of their slaves, and two other friends and neighbors. The African descendant rebels, free and enslaved, attempted to block the way from Port-au-Prince back to Fonds-Parisien by setting fire to the road. Before the 1,500 strong vigilante band of whites arrived to Desmarres' house, he and his followers had already abandoned their lands, leaving the whites to burn the plantations owned by Desmarres, the Poissons, and Renaud Robin. The blacks and freemen followed the same path that maroons had taken for generations to find freedom in Spanish Santo Domingo, where they were welcomed in Neybe. They wrote to the governor asking for asylum and were told they could become subjects of the crown if they remained in Spanish territory.[21]

Historian Thomas Madiou suggested that the fugitives remained in Santo Domingo, however other documents indicate they were executed (though possibly in effigy) in Port-au-Prince in February 1791.[22] The following were condemned to have their legs, arms, thighs, and kidneys broken alive on a scaffold at the public square: Buisson Desmarres and two of his slaves Jean-François and Jean-Joseph; three men of the Robin family, Renaud, Desruisseaux, and Ferrier; Pierre and Paris Poisson, and two of Paris' slaves Gabriel and David; Jean-François and Jean-Louis Bauge; someone named Aza; and a Spanish black man named Gustine – perhaps the one who provided them shelter in Santo Domingo. Others who were charged were Emmanuel Gonzal, a free black man and keeper of François Boe's plantation at Fond Verette; Renaud Robin's slaves François *dit* Degage, Fatime *dit* Faiman, François *dit* Tout Mon Bien, and Pierre-Louis *dit* Pompee; Charles and Nago, both slaves of Buisson Desmarres; Jean Poisson and his slaves Marie *dit* Marinette, Suzon, a young girl named Iphigenie, and Nicolas; Marie, slave of Bauge; Marie *dit* Gothon, slave of the widow Borno; Joseph *dit* Boisson, Jean-Joseph *dit* Boisson, and Denis-Victor *dit* Boisson Belleroche; and Jacques *dit* Frere, a free black named Babo, Jacques-Joseph *dit* Falaise, and a free woman named Emilie.[23]

Enslaved blacks and *mulâtres* again collaborated later that summer in July 1791 at the Fortin Bellanton plantation in Cul-de-Sac near Croix-des-Bouquets when they killed the *commandeur* for suspecting he was too loyal to whites and likely to betray their plans of a coordinated revolt. This was not the first time the Bellanton bondspeople held a grievance against plantation authorities. Some 20 years earlier, in March 1769, all the people enslaved at Bellenton went to the governor's residence in Port-au-Prince to file a claim against their white manager.[24] After the 1791 killing of the *commandeur*, the rebels escaped into the woods where they assembled with 50 other bondspeople from five neighboring plantations who had been reported as runaways. The following day, the *maréchaussée* pursued the band of 60 maroons, all of whom were armed with guns and machetes, following them to the coast. The confrontation between the *maréchaussée* and the rebel band resulted in the execution of nine rebel leaders, with two being broken alive on a scaffold.[25] On July 6, the High Court in Port-au-Prince sentenced six others to hang and have their bodies exposed on the Bellanton property for 24 hours as a warning to others.[26]

On July 18, the Count of Guitton sent a letter confirming that an armed rebellion was growing in Port-au-Prince, Vases, and Mont-Rouis at the plantations of Fortin Bellanton and Poix and Payen. Additionally, the enslaved workers at Trou-Bordet were demanding extra provisions and more time to rest. These conflicts, or "derangements" according to Guitton, were blamed on the influx of soldiers and French citizens who were supposedly imposing their ideas on the enslaved in the absence of the plantation owners.[27] Insurrection was about to engulf the Port-au-Prince area, this time at the Fessard plantation in the Montagnes Noires. Fessard was a lawyer in Port-au-Prince and managed the affairs for several planters in the area, including the recapture of runaways. An advertisement was placed for Coucoulou, a Nagô cook aged 27–30; Marc, aged 20–25, a Kongolese *commandeur*; Herode, also Kongolese, and a 35-year-old carpenter; and Desire, a 20–22-year-old creole gardener belonging to Sr. Fessard, who fled the plantation on September 1.

Before the escape, they destroyed several buildings and pieces of furniture and took with them all the guns and ammunition on the property. The four men had initially led 14 others to escape as well, but those runaways returned to report that Coucoulou, Marc, Herod, and Desire would stay put.[28] Though the 14 returned to Fessard's land, it seems that this was not the only mass desertion in the plantation's history. On September 17, 1771, almost exactly 20 years earlier, eight men and two women escaped the Montagnes Noires plantation and were suspected of being harbored by free people of color, further suggesting that in the west there had been ongoing collaboration between enslaved people and the *gens du couleur*.[29]

In late 1791, in the Cul-de-Sac region surrounding Port-au-Prince, white colonists and *gens du couleur* who were in conflict with each other both courted dissatisfied maroons – perhaps including those who survived and escaped the Fortin Bellanton conflict – and enslaved people as auxiliary armed forces, promising freedom or minimally better work conditions and a reduced working week.[30] The "Swiss," the Company of Africans, and Hyacinthe's army fought on both sides of the civil war between the whites and the freemen who took advantage of the already fermenting rebellion among the enslaved people of the region.[31] Hyacinthe was an Africa-inspired ritual leader whose following was composed of 15,000 people, including lieutenants Garion Santo, Halaou, Bebe Coustard, and Belisaire Bonaire, who emerged at Croix-des-Bouquets in 1792 during the Haitian Revolution.[32]

By July 1792, the maroon encampment at Platons in the south was growing larger by the day; and Romaine "la Prophetesse" Rivière, another charismatic leader of a folk Kongo Catholic tradition, and his following of nearly 13,000, had established control over Léogâne and Jacmel.[33] Terry Rey's *The Priest and the Prophetess* (2017) has uncovered new biographical information about Romaine Rivière and the rebellion he led in the central department. Romaine was a free man of color from Santo Domingo who at the onset of the rebellion brought together other freemen, slaves, and possibly maroons in their pillage of plantations in Léogâne and Jacmel. A letter from Léogâne, dated September 27, 1791, attests that "there have formed two camps of brigands of color who have pillaged several plantations."[34] For months, Romaine's band fortified his base at Trou Coffy with arms and spiritual protection from a huge shrine he constructed on his property. Though he was a coffee planter who may have owned slaves, Romaine's spiritual inclinations led him to build solidarities and seek an end to slavery.

The Northern Insurrection

Throughout Saint-Domingue, the foundation for the Haitian Revolution uprising was laid through maroon reclamation, organization, and the embodiment of a socio-political critique of the plantation system. In the south, marronnage was characterized by runaways creating communal spaces and using their intimate knowledge of land, space, and ecologies for subsistence farming. Western department maroons mobilized in part based on solidarity – however fragile – with free people of color. In the northern plain, where the August 1791 uprising began, maroons and enslaved people deployed transience to organize masses in small-scale and larger insurgencies. As the Haitian Revolution unfolded, their networks also appear to have been connected by women who traversed spaces to cultivate relationships, countered colonial codes by posing as the opposite sex, and performed rituals to cultivate shared consciousness and identity. As Chapter 5 demonstrated, maroons increasingly remained in fugitivity for longer periods of time, reclaiming their time and appropriating other resources during their escapes. Here, we see that acts of oppositional behavior and rebellion spread through pre-existing social ties, interpersonal relationships, and spatial connections (Morris 1984; McAdam 1988; Gould 1995).

East of Cap Français, rebellion on the Sicard plantation in Fort Dauphin may have been fermenting since an October 1784 ship revolt. Sicard, an old and wealthy planter, was traveling with a colonist named Lavalette from Martinique back to Fort Dauphin, along with a group of Lavalette's slaves. Sicard's servant Jean-Pierre, aged 14, and Lavalette's captives – all of whom were likely French speakers – successfully conspired to kill their owners and throw them overboard before arriving in Fort Dauphin. Their ship landed on the English island Tortol, where the rebels were arrested and sent to Martinique, then back to Cap Français. Later that month, Jean-Pierre was sentenced to be hanged and burned. The other five, Léveillé, Pharaon, Mercure, Luc and Azor, were condemned to publicly apologize by standing with a sign board describing their crime. Afterward, Léveillé and Pharaon had their right hands cut off, and all five were broken alive on the wheel and burned.[35]

Word of Sicard's murder and the uprising of his servant Jean-Pierre likely made its way back to Fort Dauphin, which had already been a hotbed for raids by maroon bands. Three years after the 1784 ship revolt, several individuals owned by the Sicard estate, but leased to Madame Sommanvert, escaped; some of them may have fought with the maroon leader Louis Gillot *dit* Yaya, who, along with several associates, was arrested in February 1787 for pillaging plantations in Fort Dauphin. Yaya's associates, Pierre Sicard, Jean (Louis or François), and Apollon may have been part of a group of seven absconders who escaped the Sicard plantation in Fort Dauphin in late 1786 or early 1787 and were still at large as late as January 28, 1788, months after Yaya's execution, possibly passing for free in Haut-du-Trou, Le Cap, or Limbé.[36] Yaya had been a maroon for 10–12 years, or perhaps even longer if he was the same Gillot in a 1766 advertisement describing a "very dangerous" creole man who stole horses and mules from Petite-Anse and sold them to the Spanish.[37] Yaya was joined by Narcisse, Manuel Damas, Jean François, Pierre Sicard, Pantaleon, Apollon, Dominique, Jean Louis, and an unnamed *mulâtre* woman. The rebels confronted the *maréchaussée* armed with machetes, and later several of the accused were interrogated repeatedly and dozens of witnesses were interviewed. Yaya was charged for attacking plantations and receiving arms, pillaging plantations in Trou and Terrier Rouge, and public notoriety, crimes for which he was sentenced to execution in September 1787.[38] Public knowledge of this group's escape and their open attacks on the plantation system may have influenced enslaved people on their respective plantations. On January 1, 1788, probably during or after New Year celebrations, another group of seven ran away from the Sicard plantation: César, Parisien, Jason, and Marie, all Kongolese, and Marie's creole children Vincent, Scolastique, and Marie-Thérèse.

The influence of Yaya's confrontation with the *maréchaussée* – as well as those by earlier maroon bands led by Noël Barochin, Thélémaque Canga, Isaac Candide, and Pirrhus – may have spread beyond the Sicard plantation to other parts of Fort Dauphin. From early 1787 into 1788, letters between Marie Tousard and her husband, career military officer and recent coffee planter Colonel Louis Tousard, reveal that escapes consistently occurred on their Fort Dauphin plantation that Marie managed while Louis traveled. Louis attempted to support to his wife by advising that they use iron collars as punishment, yet bondspeople on the Tousard plantation continued to escape and steal equipment to sell in town. On January 10, 1787, the colonel wrote to his mother-in-law, Madame de St. Martin, assuring her that though several slaves had escaped, among them Pompice (Pompée) and Antoine, they would be captured soon. She responded in February that she was concerned that the runaways had not returned and that they had traveled to the Spanish territory. By June 21, Louis himself began to worry that the four runaways had potentially reached Santo Domingo. He planned to place an advertisement for them and to brand Jean-Louis and Michel as punishment upon their return. By July 26, there was no mention of the runaways in the Fort Dauphin jail. Colonel Tousard did eventually place an advertisement for Pierre Loulou, a driver on this plantation; yet, as Marie's letters and the November 17, 1787, runaway advertisement claimed, Pierre was "uncontrollable" and was well known in Maribaroux and Ouanaminthe, where he frequented the Philibert, de Pontac, and de Vaublanc plantations.[39]

Loulou was eventually returned to the Tousards, though his past escape loomed in their minds. On January 17, 1788, the colonel suggested that Loulou should receive a new coat as a gift to keep him obliged to his owner – but sternly reminded Madame St. Martin that Loulou was to be kept under close watch. Tousard also suggested that another foreman, Jean-Baptiste, needed to be kept in his place because his position afforded him the potential to influence others toward chaos and disorder.[40] The concerns about Loulou and Jean-Baptiste were well-founded, as they seem to have been intent on freeing themselves by repeatedly escaping. After being captured and returned to Tousard, Pierre Loulou escaped again in August 1788; this time he, Pompée, and Jean-Baptiste managed to evade the Tousards until at least February 1789.[41] Marie sent Antoine to find Pompée, who was a Mandingue and had been missing for a year but was never found. These rebels, especially Loulou, demonstrated consistent hostility at the Tousard plantation, which spilled over into the Haitian Revolution when Loulou became part of the insurgency under Jean-François Papillon in 1792.[42] Ironically, Tousard and Jean-François' troops became acquainted when the former was dispatched to put down the revolt at Le Cap in the summer of 1791.[43] It may be possible that Loulou and Papillon knew each other before the uprising. Two weeks before Loulou's November 1787 escape, Jean-François, an early leader of the 1791 revolt along with Georges Biassou, fled the Papillon property in Le Cap.[44] That they escaped within weeks of each other (and around All Soul's Day on November 1) may hint at a wider gathering that took place among the future insurgents. It took an additional year after the initial revolt for Pierre Loulou to join Jean-François' ranks. Pierre was a leader in his own right in the areas of Fort Dauphin, Maribaroux, and Ouanaminthe, where he was well known; while Papillon was voted king of the Gallifet plantations closer to Le Cap. During the early years of the Haitian Revolution, Fort Dauphin continued to be an important location for rebels to trade for weapons, food, and resources from the Spanish.[45]

Planters worried that ties forged by runaways could easily facilitate the spread of insurrection from the city to the countryside if measures were not taken to thwart even short-term marronnage. Villevaleix was the lawyer for the Breda plantations surrounding Cap Français, one of which previously held Toussaint Louverture in bondage.[46] On March 31, 1790, Villevaleix wrote that there had been drought conditions recently and fires started by nearby maroons were destroying plantations in the plain of Le Cap. His account casually acknowleges there was indeed a regular presence of runaway communities just outside the bustling port city. These maroons may have been joined a few weeks later by a young, newly arrived African who escaped the Breda pottery on the night of April 18 or 19.[47] Nine others escaped Breda after an enslaved man was killed due to violent mistreatment, and they refused to return until they were assured that no punishment would be given. Later in September, the Breda overseer found and arrested 27 runaways at the pottery and others hiding in the slaves' housing quarters.[48]

Lieutenant Milscent's account from 1791 corroborates Villevaleix's mention of maroons gathered around Le Cap to organize a revolt, stating that:

in 1790, being a deputy of the assembly of the north, it was suddenly reported that there was a considerable assemblage of negroes in the mountains of Le Cap, well furnished with guns, canons, etc., which formed the nucleus of a general uprising of negroes in the colony... My inquiries taught me that there were about thirty negro maroons of this mountain, armed, some with machetes, others with sickles.[49]

One of these runaways may have been Étienne, a *mulâtre* carpenter and cook who escaped in the summer of 1790 with a brown horse, a gun, and a machete, claiming to be free. While the advertisement for Étienne was placed by Mr. Archambau in Le Cap, Étienne had been seen in multiple locations, including Port-Margot, Gonaïves, Artibonite, and as far south as Saint-Marc, clearly using the horse to reach different parishes. In Étienne's case, his self-identification as a free man may not have been only an individualized posturing to "pass," as was the case for many runaways, but perhaps was a public proclamation and rallying cry to galvanize other enslaved people and runaways in the northern plain for a meeting in or around Le Cap. Étienne's escape was advertised alongside that of a Senegalese woman named Martonne. She had been leased to a surgeon but eventually escaped and was later seen in Grand-Riviere, Dondon, and at Maribaroux on the Philibert plantation – one of the sites

Pierre Loulou frequented while he traversed the north.[50] The chase that Milscent attempted to organize to re-capture these runaways outside Le Cap never happened, because their camp was informed and scattered before the detachment could reach them.[51]

Bwa Kayman and "Zamba" Boukman Dutty

Like *calendas* and *vaudoux* ritual gatherings where people like François Mackandal and Dom Pedro were central leaders, the Bwa Kayman ceremony was also a free space where participants assembled outside the scope of colonial surveillance to draw upon spiritual power, strengthen oppositional consciousness, forge solidarities, and incite rebellion (see Chapter 3). There has been some scholarly debate on the validity of the Bwa Kayman ceremony as a historical fact, in addition to some confusion about its actual date and location. While few have argued that the ceremony did not happen, contemporary accounts and oral histories contribute to a consensus that this significant ritual ceremony did take place soon before the Haitian Revolution began and that it was a significant vehicle for mobilizing the enslaved population in the northern plain (Fick 1990; Geggus 2002: 81–92; Beauvoir-Dominique 2010). The Bwa Kayman ceremony is known as an exemplary case within the African Diaspora of ritual influence on impending revolt against enslavement. Less than seven days prior to the August 22, 1791, mass insurgency on Saint-Domingue's northern plain, two gatherings occurred near the Lenormand de Mezy plantation in Morne Rouge. It is believed that the first gathering was a meeting of creole coachmen, *commandeurs*, and high-ranking slaves on August 14 to outline the strategy for the revolt, and the other was held on August 21 to summon spirits for protection and sacralize the revolt.[52] However, we lack clarity about the actual date of the ceremony; although the August 14 meeting may have been an organizing meeting, it also coincides with present-day celebrations for *lwa* Ezili Kawoulo and was the feast day for the Notre Dame de l'Assomption, patron saint of the colony. This would have been particularly important to free people of color and enslaved Kongo Catholics who followed the cult of the Virgin. Also, August 15 is the date for honoring Kongo *lwa* in Gonaïves, not far from northern plain.[53]

Regardless of the ceremony's date, oral historical evidence suggests that the Bwa Kayman spiritual gathering was the culmination of ritual collaboration between the varying African ethnic groups. Participants sacrificed a pig – which in contemporary Haitian society signifies a militaristic undercurrent of the *petwo* rite – and drank its blood, indicating a Dahomean oath of secrecy done in conjunction with the *orisha* Ogou.[54] Spirits from the Nagô and Rada pantheons held more spiritual capital because Bight of Benin Africans were the first ethnic majority in the colony. These spirits were then paired with and/or transferred to the Kongolese rite.[55] Ethnographic evidence is supported by historical evidence from the Catholic tradition in the Kongolands, where petitions to the Virgin and Saint James were commonplace in the seventeenth and eighteenth centuries.[56] Therefore, we might surmise that a manifestation of the maternal water spirit Ezili, often depicted as the Catholic Virgin Mary, and the *orisha* of war and iron Ogou, appearing as Saint James, were the main forces called upon at Bwa Kayman. Ezili and Ogou from the Bight of Benin merged with the Virgin Mary and Saint James from the Kongo to reinforce the shared bond of the ritual between the two ethnic clusters.

Antoine Dalmas first detailed the Bwa Kayman ceremony; later, Antoine Metral described a woman who performed significant rituals. Then in the 1950s, the grandson of a mixed-race woman named Cécile Fatiman and former Haitian president Jean-Louis Pierrot confirmed to historian Étienne Charlier that Cécile had been the ceremony's main presider.[57] Along with Fatiman, "Zamba" Boukman Dutty orchestrated the ceremony and directed the initial attacks on the northern plantations from August until his death in November 1791. Boukman was brought from Jamaica illegally, and a lawyer in Limbé, named Leclerc, bought him. Boukman was known as a "bad slave" whose frequent marronnage resulted one night in being caught, shot, then sold to the Clement plantation in Acul, where he was for some reason promoted to either *commandeur* or coachman.[58] He was reportedly a leader of the ceremony and in Haitian historical memory was a *boko(r)*, someone who does "mystical work through his own strength" rather than through learned rituals.[59] Further, his experience in an English colony may have contributed to an understanding of inter-imperial geopolitics, providing a basis for knowledge about how to exploit conflicts between the French, English, and Spanish. If a trader brought Boukman from Jamaica during an English blockade against the French, Boukman would have arrived either during the Seven Years War (1754–1763) or during the North American War of Independence (1776–1783). In either case, Boukman probably would have been aware of the Akan-led Tacky's Revolt in 1760 and the subsequent Coromantee Wars.

Additionally, Boukman would have understood the power of African-based sacred practices in bringing together mobilizers. Tacky's Revolt was organized by *obeahmen* who hid the conspiracy using loyalty oaths and employed ritual packets as protective armaments. However, in the aftermath of the revolt, the Jamaican colonial government increased repression against ritualists, which "threw the direct competition among different forms of sacred authority into stark relief."[60] Maroons who allied with Anglo-Jamaican planters eventually betrayed Tacky. Given the conflicts between African ritualists and maroons in Jamaica, Boukman would have understood the importance of pan-African alliances and employed these lessons as he organized the August 1791 insurrection. It therefore should come as no surprise that accounts of the Bwa Kayman ceremony indicate the use of symbols and practices from multiple ethnic backgrounds. Further biographical research is needed to identify when Boukman was taken from Jamaica, then brought to Saint-Domingue. If indeed he was brought after the Coromantee Wars, any connection between these events in Jamaica and the beginnings of the Haitian Revolution would prove compelling.

The attempted killing of Galliffet's manager at La Gossette, the same plantation that experienced marronnage as labor strikes in 1785 and 1789, triggered the northern uprisings in 1791.[61] It seems clear that the masses of northern Saint-Domingue had for some time been planning the revolt that began on August 22. Georges Biassou, Jean-François Papillion, Jeanot Bullet, and Boukman Dutty were the central emerging leaders, while Toussaint Louverture was likely part of the planning but waited until fall to leave the Breda plantation and join the rebel ranks. Boukman Dutty was not the only rebel leader who recruited sacred power to enhance his ability to command thousands of insurrectionists. Georges Biassou was originally an enslaved person from the hills surrounding Cap Français. His mother was a nurse in a Jesuit hospital, where Toussaint Louverture may have also been employed. Louverture and Biassou had familiarity with one another from their early years, and Louverture would later become the doctor for Biassou's rebel camp. Georges Biassou was considered one of the more colorful revolutionary leaders, particularly because of his open dedication to African-based practices. His war tent was known to include sacred items and animals. At night, he held ceremonies featuring African dances and chants. Additionally, his military cadre included several religious specialists whom he regularly consulted for advice.[62] By November, Boukman had been killed in battle while defending his post after several attempts to sack Cap Français, and his body was decapitated and burned. Upon learning of Boukman's death, insurgents in Jean-François' camp held a three-day *calenda* in commemoration. The militaristic rituals of the *calenda* involved mocking enemy forces, as the rebels symbolically proclaimed the death of Colonel Tousard and ridiculed their white prisoners with stories of their battle successes.[63] Even after Boukman's death, fighting in the north continued. On July 2, 1793, Duvallon-L'etang sent a letter from Le Cap to his brother detailing the murder of their parents and the apparent kidnapping of their younger siblings, whose heads and hands were the only body parts that remained.[64] The rebels' persistence in fighting – eventually on behalf of the French against British and Spanish forces – and acts of self-liberation were the singular influences that led to the general emancipation of enslaved people later in 1793.

Women Bridge Leaders

Accounts of women ritualists during the early days of the Haitian Revolution uprising demonstrate that "the subversion of cultural expressions, symbols and aesthetics has been a recurrent theme in African women's resistance across divergent contexts, locations and herstorical moments" (Kuumba 2006: 116). Enslaved African and African-descended women, like the midwife Marie Catherine Kingué and Cécile Fatiman, deployed their spiritual practices to support the liberation struggle. In the weeks after Bwa Kayman, Boukman went on to lead an insurgency of tens of thousands of slaves in systematically pillaging and burning dozens of sugar plantations throughout the northern plain. Accounts from nuns of the Communauté des Religieuses Filles de Notre-Dame du Cap-Français, an expensive boarding school for black and white girls, claimed that rebel band leader Boukman Dutty attempted to capture Cap Français days after Bwa Kayman.[65] In their letters describing the insurgency's destruction, the nuns describe a former student known as "Princess" Amethyste, a young mixed-race woman who had been initiated into the Arada tradition of *Gioux* or *vaudoux* and who had persuaded other students to follow her lead. This group was referred to as "Amazons," to imply that they were female insurgents that actively assisted Boukman in sacking Le Cap, and that they were members of his spiritual sect.[66]

Besides Cécile Fatiman and Amethyste, women's spiritual role was consistent in facilitating sacred protections for the rebel forces. In February 1792, Colonel Charles Malenfant led a military excursion against a camp in Fonds-Parisien at Cul-de-Sac when he witnessed a *vaudoux* ceremony led by a priestess who had placed ritual artifacts along the road to the encampment to block foreign entry. Black and white chickens were speared on large stakes and trailed along the road, leading to a set of eight to ten large eggs, which created an entryway to an encampment covered in vines. There, over 200 women and a few men, some of whom were from the Gouraud plantation, were found singing and dancing; the militiamen chased them toward the Santo Domingo border, killing 20 women en route. The leader was described as a finely dressed woman from the Boynes plantation, but Malefant's troops executed her without due process. Malenfant was particularly annoyed by the premature killing because he was no longer able to obtain information from her about the nearby rebels. Malenfant discovered another *vaudoux* queen in the Sainte Suzanne mountains of Limonade. She was an Arada woman who had recently arrived in the colony and though she spoke no Kreyol, initiates claimed that she was all-powerful. She was questioned in Cap Français and showed interrogators a secret handshake akin to those of the Freemasons, but she never divulged other secrets that would identify other members of the sect – thereby protecting the rebels and any information they might have.[67]

The fear of marronnage as an organizing principle to build a regional or colony-wide network of rebels was legitimate, especially when considering rebels' propensity to use women as bridge leaders: couriers, spies, nurses, and smugglers.[68] After Jean-François escaped the Papillon plantation at Le Cap in November 1787, his girlfriend Charlotte, a Poulard woman, ran away from the same owner in March 1791. She had been missing for five months before an advertisement for her was placed in *Gazette de Saint Domingue* in early August. It was suspected that Charlotte was abusing the temporary pass she was given and had been moving about in different quarters. By the time the advertisement was published, it was believed that she was in or around Port-au-Prince.[69] We may never know exactly what Charlotte was doing in those five months, the different parishes she visited, or with whom she was in contact. However, it may be possible that she left in the spring on behalf of Jean-François to help coordinate the rebellions that would begin a few months later. While Charlotte was traveling in the greater Port-au-Prince area, smaller uprisings began there in July that anticipated the August 1791 mass revolt in the northern plain. By September, she was back north with Jean-François, and rebels at the former Galliffet plantation named them king and queen.[70] The election of kings and queens was common among the rebels in the north and at Platons whenever they gained military control of a parish.[71] There is no direct evidence that Jean-François and Charlotte's coronation was related to the secret *vaudoux* gatherings or Kongo-Catholic confraternity celebrations where kings and queens were the central leadership figures; however, we do know that initiates of the former were asked to perform rebellious tasks such as stealing before they could enter the secret organization. In such a case, we might then think of Charlotte's crowning as a reward for her role in coordinating the northern and western revolts.

Similarly, rebel leader Hyacinthe's partner Magdeleine escaped enslavement in August 1790 – an advertisement suggests he lured her away to the Ducoudray plantation where he was held.[72] Magdeleine was described as a creole woman who had free family members in Petit Goâve, and transgressed gender norms by dressing in men's clothes. Her apparent eschewal of conventionally gendered activity might indicate that Magdeleine was intentionally hiding herself not just as a maroon but as an active participant during the western uprisings. This supports later reports that women in Hyacinthe's camp commonly ran errands to exchange weapons and food.[73] Other women fought and died alongside husbands who were generals in the black military forces. Sanité and Charles Belair, nephew of Toussaint Louverture, were captured during the last days of the Leclerc expedition and were executed together in October 1802. Sanité was known for her hostility toward whites and her fearlessness in facing execution without a blindfold.[74] At the battle of Crête-à-Pierrot, an important turning point in the final struggle against Leclerc's forces, Marie Jeanne Lamartinière accompanied her husband "and took her share in the defense [*sic*]."[75] On the other hand, Claire Heureuse, wife of Dessalines, was sympathetic toward opposing forces and attempted to save "many of the French he had ordered massacred."[76]

MARRONNAGE AND SOLIDARITY DURING THE HAITIAN REVOLUTION

The Haitian Revolution, although not wholly dictated by Africa-inspired rituals and marronnage, benefitted from maroon bands and ritual leaders at important moments of its unfolding. The Haitian Revolution was a 13-year struggle that involved a number of divergent groups whose economic and political interests, goals, and solidarities rapidly shifted as events in France progressed and the abolition of slavery became imminent. Saint-Domingue's people of African descent – enslaved continent-born Africans of various ethnicities, colony-born creoles, and free *gens du couleur* and *affranchis* – were not a truly united force until the final movement for independence from France. During and after the 1791 uprisings, rebels were organized primarily by their ethnic or language group; for example, Toussaint Louverture allied with "Doco" maroons of Mirebalais and their leader Mademoiselle on the basis that many of the Doco and Louverture were of Arada origin and spoke the same language. There was also evidence of racial solidarity in the rebel camps as the revolution unfolded. In 1793, after declaring the abolition of slavery in Saint-Domingue, French commissioner Léger-Félicité Sonthonax invited the Nagô leader Alaou and his several thousand troops of Kongolese, Senegambian, Igbo, and Dahomean rebels to meet with him in Port-au-Prince.[77] Though the army of formerly enslaved masses was largely responsible for defeating Spanish, British, and French forces, and leveraging their own emancipation, the military elite and slave-holding free people of color were slow to join the cause of emancipation and independence.

Michel-Rolph Trouillot (1995) has argued that during the Haitian Revolution, a "war within the war" emerged as formerly enslaved and free black and mixed-race military officers elevated their economic and political statuses and diverged from the immediate interests of the formerly enslaved masses. Jean-François Papillon and Georges Biassou accepted a proposal to free themselves and their officers in exchange for putting down the general revolt – an offer that the French subsequently rebuffed, to their own chagrin. Soon after the 1793 emancipation, the other French commissioner, Étienne Poverel, instituted regulations for the formerly enslaved that hinted at the ways they sought to support themselves with subsistence farming. Freed people, then referred to as "cultivators," were forced to continue plantation work to produce the sugar and coffee that would sustain the colony's economic viability. They rebuffed the demands on their labor by insisting on having two days per week to farm for themselves. Women likely composed the larger proportion of cultivators and were especially dissatisfied with the new labor codes, which mandated that they would receive less pay than men for performing the same tasks, as they had during slavery. Women vocally protested the gendered pay gap by demanding equal wages, refusing to work, and disobeying plantation authorities.[78] Some cultivators responded with marronnage by abandoning plantations altogether and staking claims to their own land. Soon these cultivators began conspiring and staging revolts of their own, which were repressed, sometimes brutally, by Toussaint's army.[79]

It became clear that Louverture would not tolerate challenges to his authority; this may explain his regime's coercive repression of Africa-inspired rituals and leaders of maroon bands who consistently staged insurrections and labor protests against the new plantation system. Louverture and future political regimes were aware of the potential political power of marronnage and what became known as Vodou, and they attempted to control oppositional mass mobilization. For example, one *mambo* was executed in 1802 for organizing a ritual dance.[80] When Louverture's 1801 Constitution militarized labor, women cultivators were specifically targeted and prohibited from entering military camps to prevent disobedience. This restriction on women's movement and religious practices implies there was knowledge and awareness of women's role and significance as organizers of rebellion. After the French captured and exiled Toussaint Louverture, rebel officers like Jean-Jacques Dessalines defected from the insurgent army and sided with the French, but African rebels and maroons continued fighting against French forces.[81] Their military successes, especially in the south, combined with the growing evidence that the French were striving to restore slavery in Saint-Domingue, signaled to black and mixed-race officers the urgency of joining the masses to fight the French for independence. The Bwa Kayman ceremony had spiritually solidified alliances between West Central Africans and Bight of Benin Africans; and the struggle of the formerly enslaved rebels and maroons propelled racial solidarity between Africans, creoles, and free people of color toward independence in 1804. As a result, the first post-independence Constitution declared, "the Haitians shall hence forward be known only by the generic appellation of Blacks," making Haiti the first and only free and independent Black nation in the Americas.[82]

Conclusion

No nation, no race, no individual in an[y] clime or at any time, can lay claim
to civilization as its own creation or invention or exclusive personal possession. The impulse of humanity toward social progress is like the movement
in the currents of a great water system, beating ever onward toward its
eternity — the ocean.[1]

Anna Julia Cooper

The project of modernity, how, when, and where it began and who
produced it, continues to plague historians and sociologists alike.
Writing in 1925 as she accepted her diploma for completion of the
doctoral dissertation *L'Attitude de la France à l'égard de l'esclavage
pendant la révolution* [*Slavery and the French Revolutionists,
1788–1805*], Anna Julia Cooper's remarks instruct us to be constantly
in search of self-defined expressions of humanity and development
beyond the scope of the Western world. Cooper's dissertation did just
that in expanding study of the French Revolution to its imperial territories
in the Caribbean – Saint-Domingue specifically – to make the case that
without consideration of racial slavery in the colonies, the political and
philosophical ideals propagated by the Declaration of the Rights on Man
and the Citizen were woefully incomplete. That Cooper used water,
currents, and the ocean to symbolize human movement toward new,
liberated, modes of being is perhaps an irony, given that movement across
the Atlantic Ocean was largely a voyage toward unfreedom for captive
Africans. Still, even the lives of those who survived oceanic journeys and
were enslaved in the Americas were not without alternate flows, bends,

and radical turns that would alter the course of human history; the "currents" of which Cooper spoke were and are not linear.

For Anna Julia Cooper, and later C. L. R. James, slavery and colonialism were central questions in the French Revolution, highlighting the transnational nature of revolutionary processes. Indeed, just as maroons and the formerly enslaved rebels of Saint-Domingue embodied and put forward ideals of freedom and liberty that were much broader than those espoused in France, the island's centuries-long legacy of resistance that informed the Haitian Revolution stemmed from West and West Central African social, economic, cultural, religious, and militaristic sensibilities and contributions. These insights may now be considered as accepted interventions in the fields of African Diaspora Studies and Atlantic World History; yet the discipline of sociology, the field of revolutions in particular, has only recently moved toward destabilizing the limitations of Eurocentrism, methodological nationalism, and presentism (Go and Lawson 2017). Nearly 50 years after Joyce Ladner (1973) foresaw *The Death of White Sociology*, the discipline has not only recovered W. E. B. Du Bois and the Atlanta Sociological Laboratory as the true pioneers of scientific American sociology (Morris 2007, 2015), it has begun to challenge the racialized and imperial gazes that imbued the discipline and its methodologies, instead centering perspectives on humanity and modernity that emerge from the global African Diaspora and other parts of the postcolonial world (Magubane 2005; Bhambra 2011, 2014; Go 2016; Itzigsohn and Brown 2020).

The social, religious, political, and economic maroon formations explicated in this book only mark the beginning of Haiti's history as the first free and independent Black nation in the Americas. Nineteenth-century Haitians identified lifeways and freedoms that were grounded in the counter-plantation logics of marronnage: subsistence farming, landowning kin networks, the religious consolidation of Vodou, and absconding as a form of protesting unfair labor codes (Casimir 2001, 2015, 2020; Gonzalez 2019). Marronnage remains a significant orientation and mode of political action in Haiti: the Marron Inconnu statue in Port-au-Prince symbolizes this history. Similarly, the walls of the Musée du Panthéon de National Haïtien recognize the contributions of maroon leaders like François Mackandal, Polydor, Louis Gillot *dit* Yaya, Thélémaque Canga, Noël Barochin, and Colas Jambes Coupée and many others in the struggle against slavery and colonialism. Haiti's influence throughout the Black world as symbol of hope and inspiration, a locale of liberation, and, perhaps more importantly, as a wellspring of black political thought and action that represented the deepest truths of modern ideals can hopefully also be instructive to those concerned with the ideas and realities of modernity. On the other hand, the ongoing economic and militaristic aggression that Haiti has experienced in the form of the French indemnity leveled in 1825, American imperialism from 1915 to 1934, and government corruption also reveals the persistent underbelly of the ways racial capitalism and colonial legacies continue to inform our modern world. The world now awaits answers in the troubling assassination of Haitian president Jovenel Moïse in July 2021 – with many fearing that it might be a precursor to American intervention, possibly striking parallels to events that preceded the 1915 occupation.

Insights from Haiti, and African Diaspora Studies and postcolonial sociological thought more broadly, can help inform the study of social movements and revolution, especially with regard to (1) employing approaches that prioritize insurgents' long-term, emic resistance strategies (2) contextualizing Black resistance within macro-level analyses of racial capitalism, colonialism, and empire, and (3) exploring the global interconnectedness – and at times divergences – of the Black diaspora and its long legacy of international politics and transnational solidarity networks (Patterson and Kelley 2000; Martin 2005; West and Martin 2009). Analyses of the ways systems of oppression transform over time, migrate within and across empires, and re-inscribe subjugation can help illuminate connections between past and recent moments of insurrection and revolution. Both Haiti and the United States have faced economic, social, environmental, and political crises that have had disproportionately negative effects on the lives of poor and working-class people of African descent. In both countries, Black people have responded with large-scale social movements in the form of #PetroCaribeCorruption and Black Lives Matter. These events not only require analysis of Black people's micro-level mobilizing patterns, but must engage historical consideration of issues of slavery, colonialism, and imperialism to fully comprehend the ways Black struggles continue to push for democracy and political representation, economic fairness, and social justice.

Notes

Introduction

1 Métraux 1959: 187.
2 Rocha 2018: 19.
3 Geggus 1998; *Intra-American Slave Trade Database*.
4 Constitution Impériale d'Haïti (1805).
5 Geggus 2014: 29–35; Girard 2016: 54–56.
6 Shifting monikers for this field – Black Studies, Africana Studies, Africology, Pan-African Studies, African-American Studies, African and African American Studies, and African Diaspora Studies – reflect an intellectual expansion in response to an infusion of pan-African political ideals, globalization, and academic interest in diasporas and transnationalism (Hanchard 2004). I choose Black/African Diaspora Studies to acknowledge the field's original name as well as its recent trajectory.
7 I generally use "black" to describe individuals in alignment with the racial identities they were historically ascribed. However, here and in other places I use "Black" to denote the broader socio-political identity that peoples of the African Diaspora have assumed for themselves.
8 Upcoming work by Jesús Ruiz also examines the role of royalist politics in the Haitian Revolution.
9 DuBois [1896] 2007: 50.
10 James [1938] 1989: 47.
11 Taleb-Khyar 1992: 322.
12 Source: John Carter Brown Library.
13 The excludes military correspondences and declarations made during the Haitian Revolution by leaders such as Toussaint Louverture, Jean-François Papillon, Georges Biassou, and Jean-Jacques Dessalines.

1 "We Have a False Idea of the Negro": Legacies of Resistance and the African Past

1 James [1938] 1989: 356.
2 Thornton 1998: 16–17; Heywood 2009.
3 Stein 1988: 28.
4 Rodney 1982: 98–99; Law 2004: 29–30.
5 Mustakeem 2016: 31–32.
6 Geggus 2001a: 121; Pritchard, Eltis and Richardson: 206; Dubois 2009: 139; Dubois 2011: 442; Voyages Database 2009.
7 Rodney 1982: 96.
8 Dubois 2009: 140; Dubois 2011: 442.
9 31 S 50/Extrait "Correspondance de Wante, établi à Port-au-Prince, a sa famille 1787," Traite, esclavage, abolitions, Archives Bordeaux Métropole.
10 "Pétition du citoyen Sudreau afin d'obtenir l'autorisation de vendre 700 fusils pour la traite des noirs, 1790." Série F, Fonds révolutionnaire, Traite, esclavage, abolitions, Archives Bordeaux Métropole; Mustakeem 2016: 29–30.
11 66 S 70/Extrait – Compagnie des Indes, 1768. Fonds Delpit, Traite, esclavage, abolitions, Archives Bordeaux Métropole.
12 "Note du 15 novembre 1783, pour la valeur d'un noir matelot et française estimée à 2400 livres." Fonds Monneron, Traite, esclavage, abolitions, Archives Bordeaux Métropole.
13 Geggus 1989a: 25–26, 28, 37.
14 Polanyi 1966: 8, 21; Law 1991; Monroe 2014.
15 Law 2003: chapter 2; Law 1991: chapter 7.
16 Law 2004: 151.
17 Law 1991: 109–113; Sweet 2011: 17–18.
18 Bay 1998: 92, 155–157; Sweet 2011: 20–22.
19 Bay 1998: 92.
20 Law 1991: 114.
21 Bay 1998: 92–93.
22 Bay 1998: 120.
23 Bay 1998: 125.
24 Law 1977: chapter 2.
25 Law 1991: chapter 3.
26 Gomez 1998: 56–57.
27 Law 1977: 220–221; Lovejoy 2012: 55.
28 Law 1977: 52; Thornton 1991: 62.
29 Law 1977: 217, 225–227, 239–241, 306–308.
30 For more on the Nagô, see: Law 1991: 154, 227 nn. 197–198, 282–287; Law 1997; Hall 2005; Matory 2005: 5; Sweet 2011: 17–18, 24–25.
31 Debien 2000; Law 1991: chapter 1; Hall 2005: 111; for Nagôs as runaways, see Chapter 4.
32 Law 1977: 92–93, 100, 188.
33 Dalzel 1793: 182–183; Law 1997: 212–213.
34 Thornton 1991; Roberts 2005: 178.
35 Deren 1953: 82.

36 Métraux 1959: 48; Dubois 2012: 50; Jenson 2012: 620, 635–636.
37 Barry 1998: 49; Gomez 1998: 45.
38 Barry 1998: 46.
39 Barry 1998:88–93; Ware 2014: chapter 2.
40 Lovejoy 2012: 58–59.
41 "Compte de vente du navire L'Agréable de Bordeaux, capitaine Michel, 1790." Fonds Delpit, Traite, esclavage, abolitions, Archives Bordeaux Métropole; Voyages Database 2009.
42 Hall 2005: 125.
43 Gomez 2005: 28.
44 Alpers 1970: 82.
45 Gomez 2005: 28, 83.
46 Folio 123, "Contrat de vente de noirs du 10 février 1781." Fonds Fieffe, Traite, esclavage, abolitions, Archives Bordeaux Métropole.
47 "Lettre adressée par Cloupet a Louis Monneron, Ile de France, 26 juillet 1782." Fonds de la Société de géographie commerciale de Bordeaux, Traite, esclavage, abolitions, Archives Bordeaux Métropole.
48 1 S 12 Fonds Lavigne/Extrait, "Correspondance de Dominique Lavigne dans le règlement de différentes affaires, 1787." Traite, esclavage, abolitions, Archives Bordeaux Métropole.
49 Candido 2013: 75–76, 160.
50 Stein 1979: 79; Geggus 2001a: 123.
51 Debien 2000: chapter 2; Geggus 1993: 81; Geggus 1999: 39; Geggus 2001a: 131, 138; Daniels 2012: 142–143.
52 Miller 1989; Richardson 1989; Miller 2002; Heywood and Thornton 2007: 55, 106; Sommerdyck 2012: 42, 141; Domingues da Silva 2013; Mobley 2015: 170.
53 Sommerdyck 2012:42–43.
54 Thornton 1991: 60–61; Thornton 1993b: 184; Miller 2002: 56–57; Mobley 2015: 168–184.
55 Thornton 1998; Heywood 2009: 19.
56 Raimondo da Dicomano, *O Reino do Congo: A decadência final do Reino do Congo*; Raphael de Castello de Vide, *Viagem do Congo do Missionário*; Thornton 1991: 60–61; Thornton 1993b: 183; Heywood 2009.
57 Herskovits [1937] 2007: 150; Métraux 1959: 39–40.
58 Heywood and Thornton 2007: 55, 106, 206.
59 Mobley 2015: 42.
60 Heywood 2017: 34.
61 Mobley 2015: 200.
62 Janzen 1982; MacGaffey 1986; Daniels 2013.
63 Thornton 1998: 102; Thornton 2003.
64 Dubois 2016: 212–215.
65 Rodney 1982: 96.
66 Law 2004: 81.
67 66 S 81/Extrait, Papiers Dommenget, 1776. Fonds Delpit, Traite, esclavage, abolitions, Archives Bordeaux Métropole; Voyages Database 2009.
68 Harms 2002: 312–313.

69 Rodney 1982: 80–81; Inikori 2003; Lovejoy 2012: 66–68.
70 Heywood 2017: 24–28, chapters 3–5.
71 Thornton 1998: 112–114, 158, 162, 206–214; Thornton 2003: 291–293.
72 Voyages Database 2009.
73 Barry 1998: 50–54.
74 Gomez 1998: 64–65; Gomez 2005: 9–12, 50–51.
75 Ware 2014: chapter 3; Lovejoy 2016: chapter 2.
76 Soumonni 2003: 26–32.
77 Newitt 2010: 63–65.
78 Thornton 1999: 102; Green 2019: 189, 220–222, 239.
79 Ferreira 2014: 71, 76–77.
80 Ferreira 2011: 127.
81 Thompson 1983: 108–109; MacGaffey 1986: 43–46; Gomez 1998: 148; Fennel 2003: 6.
82 Mettas 1978: 710; Voyages Database 2009.
83 Richardson 2003: 204.
84 *Les Affiches américaines* (hereafter *LAA*) March 10, 1773; *LAA* September 13, 1775; Voyages Database 2009.
85 Voyages Database 2009.
86 *LAA* July 20, 1774; *LAA* October 19, 1774; *LAA* March 1, 1775.

2 In the Shadow of Death

1 James [1938] 1989: 86.
2 Moreau de Saint-Méry 1797 (Vol. 1): 74–75, 80–81; Moreau de Saint-Méry 1798: 42.
3 Stone 2013: 200–201.
4 Moreau de Saint-Méry 1798: 33–34.
5 Monzote 2011: 88.
6 Wilson 1990: chapter 3.
7 Guitar 2006: 43–45; Pons 2007: 7; Stone 2013: 198.
8 Guitar 2006: 45; Landers 2009; Sued-Badillo 2011: 107–109; Wheat 2016.
9 1504, August 26. Medina del Camp, Spain. PARES, Portal Archivos Españoles, Archivo General de Indias, INDIFERENTE, 418, L.1, F.132R.-133R.; 1527, June 28. Valladolid, Spain. PARES, Portal Archivos Españoles, Archivo General de Indias, INDIFERENTE, 421, L.12, F.151R-152R. CUNY Dominican Studies Institute, *First Blacks in the Americas*.
10 Guitar 2006: 49; Stone 2013: 203–204; Schwaller 2018: 625–626; Voyages 2009.
11 Pratt 1992: 6.
12 Guitar 2006.
13 Goveia 1960.
14 1503, March 29. Zaragoza, Spain, Archivo General de Indias, INDIFERENTE, 418 L.1,100R-102V, CUNY Dominican Studies Institute, *First Blacks in the Americas*.; Stone 2013: 203.
15 Stone 2013: 203–204.

16 Fouchard 1972: 300–307; Gomez 2005: 3–46; Guitar 2006: 41, 49; Landers 2009: 35.

17 Stone 2013: 209–210.

18 Rudolph Ware lecture, October 11, 2015 at the University of Michigan, Ann Arbor.

19 Landers 2015; Gomez 1998: 62–64; Gomez 2005: 16.

20 Landers 2004: 5.

21 1521, December 27. Pamplona, Spain. Archivo General de Indias, PATRONATO, 20, N.2, R.2 – Imagen Núm.: ¼, CUNY Dominican Studies Institute, *First Blacks in the Americas*.

22 1528, April 6. Madrid, La Espanola. Archivo General de Indias, PATRONATO, 295, No. 89, CUNY Dominican Studies Institute, *First Blacks in the Americas*.

23 1537, February 3. Valladolid, Spain. Archivo General de Indias, SANTO_DOMINGO, 868, L.1, F.33R-34V, CUNY Dominican Studies Institute, *First Blacks in the Americas*.

24 Landers 2000, 2002: 234; Guitar 2006: 49–52; Thompson 2006: 304; Landers 2015.

25 Guitar 2006: 53.

26 Landers 2000; Matibag 2003: 32; Guitar 2006: 53.

27 Schwaller 2018: 621.

28 Ponce-Vázquez 2016: 17–23

29 1545, April 24. Valladolid, Spain. PARES, Archivo General de Indias, SANTO_DOMINGO, 868, L.2-245 RECTO-IMAGEN NUM: 489/766; 1545, April 24. Valladolid, Spain. PARES, Archivo General de Indias, SANTO_DOMINGO, 868, L.2-250 RECTO-IMAGEN NUM: 499/766, 501/766, CUNY Dominican Studies Institute, *First Blacks in the Americas*.

30 Guitar 2006: 41, 62–63.

31 Thornton 1988b: 368.

32 Landers 2002: 235; Guitar 2006: 39–41.

33 1553. Archivo General de Indias, Justicia, 76, fo. 1593v.-1594R., CUNY Dominican Studies Institute, *First Blacks in the Americas*.

34 Landers 2015.

35 Schwaller 2018: 630.

36 Ponce-Vázquez 2016: 26.

37 Landers 2002: 235; Landers 2015.

38 Ponce-Vázquez 2016: 707, 716; Ricourt 2016: 55–56.

39 Ricourt 2016: 90.

40 Gomez 2005: 16.

41 Landers 2004: 5; Landers 2015.

42 Munford 1991: vii; Stein 1979: 4.

43 Polanyi 1966: 18; Law 1991:126; Munford 1991: 505–522; Boucher 2011: 218–219.

44 Heinl Jr. and Heinl 1978: 17; Knight 1990: 48–54; Pons 2007: 93.

45 Scott 2018: chapter 1.

46 Geggus 2001a: 126.

47 Fick 1990: 26.
48 Hall 1972; Garrigus 2006.
49 McClellan 1992: 61–62.
50 Moreau de Saint-Méry 1797 (Vol. 1): 71–74; Garraway 2005a.
51 Garrigus 1993; Socolow 1996.
52 Rogers and King 2012.
53 Dubois 2004: chapter 3; Garrigus 2006: chapter 8; Garrigus 2010.
54 Girard and Donnadieu 2013: 50.
55 Geggus 2013: 103.
56 Weaver 2012.
57 Geggus 1999: 33–36.
58 Geggus 2013: 103–107, 115.
59 Reproduced from Rainsford [1805] 2013, Appendix xviii: 270.
60 Geggus 1991b.
61 McClellan 1992: 64.
62 Geggus 1996: 260; Moitt 2001: chapter 2; Walton 2012: 18.
63 Moitt 1995: 157; Moitt 2001: chapter 3.
64 Garrigus 1993.
65 Geggus 1998.
66 Geggus 1998: 204.
67 Bayle 2008: 1–16.
68 Laborie 1798: 162–163.
69 Monnereau 1769: 65.
70 Trouillot 1982: 344.
71 "Extrait du Tableau des Population et Culture de St. Domingue en 1784"
   27AP/12 Francois Neufchateau Papers Dossiers 2–3, AN; Trouillot 1982:
   344–347; Geggus 1993: 78; Manuel 2005.
72 Mintz 1985.
73 Dupuy 1989: 21; Munford and Zeuske 1988: 13.
74 Geggus 1993: 74.
75 Galliffet inventory 107AP/127, dossier 6, AN.
76 Dupuy 1989.
77 Stein 1988: 43, 60; Fick 1990: 28–29.
78 Geggus 1993: 80, 84–86; Geggus 1999: 39.
79 Guillet 2009: 178.
80 Dubois 2004: 39.
81 Fick 1990: 26.
82 Monnereau 1769: 96
83 Mémoire de Assemblée Nationale 18 Juin 1790: 70, No. 4 *Nouvelles de Saint
   Domingue: Extrait du no. 66 des Affiches américaines du 19 août 1790*, John
   Carter Brown Library.
84 *LAA* November 8, 1787.
85 Munford and Zeuske 1988: 17; Fick 1990: 26.
86 Moitt 2001: chapter 5; Walton 2012: 65.
87 McClellan 1992: 29–30; Weaver 2002: 452.
88 de Vastey [1814] 2014: 109–111.
89 Garraway 2005b: 244.

90 "Interrogation d'un négres de l'habitation de la Dame de l'Isle Adam du janvier 1775" ANOM F3 90: 160; Ghachem 2012: 141–143.
91 Brown 2007: 25.
92 Métraux 1959; Fleurant 1996: 102–104; Bay 1998: 48.
93 Montilus [1982] 1993.
94 Geggus 2014: 17.
95 Vaissière 1909: 201–202; Desmangles 1992: 25.
96 Moreau de Saint-Méry 1797 (Vol. 1): 41–42.
97 Malenfant 1814: 212–213; Fouchard 1988: 15–19; Diouf 1998: chapter 4; Gomez 2005: 81–90.
98 Moreau de Saint-Méry 1797 (Vol. 1): 60-64; Fick 1990: 44; Dubois 2004: 42
99 Monnereau 1769: 56–58.
100 Moreau de Saint-Méry [1796] 1975: 64–65; Descourtilz 1809 (Vol. 3): 197.
101 Quoted from Pluchon 1987: 77–78; Debien 2000: 27, 223.
102 Brown 2008: 63–71.
103 Oldendorp [1770] 1987: 183.
104 McClellan 1992: 88.
105 Moreau de Saint-Méry 1797 (Vol 1): 557–558; Dubois 2004: 12; Munro 2010: 28.
106 Quoted from Geggus 2013: 118.
107 Moreau de Saint-Méry 1797 (Vol. 1): 60–64.
108 Walker 1996; Childs 2006; Borucki 2015; Dewulf 2015.
109 Oldendorp [1770] 1987: 187–202.
110 Cauna 1996: 335; Fick 2000: 40–45; Vanhee 2002: 246–250, 254; Dubois 2004: 49.
111 Fick 1990: 40–45; Ramsey 2011: 35–36.
112 Sosis 1971: chapter 10; conversation with John Thornton.
113 Rigaud 1953: 141–156; Hebblethwaite 2014: 6.
114 Herskovits [1937] 2007: 25; Métraux 1959: 27; Pluchon 1987: 55; Desmangles 1992.
115 Sweet 2011: 25.
116 Moreau de Saint-Méry 1797 (Vol. 1): 46–51; Geggus 2014: 20–22.
117 Pluchon 1987: 107; Vanhee 2002: 247.
118 Alpers 1970: 105.
119 Voyages 2009.
120 Stuckey 1988: 16.
121 Descourtilz 1809 (Vol. 3): 196; Fick 1990: 41.
122 Moreau de Saint-Méry 1797 (Vol. 1): 38; Fick 1990: 41.
123 Thornton 1992: 246.
124 Moreau de Saint-Méry 1797 (Vol. 1): 30–31; Gomez 1998: 128–130.
125 Ware 2014: 103.
126 "Vocabulary Creole" Du Simitière Collection Folder 9–10b, Library Company of Philadelphia; Malenfant 1814: 212–213; Diouf 1998: chapter 4; Gomez 2005: 81–90.
127 Ware 2014.
128 Fouchard 1988: 142; Diouf 1998: 165.

129 Translation from email correspondence between Bruce Hall and Laurent Dubois, Du Simitière Collection, Library Company of Philadelphia.
130 *LAA* August 14, 1768.
131 Gomez 1998: chapter 2; Hall 2005: 54.
132 Thornton 2003: 289.
133 "Vocabulary Creole" Du Simitière Collection Folder 9–10b, Library Company of Philadelphia; Sweet 2006: 65.
134 Labat [1722] 1724 (Vol. 2): 52–53; Thompson 1983: 108–109; MacGaffey 1986: 43–46; Fennel 2003: 6.
135 Moreau de Saint-Méry 1797 (Vol. 1): 44; Sweet 2006: 64–65, 73.
136 Thornton 2002: 79–80.
137 Sweet 2006: 70–71.
138 Labat [1722] 1724 (Vol. 2): 53.
139 Thornton 1988a.
140 Moreau de Saint-Méry 1784 (Vol. 4): 352; Peabody 2002: 82; Geggus 2013: 118.
141 Peabody 2002: 79.
142 Thornton 1988a; Kananoja 2010: 448; Thornton 2016.
143 Sosis 1971: 285–286.

3 "God Knows What I Do"

1 Labat [1722] 1724 (Vol. 2): 53.
2 Alpern 1998a, 1998b; Bay 1997, 1998.
3 Thornton 1998a, 1998b; Heywood 2017.
4 1530, April 10. Santo Domingo, La Española. PARES, Portal de Archivos Españoles, Archivo General de Indias, SANTO_DOMINGO, 49, R.1, N.2.
5 Moreau de Saint-Méry 1784 (Vol. 3): 48–49; Hall 1968: 46; Pluchon 1987: 152–153.
6 For other interpretations of the Mackandal case, see Fouchard 1972; Pluchon 1987; Fick 1990; Diouf 1998; Vanhee 2002; Gomez 2005; Ramsey 2011; Khan 2012; Paton 2012; Mobley 2015; and Burnard and Garrigus 2016.
7 Bourgeois 1788: 470.
8 Jouin [1758] 1761; *Extrait du Mercure de France: Makandal, Histoire véritable* 1787; Moreau de Saint-Méry 1798 (Vol. 1): 651–653; Fouchard 1972: 317–320; Fick 1990: 62; Diouf 1998: 150–152; Gomez 2005: 81–89; Ramsey 2011: 33–35.
9 Diouf 1998: 128–130.
10 These ingredients also match descriptions of *nkisis*, as well as *mandinga* pouches found during eighteenth-century Kongolese inquisitions (Kananoja 2010: 453; Daniels 2013); but the word *mandinga* might easily be linked to the Mandinga ethnic group of Africans from the Upper Guinea region. This apparent conflation of terminology – *macandal, gris-gris, mandingas* – might indicate a circulation of these ritual technologies throughout the French Atlantic, either in the material sense or in the popular imagination of

enslavers, planters, overseers, or others who came into contact with Africans and their sacred artifacts but did not know how to correctly identify them or interpret their utility.

11 Courtin 1758, "Memoire Sommaire sur les pretendues pratiques magiques est empoisonnements…" ANOM F3 88: 240; Pluchon 1987: 165–182, 201, 210–211; Gomez 2005: 89; Ramsey 2011: 34; Mobley 2015: 311–313; Burnard and Garrigus 2016: 109.

12 Courtin 1758, "Memoire Sommaire sur les pretendues pratiques magiques est empoisonnements…" ANOM F3 88: 240; Pluchon 1987: 175; Mobley 2015: 218–219.

13 Moreau de Saint-Méry 1784 (Vol. 4): 229–230; Fick 1990: 73.

14 Recently, scholars (Vanhee 2002; Mobley 2015; Burnard and Garrigus 2016) have followed David Geggus' (1991b: 32–33) argument that François Mackandal was a West Central African, given the dominance of that group in Saint-Domingue after 1750 and that the Kongo meaning for amulet is *makunda* or *makwanda*, for which the term *macandal* might be a "corruption." However, others, including African Diaspora historians especially (Fick 1990: 59–61; Diouf 1998: 150–152; Gomez 2005: 85–89; Khan 2012), have maintained closer interpretation of the archive's relatively clear descriptions of Mackandal's origins.

15 Thornton 1992: chapter 9.

16 Geggus 1999.

17 Fouchard 1972: 317–320; Fick 1990: 62–72; Ramsey 2011: 33–35; Burnard and Garrigus 2016: 101–122.

18 *Extrait du Mercure de France: Makandal, Histoire véritable* 1787; Fick 1990: 64, 251–252, 258–259; Dubois and Garrigus [2006] 2017: 42; Burnard and Garrigus 2016: 118.

19 The word *ouaïe* was described as a secret code word, but the origins and meaning of *Mayangangué* have not yet been identified. Courtin 1758, "Memoire Sommaire sur les pretendues pratiques magiques est empoisonnements…" ANOM F3 88: 240; Pluchon 1987: 212–213.

20 Métraux 1959: 114; Pluchon 1987: 221.

21 Gomez 1998: 94–98.

22 Gomez 1998: 49, 94, 111–112, 130; Thornton 2002: 74.

23 Moreau de Saint-Méry 1784 (Vol. 4): 225–228.

24 Moreau de Saint-Méry 1784 (Vol. 4): 222.

25 d'Auberteuil 1776: 137–138; Ramsey 2011: 38.

26 Burnard and Garrigus 2016: 120.

27 *LAA* April 2, 1766.

28 Moitt 2001: 106; Burnard and Garrigus 2016: 121.

29 Debien 1980: 59–60.

30 d'Auberteuil 1776: 138.

31 Cauna 1996: 329.

32 Moreau de Saint-Méry 1784 (Vol. 5): 805; Fick 1990: 73.

33 Moreau de Saint-Méry 1784 (Vol. 6): 75–78; Fick 1990: 73; Desmangles 1992: 26; Munro 2010: 27.

34 "Procédure relative à l'affaire d'Antoine dit Kengal et de sa mère Lisette contre Avalle, régisseur des biens du marquis de Paroy à Saint-Domingue (1776/ 1780)" ANOM Archives privées, Le Gentil de Paroy; Arrêt qui casse et annule celui du Conseil Supérieur du Cap du 5 février 1779, obtenu par la négresse Lizette, contre Guy Le Gentil, marquis de Paroy, et qui évoque au Conseil du Roi les contestations sur lesquelles l'arrêt est intervenu; l'arrêt stipule que le marquis de Paroy remboursera à la négresse Lizette les 3 000 livres qu'il a reçues d'elle pour l'affranchissement du nègre Antoine, son fils, et autorise le marquis de Paroy à faire arrêter ledit Antoine, soupçonné d'empoisonnement (27 novembre 1779), ANOM A17: 214.

35 Moreau de Saint-Méry 1784 (Vol. 6): 257–258; Fick 1990: 73.

36 Moitt 2001: 143.

37 Moreau de Saint-Méry 1784 (Vol. 6): 429; Fick 1990: 73.

38 *LAA* May 8, 1781.

39 Moreau de Saint-Méry 1784 (Vol. 6): 370; Fick 1990: 295 n. 132.

40 Fick 1990: 37; Vanhee 2002: 250; for in-depth discussion of this case, see Ghachem 2011.

41 Janzen 1982: 55.

42 Moreau de Saint-Méry 1797 (Vol. 1): 51; Sosis 1971: 275; Geggus 2014: 22.

43 Descourtilz 1809 (Vol. 3): 181; Mobley 2015: 325–326.

44 Janzen 1982: 13–14.

45 Ferrand de Beaudiere, Joseph Alexandre, juge de la juridiction et de l'amirauté du Petit-Goave, à Saint-Domingue 1765/1785, ANOM Series E: 112; Sosis 1971: 273; Pluchon 1987: 111; Geggus 2014: 24–25.

46 Janzen 1982: 5–6.

47 Thornton 2003: 293.

48 Thornton 1993a: 735.

49 Fick 1990: 114, 141; Sweet 2017: 93.

50 Thornton 1991: 60–61; Thornton 1993b: 183; Thornton 1998; Heywood 2009: 19.

51 Raimondo da Dicomano, *O Reino do Congo: A decadência final do Reino do Congo*; Raphael de Castello de Vide, *Viagem do Congo do Missionário*; Thornton 1991: 60–61.

52 MacGaffey 2002; Mobley 2015: 42.

53 Baudry 1803 (Vol. 2): 83; Janzen 1982: 33; Martin 1986; Sweet 2017: 95.

54 Garrigus 2006: 202–203; Vanhee 2002: 248.

55 Vanhee 2002: 248–253; Mobley 2015: 311–312.

56 Malenfant 1814: 212; Diouf 1998: 131; Gomez 2005: 87.

57 Dubois 2004: 42.

58 Thornton 1991: 61–62.

59 Sweet 2006.

60 Desch-Obi 2010: 246–250.

61 Desch-Obi 2008: 147.

62 Desch-Obi 2008: 21–22, 36–41.

63 Desch-Obi 2008: 138.

64 Hebblethwaite 2012: 49.

65 Debien 1972; Geggus 1991b: 32–34; Vanhee 2002: 252; Weaver 2006: 103–111; Desch-Obi 2008: 143–151; Ramsey 2011: 38–39.

66 Moreau de Saint-Méry 1797 (Vol. 1): 53–54; Ogle 2013: 243–244.

67 Thornton 1991; Desch-Obi 2008: 145–151.

68 Desmangles 1992: 26; Munro 2010: 27; Ramsey 2011: 34.

69 Moreau de Saint-Méry 1784 (Vol. 4): 234; Ramsey 2011: 36.

70 *Almanach historique et chronologique de Saint-Domingue, pour l'année bissextile 1788*, John Carter Brown Library; Rey 2005.

71 Desch-Obi 2002: 359; Thornton 2002: 85; Desch-Obi 2008: 22.

72 Geggus 2013: 119–120.

73 Geggus 2013: 119–120.

74 Moreau de Saint-Méry 1784 (Vol. 4): 829; Munro 2010: 27.

75 *LAA* April 30, 1766.

76 *LAA* September 16, 1767.

77 *LAA* June 20, 1768. Another possibility is that Jolicouer was a drummer for the military (King 2001: 55).

78 *LAA* November 14, 1772.

79 Moreau de Saint-Méry 1784 (Vol 6): 252; Fick 1990: 295 n. 139.

80 *LAA* December 15, 1784.

81 "Ordonnance du Roi, qui attribué aux Commandants & Officiers des Etats-Majors, danses des Gens de couleur & celle des Spectacles. Du 11 Mars 1785" ANOM C9B 36; Moreau de Saint-Méry 1784 (Vol. 5): 384; Moreau de Saint-Méry 1784 (Vol. 6): 727; Desch-Obi 2008: 273; Ramsey 2011: 38.

82 *LAA* December 16, 1789.

83 *LAA* June 12, 1790.

84 "Arrêt de la Cour, Qui défend aux Gens de couleur l'Exercice du Magnétisme, & renouvelle les défenses des Attroupements illicites, du 16 Mai 1786," 27AP/12 François Neufchâteau Papers Dossiers 2–3, AN.

85 Debien 1972; Desch-Obi 2008: 147.

86 "Arrêt de la Cour, Qui condamne à être pendus les Moteurs des Attroupements nocturnes & Assemblées prétendues Magnétiques d'Esclaves, du quartier de la Marmelade. Du 23 Novembre 1786." 27AP/12 François Neufchâteau Papers Dossiers 2–3, AN; Debien 1972; Fick 1990: 74; Weaver 2006: 103–111; Ramsey 2011: 40.

87 Voyages 2009.

88 Moitt 2001: 39–40, 59; Geggus 1996: 261; Walton 2012: 21

89 Moitt 2001: 63–68.

90 27AP/12, François Neufchateau Papers Dossiers 2-3, AN; Pluchon 1987: 223–23; Weaver 2006: chapter 7.

91 Sommerdyk 2012: 142; Mobley 2015: 75.

92 Weaver 2006: 115

93 Thornton 2002; Sommerdyk 2012: 142; Mobley 2015: 159–160, 231.

94 *LAA* December 31, 1774.

95 27AP/12, François Neufchâteau Papers Dossiers 2-3, AN: Letter 2.

96 27AP/12, François Neufchâteau Papers Dossiers 2-3, AN: Letter 4.

97 27AP/12, François Neufchâteau Papers Dossiers 2-3, AN: Letter 1; Pluchon 1987: 223–223; Weaver 2006: ch. 7.

98 27AP/12, François Neufchâteau Papers Dossiers 2-3, AN; Pluchon 1987: 223–23.
99 27AP/12, François Neufchâteau Papers Dossiers 2-3, AN: Letter 4.
100 Janzen 1982: 56.
101 Thornton 1993b: 194.
102 Weaver 2004.
103 Morrissey 1989: 115–116.
104 Moitt 2001: 63.
105 Weaver 2004: 98.
106 *LAA* March 1, 1786.
107 *LAA* October 20, 1778.
108 *LAA* April 28, 1784.
109 *LAA* June 19, 1788; Peabody 2002: 77; Gomez 2005: 89; Ramsey 2011: 58–59; Mobley 2015: 308.

4 Mobilizing Marronnage

1 *Les Affiches américaines*, December 15, 1790.
2 McClellan 1992: 97–98.
3 Moitt 1995: chapters 1–2; Geggus 1996: 260; Moitt 2001; Walton 2012: 17–18.
4 Broadhead 1983; Ferreira 2014: 72.
5 Moitt 1995; Moitt 2001: chapter 3.
6 Habitation du Quartier Morin, État du Mobilier des Nègres, Nègrillons, Nègresses et Nègrittes avec leurs Noms, Age, Nations, au 31 Décembre 1786, ANOM C9B 7.
7 Moreau de Saint-Méry 1797 (Vol. 1): 40–41; Geggus 1993: 93; Walton 2012: 57.
8 *LAA* April 8, 1786.
9 Only the most numerous ethnic groups are listed in Table 4.6.
10 Hall 2005: chapter 2.
11 Hall 2005: 47.
12 Thornton 1991: 60; Hall 2005: 65; Mobley 2015.
13 Mobley 2015: 168.
14 Hall 2005: 123.
15 Hall 2005: 107.
16 Alpers 1970: 105.
17 *LAA* August 1, 1768.
18 Geggus 1989b: 35.
19 Eddins 2019.
20 *LAA* October 16, 1769; *LAA* January 31, 1776; *LAA* December 2, 1786; *LAA* October 11, 1787; *LAA* August 30, 1788.
21 *LAA* September 22, 1787.
22 *LAA* September 23, 1775.
23 *LAA* February 15, 1786.
24 *LAA* October 28, 1789.
25 *LAA* July 24, 1773.

26 *LAA* December 13, 1783.

27 *LAA* August 27, 1766.

28 *LAA* October 25, 1769.

29 *LAA* December 28, 1785.

30 *LAA* September 5, 1789.

31 *The Intra-American Slave Trade Database*, Voyages 2009.

32 *LAA* December 11, 1788; *LAA* July 12, 1769.

33 *LAA* July 18, 1788; *LAA* October 24, 1780.

34 Garraway 2005b: chapter 1.

35 Guitar 2002.

36 Moreau de Saint-Méry 1797 (Vol. 1): 74–75, 80–81.

37 *LAA* August 16, 1783.

38 Harris 2003.

39 *LAA* October 17, 1789.

40 *LAA* July 11, 1770.

41 Moitt 2001: 134.

42 *LAA* September 12, 1780.

43 *LAA* November 1, 1788.

44 Geggus 1996.

45 *LAA* October 7, 1767.

46 *LAA* April 7, 1770; *LAA* September 12, 1770; *LAA* May 16, 1772.

47 *LAA* March 18, 1775.

48 *LAA* November 9, 1779.

49 *LAA* July 19, 1788.

50 *LAA* February 10, 1787.

51 *LAA* November 10, 1773.

52 *LAA* March 19, 1774.

53 *LAA* July 17, 1781.

54 *LAA* June 4, 1766.

55 *LAA* October 1, 1783; *LAA* October 15, 1783.

56 Labat [1722] 1724: 58; Munford 1991 (Vol. 3): 955.

57 *LAA* December 15, 1784.

58 *LAA* June 4, 1766.

59 *LAA* July 2, 1783.

60 Sweet 2017: 89–91.

61 *LAA* January 30, 1773; *LAA* March 28, 1780; Sweet 2017: 89–92.

62 *LAA* August 15, 1789.

63 La Grange, chargé du recouvrement des nègres marrons dans la partie espagnole de Saint-Domingue, par MM. de Sorel et de Montholan, 1730, ANOM E: 248.

64 *LAA* June 16, 1787.

65 *LAA* February 26, 1766.

66 *LAA* February 7, 1789.

67 Moreau de Saint-Méry 1784 (Vol. 4): 228; Moreau de Saint-Méry 1784 (Vol. 5): 165.

68 "Arrêt de la Cour, qui condamne plusieurs Nègres, voleurs, et receleurs, 1 Juin 1786," 27AP/12, AN; Fouchard 1972: 272.

69 *LAA* October 11, 1788; *LAA* November 20, 1771.

70 *LAA* May 9, 1772.

71 *LAA* June 26, 1769.
72 Madiou 1847: 105; Thornton 1991; Thornton 1993b.

5 Marronnage as Reclamation

1   1685. *Le Code Noir*, John Carter Brown Library; Moreau de Saint-Méry 1784 (Vol. 4): 225–228; Burnard and Garrigus 2016.
2   Anne-Louis de Tousard Papers, 1659–1932: Box 1 and 2, University of Michigan William L. Clements Library; Geggus 2014: 29–33.
3   Arrêt qui reçoit Morisseau d'Ester, habitant de Saint-Domingue, comme appelant d'une ordonnance rendue le 24 mai 1774 par les administrateurs de cette colonie, à propos de la désertion de plusieurs esclaves de l'habitation de feu Philippe Morisseau, son frère, 22 décembre 1775, ANOM A15: 147; Arrêt qui casse et annule celui du conseil supérieur du Cap du 25 novembre 1777, obtenu par Fleury, habitant du Dondon, contre Soubira, habitant de Dondon puis du Cap, ainsi que la sentence du juge du 23 mai 1776. L'arrêt déclare, en conséquence, nul l'affranchissement de la négresse Zabeth, créole, et de sa fille, Adélaïde, mulâtresse, et en ordonne la remise à Soubira, leur maître, 4 janvier 1779, ANOM A17: 16; Ghachem 2012: 105–111.
4   "Lettre des … au minister sur le nègres marons, Au Port au Prince 10.9.1767" ANOM F3 94: 88; Ghachem 2012: 11.
5   *LAA* November 30, 1771.
6   Moreau de Saint-Méry 1784 (Vol. 5): 385, 702.
7   *LAA* November 23, 1771.
8   *LAA* December 30, 1790.
9   *LAA* January 28, 1767; *LAA* December 5, 1768.
10 *LAA* August 15, 1789.
11 *LAA* November 13, 1790.
12 *LAA* February 13, 1781; *LAA* June 14, 1783.
13 *LAA* October 25, 1788.
14 *LAA* December 13, 1783.
15 Geggus 2013: 103–107, 115.
16 King 2004; Girard 2016: 97.
17 "Arrêt de la Cour, qui condamne plusieurs Nègres, voleurs, et receleurs, 1 Juin 1786," 27AP/12, François Neufchâteau Papers Dossiers 2-3, AN; Fouchard 1972: 272; Geggus 2013: 115.
18 "Arrêt de la Cour, qui condamne plusieurs Nègres, voleurs, et receleurs, 1 Juin 1786," 27AP/12, François Neufchâteau Papers Dossiers 2-3, AN; Fouchard 1972: 272; Geggus 2013: 115.
19 "Arrêt du Conseil Supérieur du Cap, Du 12 Janvier 1775, Extrait des Registres du Conseil Supérieur du Cap" ANOM C9A.
20 Moreau de Saint-Méry 1784 (Vol 6): 640.
21 Munford and Zeuske 1988: 19.
22 "Arret de la Cour, qui condamne le Nègre CEZAR à être Pendu, pour crime de Plaigaire ou Vol d'Esclaves" ANOM C9B 36; Geggus 2013: 115.
23 *LAA* July 30, 1766.
24 *LAA* April 7, 1787.
25 *LAA* December 19, 1770.

26 *LAA* July 10, 1782.

27 *LAA* February 6, 1771.

28 *LAA* August 3, 1776.

29 *LAA* April 29, 1786; *LAA* May 6, 1786; *LAA* November 20, 1788; *LAA* November 27, 1788; *LAA* December 4, 1788; *LAA* December 26, 1789; *LAA* January 2, 1790; *LAA* January 7, 1790; Geggus 2014: 33.

30 Burnard and Garrigus 2016: 167.

31 Brevet de grâce en faveur de Marot, habitant de Saint-Domingue et économe de l'habitation de Doyte, condamné pour le meurtre commis, le 31 août 1775, sur Sabournin, qui avait recueilli Francisque, nègre marron de l'habitation, 4 janvier 1779, ANOM A17: 26.

32 Moreau de Saint-Méry 1784 (Vol. 5): 741, 744; de Vastey [1814] 2014: 109–110.

33 Moreau de Saint-Méry 1784 (Vol. 5): 906.

34 Manigat 1977: 432; Manigat 2007: 54.

35 Moreau de Saint-Méry 1784 (Vol 6): 474.

36 "Arrêt de la Cour, qui condamne le nomme LAFORTUNE, Nègre esclave, assassin de son Maitre" 27AP/12, François Neufchâteau Papers Dossiers 2-3, AN; Munford and Zeuske 1988: 19.

37 *LAA* July 24, 1790.

38 *LAA* June 17, 1790.

39 *LAA* July 22, 1767.

40 *LAA* July 29, 1767.

41 *LAA* January 22, 1775.

42 *LAA* March 6, 1773.

43 *LAA* September 26, 1789.

44 Debien [1973] 1996: 111.

45 "Inventaire des effets trouves dans les habitations de M. de Galliffet a la sortie de M. Masson en 1775"; "Recensement des nègres, nègresses, nègrillons et nègrittes existants au premier janvier 1783 sur les cinq habitations de Mr. le Marquis de Galliffet"; "Etat du mobilier existant au premier Janvier 1786 sur les ..."; and "Etat par métier des nègres des cinq habitations de Monsieur le Marquis de Galliffet au premier de Janvier 1791," 107AP/127 dossier 2, AN.

46 *LAA* December 3, 1774.

47 *LAA* July 5, 1775.

48 Debien [1973] 1996: 120–122.

49 *LAA* January 18, 1783; *LAA* January 25, 1783; *LAA* February 22, 1783.

50 *LAA* July 15, 1789; *LAA* July 22, 1789; *LAA* July 29, 1789.

6 Geographies of Subversion: Maroons, Borders, and Empire

1 Moreau de Saint-Méry 1797 (Vol. 2): 62; McClellan 1992: 142.

2 Lindskog 1998: 74–75.

3 Lindskog 1998: 75–77.

4 "Déclaration du Roi pour la police des Noirs. Donnée à Versailles le neuf août 1777. Registrée en Parlement le 27 août 1777," John Carter Brown Library.

5 McClellan 1992: 64.

6 Geggus 1999: 35.

7 Fouchard and Debien 1969: 31; Scott [1986] 2018: 21.

8 Sweeney 2019: 205.

9 *LAA* April 22, 1770.

10 *LAA* May 21, 1766.

11 *LAA* October 31, 1768.

12 *LAA* December 17, 1783.

13 Heinl Jr., Debs, and Heinl 1978: 11; Wilson 1990: 59; Bellegarde-Smith 2004: 14.

14 McClellan 1992: 25.

15 Moreau de Saint-Méry 1797 (Vol. 1): 200; Fouchard 1972: 316; Beauvoir-Dominique 2009: 84.

16 Beauvoir-Dominique 2009: 80–81.

17 Moreau de Saint-Méry 1797 (Vol. 1): 118.

18 Geggus 1991a: 99, 101.

19 Moreau de Saint-Méry 1797 (Vol. 1): 124.

20 Burnard and Garrigus 2016: 113–119.

21 *LAA* November 25, 1766.

22 *LAA* June 22, 1776.

23 Moreau de Saint-Méry 1797 (Vol. 1): 154.

24 Moreau de Saint-Méry 1797 (Vol. 1): 200.

25 Fouchard 1972: 312–313; Debien [1973] 1996: 110; Manigat 1977: 432–433; Cauna 1996: 327–328; Debien 2000: 419.

26 Labat [1722] 1724 (Vol. 2): 266.

27 *LAA* August 15, 1770.

28 *LAA* February 8, 1772.

29 *LAA* September 1, 1773.

30 *LAA* May 17, 1769.

31 *LAA* May 19, 1773.

32 *LAA* March 21, 1780.

33 Foubert 1988: 297.

34 *LAA* May 31, 1783.

35 *LAA* December 25, 1788.

36 Beauvoir-Dominque 2009: 80.

37 "Mémoire sur les nègres marrons a S. Domingue et les moyenne d'un diminuer le nombre le danger, 1775," and "Mémoire sou les moyenne à employer pas le S. Amant, lorsqu'il sera chargé de poursuivre et faire arrêtes les nègres marron de S. Domingue," ANOM F3 94: 116–118.

38 Miller 1989: 15–17; Heywood 2017: 8–10.

39 Miller 1989: chapter 1; Heywood 2017: 8–9.

40 Gomez 1998: 117–120.

41 Dawson 2018: 27; Soumonni 2003: 26–30.

42 McClellan 1992: 78.

43 McClellan 1992: 26.

44 *LAA* August 15, 1789.

45 *Gazette de Saint Domingue* June 22, 1791: 635.

46 *LAA* February 10, 1768.
47 *LAA* April 10, 1781.
48 *LAA* February 1, 1783.
49 *LAA* April 24, 1781.
50 Munford 1991 (Vol. 3): 902–903; Ghachem 2012: 55–60.
51 Thornton 1992: 278.
52 Berquist 2010: 184–186; Phillips 2011: 342–246; Hontanilla 2015.
53 Ponce-Vázquez 2016.
54 Landers 2002: 235–236; Landers 2015.
55 Ghachem 2012: 33.
56 Moreau de Saint-Méry 1797 (Vol. 1): 694; Fouchard 1972: 307–308; Manigat 1977: 432–433; Munford 1991 (Vol. 3): 900–902; Cauna 1996: 327–328.
57 Pritchard 2004: chapter 7.
58 Moreau de Saint-Méry 1798 (Part 1): vi, 161.
59 "de l'introduction des nègres à Saint Domingue de leurs révoltes, de leur traitement, etc. 1501/1718" ANOM F3 94: 1–8; Fouchard 1972: 307; Manigat 1977: 432–433; Fouchard 1988: 34; Cauna 1996: 327–328.
60 Moreau de Saint-Méry 1784 (Vol. 1): 500–502; de Vaissière 1909: 232; Munford 1991 (Vol. 3): 903.
61 Fouchard 1972: 309; Heinl Jr., Debs and Heinl 1978: 27; Munford 1991 (Vol. 2): 904.
62 Heinl Jr., Debs and Heinl 1978: 27.
63 Munford 1991 (Vol. 3): 944–945.
64 Moreau de Saint-Méry 1784 (Vol. 2): 158, 228, 234; Moreau de Saint-Méry 1798 (Part 2): 170–171; Munford 1991 (Vol. 3): 939.
65 Moreau de Saint-Méry 1784 (Vol. 2): 253.
66 Moreau de Saint-Méry 1784 (Vol. 2): 726; Moreau de Saint-Méry 1784 (Vol. 3): 344; King 2004.
67 "Lettre de Dubois au sujet des marrons a Saint Domingue, 18 mars 1715" ANOM F3 94: 29.
68 Moreau de Saint-Méry 1798 (Part 2): 172–173.
69 Moreau de Saint-Méry 1797 (Vol. 2): 497.
70 "de l'introduction des nègres à Saint Domingue de leurs révoltes, de leur traitement, etc. 1501-1718" ANOM F3 94: 1.
71 Moreau de Saint-Méry 1797 (Vol. 2): 497; Sosis 1971: 169; Fouchard 1988: 34; Matibag 2003: 47.
72 Moreau de Saint-Méry 1798 (Part 1): 161.
73 Moreau de Saint-Méry 1798 (Part 2): 173; Hall 1971: 65.
74 Moreau de Saint-Méry 1798: xiii.
75 La Grange, chargé du recouvrement des nègres marrons dans la partie espagnole de Saint-Domingue, par MM. de Sorel et de Montholan, 1730, ANOM E: 248.
76 Moreau de Saint-Méry 1798 (Part 1): xxvi–lii; Ghachem 2012: 35.
77 Moreau de Saint-Méry 1798: xviii.
78 Geggus 1991a.

79 Moreau de Saint-Méry 1798 (Part 2): 174.

80 Fouchard 1972: 316; Fouchard 1988: 34; Matibag 2003: 54.

81 McClellan 1992: 27.

82 Nessler 2016: 12–13.

83 Moreau de Saint-Méry 1798: xix.

84 Moreau de Saint-Méry 1798 (Part 2): 175.

85 Moreau de Saint-Méry 1798 (Part 1): 78–79; Matibag 2003: 56.

86 "Nègre maron et Espagnol" ANOM F3 132: 257.

87 Moreau de Saint-Méry 1784 (Vol 4): 812–815; Fouchard 1972: 218.

88 "Traité fait entre Manuel de Aslor, gouverneur de la partie espagnole de Saint-Domingue, et le prince de Rohan, gouverneur général de la partie française de l'île, pour la restitution des nègres marrons ou volés, ainsi que des soldats déserteurs et pour la répression des marchands qui font passer des bêtes à cornes sans droits de sortie, 11 décembre 1766" ANOM A27: 129.

89 Moreau de Saint-Méry 1798 (Part 2): 176.

90 Moreau de Saint-Méry 1798 (Part 1): xx–xxii.

91 *LAA* October 17, 1789.

92 "Lettre des … un proposition al … detruire les nègres marons 14 fev 1775," ANOM F3 94: 112.

93 Landers 2002: 238; Landers 2015.

94 Girard 2016: 274 n. 16.

95 Moreau de Saint-Méry 1784 (Vol. 5): 658–659, 687–688.

96 Moreau de Saint-Méry 1784 (Vol. 5): 848; Moreau de Saint-Méry 1797 (Vol. 2): 498–499; Fouchard 1972: 330–331.

97 "Extrait des Registres du Conseil Supérieur du Cap, Traite définitif de Police entre les Cours de France & d'Espagne sur divers points concernant leurs Sujets respectifs à Saint Domingue." Cap Français: de l'Imprimerie Royale du Cap, 1777, John Carter Brown Library; Moreau de Saint-Méry 1784 (Vol. 5): 774; Moreau de Saint-Méry 1798 (Part 2): 176–177.

98 Moreau de Saint-Méry 1784 (Vol. 5): 666, 810.

99 Moreau de Saint-Méry 1797 (Vol. 2): 497–503.

100 Fick 1990: 297 n. 20.

101 Munford and Zeuske 1988: 18.

102 Berquist 2010: 184–186; Hontanilla 2015.

103 Hall 1971: 102–110.

104 Eddins 2020.

7 "We Must Stop the Progress of Marronage": Repertoires and Repression

1 Voyages 2009.

2 Hall 1968: 44; Fick 1990: 52.

3 "Lettre du ministre au Sieur de Brach au sujet des nègres marrons, 2 juin 1700" ANOM F3 94: 18; Saint-Méry 1797 (Vol. 1): 382; Fick 1990: 52; Munford 1991 (Vol. 3): 923, 945.

4 Moreau de Saint-Méry 1784 (Vol. 2): 585.

5 Labat [1722] 1724 (Vol. 2): 266; Debien [1973] 1996: 115.

6 Moreau de Saint-Méry 1784 (Vol. 2): 753; Hall 1971: 65.

7 Moreau de Saint-Méry 1784 (Vol. 2): 781–782.

8 Moreau de Saint-Méry 1784 (Vol. 3): 111.

9 Moreau de Saint-Méry 1784 (Vol. 3): 48–49; Moreau de Saint-Méry 1797 (Vol. 1): 200.

10 Sosis 1971: 170.

11 Moreau de Saint-Méry 1784 (Vol. 3): 48–49; Hall 1968: 46; Pluchon 1987: 152–153.

12 "Nomination, par Sorel et Montholon, de Duclos comme lieutenant de Colin, prévôt général au quartier du Petite-Goave, afin de lutter contre le marronnage, 31 juillet 1722" ANOM A28: 105.

13 "Lettre de la Rochalar au sujet des nègres marrons, 7 juin 1726" ANOM F3 94: 56.

14 Debien 2000: 419.

15 Laguerre 1989: 43; Munford 1991 (Vol. 3): 944.

16 Sosis 1971: 171; Fouchard 1972: 312–313; Debien [1973] 1996: 110; Manigat 1977: 432–433; Cauna 1996: 327–328; Debien 2000: 419; Garrigus 2006: 96.

17 "Ordonnance du Marquis de Fayet et de Jean Baptiste Duclos qui institue un lieutenant de prévôt de la maréchaussée pour le seul quartier de Nippes, très étendu, où se réfugient de nombreux nègres marrons, 25 octobre 1733" ANOM A28: 156; Moreau de Saint-Méry 1784 (Vol. 3): 344, 379; Debien [1973] 1996: 115.

18 "Arrêt annulant l'arrêt du conseil supérieur du Petite-Goave du 6 mai 1726 qui promettait une somme de 300 livres par tête d'esclave fugitive ramené ou la liberté aux noirs qui auraient participé aux poursuites, 30 septembre 1726," COL A28: 131v; "Arrêt qui annule celui du conseil supérieur du Petit-Goave du 6 mai 1726, en ce qu'il met à prix les têtes du plusieurs nègres fugitifs et contumaces, et qu'il accorde la liberté aux esclaves qui amèneraient morts ou vifs, 30 septembre 1726," ANOM A27: 34.

19 Moreau de Saint-Méry 1784 (Vol. 3): 399.

20 "Laurent, nègre qui a contribué à la capture du fameux Polidar, nègre marron de Saint-Domingue, son affranchissement, 1734" ANOM E: Lettre L-261; Moreau de Saint-Méry 1797 (Vol. 1): 175–176.

21 Moreau de Saint-Méry 1797 (Vol. 1): 163, 183; Debien [1973] 1996: 110; Dubois 2004: 52.

22 Lettres de déclaration de noblesse en faveur des enfants de François Narp, habitant du quartier du Cap, à Saint-Domingue, célèbre adversaire du nègre Polidore et de son parti d'esclaves révoltes, 27 mai 1774 ANOM A14: 242.

23 Milscent 1791: 4.

24 Moreau de Saint-Méry 1784 (Vol. 3): 418–419.

25 Moreau de Saint-Méry 1784 (Vol. 2): 25; Fouchard 1988: 34.

26 Moreau de Saint-Méry 1784 (Vol. 3): 568–571, 673.

27 Moreau de Saint-Méry 1784 (Vol. 3): 162

28 Moreau de Saint-Méry 1784 (Vol. 3): 660; Debien [1973] 1996: 114; Moitt 2004: 62.

29 "Tableau de comparaison des Nègres, depuis 1730, jusqu'a 1786, dans la Colonie de Saint-Domingue," *LAA* November 8, 1787.

30 Moreau de Saint-Méry 1784 (Vol. 3): 685.

31 Moreau de Saint-Méry 1784 (Vol. 3): 847; Moreau de Saint-Méry 1797 (Vol. 2): 497.

32 Manigat 1977: 432–433; Dubois 2004: 53.

33 25 September 1744 Royal Statement on Maroons, Mangones Collection, University of Florida at Gainesville Library.

34 Moreau de Saint-Méry 1784 (Vol. 4): 226–228; Moreau de Saint-Méry 1784 (Vol. 5): 142–144; Manigat 1977: 435; Fick 1990: 53; Manigat 2007: 66.

35 Moreau de Saint-Méry 1784 (Vol. 4): 619.

36 Moreau de Saint-Méry 1784 (Vol. 4): 706.

37 Debien 1966: 10.

38 "Arrêt qui casse l'ordonnance rendue le 23 mars 1764 par Jean Étienne de Clugny de Nuits, intendant de Saint-Domingue, et l'arrêt du Conseil supérieur du Cap du 4 avril dernier, au sujet de la suppression de la vente des nègres marrons comme épaves, en raison des pouvoirs insuffisants de l'intendant et du conseil pour légiférer en cette matière, 18 novembre 1767" ANOM COL A11: 414; Moreau de Saint-Méry 1784 (Vol. 4): 717–718; Moitt 2004: 62.

39 "Ordonnance qui règle la vente comme épaves des nègres marrons, à Saint-Domingue, 18 novembre 1767," ANOM COL A11: 416; Moreau de Saint-Méry 1784 (Vol. 5): 139–141.

40 Moreau de Saint-Méry 1784 (Vol. 5): 427.

41 Moreau de Saint-Méry 1784 (Vol. 5): 512; Moreau de Saint-Méry 1784 (Vol. 6): 19; Moitt 2004: 63.

42 "Du Bourgneuf, Bernard Olivier, ancien habitant de Saint-Domingue et prévôt de maréchaussée, memoire sur les nègres marrons, 1770" ANOM E140: 793.

43 Schultz 2014.

44 Milscent 1791: 7.

45 "Lettres du Ministre du Vallière sur une proposition pour la chasse des nègres marrons, 21 november 1774," ANOM F3 94: 110.

46 Hall 1971: 76.

47 *LAA* November 18, 1775.

48 Moreau de Saint-Méry 1784 (Vol. 5): 550.

49 Debien 1961.

50 Milscent 1791: 8.

51 Laguerre 1989: 47–48.

52 Milscent 1791: 8.

53 Thornton 1991.

54 King 2001: 112–113.

55 Ghachem 2012: 114–116.

56 "Lettre du ministre a M. d'Argout sur les chasses de nègres marron et les chatiments à infliger aux nègres libres qui participent aux chasses et désertent au cours de l'operations 28 juillet 1778," ANOM F3 94: 136.

57 Moreau de Saint-Méry 1784 (Vol. 3): 751; Ghachem 2012: 114–116.

58 Milscent 1791: 8.

59 Moreau de Saint-Méry 1784 (Vol. 5): 800.

60 *Les Affiches américaines* (*LAA*) August 29, 1768.
61 "Modele d'un ordre de chasse à nègres marrons, du 21.9.1778," ANOM F3 94: 138 .
62 Moreau de Saint-Méry 1784 (Vol. 5): 847.
63 "Lettre du gouvernement au sujet d'un nègres tué comme marron alors qu'il n'était pas, 1779" ANOM F3 94: 139.
64 Moreau de Saint-Méry 1797 (Vol. 1): 200.
65 *LAA* January 18, 1780.
66 *LAA* May 6, 1786; Fouchard 1972: 272.
67 Moreau de Saint-Méry 1784 (Vol. 6): 6–7, 253.
68 Ogle 2005: 231.
69 Moreau de Saint-Méry 1784 (Vol. 6): 528–529.
70 Moreau de Saint-Méry 1784 (Vol 6): 718.
71 "Lettre de M. de Reynaud a M. de Vincent sur la chasse des nègres marrons, 7 aout 1780," ANOM F3 94: 140.
72 "Lettre du ministre a M. de Bellecombe sur les nègres marrons, 8 novembre 1782," ANOM F3 94: 142.
73 "18 mai 1786 Saint-Domingue" ANOM C9B 36.
74 Debien [1973] 1996: 129; McClellan 1992: 28.
75 Cheney 2013: 50–51.
76 Voyages 2009.
77 Moreau de Saint-Méry 1797 (Vol. 1): 526; Girard 2016: 74.
78 McClellan 1992: 27; Cheney 2013: 57.
79 Clark 1980.
80 *LAA* July 31, 1781.
81 *LAA* July 30, 1783.
82 Thornton 1991.
83 Ordonnance du Roi, concernant les procureurs & économes-gérans des habitations situées aux Isles sous le Vent, du 17 décembre 1784, John Carter Brown Library.
84 Fick 1990: 98; Geggus 2014: 25–29.
85 "Cappeau, Joseph Antoine, commis dans les bureaux de l'administration a Saint-Domingue, demande un brevet d'écrevain des colonies, auteur d'un mémoire sur les nègres marrons, 1784-1789" ANOM E62.
86 Laguerre 1989: 43.
87 "Louis-Joseph-Donnadieu de Pelissier Chevalier du Greg, Chevalier de l'ordre Royal et Militaire de Saint-Louis, Colonel l'Infanterie, commandant particulier du Cap, et en second par interim de la partie du nord de Saint-Domingue, au Cap, le 9 Mars 1785" ANOM F3 94: 170; Geggus 2002: 71.
88 Milscent 1791: 10.
89 Fouchard 1972: 316; Garrigus 2006: 96; Beauvoir Dominique 2009.
90 Moreau de Saint-Méry 1797 (Vol. 2): 497–498.
91 Moreau de Saint-Méry 1797 (Vol. 1): 154.
92 Milscent 1791.
93 Moreau de Saint-Méry 1784 (Vol. 5): 284.
94 "Memoire sur les nègres marrons a S. Domingue et les moyenne d'un diminuier le nombre le danger, 1775," and "Memoire sou les moyenn à

employer pas le S. Amant, lorsqu'il sera chargé de poursuivre et faire arrêtes les nègres marron de S. Domingue," ANOM F3 94: 116–118.

95 Lettre du père Charles-François de Coutances au sujet de l'installation de deux maîtres, 11 juillet 1777, ANOM F5 A: 18.

96 Thompson 2006: 309–310.

97 Turner 2011: 690–693; Brown 2012; Kars 2016.

98 Long [1774] 2002 (Vol. 2): 444–445.

99 Gomez 1998: 1–3; Edgerton and Paquette 2017: 2.

100 Scott [1986] 2018: 17–22.

101 King 2004; Geggus 2009: 8.

102 15 Mai 1788, Règlement du Roi, Concernant les Nègres épaves, Extrait des minutes du Conseil-Supérieur de Saint-Domingue, BNF.

8 Voices of Liberty: The Haiitian Revolution Begins

1 James [1938] 1989: 87.

2 Fick 1990: 49.

3 Manigat 1977: 433; Manigat 2007: 60.

4 Moreau de Saint-Méry 1798 (Part 1): 82.

5 *LAA* March 1, 1787.

6 McClellan 1992: 27.

7 Scott [1986] 2018: 69–72; McClellan 1992: 67.

8 "Dénonciation que fait M. Lamothe Vedel de ses Nègres marrons, & des faits résultants de leur marronnage, Le 6 Avril 1791," *Gazette de Saint Domingue Vol. 1* April 13, 1791, p. 382, John Carter Brown Library; "Avis divers" and "suivent les annexes," *Supplement a la Gazette de St. Domingue*, August 27, 1791, p. 839, John Carter Brown Library; Fouchard 1972: 254–255.

9 "Concernant les nègres marrons au Port-au-Prince, 6 fevrier 1786" ANOM C9B 36; Moreau de Saint-Méry 1797 (Vol. 2): 501–502; Yingling 2015: 34.

10 "Letter commune nègres maron, au Port-au-Prince, 30 avril 1786" ANOM C9B 36; "6 mai 1786: Saint Domingue" ANOM C9B 36.

11 Moreau de Saint-Méry 1797 (Vol. 2): 499.

12 "Concernant les nègres marrons au Port-au-Prince, 8.7.1786" ANOM C9B 36; Moreau de Saint-Méry 1797 (Vol. 2): 502.

13 "A Versailles le 16 aout 1786" ANOM C9B 36; "10 aout 1786" ANOM C9B 36.

14 Fick 1990: 137–138, 143.

15 Fick 1990: chapter 6; Becker 2017.

16 Fick 1990: chapter 9.

17 "Déclaration du Roi, Pour la Police des Noirs, Du 9 Aout 1777," John Carter Brown Library.

18 Klooster 2014.

19 Munford and Zeukse 1988: 18; Benot 2009: 102.

20 "Arrêt du Conseil Supérieur de Saint Domingue du 22 février 1791," John Carter Brown Library.

21 Lespinasse [1882] 2015: 309–310; Leger 1907: 44; King 2001: 219–220.

22 Madiou 1847: 65–66, 81.
23 "Arrêt du Conseil Supérieur de Saint Domingue du 22 février 1791," John Carter Brown Library.
24 Manigat 1977: 435; Manigat 2007: 66.
25 Fick 1990: 86–87.
26 *Gazette de Saint Domingue Vol.* 2 July 9, 1791 "du Port-au-Prince," p. 700, John Carter Brown Library.
27 Pluchon 1987: 128–129, n. 20.
28 *Gazette de Saint Domingue Vol.* 2 October 1, 1791, "Esclaves en marronnage" p. 925, John Carter Brown Library.
29 *LAA* November 20, 1771.
30 Fick 1990: 120; Geggus 2002: 102.
31 Geggus 2006: 214–218.
32 Malenfant 1814: 41; Madiou 1847 (Vol. 1): 100–103; Ardouin 1853: 325
33 Fick 1990: 127–129; Rey 2017.
34 "Lettre de Dusoles a C. Faure, Léogâne, 27 Septembre 1791," Fonds Pedroni, Atelier Monumerique/Archimerique Traite, esclavage, abolitions, Archives Bordeaux Metropole.
35 *LAA* 23 October 1784; Moreau de Saint-Méry 1784 (Vol. 6): 623–625; Fouchard 1972: 261.
36 *LAA* December 27, 1786; *LAA* January 26, 1788.
37 *LAA* February 26, 1766.
38 "Rapport du procès criminel instruit contre des nègres marrons, 1787," ANOM F3 94: 174; Moreau de Saint-Méry 1797 (Vol. 1): 176.
39 *LAA* November 17, 1787.
40 Anne-Louis de Tousard Papers, 1659–1932: Box 1 and 2, University of Michigan William L. Clements Library; Geggus 2014: 29–33.
41 *LAA* February 7, 1789.
42 Geggus 2014: 16, 32.
43 1791. "A Particular Account of the Insurrection of the Negroes of St. Domingo, Begun in August, 1791." Translated from the French, 4th Ed.
44 *LAA* November 3, 1787; Geggus 2014: 35.
45 Geggus 2002: 19, 180; Landers 2015: 2; Nessler 2016: 57–60.
46 Girard and Donnadieu 2013; Girard 2016: chapters 2–3.
47 *LAA* April 21, 1790.
48 Debien 1956: 164–170; Scott [1986] 2018: 25.
49 Milscent 1791: 11.
50 *LAA* August 28, 1790.
51 Milscent 1791: 11–12.
52 Geggus 2002: chapter 6.
53 Rey 2005: 5.
54 Sosis 1971: 404–405, n. 48; Pluchon 1987: 74–77; Law 1999.
55 Hebblethwaite 2012: 7.
56 Rey 2005: 3–4.
57 Dalmas 1814: 116–127; Metral 1818: 15–20; Dumesle 1824; Ardouin 1853; Charlier 1954: 49; Fick 1990: 93–94; Geggus 2002: 82; Dubois 2004: 99–100.

58 Sosis 1971: 405 n. 49; Fouchard 1972: 339; Benot 2009: 102.
59 Deren 1953: 63; Hebblethwaite and Payton interview with Sevite Dorsainville Estime, November 1, 2012, *The Vodou Archive*, UF Digital Collections.
60 Brown 2008: 148–149.
61 Geggus 2014: 25–29.
62 Fouchard 1972: 346–347; Fick 1990: 113; Landers 2010: chapter 2.
63 Dubois 2004: 124; Garrigus and Dubois 2004: 93–94; Munro 2010: 29.
64 "Lettre de Duvallon-L'etang a son frere" Series F: F7 Extrait, Atelier Monumerique/Archimerique Traite, esclavage, abolitions, Archives Bordeaux Metropole.
65 Geggus 2013: 107.
66 Fouchard 1988: 39–40; Fick 1990: 104, 265–266; Vanhee 2002: 248–249.
67 Malenfant 1814: 217–219; Sosis 1971: 263; Fouchard 1972: 344–345.
68 Moitt 2001: chapter 7; Girard 2009: 68–72.
69 *Gazette de Saint Domingue Vol. 2* August 6, 1791 "Esclaves en marronnage," pg. 776, John Carter Brown Library.
70 Geggus 2014: 33.
71 Thornton 1993b: 207–210.
72 *LAA* November 13, 1790.
73 Malenfant 1814: 76, 235.
74 James [1938] 1989: 257, 352.
75 James [1938] 1989: 315.
76 Dayan 1995: 47.
77 Dubois 2004: 167–168, 184.
78 Kafka 1997.
79 Dubois 2004: 184–193.
80 Girard 2009: 71.
81 Fick 1990; Gerard 1997; Girard 2011.
82 Constitution Impériale d'Haïti (1805).

Conclusion

1 Anna Julia Cooper Address Accepting Her Diploma from the Sorbonne, University of Paris (1925). Manuscripts and Addresses, 16. Anna Julia Cooper Collection, Digital Howard.

References

ARCHIVES

Archives Bordeaux Métropole
Archives Nationales of France (AN)
Archives Nationales d'Outre-Mer (ANOM)
Bibliothèque Nationale de France
Conseil Départemental de la Haute-Garonne Archives Départementales
John Carter Brown Library
The Library Company of Philadelphia
The Schomburg Center for Research in Black Culture
University of Florida George A. Smathers Libraries
University of Michigan William L. Clements Library

Newspapers

Les Affiches américaines
Courrier Nationale de Saint Domingue
Gazette de Saint Domingue

PRIMARY SOURCES

([1685] 1980). *Le Code Noir ou recueil des règlements rendus jusqu'à présent.* Société, d'Histoire de la Guadeloupe.

(1787). *Extrait du Mercure de France: Makandal, Histoire véritable.*

(1791). "A Particular Account of the Insurrection of the Negroes of St. Domingo, Begun in August, 1791." Translated from the French, 4th ed.

d'Auberteuil, Hilliard. (1776). *Considérations sur l'état présent de la colonie française de Saint Domingue.* Paris: Imprimeur-Libraire.

Ardouin, Beaubrun. (1853). *Etudes sur l'histoire d'Haiti.* Paris: Dézobry et E. Magdeleine.

Baudry, Louis. (1803). *Second Voyage à la Louisiane*. Paris: Chez Charles.

Bourgeois, Nicolas Louis. (1788). *Voyages Intéressans dans Différentes Colonies Françaises, Espagnoles, Anglaises, etc.* Paris: Jean-François Bastien.

Dalmas, Antoine. (1814). *Histoire de la Revolution de Saint-Domingue*. Paris: Meme Frères.

Dalzel, Archibald. (1793). *The History of Dahomy: An Inland Kingdom of Africa*. London: Spilsbury and Son, Snowhill.

Descourtilz, Michel Etienne. (1809). *Voyages d'un Naturaliste, et ses Observations*. Paris: Dufart.

Dumesle, Herard. (1824). *Voyage dans le Nord d'Haiti, ou, Revelation des Lieux et des Monuments Historiques*. Les Cayes: Imprimerie du Gouvernement.

Jouin, Nicolas. ([1758] 1761). "Relation d'une Conspiration Tramée par les Negres, dans l'Isle de S. Domingue." In *Procès Contre les Jésuites: Pour Servir de Suite aux Cause Célèbres*. A Douai: MDCCLXI.

Labat, Jean Baptiste. ([1722] 1724). *Nouveau Voyage aux Isles de l'Amérique*. Paris.

Laborie, P. J. (1798). *The Coffee Planter of Saint Domingo*. London: T. Cadell and W. Davies.

Lespinasse, Beauvais. ([1882] 2015). *Histoire des Affranchis de Saint-Domingue, Tome Premier*. Port-au-Prince: Les Editions Fardin.

Long, Edward. ([1774] 2002). *The History of Jamaica, Volume 2*. Montreal: McGill-Queen's University Press.

Madiou, Thomas. (1847). *Histoire d'Haiti*. Port-au-Prince: Editions Henri Deschamps.

Malenfant, Colonel Charles. (1814). *Des Colonies, et Particulièrement de celle de Saint Domingue; Mémoire Historique et Politique*. Paris: Chez Audibert.

Metral, Antoine. (1818). *Histoire de l'Insurrection des Esclaves dans le Nord de Saint-Domingue*. Paris: F. Scherff.

Milscent de Mussé, Claude. (1791). *Sur les Troubles de Saint-Domingue*. Paris: De l'Imprimerie du Patriote François.

Monnereau, Elias. 1769. *The Complete Indigo-Maker*. London: P. Elmsly.

Moreau de Saint-Méry, M. L. E. (1784). *Loix et Constitutions des Colonies Françoises de l'Amérique Sous le Vent (Vol. 1–6)*. Paris: Chez l'Auteur.

([1796] 1975). *Dance: An Article Drawn from the Work by M. L. E. Moreau de St.-Méry*. Translated by Lily and Baird Hastings. Brooklyn: Dance Horizons.

(1797). *Description Topographique, Physique, Civile, Politique et Historique de la Partie Française de l'Isle Saint Domingue*. Paris: Société de l'Histoire des Colonies Françaises.

(1798). *A Topographical and Political Description of the Spanish Part of Saint-Domingo*. Translated by William Cobbett. Philadelphia.

Oldendorp, Christian Georg Andreas. ([1770] 1987). *History of the Mission of the Evangelical Brethren on the Caribbean Islands of St. Thomas, St. Croix, and St. John*, edited by Johann Jakob Bossard. Ann Arbor: Karoma Publishers, Inc.

Rainsford, Marcus. ([1805] 2013). *An Historical Account of the Black Empire of Hayti*, edited by Paul Youngquist and Grégory Pierrot. Durham: Duke University Press.

de Vaissière, Pierre. (1909). *Saint-Domingue: La Société et la Vie Créoles sous l'Ancien Régime (1629–1789)*. Paris: Perrin.

de Vastey, Baron. ([1814] 2014). *The Colonial System Unveiled*. Translated and edited by Chris Bongie. Liverpool: Liverpool University Press.

SECONDARY SOURCES

Books, Chapters, and Articles

Adams, Julia, Elisabeth S. Clemens, and Anna Shola Orloff, eds. (2005). *Remaking Modernity: Politics, History and Sociology*. Durham: Duke University Press.

Alpern, Stanley B. (1998a). *Amazons of Black Sparta: The Women Warriors of Dahomey*. Washington Square, New York: New York University Press.

(1998b). "On the Origins of the Amazons of Dahomey." *History in Africa* 25: 9–25.

Alpers, Edward A. (1970). "The French Slave Trade in East Africa (1721–1810)." *Cahiers d'Études Africaines* 10 (37): 80–124.

Ansell, Christopher K. (1997). "Symbolic Networks: The Realignment of the French Working Class, 1887–1894." *American Journal of Sociology* 103 (2): 359–390.

Aptheker, Herbert. ([1943] 1969). *American Negro Slave Revolts*. New York: International Publishers.

Barcia, Manuel. (2014). *West African Warfare in Bahia and Cuba: Soldier Slaves in the Atlantic World, 1807–1844*. New York: Oxford University Press.

Barry, Boubacar. (1998). *Senegambia and the Atlantic Slave Trade*. New York: Cambridge University Press.

Bay, Edna G. (1997.) "The Kpojito or "Queen Mother" of Precolonial Dahomey: Towards an Institutional History" In *Queens, Queen Mothers, Priestesses, and Power: Case Studies in African Gender*, edited by Flora E. S. Kaplan, 19–41. New York: The New York Academy of Sciences.

(1998). *Wives of the Leopard: Gender, Politics, and Culture in the Kingdom of Dahomey*. Charlottesville: University of Virginia Press.

Bayle, Mme Jeanne. (2008). "Vente d'une Plantation à Saint-Domingue en 1784." *Petite Bibliothèque* 161: 1–16. Les Amis des Archives de la Haute-Garonne.

Beauvoir-Dominique, Rachel. (2009). "The Rock Images of Haiti: A Living Heritage." In *Rock Art of the Caribbean*, edited by Michele Hayward, Lesley-Gail Atkinson, and Michael Cinquino, 78–89. Tuscaloosa: University of Alabama Press.

(2010). "The Social Value of Voodoo throughout History: Slavery, Migrations and Solidarity." *Museum International* 62 (4): 99–105.

Beck, Colin J. (2017). "Revolutions: Robust Findings, Persistent Problems, and Promising Frontiers." In *The Handbook of Political Conflict*, edited by Mark Lichbach, Michael Stohl, and Peter Grabosky, 2–26. Routledge.

Becker, Michael. (2017). "Revolution at the Crossroads: Re-Framing the Haitian Revolution from the Heights of Platons." In *Human Rights, Race, and*

Resistance in Africa and the African Diaspora, edited by Toyin Falola and Cacee Hoyer, 170–187. New York: Routledge.

Bellegarde-Smith, Patrick. (2004). *Haiti: The Breached Citadel, Revised and Updated Edition*. Toronto: Canadian Scholars' Press.

Bennett, Herman. (2018). *African Kings and Black Slaves: Sovereignty and Dispossession in the Early Modern Atlantic*. Philadelphia: University of Pennsylvania Press.

Benot, Yves. (2009). "The Insurgents of 1791, Their Leaders, and the Concept of Independence." In *The World of the Haitian Revolution*, edited by David Patrick Geggus and Norman Fiering, 99–110. Bloomington: Indiana University Press.

Berger, Peter L. and Thomas Luckmann. (1966). *The Social Construction of Reality: A Treatise in the Sociology of Knowledge*. New York: Anchor Books.

Berlin, Ira. (1996). "From Creole to African: Atlantic Creoles and the Origins of African American Society in Mainland North America." *The William and Mary Quarterly* 53 (2): 251–288.

Berquist, Emily. (2010). "Early Anti-Slavery Sentiment in the Spanish Atlantic World, 1765–1817." *Slavery & Abolition* 31 (2): 181–205.

Berry, Daina Ramey. (2017). *The Price for Their Pound of Flesh: The Value of the Enslaved, from Womb to Grave, in the Building of a Nation* Boston: Beacon Press.

Bhambra, Gurminder K. (2011). "Historical Sociology, Modernity, and Postcolonial Critique." *American Historical Review* 116 (3): 653–662.

(2014). "A Sociological Dilemma: Race, Segregation and U.S. Sociology." *Current Sociology Monography* 62 (4): 472–492.

(2015). "On the Haitian Revolution and the Society of Equals." *Theory, Culture & Society* 32 (7–8): 267–274.

(2016). "Undoing the Epistemic Disavowal of the Haitian Revolution: A Contribution to Global Social Thought." *Journal of Intercultural Studies* 37 (1): 1–16.

Biggs, Michael. 2013. "How Repertoires Evolve: The Diffusion of Suicide Protest in the Twentieth Century." *Mobilization: An International Quarterly* 18 (4): 407–428.

Blackburn, Robin. (2011). *Overthrow of Colonial Slavery, 1776–1848*. London: Verso.

Borucki, Alex. (2015). *From Shipmates to Soldiers: Emerging Black Identities in the Rio de la Plata*. Albuquerque: University of New Mexico Press.

Boucher, Philip. (2011). "The French and Dutch Caribbean, 1600–1800." In *The Caribbean: A History of the Region and its Peoples*, edited by Stephan Palmié and Francisco A. Scarano, 217–230. Chicago: The University of Chicago Press.

Boudreau, Vince. (2005). "Precarious Regimes and Matchup Problems in the Explanation of Repressive Policy." In *Repression and Mobilization*, edited by Christian Davenport, Hank Johnston, and Carol Mueller, 33–57. Minneapolis: University of Minnesota Press.

Bracey II, Glenn E. (2016). "Black Movements Need Black Theorizing: Exposing Implicit Whiteness in Political Process Theory." *Sociological Focus* 49 (1): 11–27.

Broadhead, Susan Herlin. (1983). "Slave Wives, Free Sisters: Bakongo Women and Slavery c. 1700–1850." In *Women and Slavery in Africa*, edited by Claire C. Robertson and Martin Klein, 160–180. Madison: University of Wisconsin Press.

Brown, Karen McCarthy. (2007). "Afro-Caribbean Spirituality: A Haitian Case Study." In *Vodou in Haitian Life and Culture: Invisible Powers*, edited by Claudine Michel and Patrick Bellegarde-Smith, 1–26. New York: Palgrave Macmillan.

Brown, Vincent. (2008). *The Reaper's Garden: Death and Power in the World of Atlantic Slavery*. Cambridge: Harvard University Press.

(2020). *Tacky's Revolt: The Story of an Atlantic Slave War*. Cambridge: Harvard University Press.

Browne, Simone. (2015). *Dark Matters: On the Surveillance of Blackness*. Durham: Duke University Press.

Brubaker, Rogers. (2005). "The 'Diaspora' Diaspora." *Ethnic and Racial Studies* 28 (1): 1–19.

Buck-Morss, Susan. (2009). *Hegel, Haiti, and Universal History*. Pittsburgh: University of Pittsburgh Press.

Burnard, Trevor and John Garrigus. (2016). *The Plantation Machine: Atlantic Capitalism in French Saint-Domingue and British Jamaica*. Philadelphia: University of Pennsylvania Press.

Butler, Kim D. (1998). *Freedoms Given, Freedoms Won: Afro-Brazilians in Post-Abolition São Paulo and Salvador*. New Brunswick: Rutgers University Press.

(2001). "Defining Diaspora, Refining a Discourse." *Diaspora: A Journal of Transnational Studies* 10: 189–219.

Camp, Stephanie M. H. (2004). *Closer to Freedom: Enslaved Women and Everyday Resistance in the Plantation South*. Chapel Hill: University of North Carolina Press.

Candido, Mariana P. (2013). *An African Slaving Port and the Atlantic World: Benguela and its Hinterland*. New York: Cambridge University Press.

Casimir, Jean. (2001). *La Culture Opprimée*. Delmas: Imprimer Lakay.

(2015). "The Sovereign People of Haiti during the Eighteenth and Nineteenth Centuries." In *The Haitian Declaration of Independence*, edited by Julia Gaffield. Charlottesville: University of Virginia Press.

(2020). *The Haitians: A Decolonial History*. Chapel Hill: University of North Carolina Press.

Cauna, Jacques. (1996). "The Singularity of the Saint-Domingue Revolution: Marronage, Voodoo, and the Color Question." *Plantation Society in the Americas* III 3: 321–345.

Charlier, Etienne. (1954). *Aperçu sur la Formation Historique de la Nation Haïtienne*. Port-au-Prince: Presses Libres.

Cheney, Paul. (2013). "A Colonial Cul de Sac: Plantation Life in Wartime Saint-Domingue, 1775–1782." *Radical History Review* 115: 45–64.

Childs, Matt D. (2006). *The 1812 Aponte Rebellion in Cuba and the Struggle against Atlantic Slavery*. Chapel Hill: University of North Carolina Press.

Clark, George P. (1980). "The Role of the Haitian Volunteers at Savannah in 1779: An Attempt at an Objective View." *Phylon* 41 (4): 356–366.

Clemens, Elisabeth S. and Martin D. Hughes. (2002). "Recovering Past Protest: Historical Research on Social Movements." In *Methods of Social Movement Research*, edited by Bert Klandermans and Suzanne Staggenborg, 201–230. Minneapolis: University of Minnesota Press.

Cohen, Robin. (1992). "The Diaspora of a Diaspora: The Case of the Caribbean." *Social Science Information* 31 (1): 159–169.

(2008). *Global Diasporas: An Introduction, 2nd Edition*. London: Routledge

Cooper, Anna Julia. ([1925] 1988). *Slavery and the French Revolutionists, 1788–1805*. New York: The Edwin Mellen Press.

Couto, Richard A. (1993). "Narrative, Free Space, and Political Leadership in Social Movements." *The Journal of Politics* 55: 57–79.

Covin, David. (1997). "Narrative, Free Spaces, and Communities of Memory in the Brazilian Black Consciousness Movement." *Western Journal of Black Studies* 21 (4): 272–279.

Creasap, Kimberly. (2012). "Social Movement Scenes: Place-based Politics and Everyday Resistance." *Sociology Compass* 6 (2): 182–191.

Crush, Jonathan. (1994). "Post-colonialism, De-colonization, and Geography." In *Geography and Empire*, edited by Anne Godlewska and Neil Smith, 333–350. Oxford: Blackwell.

Daniels, Jason. (2012). "Recovering the Fugitive History of Marronage in Saint Domingue, 1770–1791." *The Journal of Caribbean History* 46 (2): 121–153.

Daniels, Kyrah Malika. (2013). "The Undressing of Two Sacred Healing Bundles: Curative Arts of the Black Atlantic in Haiti and Ancient Kongo." *Journal of Africana Religions* 1 (3): 416–429.

Daut, Marlene L. (2015). *Tropics of Haiti: Race and the Literary History of the Haitian Revolution in the Atlantic World, 1789–1865*. Liverpool: Liverpool University Press.

Davenport, Christian. (2005). "Repression and Mobilization: Insights from Political Science and Sociology." In *Repression and Mobilization*, edited by Christian Davenport, Hank Johnston, and Carol Mueller, vii–xii. Minneapolis: University of Minnesota Press.

Dawson, Kevin. (2018). *Undercurrents of Power: Aquatic Culture in the African Diaspora*. Philadelphia: University of Pennsylvania Press.

Dayan, Joan. (1995). *Haiti, History, and the Gods*. Berkeley: University of California Press.

Debbasch, Yvan. ([1973] 1996). "Le Maniel: Further Notes." In *Maroon Societies: Rebel Slave Communities in the Americas*, edited by Richard Price, 143–148. Garden City: Anchor Books.

Debien, Gabriel. (1956). *Etudes Antillaises (XVIIe Siècle)*. Paris: Librairie Armand Colin.

(1961). "Les Origines des Esclaves des Antilles." *Bulletin de l'Institut Français d'Afrique Noire Série B, Sciences Humaines* 23 (3–4): 363–387.

(1966). "Les Marrons de Saint-Domingue en 1764." *Jamaican Historical Review* 6 (1): 9–20.

(1972). "Assemblées Nocturnes d'Esclaves a Saint Domingue, 1786 (Night-Time Slave Meetings in Saint Domingue)." *Translated by John Garrigus.* Des Annales historiques de la Révolution 208: 273–284.

([1973] 1996). "Marronage in the French Caribbean." In *Maroon Societies: Rebel Slave Communities in the Americas,* edited by Richard Price, 107–134. Garden City: Anchor Books.

(1980). "Les Esclaves des Plantations Mauger a Saint Domingue (1763–1802)." *Notes d'Histoire Coloniale – No. 201. Extrait du Bulletin de la Societe d'Histoire de la Guadeloupe* 43–44.

(2000). *Les Esclaves aux Antilles Françaises (XVIIème –XVIIIème Siècles).* Gourbeyre: Société d'Histoire de la Guadeloupe.

della Porta, Donatella. (2013). "Repertoires of Contention." In *The Wiley-Blackwell Encyclopedia of Social and Political Movements,* edited by David A. Snow. Blackwell Publishing.

Deren, Maya. (1953). *Divine Horsemen: The Living Gods of Haiti.* New York: McPherson & Company.

Desch-Obi, T. J. (2002). "Combat and the Crossing of the Kalunga." In *Central Africans and Cultural Transformations in the American Diaspora,* edited by Linda Heywood, 353–370. Cambridge: Cambridge University Press.

(2008). *Fighting for Honor: The History of African Martial Art Traditions in the Atlantic World.* Columbia: University of South Carolina Press.

(2010). "'Koup Tet': A Machete Wielding View of the Haitian Revolution." In *Activating the Past: History and Memory in the Black Atlantic World,* edited by Andrew Apter and Lauren Derby, 245–266. Newcastle upon Tyne: Cambridge Scholars.

Desmangles, Leslie. (1992). *The Faces of the Gods: Vodou and Roman Catholicism.* Chapel Hill: The University of North Carolina Press.

Dewulf, Jeroen. (2015). "Black Brotherhoods in North America: Afro-Iberian Central African Influences." *African Studies Quarterly* 15(3): 19–38.

Diani, Mario. (1997). "Social Movements and Social Capital: A Network Perspective on Movement Outcomes." *Mobilization: An International Journal* 2 (2): 129–147.

(2003). "Networks and Social Movements: A Research Programme." In *Social Movements and Networks: Relational Approaches to Collective Action,* edited by Mario Diani and Doug McAdam, 299–319. New York: Oxford University Press.

Diehl, David and Daniel McFarland. (2010). "Toward a Historical Sociology of Social Situations." *American Journal of Sociology* 115 (6): 1713–1752.

Diouf, Sylviane A. (1998). *Servants of Allah: African Muslims Enslaved in the Americas.* New York: New York University Press.

ed. (2003). *Fighting the Slave Trade: West African Strategies.* Athens: Ohio University Press.

(2014). *Slavery's Exiles: The Story of the American Maroons.* New York: New York University Press.

Domingues da Silva, Daniel B. (2013). "The Atlantic Slave Trade from Angola: A Port-by-Port Estimate of Slaves Embarked, 1701–1867." *International Journal of African Historical Studies* 46(1): 105–123.

(2017). *The Atlantic Slave Trade from West Central Africa, 1780–1867.* Cambridge: Cambridge University Press.

Dubois, Laurent. (2004). *Avengers of the New World: The Story of the Haitian Revolution.* Cambridge: Harvard University Press.

(2009). "The French Atlantic." In *Atlantic History: A Critical Appraisal,* edited by Jack P. Greene and Philip D. Morgan, 137–162. Oxford: Oxford University Press.

(2011). "Slavery in the French Caribbean, 1635–1804." In *The Cambridge World History of Slavery, Volume 3: AD 1420–AD 1804,* edited by David Eltis and Stanley L. Engerman, 431–449. Cambridge: Cambridge University Press.

(2012). *Haiti: The Aftershocks of History.* New York: Metropolitan Books.

(2016). "Thinking Haitian Independence in Haitian Vodou." *In The Haitian Declaration of Independence: Creation, Context, and Legacy,* edited by Julia Gaffield, 201–218. Charlottesville: University of Virginia Press.

Dubois, Laurent and John D. Garrigus. ([2006] 2017). *Slave Revolution in the Caribbean, 1789–1804: A Brief History with Documents.* Boston: Bedford/St. Martin's.

Du Bois, W. E. B. ([1896] 2007). *The Suppression of the African Slave Trade to the United States of America, 1638–1870.* New York: Oxford University Press.

([1903] 1994). *The Souls of Black Folk.* Mineola: Dover Publications.

([1935] 1992). *Black Reconstruction in America.* New York: Atheneum.

Dufoix, Stéphane. (2008). *Diasporas.* Translated by William Rodarmor. Berkeley: University of California Press.

Dupuy, Alex. (1989). *Haiti in the World Economy: Class, Race, and Underdevelopment since 1700.* Boulder: Westview Press.

Durkheim, Emile. (1912). *The Elementary Forms of Religious Life.* New York: Collier Books.

Earl, Jennifer. (2003). "Tanks, Tear Gas, and Taxes: Toward a Theory of Movement Repression." *Sociological Theory* 21 (1): 44–68.

(2006). "Introduction: Repression and the Social Control of Protest." *Mobilization: An International Journal* 11 (2): 129–143.

(2011). "Political Repression: Iron Fists, Velvet Gloves, and Diffuse Control." *Annual Review of Sociology* 37: 261–284.

Eddins, Crystal Nicole. (2019). "Runaways, Repertoires, and Repression: Antecedents to the Haitian Revolution 1766–1791." *Journal of Haitian Studies* 25 (1): 4–38.

(2020). "'Rejoice! Your wombs will not beget slaves!' Marronnage as Reproductive Justice in Colonial Haiti." *Gender & History* 32 (3): 562–580.

Edgerton, Douglas R. and Robert L. Paquette, eds. (2017). *The Denmark Vesey Affair: A Documentary History.* Gainesville: University Press of Florida.

Evans, Sara M. and Harry C. Boyte. (1986). *Free Spaces: The Sources of Democratic Change in America.* New York: Harper & Row, Publishers.

Fantasia, Rick. (1988). *Cultures of Solidarity: Consciousness, Action, and Contemporary American Workers.* Berkeley: University of California Press.

Fantasia, Rick and Eric Hirsch. (1995). "Culture in Rebellion: The Appropriation and Transformation of the Veil in the Algerian Revolution." In *Social*

Movements and Culture, edited by Hank Johnston and Bert Klandermans, 144–178. Minneapolis: University of Minnesota Press.

Fennell, Christopher C. 2003. "Group Identity, Individual Creativity, and Symbolic Generation in a BaKongo Diaspora." *International Journal of Historical Archaeology* 7 (1): 1–31.

Ferreira, Roquinaldo. (2011). "Slaving and Resistance to Slaving in West Central Africa." *In The Cambridge World History of Slavery*, edited by David Eltis and Stanley L. Engerman, Cambridge University Press.

(2014). "Slave Flights and Runaway Communities in Angola (17th–19th Centuries)." *Anos 90, Porto Alegre* 21 (40): 65–90.

Fick, Carolyn E. (1990). *The Making of Haiti: The Saint Domingue Revolution from Below*. Knoxville: The University of Tennessee Press.

(2000). "The St. Domingue Slave Insurrection of 1791: A Socio-Political and Cultural Analysis." In *Caribbean Slavery in the Atlantic World: A Student Reader*, edited by Verene A. Shepard and Hilary M. Beckles, 961–982. Kingston: Ian Randle.

Fleurant, Gerdès. (1996). *Dancing Spirits: Rhythms and Rituals of Haitian Vodun, the Rada Rite*. Wesport: Greenwood Press.

Foran, John. (1993). "Theories of Revolution Revisited: Toward a Fourth Generation?" *Sociological Theory* 11 (1): 1–20.

(2001). "Studying Revolutions through the Prism of Race, Gender, and Class: Notes toward a Framework." *Race, Gender & Class* 8 (2): 117–141.

(2009). *Taking Power: On the Origins of Third World Revolutions*. New York: Cambridge University Press.

Foubert, Bernard. (1988). "Le marronage sur les habitations Laborde à Saint-Domingue dans la seconde moitié du XVIIIe siècle." *Annales de Bretagne et des pays de l'Ouest* 95 (3): 277–310.

Foucault, Michel. (1977). *Discipline & Punish: The Birth of the Prison*. New York: Vintage Books.

Fouchard, Jean. (1972). *The Haitian Maroons: Liberty or Death*. New York: E. W. Blyden Press.

(1988). *Les Marrons du Syllabaire: Quelques Aspects du Problème de l'Instruction et de l'Education des Esclaves et Affranchis de Saint-Domingue*. Port-au-Prince: Les Editions Henri Deschamps.

Fouchard, Jean and Gabriel Debien. (1969). "Aspects de l'esclavage aux Antilles Françaises: le petit marronage à Saint Domingue autour du Cap, 1790–1791." *Cahiers des Amériques Latines* 3: 31–67.

Gamson, William A. (1992). "The Social Psychology of Collective Action." In *Frontiers in Social Movement Theory*, edited by Aldon D. Morris and Carol McClurg Mueller, 53–76. New Haven: Yale University Press.

Garraway, Doris. (2005a). "Race, Reproduction and Family Romance in Moreau de Saint-Mery's Description ... de la Partie Française de l'Isle Saint Domingue." *Eighteenth-Century Studies* 38 (2): 227–246.

(2005b). *The Libertine Colony: Creolization in the Early French Caribbean*: Durham: Duke University Press.

Garrigus, John David. (1993). "Blue and Brown: Contraband Indigo and the Rise of a Free Colored Planter Class in French Saint-Domingue." *The Americas* 50 (2): 233–263.

(2006). *Before Haiti: Race and Citizenship in French Saint-Domingue.* New York: Palgrave MacMillan.

(2010). "'Thy coming fame, Oge! Is sure' New Evidence on Oge's 1790 Revolt and the Beginnings of the Haitian Revolution." In *Assumed Identities: The Meanings of Race in the Atlantic World*, edited by John D. Garrigus and Christopher Morris, 19–45. Arlington: Texas A&M University Press.

Gautier, Arlette. (1985). *Les Sœurs de Solitude: La Condition Féminine dans l'Esclavage aux Antilles du XVIIe au XIXe siècle.* Paris: Editions Caribéennes.

Gaventa, John. (1980). *Power and Powerlessness: Quiescence and Rebellion in an Appalachian Valley.* Urbana: University of Illinois Press.

Geggus, David Patrick. (1986). "On the Eve of the Haitian Revolution: Slave Runaways in Saint Domingue in the Year 1790." In *Out of the House of Bondage: Runaways, Resistance and Marronage in Africa and the New World*, edited by Gad Heuman, 112–128. Great Britain: Frank Cass and Company.

(1989a). "Sex Ratio and Ethnicity: A Reply to Paul E. Lovejoy." *The Journal of African History* 30 (2): 395–397.

(1989b). "Sex Ratio, Age and Ethnicity in the Atlantic Slave Trade: Data from French Shipping and Plantation Records." *The Journal of African History* 30 (1): 23–44.

(1991a). "Haitian Voodoo in the Eighteenth Century: Language, Culture Resistance." *Jahrbuch für Geschichte von Staat, Wirtschaft und Gesellschaft Lateinamerikas* 28: 21–51.

(1991b). "The Major Port Towns of Saint Domingue in the Later Eighteenth Century." In *Atlantic Port Cities: Economy, Culture, and Society in the Atlantic World, 1650–1850*, edited by Franklin W. Knight and Peggy K. Liss, 87–116. Knoxville: The University of Tennessee Press.

(1993). "Sugar and Coffee Cultivation in Saint Domingue and the Shaping of the Slave Labor Force." In *Cultivation and Culture: Labor and the Shaping of Slave Life in the Americas*, edited by Ira Berlin and Philip D. Morgan, 73–98. Charlottesville: University Press of Virginia.

(1996). "Slave and Free Colored Women in Saint Domingue." In *More Than Chattel: Black Women and Slavery in the Americas, edited by David Barry Gaspar and Darlene Clark Hine*, 259–278. Bloomington: Indiana University Press.

(1998). "Indigo and Slavery in Saint-Domingue." *Plantation Society in the Americas III* 5 (2 & 3): 189–204.

(1999). "Slave Society in the Sugar Plantation Zones of Saint Domingue and the Revolution of 1791–93." *Slavery & Abolition* 20 (2): 31–46.

(2001a). "The French Slave Trade: An Overview." *The William and Mary Quarterly* 58 (1): 119–138.

(2002). *Haitian Revolutionary Studies.* Bloomington: Indiana University Press.

(2006). "The Arming of Slaves in the Haitian Revolution." In *Arming Slaves: From Classical Times to the Modern Age*, edited by Christopher Leslie Brown and Philip D. Morgan, 209–232. New Haven: Yale University Press.

(2009). "Saint Domingue on the Eve of the Haitian Revolution." In *The World of the Haitian Revolution*, edited by David Patrick Geggus and Norman Fiering. Bloomington: Indiana University Press.

(2013). "The Slaves and Free People of Color in Cap Français." In *Early Modern Americas: Black Urban Atlantic in the Age of the Slave Trade*, edited by Jorge Canizares-Esguerra, Matt Childs, and James Sidbury, 101–121. Philadelphia: University of Pennsylvania Press.

ed. (2014). *The Haitian Revolution: A Documentary History*. Indianapolis: Hackett Publishing Company.

Genovese, Eugene D. (1979). *From Rebellion to Revolution: Afro-American Slave Revolts in the Making of the Modern World*. Baton Rouge: Louisiana State University Press.

Gerard, Barthelemy. (1997). "Le Rôle des Bossales dans l'Emergence d'une Culture de Marronnage en Haiti." *Cahiers d'Etudes Africaines* 37 (148): 839–862.

Getachew, Adom. (2016). "Universalism after the Post-colonial Turn: Interpreting the Haitian Revolution." *Political Theory*: 1–25.

Ghachem, Malick W. (2011). "Prosecuting Torture: The Strategic Ethics of Slavery in Pre-Revolutionary Saint Domingue (Haiti)." *Law and History Review* 29 (4): 985–1029.

(2012). *The Old Regime and the Haitian Revolution*. Cambridge: Cambridge University Press.

Gilroy, Paul. (1992). *The Black Atlantic: Modernity and Double Consciousness*. Cambridge: Harvard University Press.

Girard, Phillippe R. (2009). "Rebelles with a Cause: Women in the Haitian War of Independence, 1802–1804." *Gender & History* 21 (1): 60–85.

(2011). *The Slaves Who Defeated Napoleon: Toussaint Louverture and the Haitian War of Independence*. Tuscaloosa: University of Alabama Press.

(2013). "The Haitian Revolution, History's New Frontier: State of the Scholarship and Archival Sources." *Slavery & Abolition* 34 (3): 485–507.

(2016). *Toussaint Louverture: A Revolutionary Life*. New York: Basic Books.

Girard, Phillippe and Jean-Louis Donnadieu. (2013). "Toussaint before Louverture: New Archival Findings on the Early Life of Toussaint Louverture." *The William and Mary Quarterly* 70 (1): 41–78.

Go, Julian. (2016). *Postcolonial Thought and Social Theory*. New York: Oxford University Press.

Go, Julian and George Lawson, eds. (2017). *Global Historical Sociology*. Cambridge: Cambridge University Press.

Goldstone, Jack A. (1991). *Revolution and Rebellion in the Early Modern World*. Berkeley: University of California Press.

(2001). "Toward a Fourth Generation of Revolutionary Theory." *Annual Review of Political Science* 4: 139–187.

Goldstone, Jack A. and Daniel P. Ritter. (2019). "Revolutions and Social Movements." In *The Blackwell Companion of Social Movements, Second*

Edition, edited by David A. Snow, Sarah A. Soule, Hanspeter Kriesi, and Holly J. McCammon, 682–697. Malden: Blackwell Publishing

Gomez, Michael A. (1998). *Exchanging Our Country Marks: The Transformation of African Identities in the Colonial and Antebellum South*. Chapel Hill: The University of North Carolina Press.

(2005). *Black Crescent: The Experience and Legacy of African Muslims in the Americas*. Cambridge: Cambridge University Press.

Gonzalez, JohnHenry. (2019). *Maroon Nation: A History of Revolutionary Haiti*. New Haven: Yale University Press.

Gould, Roger V. (1995). *Insurgent Identities: Class, Community, and Protest in Paris from 1848 to the Commune*. Chicago: The University of Chicago Press.

(2005). "Historical Sociology and Collective Action." In *Remaking Modernity: Politics, History and Sociology*, edited by Julia Adams, Elisabeth S. Clemens, and Ann S. Orloff, 286–299. Durham: Duke University Press.

Goveia, Elsa V. (1960). "The West Indian Slave Laws of Eighteenth Century." *Revista de Ciencias Sociales* 75–105.

Granovetter, Mark S. (1973). "The Strength of Weak Ties." *American Journal of Sociology* 78 (6): 1360–1380.

Green, Toby. (2019). *A Fistful of Shells: West Africa from the Rise of the Slave Trade to the Age of Revolution*. Chicago: University of Chicago Press.

Guillet, Bertrand. (2009). *La Marie-Séraphique, Navire Negrier*. Nantes: Musée d'histoire de Nantes.

Guitar, Lynne. (2002). "Documenting the Myth of Taíno Extinction." *KACIKE: Journal of Caribbean Amerindian History and Anthropology*: 1–15.

(2006). "Boiling It Down: Slavery on the First Commercial Sugarcane *Ingenios* in the Americas (Hispaniola, 1530–45)." In *Slaves, Subjects, and Subversives: Blacks in Colonial Latin America*, edited by Jane G. Landers and Barry M. Robinson, 39–82. Albuquerque: University of New Mexico Press.

Hall, Gwendolyn Midlo. (1968). "Black Resistance in Colonial Haiti." *Black World/Negro Digest* 17 (4): 40–48.

(1971). *Social Control in Slave Plantation Societies: A Comparison of St. Domingue and Cuba*. Baton Rouge: Louisiana State University Press.

(1972). "Saint Domingue." In *Neither Slave nor Free: The Freedman of African Descent in the Slave Societies of the New World*, edited by David W. Cohen and Jack P. Greene, 172–192. Baltimore: John Hopkins University Press.

(2005). *Slavery and African Ethnicities in the Americas: Restoring the Links*. Chapel Hill: University North Carolina Press.

Hall, John R. (1990). "Social Interaction, Culture, and Historical Studies." In *Symbolic Interaction and Cultural Studies*, edited by Howard S. and Michal McCall Becker, 2–45. Chicago: University of Chicago Press.

Hamilton, Ruth Simms. (1988). "Toward a Paradigm for African Diaspora Studies." *Monograph No. 1, African Diaspora Research Project*. East Lansing: Michigan State University.

ed. (2007). *Routes of Passage: Rethinking the African Diaspora*. East Lansing: Michigan State University Press.

Hanchard, Michael George. (1999). "Afro-Modernity: Temporality, Politics, and the African Diaspora." *Public Culture* 11 (1): 245–268.

(2004). "Black Transnationalism, Africana Studies, and the 21st Century." *Journal of Black Studies* 35 (2):139–153.

Harms, Robert. (2002). *The Diligent: A Voyage through the Worlds of the Slave Trade*. New York: Basic Books.

Harris, Fredrick C. (2001). "Religious Resources in an Oppositional Civic Culture." In *Oppositional Consciousness: The Subjective Roots of Social Protest*, edited by Jane Mansbridge and Aldon Morris, 38–64. Chicago: The University of Chicago Press.

Harris, Joseph E., ed. ([1982] 1993). *Global Dimensions of the African Diaspora, Second Edition*. Washington, DC: Howard University Press.

(2003). "Expanding the Scope of African Diaspora Studies: The Middle East and India, A Research Agenda." *Radical History Review* 157–168 (87): 157–168.

Hayes, Robin J. (2008). "'A Free Black Mind Is a Concealed Weapon': Institutions and Social Movements in the African Diaspora." In *Transnational Blackness: Navigating the Global Color Line*, edited by Manning Marable and Vanessa Agard-Jones, 175–187. New York: Palgrave Macmillan.

Hebblethwaite, Benjamin. (2012). *Vodou Songs in Haitian Creole and English*. Philadelphia: Temple University Press.

(2014). "Historical Linguistic Approaches to Haitian Creole Vodou Rites, Spirit Names and Songs: The Founders' Contributions to Asogwe Vodou."

Heinl, Jr., Robert Debs, and Nancy Gordon Heinl. (1978). *Written in Blood: The Story of the Haitian People, 1492–1971*. Boston: Houghton Mifflin Company.

Herskovits, Melville J. ([1937] 2007). *Life in a Haitian Valley*. Princeton: Markus Wiener Publishers.

(1958). *The Myth of the Negro Past*. Boston: Beacon Press.

Heuman, Gad, ed. (1986). *Out of the House of Bondage: Runaways, Resistance and Marronage in Africa and the New World*. Great Britain: Frank Cass and Company.

Heywood, Linda M. (2009). "Slavery and Its Transformation in the Kingdom of Kongo: 1491–1800." *The Journal of African History* 50 (1): 1–22.

(2017). *Njinga of Angola: Africa's Warrior Queen*. Cambridge: Harvard University Press.

Heywood, Linda and John K. Thornton. (2007). *Central Africans, Atlantic Creoles, and the Foundation of the Americas, 1585–1660*. New York: Cambridge University Press.

Hontanilla, Ana. (2015). "Sentiment and the Law: Inventing the Category of the Wretched Slave in the Real Audiencia of Santo Domingo, 1783–1812." *Eighteenth-Century Studies* 48 (2): 181–200.

Hounmenou, Charles. (2012). "Black Settlement Houses and Oppositional Consciousness." *Journal of Black Studies* 43 (6): 636–666.

Hunt, Scott A. and Robert D. Benford. (2004). "Collective Identity, Solidarity, and Commitment." In *The Blackwell Companion of Social Movements*, edited by David A. Snow, Sarah A. Soule and Hanspeter Kriesi, 433–457. Malden: Blackwell Publishing.

Hutter, Swen. (2014). "Protest Event Analysis and Its Offspring." In *Methodological Practices in Social Movement Research*, edited by Donatella della Porta, 335–367. Oxford: Oxford University Press.

Inikori, Joseph E. (2003). "The Struggle against the Transatlantic Slave Trade: The Role of the State." In *Fighting the Slave Trade: West African Strategies*, edited by Sylvian Diouf, 170–198. Athens: Ohio University Press.

Itzigsohn, Jose and Karida Brown. (2020). *The Sociology of W. E. B. Du Bois: Racialized Modernity and the Global Color Line*. New York: New York University Press.

James, C. L. R. ([1938] 1989). *The Black Jacobins: Toussaint L'Ouverture and the San Domingo Revolution*. New York: Vintage Books.

Janzen, John M. (1982). *Lemba, 1650–1930: A Drum of Affliction in Africa and the New World*. New York: Garland Publishing.

Jenson, Deborah. (2012). "Sources and Interpretations: Jean-Jacques Dessalines and the African Character of the Haitian Revolution." *The William and Mary Quarterly* 69 (3): 615–638.

Johnson, Jessica Marie. (2020). *Wicked Flesh: Black Women, Intimacy, and Freedom in the Atlantic World*. Philadelphia: University of Pennsylvania Press.

Johnston, Hank. (2009). "Protest Cultures: Performance, Artifacts, and Ideations," In *Culture, Social Movements, and Protest*, edited by Hank Johnston, 3–29. Burlington: Ashgate Publishing Company.

Joseph, Celucien L. (2012). "'The Haitian Turn': An Appraisal of Recent Literary and Historiographical Works on the Haitian Revolution." *The Journal of Pan African Studies* 5 (6): 37–55.

Kananoja, Kalle. (2010). "Healers, Idolaters, and Good Christians: A Case Study of Creolization and Popular Religion in Mid-Eighteenth Century Angola." *The International Journal of African Historical Studies* 43 (3): 443–465.

Kane, Anne. (2000). "Reconstructing Culture in Historical Explanation: Narratives as Cultural Structure and Practice." *History and Theory* 39 (3): 311–330.

  (2011). *Constructing Irish National Identity: Discourse and Ritual during the Land War, 1879–1882*. New York: Palgrave MacMillan.

Kars, Marjoleine. (2016). "Dodging Rebellion: Politics and Gender in the Berbice Slave Uprising of 1763." *American Historical Review* 39–69.

Khan, Aisha. (2012). "Islam, Vodou, and the Making of the Afro-Atlantic." *New West Indian Guide/Nieuwe West-Indische Gids* 86 (1/2): 29–54.

King, Stewart R. (2001). *Blue Coat or Powered Wig: Free People of Color in Pre-Revolutionary Saint Domingue*. Athens: The University of Georgia Press.

  (2004). "The Maréchaussée of Saint-Domingue: Balancing the Ancient Regime and Modernity." *Journal of Colonialism and Colonial History* 5 (2).

Klooster, Wim. ([2009] 2018). *Revolutions in the Atlantic World: A Comparative History, New Edition*. New York: New York University Press.

  (2014). "Slave Revolts, Royal Justice, and a Ubiquitous Rumor in the Age of Revolutions." *The William and Mary Quarterly* 71 (3): 401–424.

Knight, Franklin W. (1990). *The Caribbean: The Genesis of a Fragmented Nationalism, Second Edition*. New York: Oxford University Press.

(2000). "The Haitian Revolution." *The American Historical Review* 105 (1): 103–115.

Koopmans, Ruud and Dieter Rucht. (2002). "Protest Event Analysis." In *Methods of Social Movement Research*, edited by Bert Klandermans and Suzanne Staggenborg, 231–259. Minneapolis: University of Minnesota Press.

Kuumba, M. Bahati. (2002). "'You've Struck a Rock': Comparing Gender, Social Movements, and Transformation in the United States and South Africa." *Gender and Society* 16 (4): 504–523.

(2006). "African Women, Resistance Cultures and Cultural Resistances." *Agenda: Empowering Women for Gender Equity* 68: 112–121.

Kuumba, M. Bahati and Femi Ajanaku. (1998). "Dreadlocks: The Hair Aesthetics of Cultural Resistance and Collective Identity Formation." *Mobilization: An International Journal* 3 (2): 227–243.

Ladner, Joyce A, ed. (1973). *The Death of White Sociology*. New York: Vintage Books.

Laguerre, Michel. (1989). *Voodoo and Politics in Haiti*. London: Macmillan.

Landers, Jane G. (2000). "Maroon Ethnicity and Identity in Ecuador, Colombia, and Hispaniola." Paper prepared for delivery at the meeting of the 2000 Latin American Studies Association. Miami. Used with permission.

(2002). "The Central African Presence in Spanish Maroon Communities." In *Central Africans and Cultural Transformations in the American Diaspora*, edited by Linda Heywood, 227–241. Cambridge: Cambridge University Press.

(2004). "Maroon Women in Colonial Spanish America: Case Studies in the Circum-Caribbean from the Sixteenth through the Eighteenth Centuries" In *Beyond Bondage: Free Women of Color in the Americas*, edited by David Barry Gaspar and Darlene Clark Hine, 3–18. Urbana: University of Illinois Press.

(2009). "Cimarron Ethnicity and Cultural Adaptation in the Spanish Domains of the Circum-Caribbean, 1503–1763." In *Identity in the Shadow of Slavery*, edited by Paul E. Lovejoy, 30–54. London: Continuum.

(2010). *Atlantic Creoles in the Age of Revolutions*. Cambridge: Harvard University Press.

(2015). "A View from the Other Side: Spanish Sources on the Slave Revolt in Saint Domingue." Nathan I. Huggins Lecture Series, Harvard University.

Law, Robin. (1977). *The Oyo Empire, c. 1600–c. 1836: A West African Imperialism in the Era of the Atlantic Slave Trade*. Oxford: Clarendon Press.

(1991). *The Slave Coast of West Africa, 1550–1750: The Impact of the Atlantic Slave Trade on an African Society*. Oxford: Clarendon Press.

(1997). "Ethnicity and the Slave Trade: "Lucumi" and "Nago" as Ethnonyms in West Africa." *History in Africa* 24: 205–219.

(1999). "On the African Background to the Slave Insurrection in Saint-Domingue (Haiti) in 1791: The Bois Caiman Ceremony and the Dahomian 'Blood Pact'." *Harriet Tubman Seminar*, Department of History: York University.

(2004). *Ouidah: The Social History of a West African Slaving 'Port', 1727–1892*. Athens: Ohio University.

Lawson, George. (2017). "A Global Historical Sociology of Revolution." In *Global Historical Sociology*, edited by Julian Go and George Lawson, 76–98. Cambridge: Cambridge University Press.

Leger, Jacques. (1907). *Haiti, Her History and Her Detractors*. New York: Neale.

Lindskog, Per. (1998). "From Saint Domingue to Haiti: Some Consequences of European Colonisation on the Physical Environment of Hispaniola." *Caribbean Geography* 9 (2): 71–86.

Linebaugh, Peter and Marcus Rediker. (2000). *The Many-Headed Hydra: Sailors, Slaves, Commoners, and the Hidden History of the Revolutionary Atlantic*. Boston: Beacon Press.

Lovejoy, Paul E. (1997). "The African Diaspora: Revisionist Interpretations of Ethnicity, Culture and Religion under Slavery." *Abolition and Emancipation* 2: 1–23.

(2012). *Transformations in Slavery: A History of Slavery in Africa, Third Edition*. Cambridge: Cambridge University Press.

(2016). *Jihad in West Africa during the Age of Revolution*. Athens: Ohio University Press.

MacGaffey, Wyatt. (1986). *Religion and Society in Central Africa: The BaKongo of Lower Zaire*. Chicago: University of Chicago Press.

(2002). "Twins, Simbi Spirits, and Lwas in Kongo and Haiti." In *Central Africans and Cultural Transformations in the American Diaspora*, edited by Linda Heywood, 211–226. Cambridge: Cambridge University Press.

Magubane, Zine. (2005). "Overlapping Territories and Intertwined Histories: Historical Sociology's Global Imagination." In *Remaking Modernity: Politics, History, and Sociology*, edited by Julia Adams, Elisabeth Clemens, and Ann Shola Orloff, 92–108. Durham: Duke University Press.

Manigat, Leslie F. (1977). "The Relationship between Marronage and Slave Revolts and Revolution in St. Domingue." *Annals of the New York Academy of Sciences* 292 (1): 420–438.

(2007). "Evolution et Révolutions: Marronnage et Révoltes puis Révolution à Saint Domingue." *Les Petites Classiques de l'Histoire Vivante d'Haiti No. 2*. Port-au-Prince: Media-Texte.

Mann, Kristin. (2001). "Shifting Paradigms in the Study of the African Diaspora and of Atlantic History and Culture." *Slavery & Abolition* 22 (1): 3–21.

Martin, Phyllis M. (1986). "Power, Cloth and Currency on the Loango Coast." *African Economic History* 15: 1–12.

Martin, William G. (2005). "Global Movements before 'Globalization': Black Movements as World-Historical Movements." *Review (Fernand Braudel Center)* 28 (1): 7–28.

Marx, Karl and Frederick Engels. (2001). *German Ideology*. London: Electric Book Co.

Matibag, Eugenio. (2003). *Haitian-Dominican Counterpoint: Nation, State, and Race on Hispaniola*. New York: Palgrave.

Matory, James. (2005). *Black Atlantic Religion: Tradition, Transnationalism and Matriarchy in the Afro-Brazilian Candomblé*. Princeton: Princeton University Press.

Mbiti, John S. (1990). *African Religions and Philosophy.* Oxford: Heinemann Educational Publishers.

McAdam, Doug. ([1982] 1999). *Political Process and the Development of Black Insurgency, 1930–1970 Second Edition.* Chicago: The University of Chicago Press.

(1986). "Recruitment to High-Risk Activism: The Case of Freedom Summer." *American Journal of Sociology* 92 (1): 64–90.

(1988). *Freedom Summer.* Oxford: Oxford University Press.

McAdam, Doug, Sidney Tarrow and Charles Tilly. (1996). "To Map Contentious Politics." *Mobilization* 1 (1): 17–34.

McClellan, James E. (1992). *Colonialism and Science: Saint Domingue and the Old Regime.* Chicago: The University of Chicago Press.

Melucci, Alberto. (1985). "The Symbolic Challenge of Contemporary Movements." *Social Research* 52: 789–816.

(1989). *Nomads of the Present: Social Movements and Individual Needs in Contemporary Society.* Philadelphia: Temple University Press.

Métraux, Alfred. (1959). *Voodoo in Haiti.* New York: Oxford University Press.

Mettas, Jean. (1978). *Répertoire des Expéditions Négrières Françaises au XVIIIème Siècle.* Paris: Société Française d'Histoire d'Outre-Mer.

Midy, Franklin. (2006). "The Congos in Santo Domingo from Imagination to Reality." *Ethnologies* 28 (1): 173–201.

Mignolo, Walter D. (2011). *The Darker Side of Western Modernity: Global Futures, Decolonial Options.* Durham: Duke University Press.

Miki, Yuko. (2012). Fleeing into Slavery: The Insurgent Geographies of Brazilian Quilombolas (Maroons), 1880–1881,' *The Americas* 68: 495–528.

Miller, Joseph C. (1989). "The Numbers, Origins, and Destinations of Slaves in the Eighteenth-Century Angolan Slave Trade." *Social Science History* 13: 381–419.

(2002). "Central Africa during the Era of the Slave Trade, c. 1490s–1850s." In *Central Africans and Cultural Transformations in the American Diaspora,* edited by Linda Heywood, 21–69. Cambridge: Cambridge University Press.

Mills, Charles. (2014). "White Time: The Chronic Injustice of Ideal Theory." *Du Bois Review* 11 (1): 27–42.

Mintz, Sidney W. (1985). *Sweetness and Power: The Place of Sugar in Modern History.* New York: The Penguin Group.

Mintz, Sidney W. and Richard Price. (1976). *The Birth of African-American Culture: An Anthropological Perspective.* Boston: Beacon Press.

Moitt, Bernard. (1995). "Women, Work and Resistance in the French Caribbean during Slavery, 1700–1848." In *Engendering History: Caribbean Women in Historical Perspective,* edited by Bridget Brereton Verene Shepherd, and Barbara Bailey, 155–175. New York: St. Martin's Press.

(2001). *Women and Slavery in the French Antilles, 1635–1848.* Bloomington: Indiana University Press.

(2004). "Sugar, Slavery, and Marronnage in the French Caribbean: The Seventeenth to the Nineteenth Centuries." In *Sugar, Slavery, and Society: Perspectives on the Caribbean, India, the Mascarenes, and the United States,* edited by Bernard Moitt, 57–71. Gainesville: University Press of Florida.

Monroe, J. Cameron. (2014). *The Precolonial State in West Africa: Building Power in Dahomey*. New York: Cambridge University Press.

Montilus, Guerin C. ([1982] 1993). "Guinea versus Congo Lands: Aspects of the Collective Memory in Haiti." In *Global Dimensions of the African Diaspora*, edited by Joseph E. Harris, 159–165. Washington, DC: Howard University Press.

Moomou, Jean and l'APFOM, ed. (2015). *Sociétés marronnes des Amériques: mémoires, patrimoines, identitéset histoire du XVIIe au XXe siècles*. Matoury: Ibis Rouge Editions.

Monzote, Reinaldo Funes. (2011). "The Columbian Moment: Politics, Ideology, and Biohistory." In *The Caribbean: A History of the Region and its Peoples*, edited by Stefan Palmié and Fransisco Scarani, 83–95. Chicago: The University of Chicago Press.

Morgan, Jennifer L. (2018). "Partus sequitur ventrem: Law, Race, and Reproduction in Colonial Slavery." *Small Axe* 22 (1): 1–17.

Morgan, Philip D. (1997). "The Cultural Implications of the Atlantic Slave Trade: African Regional Origins, American Destinations and New World Developments." *Slavery & Abolition* 18 (1): 122–145.

Morris, Aldon. (1984). *The Origins of the Civil Rights Movement: Black Communities Organizing for Change*. New York: The Free Press.

(1992). "Political Consciousness and Collective Action." In *Frontiers in Social Movement Theory*, edited by Aldon D. Morris and Carol McClurg Mueller, 351–373. New Haven: Yale University Press.

(2007). "Sociology of Race and W. E. B. DuBois: The Path Not Taken." In *Sociology in America: A History*, edited by Craig Calhoun, 503–534. Chicago: University of Chicago Press.

(2015). *The Scholar Denied: W. E. B. DuBois and the Birth of Modern Sociology*. Oakland: University of California Press.

Morris, Aldon and Naomi Braine. (2001). "Social Movements and Oppositional Consciousness." In *Oppositional Consciousness: The Subjective Roots of Social Protest*, edited by Jane Mansbridge and Aldon Morris, 20–37. Chicago: The University of Chicago Press.

Morrissey, Marietta. (1989). *Slave Women in the New World: Gender Stratification in the Caribbean*. Lawrence: University Press of Kansas.

Mueller, Carol McClurg and Morris, Aldon D., eds. (1992). *Frontiers in Social Movement Theory*. New Haven: Yale University Press.

Munford, Clarence J. (1991). *The Black Ordeal of Slavery and Slave Trading in the French West Indies, 1625–1715, Vol. 1–3*. Lewiston: The Edwin Mellen Press.

Munford, Clarence J. and Michael Zeuske. (1988). "Black Slavery, Class Struggle, Fear and Revolution in St. Domingue and Cuba, 1785–1795." *The Journal of Negro History* 73 (1/4): 12–32.

Munro, Martin. (2010). *Different Drummers: Rhythm and Race in the Americas*. Berkeley: University of California Press.

Mustakeem, Sowande M. (2016). *Slavery at Sea: Terror, Sex, and Sickness in the Middle Passage*. Urbana-Champaign: The University of Illinois Press.

Nessler, Graham T. (2016). *An Islandwide Struggle for Freedom: Revolution, Emancipation, and Reenslavement in Hispaniola, 1789–1809.* Chapel Hill: The University of North Carolina Press.

Newitt, Malyn. (2010). *The Portuguese in West Africa, 1415–1670: A Documentary History.* New York: Cambridge University Press.

Ogle, Gene E. (2005). "Natural Movements and Dangerous Spectacles: Beatings, Duels, and 'Play' in Saint Domingue." In *New World Orders: Violence, Sanction, and Authority in the Colonial Americas,* edited by John Smolenski and Thomas J. Humphrey, 226–248. Philadelphia: University of Pennsylvania Press.

(2013). "Natural Movements and Dangerous Spectacles: Beatings, Duels, and 'Play' in Saint Domingue." In *New World Orders: Violence, Sanction, and Authority in the Colonial Americas,* edited by John Smolenski and Thomas J. Humphrey, 226–248. Philadelphia: University of Pennsylvania Press.

Oliver, Pamela. (2008). "Repression and Crime Control: Why Social Movement Scholars Should Pay Attention to Mass Incarceration as a Form of Repression." *Mobilization: An International Journal* 13 (1): 1–24.

(2013). "Collective Action (Collective Behavior)" In *The Wiley-Blackwell Encyclopedia of Social and Political Movements,* edited by David A. Snow. London: Blackwell Publishing.

Oliver, Pamela and Gerald Marwell. (1992). "Mobilizing Technologies for Collective Action." In *Frontiers in Social Movement Theory,* edited by Aldon D. Morris and Carol McClurg Mueller, 251–272. New Haven: Yale University Press.

Palmer, Colin A. (2000). "Defining and Studying the Modern African Diaspora." *The Journal of Negro History* 85 (1/2): 27–32.

Paton, Diana. (2012). "Witchcraft, Poison, Law, and Atlantic Slavery." *The William and Mary Quarterly* 69 (2): 235–264.

Patterson, Orlando. (1982). *Slavery and Social Death: A Comparative Study.* Cambridge: Harvard University Press.

Patterson, Tiffany Ruby and Robin D. G. Kelley. (2000). "Unfinished Migrations: Reflections on the African Diaspora and the Making of the Modern World." *African Studies Review* 43 (1): 11–45.

Pattillo-McCoy, Mary. (1998). "Church Culture as a Strategy of Action in the Black Community." *American Sociological Review* 63 (6): 767–784.

Peabody, Sue. (2002). "'A Dangerous Zeal': Catholic Missions to Slaves in the French Antilles, 1635–1800." *French Historical Studies* 25 (1): 53–90.

Perry, Keisha-Khan Y. (2009). "'If We Didn't Have Water': Black Women's Struggle for Urban Land Rights in Brazil." *Environmental Justice* 2 (1): 1–7.

Peterson, David K. (2013). "Slave Rebellions." In *The Wiley-Blackwell Encyclopedia of Social and Political Movements,* edited by David A. Snow. London: Blackwell Publishing.

Pettinger, Alasdair. (2012). "'Eh! Eh! Bomba, Hen! Hen!': Making Sense of a Vodou Chant." In *Obeah and Other Powers: The Politics of Caribbean Religion and Healing,* edited by Diana Paton and Maarit Forde, 80–102. Durham: Duke University Press.

Phillips, William D. (2011). "Slavery in the Atlantic Islands and the Early Modern Spanish Atlantic World." In *The Cambridge World History of Slavery, Volume 3: AD 1420–AD 1804*, edited by David Eltis and Stanley L. Engerman, 325–347. Cambridge: Cambridge University Press.

Pluchon, Pierre. (1987). *Vaudou, Sorciers, Empoisonneurs: de Saint-Domingue a Haiti*. Paris: Karthala Editions.

Polanyi, Karl. (1966). *Dahomey and the Slave Trade: An Analysis of an Archaic Economy*. Seattle: University of Washington Press.

Polletta, Francesca. (1999). "'Free Spaces' in Collective Action." *Theory and Society* 28: 1–38.

Polletta, Francesca and James M. Jasper. (2001). "Collective Identity and Social Movements." *Annual Review of Sociology* 27: 283–305.

Polletta, Francesca and Kelsy Kretschmer. (2013). "Free Spaces." In *The Wiley-Blackwell Encyclopedia of Social and Political Movements*, edited by David A. Snow. London: Blackwell Publishing.

Ponce-Vázquez, Juan José. (2016). "Unequal Partners in Crime: Masters, Slaves, and Free People of Color in Santo Domingo, c. 1600–1650." *Slavery & Abolition* 37 (4): 704–723.

Pons, Frank Moya. (2007). *History of the Caribbean: Plantations, Trade and War in the Atlantic World*. Princeton: Markus Wiener Publishers.

Pratt, Mary Louise. ([1992] 2007). *Imperial Eyes: Travel Writing and Transculturation, Second Edition*. New York: Routledge.

Price, Richard, ed. ([1973] 1996). *Maroon Societies: Rebel Slave Communities in the Americas*. Garden City: Anchor Press.

Price-Mars, Jean. (1938). "Lemba-Pétro, Un Culte Secret: Son Histoire, Sa Localisation Géographique, Son Symbolisme." *Revue de La Société d'Histoire et de Géographie d'Haïti* 9 (28): 12–31.

Pritchard, James. (2004). *In Search of Empire: The French in the Americas, 1670–l1730*. Cambridge: Cambridge University Press.

Pritchard, James, David Eltis, and David Richardson. (2008). "The Significance of the French Slave Trade to the Evolution of the French Atlantic World before 1716." In *Extending the Frontiers: Essays on the New Transatlantic Slave Trade Database*, edited by David Eltis and David Richardson, 205–227. New Haven: Yale University Press.

Ramsey, Kate. (2011). *The Spirits and the Law: Vodou and Power in Haiti*. Chicago: The University of Chicago Press.

Reis, João José. (1993). *Slave Rebellion in Brazil: The Muslim Uprising of 1835 in Bahia*. Baltimore: The Johns Hopkins University Press.

Rey, Terry. (2005). "Toward an Ethnohistory of Haitian Pilgrimage." *Journal de la Société des Américanistes* 91 (1): 1–17.

(2017). *The Priest and the Prophetess: Abbé Ouvrière, Romaine Rivière, and the Revolutionary Atlantic World*. New York: Oxford University Press.

Richardson, David. (1989). "Slave Exports from West and West-Central Africa, 1700–1810: New Estimates of Volume and Distribution." *The Journal of African History* 30: 1–22.

(2003). "Shipboard Revolts, African Authority, and the Atlantic Slave Trade." In *Fighting the Slave Trade: West African Strategies*, edited by Sylvian Diouf, 199–218. Athens: Ohio University Press.

Ricourt, Milagros. (2016). *The Dominican Racial Imaginary: Surveying the Landscape of Race and Nation in Hispaniola*. New Brunswick: Rutgers University Press.

Rigaud, Milo. (1953). *La Tradition Voudoo et le Voudoo Haïtien: Son Temps, Ses Mystères, Sa Magie*. Port-au-Prince: Editions Fardin.

Ring-Ramirez, Misty, Heidi Reynolds-Stenson, and Jennifer Earl. (2014). "Culturally Constrained Contention: Mapping the Meaning Structure of the Repertoire of Contention." *Mobilization: An International Quarterly* 19 (4): 405–419.

Roberts, Kevin. (2005). "The Influential Yoruba Past in Haiti." In *Yoruba Diaspora in the Atlantic World*, edited by Toyin Falola and Matt D. Childs, 177–182. Bloomington: Indiana University Press.

Roberts, Neil. (2015). *Freedom as Marronage*. Chicago: The University of Chicago Press.

Robinson, Cedric J. (1983). *Black Marxism: The Making of the Black Radical Tradition*. Chapel Hill: University of North Carolina Press.

Robnett, Belinda. (1997). *How Long? How Long? African-American Women in the Struggle for Civil Rights*. New York: Oxford University Press.

Rocha, Gabriel de Avilez. (2018). "Maroons in the *Montes*: Toward a Political Ecology of Marronage in the Sixteenth-Century Caribbean," in *Early Modern Black Diaspora Studies: A Critical Anthology*, edited by Cassander L. Smith, Nicholas R. Jones, and Miles P. Grier, 15–35. Palgrave Macmillan.

Rodney, Walter. (1982). *How Europe Underdeveloped Africa*. Washington, DC: Howard University Press.

Rogers, Dominique and Stewart King. (2012). "Housekeepers, Merchants, Rentières: Free Women of Color in the Port Cities of Colonial Saint Domingue, 1750-1790." In *Women in Port: Gendering Communities, Economies, and Social Networks in Atlantic Port Cities, 1500–1800*, edited by Douglas and Jodi Campbell Catterall, 357–397. Leiden: Brill.

Rucker, Walter. (2015). *Gold Coast Diasporas: Identity, Culture, and Power*. Bloomington: Indiana University Press.

Santiago-Valles, Kelvin. (2005). "World-Historical Ties among 'Spontaneous' Slave Rebellions in the Atlantic." *Review (Fernand Braudel Center)* 28 (1): 51–83.

Schultz, Alexandra Tolin. (2014). "The *Créole Patriote*: The Journalism of Claude Milscent." *Atlantic Studies* 11 (2): 175–194.

Schwaller, Robert C. (2018). "Contested Conquests: African Maroons and the Incomplete Conquest of Hispaniola, 1519–1620," *The Americas* 75 (4): 609–638.

Scott, James. (1985). *Weapons of the Weak: Everyday Forms of Peasant Resistance*. New Haven: Yale University Press.

(1990). *Domination and Arts of Resistance: Hidden Transcripts*. New Haven: Yale University Press.

Scott, Julius S. ([1986] 2018). *The Common Wind: Currents of Afro-American Communication in the Era of the Haitian Revolution*. London: Verso.

Scott, Rebecca J. and Jean M. Hebrard. (2012). *Freedom Papers: An Atlantic Odyssey in the Age of Emancipation*. Cambridge: Harvard University Press.

Selbin, Eric. (1997). "Revolution in the Real World: Bringing Agency Back in." In *Theorizing Revolutions: New Approaches from Across the Disciplines*, edited by John Foran, 118–132. London: Routledge.

   (2010). *Revolution, Rebellion, Resistance: The Power of Story*. London: Zed Books.

Sewell, William H. (1992). "A Theory of Structure: Duality, Agency, and Transformation." *American Journal of Sociology* 98 (1): 1–29.

   (1996a). "Three Temporalities: Toward an Eventful Sociology." In *The Historic Turn in the Human Sciences*, edited by Terrence J. McDonald, 245–280. Ann Arbor: The University of Michigan Press.

   (1996b). "Historical Events as Transformations of Structures: Inventing Revolution at the Bastille." *Theory and Society* 25 (6): 841–881.

Sheffer, Gabriel. (2012). "The Historical, Cultural, Social, and Political Backgrounds of Ethno-national Diasporas." In *Routledge International Handbook of Migration Studies*, edited by Steven J. Gold and Stephanie J. Nawyn, 437–449. London: Routledge.

Sheller, Mimi. (2012). *Citizenship from Below: Erotic Agency and Caribbean Freedom*. Durham: Duke University Press.

Shilliam, Robert. (2008). "What the Haitian Revolution Might Tell Us about Development, Security, and the Politics of Race." *Comparative Studies in Society and History* 50 (3): 778–808.

   (2017). "Race and Revolution at Bwa Kayiman." *Millennium: Journal of International Studies* 45 (3): 269–292.

Shuval, Judith T. (2000). "Diaspora Migration: Definitional Ambiguities and a Theoretical Paradigm." *International Migration* 38 (5): 41–57.

Skocpol, Theda. (1979). *States & Social Revolutions: A Comparative Analysis of France, Russia, and China*. Cambridge: Cambridge University Press.

   (1994). *Social Revolutions in the Modern World*. New York: Cambridge University Press.

Smallwood, Stephanie. (2008). *Saltwater Slavery: A Middle Passage from Africa to American Diaspora*. Cambridge: Harvard University Press.

Smith, Andrea. (2012). "Indigeneity, Settler Colonialism, White Supremacy." In *Racial Formation in the Twenty-First Century*, edited by Daniel Martinez HoSang, Oneka La Bennett, and Laura Pulido, 66–90. Berkeley: University of California Press.

Snow, David A. and Roberta G. Lessor. (2013). "Consciousness, Conscience, and Social Movements." In *The Wiley-Blackwell Encyclopedia of Social and Political Movements*, edited by David A. Snow. London: Blackwell Publishing.

Socolow, Susan M. (1996). "Economic Roles of the Free Women of Color in Cap Français." In *More Than Chattel: Black Women and Slavery in the Americas*, edited by David Barry Gaspar and Darlene Clark Hine, 279–297. Bloomington: Indiana University Press.

Sohrabi, Nader. (2005). "Revolutions as Pathways to Modernity." In *Remaking Modernity: Politics, History, and Sociology*, edited by Julia Adams, Elisabeth Clemens, and Ann Shola Orloff, 300–329. Durham: Duke University Press.

Soumonni, Elisée. (2003). "Lacustrine Villages in South Benin as Refuges from the Slave Trade." In *Fighting the Slave Trade: West African Strategies*, edited by Sylvian Diouf, 3–14. Athens: Ohio University Press.

Stein, Robert L. (1979). *The French Slave Trade in the Eighteenth Century: An Old Regime Business*. Madison: The University of Wisconsin Press.

(1988). *The French Sugar Business in the Eighteenth Century*. Baton Rouge: Louisiana State University Press.

Steinberg, Marc W. (1999). *Fighting Words: Working-Class Formation, Collective Action, and Discourse in Early Nineteenth-Century England*. Ithaca: Cornell University Press.

Stern, Steve J., ed. (1987). *Resistance, Rebellion, and Consciousness in the Andean Peasant World, 18th to 20th Centuries*. Madison: The University of Wisconsin Press.

Stinchcombe, Arthur L. (1995). *Sugar Island Slavery in the Age of Enlightenment: The Political Economy of the Caribbean World*. Princeton: Princeton University Press.

Stone, Erin Woodruff. (2013). "America's First Slave Revolt: Indians and African Slaves in Española, 1500–1534." *Ethnohistory* 60 (2): 195–217.

Stuckey, Sterling. (1988). *Slave Culture: Nationalist Theory and the Foundations of Black America*. New York: Oxford University Press.

Sued-Badillo, Jalil. (2011). "From Taínos to Africans in the Caribbean: Labor, Migration, and Resistance." *In Palmié, et al.* 2011, 97–113.

Sweeney, Shauna J. (2019). "Market Marronage: Fugitive Women and the Internal Marketing System in Jamaica, 1781–1834." *The William and Mary Quarterly* 76 (2): 197–222.

(2021). "Gendering Racial Capitalism and the Black Heretical Tradition." In *Histories of Racial Capitalism*, edited by Destin Jenkins and Justin Leroy, 53–84. New York: Columbia University Press.

Sweet, James H. (2006). "The Evolution of Ritual in the African Diaspora: Central African *Kilundu* in Brazil, St. Domingue, and the United States, Seventeenth-Nineteenth Centuries." In *Diasporic Africa: A Reader*, edited by Michael A. Gomez, 64–80. New York: New York University Press.

(2011). *Domingos Alvares, African Healing, and the Intellectual History of the Atlantic World*. Chapel Hill: The University of North Carolina Press.

(2017). "Research Note: New Perspectives on Kongo in Revolutionary Haiti." *The Americas* 74 (1): 83–97.

Swidler, Ann. (1986). "Culture in Action: Symbols and Strategies." *American Sociological Review* 51 (2): 273–286.

Taleb-Khyar, Mohamed B. (1992). "Jean Fouchard." *Callaloo* 15 (2): 321–326.

Tamason, Charles A. (1980). "From Mortuary to Cemetery: Funeral Riots and Funeral Demonstrations in Lille, 1779–1870. *Social Science History*: 4 (1): 15–31.

Taylor, Verta and Nella Van Dyke. (2004). "'Get Up, Stand Up': Tactical Repertoires of Social Movements." In *The Blackwell Companion of Social Movements*, edited by David A. Snow, Sarah A. Soule and Hanspeter Kriesi, 262–293. Malden: Blackwell Publishing.

Taylor, Verta and Nancy E. Whittier. (1992). "Collective Identity in Social Movement Communities: Lesbian Feminist Mobilization." In *Frontiers in Social Movement Theory*, edited by Aldon D. Morris and Carol McClurg Mueller, 104–129. New Haven: Yale University Press.

Terborg-Penn, Rosalyn. (1996). "Slavery and Women in Africa and the Diaspora." In *Women in the African Diaspora*, edited by Rosalyn Terborg-Penn, Sharon Harley, and Andrea Benton Rushing, 217–230. Washington, DC: Howard University Press.

Thompson, Alvin O. (2006). *Flight to Freedom: African Runaways and Maroons in the Americas*. Kingston: University of the West Indies Press.

Thompson, E. P. (1980). *The Making of the English Working Class*. London: Victor Gollancz.

Thompson, Robert Farris. (1983). *Flash of the Spirit: African & Afro-American Art & Philosophy*. New York: Vintage.

Thornton, John K. (1988a). "On the Trail of Voodoo: African Christianity in Africa and the Americas." *The Americas* 44 (3): 261–278.

  (1988b). "The Art of War in Angola, 1575–1680." *Comparative Studies in Society and History* 30: 360–378.

  (1991). "African Soldiers in the Haitian Revolution." *The Journal of Caribbean History* 25 (1): 58–80.

  (1992). *Africa and Africans in the Making of the Atlantic World, 1400–1680*. Cambridge: Cambridge University Press.

  (1993a). "Central African Names and African-American Naming Patterns." *The William and Mary Quarterly* 50 (4): 727–742.

  (1993b). "'I Am the Subject of the King of Congo': African Political Ideology and the Haitian Revolution." *Journal of World History* 4: 181–214.

  (1998). *The Kongolese Saint Anthony: D Beatriz Kimpa Vita and the Antonian Movement, 1684–1706*. Cambridge: Cambridge University Press.

  (1999). *Warfare in Atlantic Africa, 1500–1800*. London: University College London Press.

  (2002). "Religious and Ceremonial Life in the Kongo and Mbundu Areas, 1500–1700." In *Central Africans and Cultural Transformations in the American Diaspora*, edited by Linda Heywood, 71–90. Cambridge: Cambridge University Press.

  (2003). "Cannibals, Witches, and Slave Traders in the Atlantic World." *The William and Mary Quarterly* 60 (2): 273–294.

  (2016). "The Kingdom of Kongo and Palo Mayombé: Reflections on an African-American Religion." *Slavery & Abolition* 37 (1): 1–22.

Tilly, Charles. (1978). *From Mobilization to Revolution*. Reading: Addison-Wesley Publishing Company.

  (1995). "Contentious Repertoires in Great Britain, 1758–1834." In *Repertoires and Cycles of Collective Action*, edited by Mark Traugott, 15–42. Durham: Duke University Press.

  (2006). *Regimes and Repertoires*. Chicago: University of Chicago Press.

Tinsley, Omise'eke Natasha. (2008). "Black Atlantic, Queer Atlantic: Queer Imaginings of the Middle Passage." *GLQ: A Journal of Lesbian and Gay Studies* 14 (2–3): 192–215.

Traugott, Mark, ed. (1995). *Repertoires & Cycles of Collective Action*. Durham: Duke University Press.

Trouillot, Michel-Rolph. (1982). "Motion in the System: Coffee, Color, and Slavery in Eighteenth-Century Saint-Domingue." *Review (Fernand Braudel Center)* 3: 331–388.

(1995). *Silencing the Past: Power and the Production of History*. Boston: Beacon Press.

Turner, Mary. (2011). "Slave Worker Rebellions and Revolution in the Americas." In *The Cambridge World History of Slavery*, edited by David Eltis and Stanley L. Engerman, 677–707. Cambridge: Cambridge University Press.

Tyler, Imogen. (2018). "Resituating Erving Goffman: From Stigma Power to Black Power." *The Sociological Review Monographs* 66 (4): 744–765.

Vanhee, Hein. (2002). "Central African Popular Christianity and the Making of Haitian Vodou Religion." In *Central Africans and Cultural Transformations in the American Diaspora*, edited by Linda Heywood, 243–264. Cambridge: Cambridge University Press.

Vertovec, Steven. (1997). "Three Meanings of 'Diaspora,'" Exemplified among South Asian Religions." *Diaspora: A Journal of Transnational Studies* 6 (3): 277–299.

Walker, Shelia S. (1996). "The Feast of the Good Death: An Afro-Catholic Emancipation Celebration in Brazil." In *Women in the African Diaspora*, edited by Rosalyn Terborg-Penn, Sharon Harley, and Andrea Benton Rushing, 203–214. Washington, DC: Howard University Press.

Ward, Matthew. (2015). "Social Movement Micromobilization." *Sociopedia.isa*. DOI: 10.1177/205684601551

(2016). "Rethinking Social Movement Micromobilization: Multi-Stage Theory and the Role of Social Ties." *Current Sociology* 64 (6): 853–874.

Ware, Rudolph T. (2014). *The Walking Qur'an: Islamic Education, Embodied Knowledge, and History in West Africa*. Chapel Hill: The University of North Carolina Press.

Weaver, Karol K. (2002). "The Enslaved Healers of Eighteenth-Century Saint Domingue." *Bulletin of the History of Medicine* 76 (3): 429–460.

(2004). "'She Crushed the Child's Fragile Skull': Disease, Infanticide, and Enslaved Women in Eighteenth-Century Saint Domingue." *French Colonial History* 5: 93–109.

(2006). *Medical Revolutionaries: The Enslaved Healers of Eighteenth-Century Saint Domingue*. Urbana: University of Illinois Press.

(2012). "Fashioning Freedom: Slave Seamstresses in the Atlantic World." *Journal of Women's History* 24 (1): 44–59.

West, Michael O. and William G. Martin. (2009). "Haiti, I'm Sorry: The Haitian Revolution and the Forging of the Black International." In *From Toussaint to Tupac: The Black International since the Age of Revolution*, edited by Michael O. West, William G. Martin, and Fanon Che Wilkins, 72–104. Chapel Hill: The University of North Carolina Press.

Wheat, David. (2016). *Atlantic Africa and the Spanish Caribbean, 1570–1640*. Chapel Hill: The University of North Carolina Press.

Williams, Eric. (1944). *Capitalism & Slavery*. Chapel Hill: The University of North Carolina Press.

Wilson, Samuel M. (1990). *Hispaniola: Caribbean Chiefdoms in the Age of Columbus*. Tuscaloosa: The University of Alabama Press.

Winant, Howard. (2001). *The World Is a Ghetto: Race and Democracy since World War II*. New York: Basic Books.

Yingling, Charlton W. (2015). "The Maroons of Santo Domingo in the Age of Revolutions: Adaptation and Evasion, 1783–1800." *History Workshop Journal* 79: 25–51.

UNPUBLISHED MANUSCRIPTS

Manuel, Keith Anthony. (2005). "Slavery, Coffee, and Family in a Frontier Society: Jérémie and Its Hinterland, 1780–1789." Master's Thesis, The University of Florida.

Mobley, Christina Frances. (2015). "The Kongolese Atlantic: Central African Slavery & Culture from Mayombé to Haiti." PhD Diss., Duke University.

Sommerdyk, Stacey Jean Muriel. (2012). "Trade and the Merchant Community of the Loango Coast in the Eighteenth Century." PhD Diss., University of Hull. ProQuest (AAT U635171).

Sosis, Howard Justin. (1971). "The Colonial Environment and Religion in Haiti: An Introduction to the Black Slave Cults in Eighteenth Century Saint Domingue." PhD Diss., Columbia University. ProQuest (AAT 7412768).

Walton, Rachel. (2012). "Enslaved Women and Motherhood: Saint Domingue on the Eve of the Haitian Revolution." Master's Thesis, The University of Florida.

Wynter, Sylvia. (n.d.). *Black Metamorphosis: New Natives in a New World*. Unpublished ms.

ONLINE SOURCES

Brown, Vincent. (2016). "Designing Histories of Slavery for the Database Age," Podcast: Comparative Media Studies. http://cmsw.mit.edu/podcast-vincent-brown-designing-histories-of-slavery-for-the-database-age/ (last accessed March 15, 2016).

da Dicomano, Raimondo. (1798). *O Reino do Congo: A decadência final do Reino do Congo*, http://arlindo-correia.com/121208.html (last accessed May 6, 2021).

de Castello de Vide, Raphael. 1780–1788. *Viagem do Congo do Missionário*, http://arlindo-correia.com/161007.html (last accessed May 6, 2021)

CUNY Dominican Studies Institute. (2016). *First Blacks in the Americas: The African Presence in the Dominican Republic*, www.firstblacks.org/en/ (last accessed December 15, 2016).

Hebblethwaite, Benjamin. *The Vodou Archive: Curating and Sharing the Sources of Vodou Religion and Culture*. University of Florida Digital Collections, http://ufdc.ufl.edu/vodou (last accessed December 8, 2016).

Le Glaunec, Jean-Pierre and Léon Robichaud. (2009). *Marronnage dans le monde Atlantique*. Montreal: The French Atlantic History Group, http://marronnage .info/fr/index.html (last accessed July 28, 2020).

Voyages Database. (2009). *Voyages: The Trans-Atlantic Slave Trade Database*, www.slavevoyages.org/ (last accessed May 7, 2021).

Index